MILTON STUDIES
XIII

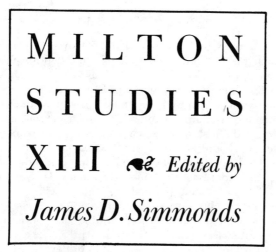

MILTON
STUDIES
XIII ❧ *Edited by*
James D. Simmonds

UNIVERSITY OF PITTSBURGH PRESS

MILTON STUDIES

is published annually by the University of Pittsburgh Press as a forum for Milton scholarship and criticism. Articles submitted for publication may be biographical; they may interpret some aspect of Milton's writings; or they may define literary, intellectual, or historical contexts—by studying the work of his contemporaries, the traditions which affected his thought and art, contemporary political and religious movements, his influence on other writers, or the history of critical response to his work.

Manuscripts should be upwards of 3,000 words in length and should conform to the *MLA Style Sheet*. Manuscripts and editorial correspondence should be addressed to James D. Simmonds, Department of English, University of Pittsburgh, Pittsburgh, Pa. 15260.

Milton Studies does not review books.

Within the United States, *Milton Studies* may be ordered from the University of Pittsburgh Press, Pittsburgh, Pa. 15260.

Overseas orders should be addressed to Feffer and Simons, Inc., 100 Park Avenue, New York, N.Y. 10017, U.S.A.

Library of Congress Catalog Card Number 69-12335
ISBN 0-8229-3174-5 (Volume I) (out of print)
ISBN 0-8229-3194-x (Volume II)
ISBN 0-8229-3218-0 (Volume III)
ISBN 0-8229-3244-x (Volume IV)
ISBN 0-8229-3272-5 (Volume V)
ISBN 0-8229-3288-1 (Volume VI)
ISBN 0-8229-3305-5 (Volume VII)
ISBN 0-8229-3310-1 (Volume VIII)
ISBN 0-8229-3329-2 (Volume IX)
ISBN 0-8229-3356-x (Volume X)
ISBN 0-8229-3373-X (Volume XI)
ISBN 0-8229-3376-4 (Volume XII)
ISBN 0-8229-3404-3 (Volume XIII)
US ISSN 0076-8820
Published by the University of Pittsburgh Press, Pittsburgh, Pa. 15260
Feffer & Simons, Inc., London
Manufactured in the United States of America

CONTENTS

MILTON STUDIES
XIII

"RATIONAL BURNING":
MILTON ON SEX AND MARRIAGE

David Aers and Bob Hodge

The immediate, natural and necessary relationship of human
being to human being is the relationship of man to woman. In
this natural relationship of the sexes, man's relationship to
nature is immediately his relationship to man, and his relationship to man is immediately his relationship to nature, his
own natural function. Thus, in this relationship is sensuously
revealed and reduced to an observable fact how far for man his
essence has become nature or nature has become man's human essence. Thus, from this relationship the whole cultural
level of man can be judged.
                —Karl Marx, "Private Property and Communism"

MILTON, AS IS well known, lived before the days of Women's
Liberation and we have many modern critics and scholars
grateful for the fact. They teach us that Milton's most repressive
and reactionary attitudes toward women are so basic to "the
seventeenth-century mind" as to be beyond criticism. We must
accept them, we are told with an earnest appeal to our historical
sense, if we are ever to appreciate the Great Work in the context of
its age. And there is a civilizing reward for making this imaginative leap. If only we can accept the initial premise that women are
naturally inferior and subordinate to men we will inhabit a mag-
nificently coherent, and yet generous, human, and moral universe.
Every time we read the Great Work we will be chastened and
purged of our inadequate "modern" responses: our "historicism"
will be part of our moral education. Or so we are promised by
critics of the neo-Christian tradition.[1]

Regrettably this whole line of criticism rests on quite unsound
"historical" and theoretical foundations. As for the latter, claims
for the coherence of the universe depicted by orthodoxy have
been seriously undermined by Empson's stimulating and exuberant *Milton's God*, in which he also points out how morally repulsive *Paradise Lost* would be if it had the kind of coherence attri-

3

buted to it by neo-Christian critics. But such critics have proved
impervious to radical criticism: Patrides, Halkett, and others proceed as though Empson had not written. It would be naive to
suppose that these critics would abandon their pieties merely because someone had demonstrated their incoherence: indeed, accepting incoherence itself becomes a criterion of true faith. Their
appeal to history, however, is also distorted and inadequate. They
write as though there was no revolution in the seventeenth century and no radical challenges to the orthodox pieties they champion. Yet Milton himself was seen as a "libertine" by such orthodox contemporaries as Clement Walker and Prynne, while Ranters
like Coppe were as much his contemporaries as the Presbyterian
Baxter or the chaste Cambridge Platonists. Too many academic
critics have presented a homogenized Milton and a homogenized
seventeenth century, resolving all tensions, blind to all contradictions and dissidence, in Milton or his society. They are certainly
not inspired by any disinterested regard for the truth or historical
fact, so sadly and reluctantly we must suspect them of ideological
motivation. It is our purpose to penetrate the ideological mists that
have gathered round "the Poet—blind, yet bold." Milton's position, in fact, was neither constant nor consistent. His attitudes to
women and sex entailed contradictions which he never fully resolved. Yet there is a development over his lifetime, from the
prose tracts on divorce to *Paradise Lost,* and this development
constitutes a critique of the neo-Christian appropriation of Milton.
He did not collapse back into orthodox pieties in his great poem,
as has been claimed: on the contrary, *Paradise Lost* shows how far
he was able to go in his heroic and radical struggle toward a more
adequate view of sexuality and the relationship between women
and men. From this struggle, as Marx said, "the whole cultural
level" of Milton and his social group can be judged. And of his
critics.

I

In thinking about sex and marriage Milton had to deal with
two aspects of what Marx called alienation: estrangement of man
from his species and man from himself.[2] It is in these terms that
we need to see both the dominant seventeenth-century ideology
governing relations between the sexes and Milton's complicity
and struggle with that ideology.

Neo-Christian critics are of course right that Milton's views
grow out of the dominant Puritan tradition. These critics do not

usually juxtapose this tradition with an account of the actual position of women in seventeenth-century society, but that is not here in dispute—discriminated against legally, economically, and socially, there is no doubt that they made up an oppressed class. There were differing degrees of servitude, and certainly there were hopeful signs of change we must not overlook and underestimate;[3] but none of these factors challenges the basic fact of massive repression at all levels of society.

But there were a number of contradictions in the position of a middle-class wife, which were inevitably registered in the dominant ideology. She was both of the class and not of it: a bourgeois but a woman, united to her husband by class, separated and subordinated by sex. She was exploited by her husband yet entrusted with the management of the household, servants, and children, perpetrator of the ideology yet a victim of it. So the ideology had to present a basically exploitative relationship as a mutually beneficial one, while also reinforcing masculine consciousness of the conviction that the right to rule was the male's. "The husband must so unite Authority and Love, that neither of them may be omitted or concealed, but both be excercised and maintained," wrote Baxter, one of the more humane of Puritan divines, anxious that men should not "omit or conceal" the real differences in authority, the difference between ruler and ruled.[4] "Love," we see, is something to be "excercised and maintained," not felt. Yet the same ideology had to mediate the wife's equivocal status as ruled and ruler, wife and lover.

The ensuing contradictions can be seen in a representative treatise, *A Godly Forme of Household Government,* by John Dod and Robert Cleaver. They begin by seeing the family in explicitly political terms: "An household is as it were a little commonwealth, by the good government whereof, God's glory may be advanced."[5] They then analyze the primary relationship as follows. "There are two sorts in every perfect family: (1) the governors; (2) those that must be ruled." In this basic scheme, the wife is one of the governors, though not absolutely. The governors, they say, "are, first, the *chief governor,* which is the *Husband,* secondly, a *fellow-helper,* which is the wife" (p. 7). This seems to present the wife as rather ruler than ruled, subordinate only to her husband, a near equal belonging to the same class. But when Dod and Cleaver reach the section on the duties of the wife they are almost exclusively concerned with her subordination to her husband: "So then the principal duty of the wife is, first to be subject to her husband, Ephes. 5.22, Coloss. 3.18, 1 Pet. 3.1, 2. To be chaste and shamefast modest and silent godly and discreet. To keep herself at home for the good government of her family, and not to stay abroad without just cause" (p. 175). Three texts buttress the announcement of her subjection. A whole section of the book reinforces it. The second "duty" repetitiously insists on her submissive behavior. The third seems as anxious that she should be bound to the home as that she should manage the household efficiently. So much for the near equality of status of this "governor."

A similar contradiction undercuts the ideology of love and companionship. Dod and Cleaver define matrimony as "a lawful knot and unto God an acceptable yoking and joining together of one man and one woman, with the good consent of them both; to the end that they may dwell together in friendship and honesty, one helping and comforting the other" (p. 85). Which one helps which? we might ask. But the ideal of marriage seems blandly benign here. "Good consent" and "friendship" and comfort (though, interestingly, not love) are part of the very definition of marriage, an image of a humane and rich social relationship.

But when Dod and Cleaver come round to advising a husband how to pick this companion of his most intimate hours, his comfort and friend, they give a useful rule of thumb. "As the echo answereth but one word for many, which are spoken to her; so a Maid's answer should be in a word" (p. 94). A lifetime of richly mutual conversations stretches out in prospect.[6] But some husbands don't see the advantage of a loving marriage early enough. Dod and Cleaver present its real and substantial attractions winningly:

And if we have regard unto commodity and profit, there is nothing that giveth so much as doth a good wife, no not horses, oxen, servants or farms: for a man's wife is the fellow and comforter of all care and thoughts, and doth more faithful and true service unto him than either maid-servant or man-servant, which do serve man for fear, or else for wages: but thy wife will be led only by love and therefore she doth everything better than all other. (pp. 145–46)

The preacher is certain that a bourgeois husband will have due regard for "commodity and profit" and will see the usefulness of "love."[7]

The Hallers' comment on Milton's relation to this tradition is just, as far as it goes: "though Milton voiced the accepted tenets of Puritan doctrine, he did not draw back as the preachers had done from its extreme implications."[8] Milton did indeed have the habit, unfortunate in an ideologue insofar as his own social group is concerned, of taking basic premises of the ideology too seriously, so that its inherent contradictions began to obtrude, its moral bromides turn into calls of action. But his idiosyncratic development of the ideology had its roots in a state of mind that was typical of his class. He came at this ideology as its victim. Shocked by his traumatic experience of marriage into realizing the alienating nature of the conventional bourgeois sexual ethic, he struggled to find in marriage the complete solution to the psychic consequences of bourgeois individualism: isolation, fragmentation of personality, crippling frustration, and hence despair.[9]

Protestantism was able to provide the ideological reflex of the economic individualism basic to the bourgeois view of man, and Weber has some relevant comments on the doctrinal basis:

The Father in heaven of the New Testament, so human and understanding, who rejoices over the repentance of a sinner as a woman over the lost piece of silver she has found, is gone. His place has been taken by a transcendental being, beyond the reach of human understanding, who with His quite incomprehensible decrees has decided the fate of every individual and regulated the tiniest details of the cosmos from eternity. God's grace is, since His decrees cannot change, as impossible for those to whom He has granted it to lose as it is unattainable for those whom He has denied it.

In its extreme inhumanity this doctrine must above all have had one consequence for the life of a generation which surrendered to its magnificent consistency. That was a feeling of unprecedented inner loneliness of the single individual. In what was for man of the age of the Reformation the most important thing in life, his eternal salvation, he was forced to follow his path alone to meet a destiny which had been decreed for him from eternity. No one could help him. No priest, for the chosen one can understand the word of God only in his own heart. No sacraments, for though the sacraments had been ordained by God for the increase of His glory, and must hence be scrupulously observed, they are not a means to the attainment of grace, but only the subjective externa subsidia of faith. No Church, for though it was held that extra ecclesiam nulla salus in the sense that whoever kept away from the true Church could never belong to God's chosen band, nevertheless the membership of the external Church included the doomed. They should belong to it and be subjected to its discipline, not in order thus to attain salvation, that is impossible, but because, for the glory of God, they too must be forced to obey His commandments. Finally, even no God. For even Christ had died only for the elect, for whose benefit God had decreed His martyrdom from eternity.[10]

Milton specifically invokes marriage as the divinely ordained cure for "loneliness," what Weber calls the "unprecedented inner loneliness" of protestant and bourgeois man.[11] "Loneliness" redefined in this way becomes an immensely important and multiple loss of connections, alienation in its many related forms. However, in his prose works, Milton was never able to relate this experience of alienation to repressive social relationships.[12] So although he made new demands on the marriage relationship and weakened the repressive forms of the basic ideology in this area, he did not bring himself to renounce totally an exploitative relationship which he as a male benefited from in seventeenth-century society (as his descendants of male gender in the twentieth century continue to benefit).

II

Milton's thinking on marriage was precipitated by his own marriage to Mary Powell and her prompt departure in 1642. At the age of thirty-three he had hastily renounced all his previous dedication to chastity and with equal speed had himself been renounced. The divorce tracts grew out of this double experience and express two potentially opposite cases: Milton's high claims for marriage and his urgent need for divorce.

The particular circumstances in which he argued the case also contributed dramatically to his education. He faced the problem, nearly fatal to his enterprise, that God's word did not say what he wanted it to. He had to wrest the Bible violently to suit his case, and this drew him toward a version of the radical Protestant position that scripture was only clearly understood by the illuminated individual spirit, the Saint. As he pressed on with his case he evolved the tacit principle that the clearest of God's commands might mean the exact opposite of what it said. So when Christ said, "What therefore God hath joined together, let no man put asunder," he should be understood to mean, "let the husband put asunder if he is dissatisfied." Milton did not assert this blatantly: the argument he used was that God could not have done the joining in the first place if the man was dissatisfied. So the man becomes the sole judge of what God intended.[13] The procedure effectively leads to the creation of an alternative deity, whose relation to his apparent commands is accessible only to the higher reason of the saints. This whole debate certainly radicalized Milton's theology and brought him closer to extreme individualistic ethics.

Another important factor shaping his thinking in these tracts was his simultaneous immersion in political controversy. He was in mid-career as an ideologue for Parliament. He was specifically aware of a connection between power relations in the family and the state (the connection was of course a commonplace) as he pointed out in the dedication of *The Doctrine and Discipline of Divorce* (1644 edition) addressed to Parliament:[14]

Advise you well, supreme Senate, if charity be thus excluded and ex-pulsed, how you will defend the untainted honour of your own actions and proceedings. He who marries, intends as little to conspire his own ruin, as he that swears allegiance: and as a whole people is in proportion to an ill government, so is one man to an ill marriage. If they against any authority, Covenant, or Statute, may by the sovereign edict of charity, save not only their lives, but honest liberties from unworthy bondage, as well may he against any private Covenant, which he never entered to his mischief, redeem himself from insupportable disturbances to honest peace and just contentment. (YP, II, p. 229)

Here the parliamentarians' ideologue is using the basic premises of their ideology against them. But what Milton says here about Parliament is surely even truer of himself. If he was sincere in his devotion to justice and individual liberty, he should be equally tender of the rights of women. In fact we shall see that he is intermittently and uneasily aware of this consequence. Neverthe-less, this paragraph does show graphically how easily ideology can be manipulated and absorb contradictions, even when the ideo-logue is actually engaged in pointing out consequences and poten-tial contradictions of a position to his masters. The analogy is lopsided in favor of males. As the "whole people" are to govern-ment, so a "man" is to marriage. But surely, for Milton, it is a man who governs in marriage: the analogy would work more naturally, in keeping with his general account of marrige, if it went, "peo-ple:government :: wife:husband." This would give the oppressed wife the full right Milton denies her, of rebellion against what she herself judges to be "unworthy bondage." The effect of Milton's use of bondage is to make women nonpeople, as the lower classes in general were in his version of the liberal ethic.[15]

The antifeminist bias which various critics acclaim in *Para-dise Lost* is present in *Doctrine and Discipline of Divorce*. But very rarely is it unqualified even there. In chapter 15 of the first book, for instance, he argues against the view that "divorce was permitted only for wives:"

Palpably uxorious! Who can be ignorant that woman was created for man, and not man for woman; and that a husband may be injured as insuffer-

ably in marriage as a wife. What an injury is it after wedlock not to be
beloved, what to be contended with in point of house-rule who shall be
head, not for any parity of wisdom, for that were something reasonable,
but out of a female pride. (YP, II, p. 324)

The vehemence of this expostulation comes from that premise
beloved of male chauvinists of all periods: "woman was created
for man, and not man for woman." But the development of the
rhetorical case is interesting. He only argues equality of suffering
for the man, so tacitly acknowledging that men can be insufferable
too. The tone is surprisingly plaintive, like a post–Women's Liberation plea for consideration for the unfortunate male, an appeal
from weakness, not strength. The parenthetical "not for any parity
of wisdom, for that were something reasonable," is also a dangerous concession. What if the woman, despite all the controls of a
male-dominated society, is as intelligent as the man, has the "parity of wisdom" that Milton does seem to demand for a valid marriage? Or worse, what if she is more intelligent? Milton is extremely vulnerable here, for the near equality necessary for fit
minds is liable to topple over into equality or even female superiority. The later *Tetrachordon* (1645) attempts to absorb these implications. For instance, discussing the key proposition, "he not
for her but she for him," he makes this qualification:

Nevertheless man is not to hold her as a servant, but receives her into a
part of that empire which God proclaims him to, though not equally, yet
largely, as his own image and glory: for it is no small glory to him, that a
creature so like him, should be made subject to him. Not but that particular exceptions may have place, if she exceed her husband in prudence
and dexterity and he contentedly yield, for then a superior and more
natural law comes in, that the wiser should govern the less wise, whether
male or female. (YP, II, p. 589)

This qualification goes counter to his text and has no text to support
it. Its motivation comes from elsewhere, perhaps Milton's God-
given insight into what God really meant. "Man is not to hold her as
a servant": why not, when wives are ordered to be "subject to your
husbands in everything"? Part of the reason is that she must participate in his rule, his "empire," as we saw Cleaver trying to explain.
Another reason is that the more equal she is, the greater the
"glory"—"to him" Milton emphasizes. To dominate "a creature so
like him" is much more satisfying than training a horse or kicking
the dog around. But "so like," he again uneasily recognizes, that
she might be superior in "prudence and dexterity" as well as in her

domestic and reproductive specialties. The "superior" law he invokes here to justify government by females is the same law he and the Fifth Monarchists invoked to justify the rule by a minority elite. Of course, as we can see in the later *Ready and Easy Way*, he made this "law" less subversive by accepting that this rational elite coincided with the property-owning elite who were in control.[16] And we are reminded that an ideologue cannot be trusted to mean what he seems to be saying. In the present case he gives with one hand and takes away with the other. He establishes a connection, gratuitously it seems, between the rights of women and the claims of the most radical elements of the bourgeoisie, the connection we saw he suppressed in the earlier *Doctrine and Discipline*. Yet he also includes an escape clause: "and he contentedly yield." So the man remains the sole judge of who is the wiser, even when Milton concedes his inferiority.

At one point in *Tetrachordon* Milton goes further than this. "The wife also, as her subjection is terminated in the Lord, being herself the redeemed of Christ, is not still bound to be the vassal of him, who is the bond-slave of Satan" (YP, II, p. 591). Here he approaches the classic radical sectarian position, with its subversive implications for the traditional view of marriage, which Keith Thomas has analysed well.[17] So Milton knew where the logic of his position took him, at least once in his intellectual life.

The position argued in *Doctrine and Discipline of Divorce*, however, was far less liberal, and remained his basic position. The man, he insists, can unilaterally decide to divorce his wife. She has not the same freedom, nor is there any outside redress for her:

Another act of papal encroachment it was to pluck the power and arbitrement of divorce from the master of the family, into whose hands God and the law of nations had put it, and Christ so left it, preaching only to the conscience, and not authorising a judicial Court to toss about and divulge the unaccountable and secret reasons of disaffection between man and wife, as a thing most improperly answerable to any such kind of trial. (YP, II, p. 343)

This leaves the husband as judge, jury, and accuser in his own case, ruling with arbitrary power. No justification is offered here for this large claim, beyond the negative pseudoreason that since "papal encroachment" took this power away it must be restored. His contention rests partly on a belief in male supremacy: "For even the freedom and eminence of man's creation gives him to be a law in this matter to himself being the head of the other sex which was made for him: whom therefore though he ought not to injure, yet neither should he be forced to retain in his society to his own overthrow, nor to hear any judge therein above himself" (YP, II, p. 347). The other basic premise here is the extreme form of individualism we have already met, unrestrained by any claims of society, including that of his rejected marriage partner. He "ought not to injure her," certainly, but he is to be sole judge in deciding whether he has or not.

On the role of law in all this Milton is merely sophistic:

The law can only appoint the just and equal conditions of divorce, and is to look how it is an injury to the divorced, which in truth it can be none, as a mere separation; for if she consents, wherein has the law to right her? or consent not, then is it either just and so deserved, or if unjust, such in all likelihood was the divorcer, and to part from an unjust man is a happiness, and no injury to be lamented. (YP, II, p. 349)

Heads he wins, tails she loses. No talk of any economic settlement, no recognition of the problems of a divorced woman in seventeenth-century society. He is totally impervious to all social considerations, here and elsewhere. He hardly mentions children, for instance, as a possible complication, and in *Colasterion* he jeers at this objection from an anonymous critic:

And for those weak supposes of Infants that would be left in their mother's belly, (which must needs be good news for Chambermaids, to bear a serving-man grown so provident for great bellies) and portions, and jointures likely to incur embezzlement hereby, the ancient civil Law instructs us plentifully how to award. (YP, II, pp. 734–35)

It seems from this that only chambermaids get pregnant and only servants need be concerned. Does Milton suppose that procreation can be left to the lower classes? Or does he trust the scrupulous generosity of the bourgeois male? The "ancient civil Law" which was rejected in *Doctrine and Discipline* as a popish imposition is hastily and perfunctorily wheeled in again, to silence the objection.[18]

What we have here is a vivid example of a central illusion in bourgeois (and Protestant) thought: the myth of individual autonomy, and the failure to grasp the truth that the life and development of individuals depend unequivocally on social reciprocity, that the individual can only become a human individual through social relationships and is essentially a social individual. In Milton's case his version of individualism coexists with his intense loneliness and felt need for human society.

His orthodox contemporaries saw the individualism in his thought clearly enough and knew where it led: to the anarchic experimentalism of the Ranters. Prynne made the connection explicitly as he commented on "the late dangerous increase of many *Anabaptistical, Antinomian, Heretical, Atheistical opinions, as of the soul's mortality, divorce at pleasure etc.* lately broached, preached, printed in this famous City, which I hope our grand Council will speedily and carefully suppress."[19] Milton indignantly repudiated Prynne's retitling of his work as *Divorce at Pleasure.* Prynne, Milton assumed, had failed to see how high-minded he really was. But Prynne was right about the tendencies of Milton's view of divorce, right about its affinities with Antinomian and extreme Protestant individualism (Milton certainly finished up a mortalist and a heretic many times over). He was right too about the vulnerability of such individualism before well-organized forces of repression. The story of the preaching lace-woman, Mrs. Attaway, shows how unorthodox contemporaries also interpreted Milton in Prynne's way. She left her husband for William Jenney, and Jenney abandoned his wife and children to elope with the female preacher: she also recommended "Master Milton's *Doctrine of Divorce*" to her audience, recognizing the implications of Milton's version of Christian liberty, just as Prynne did.[20]

Milton shared something of the Ranters' faith in his own unerring illumination, and this illuminated reason led him to doctrines which had important areas in common. "They say that for one man to be tied to one woman, or one woman to one man, is a fruit of the curse: but they say, we are freed from the curse: therefore it is our liberty to make use of whom we please."[21] (The later Milton also endorsed polygamy, though characteristically less generously than this, since he limited it to men.) For another example, here is Laurence Clarkson:

This to me by Reason is confirmed, and by Scripture declared, *That to the pure all things are pure:* So that for my part I know nothing unclean to me, no more than it is of it self, and therefore what Act soever I do, is acted by that Majesty in me. . . . So to conclude, the censures of Scriptures, Churches, Saints, and Devils, are no more to me than the cutting off of a Dog's neck.[22]

Clarkson is like Milton in believing that Scripture must be interpreted by reason and the individual's illuminated spirit: he is only more frank and vehement in dismissing any contrary authorities.

These extreme individualistic views were not truly radical in the fullest sense of "going to the roots" of the issues, based on an awareness of the concrete relations of men in that society. So it is appropriate that the most intelligent and cool critique of such views comes from the communist Winstanley. His grasp of social realities and his commitment to developing social liberty for the mass of people led him to see such individualistic autonomy as a delusion which was deeply irresponsible to the women and children concerned. His critique applies equally to Milton's views on divorce:

> The Ranting practice . . . breaks the peace in Families . . . separates those very friends, causing both sides to run into the sea of confusion, madness and destruction, to leave each other, to leave their Children, and to live in discontent. . . . And the mother and child begotten in this manner is like to have the worst of it, for the man will be gone and leave them; and regard them no more than other women, like a Bull that begets a Calf, that never takes care neither for Cow nor Calf, after he hath had his pleasure. Therefore you women beware, for this ranting practice is not the restoring, but the destroying, power of the creation.[23]

He might have added, "Beware of one John Milton too." The dominant ideology of marriage justified permanent repression of women, but at least it provided the repressed with *some* guarantees of whatever material protection was available.

III

On sexuality Milton's position changed considerably over his life, but at every stage there is a degree of tension and ambivalence all too rarely recognized. In the poetry he wrote before his marriage, the literary eroticism of his early sonnets (decently veiled in foreign tongues) gave way to the militant chastity of *Comus*, threatened on all sides by sensuous and erotic energies. The *Apology Against a Pamphlet* (1642) has the famous critique of unchaste verses and the self-portrait which attributes to himself "a certain niceness of nature, an honest haughtiness and self-esteem either of what I was or what I might be (which let envy call pride) and lastly that modesty" (YP, I, p. 890), or self-righteous priggishness arguing very little self-knowledge at the age of thirty-three.

But that was before his marriages, his strenuous attempts to come to terms with the demands of his own sexuality. In contrast to the crude split between body and soul of his earlier work, in *Christian Doctrine* he asserts their total identity. Man "is not double or separable: not, as is commonly thought, produced from and composed of two different and distinct elements, soul and body. On the contrary, the whole man is the soul, and soul the man: a body, in other words, or individual substance, animated, sensitive, and rational" (YP, VI, p. 318). In *Christian Doctrine* he holds to this belief through heresy after heresy. Certainly, in theory at least, he resolved the body-soul split. Two questions then arise. By what route did he come to this final position? And how deep did the resolution go, how totally did it modify the attitudes and values that governed his responses in human relations? To answer the second question we will go to *Paradise Lost*, not to any conjectural biography.

Even in the early *Doctrine and Discipline* Milton is capable at times of near Blakeian insights. Here he is invoking Parliament:

The greatest burden in the world is superstition; not only of Ceremonies in the Church, but of imaginary and scarecrow sins at home. What greater weakening, what more subtle stratagem against our Christian warfare, when besides the gross body of real transgressions to encounter; we shall be terrified by a vain and shadowy menacing of faults that are not: When things indifferent shall be set to over-front us, under the banners of sin, what wonder if we be routed, and by the Art of the Adversary, fall into the subjection of the worst and deadliest offences. The superstition of the Papist is, *touch not, taste not,* when God bids both: and ours is, *part not, separate not,* when God and charity both permits and commands. (YP, II, p. 228)

Superstition, mystery, prohibitions which sap energy, intelligence, and the will to resist, leading to paralyzed subjection, all seem recognized here and repudiated. The Urizenic "touch not, taste not" has, it seems, been superseded. Milton appears an affirmative revolutionary, pressing forward.

But the enemy here is the papist, whose defeat is a thing of the past although it has left some vestiges in the Protestant "part not, separate not." Milton understands the repressive uses of religion by the papists, but does not yet extend this insight, as Winstanley and others did, to Protestant strategies. He claims that "our" (i.e., Protestant) superstition is "part not, separate not." Yet, as Weber noted, Protestant individualism tended to *separate:* man from friends, from priest, from church, and even from God. This brings out again the contradictory nature of Milton's enterprise. He is arguing for marriage as a cure for "loneliness" and using this as the basic premise in his case for easier divorce. If he had not insisted on the one-sidedness of the relationship, if a woman could divorce her husband as easily as a man could divorce his wife under the Miltonic dispensation, then marriage would only intensify his loneliness and insecurity (as Mary's rapid departure must have done). No friends, no priest, no church, no god—and no reliable wife either, the last prop kicked away. Marriage is specifically the escape from individualism, yet he cannot prevent himself from seeing it in destructively individualistic terms.

The affirmation of touch and taste, the easy transcendence of papist prohibitions, is a much more equivocal matter in practice than theory in the *Doctrine and Discipline*. He argued that the grounds for divorce should be extended to include nonphysical disabilities, so it was natural that he should emphasize the nonphysical aspects of marriage. (It is interesting that it was the despised papists, in spite of their "touch not," who had included sexual incapacities as grounds for annulment.) However, Milton does not only elevate the nonphysical, he degrades the physical with intense images of disgust: "when as the mind from whence must flow the acts of peace and love, a far more precious mixture than the quintessence of an excrement" (YP, II, p. 248). The image paradoxically works against itself, for the reader's response to "acts of peace and love" is colored by the implicit comparison with the excremental quintessence: it is as if the "acts of peace and love" themselves "flow" like an excremental "mixture" from a soul-penis. Milton's control of implication is uncertain, probably a sign of an unsuccessful attempt at sublimation.

There are similar revealing shifts in his glossing of St. Paul's "It is better to marry than to burn." Papists and Protestants alike saw the sexual implications of "burn" as relevant. Milton's interpretation is at least original (it is unlikely that even St. Paul thought of it):

That desire which God saw it was not good that man should be left alone to burn in; the desire and longing to put off an unkindly solitariness by uniting another body, but not without a fit soul to his in the cheerful society of wedlock. Which if it were so needful before the fall, when man was much more perfect in himself, how much more is it needful now against all the sorrows and casualties of this life to have an intimate and speaking help, a ready and reviving associate in marriage: whereof who misses by chancing on a mute and spiritless mate, remains more alone than before, and in a burning less to be contained than that which is fleshly and more to be considered; as being more deeply rooted even in the faultless innocence of nature. (YP, II, p. 251)

He equivocates with the traditional sexual interpretation of "burn." He starts with physical union, "uniting another body," and has spiritual compatibility edge its way in ("not without"). As he continues, the place of sexuality is usurped by the intense focus on loneliness, isolation. The sense of need comes over strongly. Why is God not man's source of solace against "all the sorrows and casualties of this life"? Weber might answer, "no god." The "mute and spiritless mate" rejected so vehemently here is the perfect wife of Puritan ideology we spoke of above, who answers only like an echo, with one word.

Immediately after this he acknowledges, in order to reject,

> that other burning, which is but as it were the venom of a lusty and overbounding concoction, strict life and labour with the abatement of a full diet may keep that low and obedient enough: but this pure and more inbred desire of joining to itself in conjugal fellowship a fit conversing soul (which desire is properly called love) *is stronger than death.* (YP, II, p. 251)

Although it is "venom" (so that papists were right to warn against taste and touch?) it is easy to control. The other burning is both much more intense and more valuable. But in spite of this distinction, he has retained the same metaphor and the same basic gloss to that metaphor. He realizes that the higher burning is specifically erotic too, an urgent desire, not the wish for a chat. So although it would be logical to satisify a mere burning for conversation by visiting intelligent male friends, by joining some Platonic academy, Milton doesn't even consider that option:

> Lest therefore so noble a creature as man should be shut up incurably under a worse evil by an easy mistake ... the aggrieved person shall do more manly to be extraordinary and singular in claiming the due right whereof he is frustrated, than to piece up his lost contentment by visiting the Stews, or stepping to his neighbours bed, which is the common shift in this misfortune, or else by suffering his useful life to waste away and be lost under a secret affliction of an unconscionable size to human strength. (YP, II, p. 247)

No mention of Platonic academics here. One doesn't go to brothels ("the Stews") to cure "loneliness." The word becomes an obvious euphemism, though the sense of isolation remains part of the experience. The "due right" Milton is talking of here is a man's right to a fully satisfactory sexual relationship (a woman's right is not, of course, contemplated). Paradoxically, his means of achieving this right involves being "extraordinary and singular," isolated from the rest of society, rejecting all its constraining norms. The way out of the prison of egotistic individualism is through "extraordinary" sin-

gularity, extreme individualism. The paradox is grounded in contradictions intrinsic to bourgeois individualism.[24]

In *Tetrachordon* Milton hides less behind this pose of high-
mindedness. It did not take a Freud to see through the rationaliz-
ing that was going on in his first stance. Prynne, we saw, renamed
it *Divorce at Pleasure,* and Milton's anonymous critic in the
Answer had been able to point out that the best cure for Milton's
loneliness would have been a good friend. The answerer had para-
phrased an argument to this effect by St. Augustine, though without acknowledgement. In *Tetrachordon* Milton explicitly repudiates this view, assigning it to its source: "*Austin* contests that
manly friendship in all other regards had been a more becoming
solace for *Adam,* than to spend so many secret years in an empty
world with one woman. But our Writers deservedly reject this
crabbed opinion." (YP, II, p. 596). He maintains that Adam was
essentially "alone" until Eve was created. A host of angels as
well-informed as Raphael would not have counted as company.
Again, "our Writers," the Protestant theologians, have effortlessly
transcended the crabbed asceticism of the papist past. By this
stage Milton is more clear about his commitment to a reintegration
of reason and feelings in a sexual relationship and aware that
mutuality, if not equality, was of the essence of such a relationship. How far had his theoretical insight advanced by the 1660s?
How integrated was this theoretical awareness with attitudes that
prevailed in social relations of practical life? It is time to turn to
Milton's dramatic exploration of these concerns in *Paradise Lost.*

IV

Here is Milton's Eve, when Adam is visited by an amiable top
academic, Raphael, and is able to talk about the latest develop-
ments in astronomy. Eve goes off.

> Yet went she not, as not with such discourse
> Delighted, or not capable her ear
> Of what was high: such pleasure she reserved,
> Adam relating, she sole auditress;
> Her husband the relater she preferred
> Before the angel, and of him to ask
> Chose rather; he, she knew would intermix
> Grateful digressions, and solve high dispute
> With conjugal caresses, from his lip
> Not words alone pleased her.
>
> (*PL* VIII, 48–57)[25]

This seems a vision of reason and feelings harmoniously recon-
ciled. Adam's lips are a source of both kisses and words, erotic
sensations and reasoning. His explanations would be part of an
erotic game, but the erotic play would not invalidate or interfere
with the rational argument. This is the point of the activity. But
underlying some of the details remains a striking distrust of
women and of sexual feelings. Milton carefully denies that Eve is
unintelligent or uninterested, yet (as so many of our women students have pointed out to us) still gives the impression that she is
both. Adam can be absorbed in scientific discussion; she can't be.
It is Eve who wants astronomy mingled with love, not Adam; and
Eve being the inferior partner such intermingling is by implication inferior. The motive for it comes from the weaker partner. It
is only Adam who can "solve high dispute" with conjugal caresses, or who is allowed to solve them that way—manipulating
his partner sexually as and when he chooses, while not being
manipulated in return. Beneath the affirmation of the unity of the
pair, in the unity of body and soul, reason and feelings, lie unresolved tensions, unexorcised anxieties. The paradox is that Milton's conscious mind affirmed the value of the body and its essen-
tiality to human relationships, while he still deeply feared and
resisted the dissolution of the ego. The tension appears in the
poetry partly through slight uncertainties of tone—as in "from his
lip / Not words alone pleased her." Why veil a kiss in a coy negative? It is as though Eve/Milton is proud of having gone so far in
overcoming her/his inhibitions.

The particular discussion into which this passage is set also
bears obliquely on Eve's position. Adam's question is about hierarchies in heaven. Why is the "sedentary earth / . . . Served by
more noble than herself"? (*PL* VIII, 15–38). Raphael's answer,
given after Eve has left, is this:

> consider first, that great
> Or bright infers not excellence: the earth
> Though in comparison of heaven, so small
> Nor glistering, may of solid good contain
> More plenty than the sun that barren shines,
> Whose virtue on it self works no effect,
> But in the fruitful earth; there first received
> His beams, unactive else, their vigour find.   (VIII, 90–97)

The parallel with human sexuality is explicit: the earth as female,
the sun as male. The lesson is clear too. The apparent excellence
of the active male principle is illusory: without the earth it is

barren, since its beams find their "vigour" in the fruitful earth. In spite of its apparent greatness the sun exists for the earth. So man, in spite of doctrine to the contrary, exists for woman? It is just as well that Eve is not around to hear (though later we find she has been listening behind a bush: she was not so uninterested in Raphael's discourse, unaccompanied by "conjugal caresses," after all). What we are presented with is Milton's covert rejection of hierarchy, again, now in connection with the role of woman.

What Eve is described as doing makes a complex comment. She

> went forth among her fruits and flowers,
> To visit how they prospered, bud and bloom,
> Her nursery; they at her coming sprung
> And touched by her fair tendance gladlier grew.
>
> (VIII, 44–47)

She functions here partly as a gardener, but also unmistakably as sun, active principle of growth and hence a male force. As she leaves, graces

> from about her shot darts of desire
> Into all eyes to wish her still in sight.   (VIII, 62–63)

Again, images of masculine aggression (Cupid? Apollo?). Not only does Milton imply, through the earth-sun analogy, that the woman may be the superior being, he also, inconsistently, attributes male potency to her. (Perhaps the lines just quoted also relate *typologically* to Christ's aggression in VI, 844–52?[26]) Here she represents the transcendence of the conventional categories of male and female, and so momentarily we glimpse a Hegelian supersession of opposed categories. But only glimpse. For it is only in types and images that Milton can allow Eve to achieve such a transcendence, not as human being, however unfallen.

What we have in this section is a microcosm of the poem as a whole: a timid doctrine of near equality and partial integration of body and mind, undercut by a dramatization which implies the opposite, glossed by a context which by way of analogy implies an extraordinarily radical concept of sexual relationships which manifestly does not prevail in Eden, in practice or in theory. Milton's sense of a conceivably perfect union, transcending the opposites of body and soul, male and female, is thus not directly represented in *Paradise Lost*, not dramatically created. In fact, he uses angelology to indicate schematically what it would involve. Here all his departures from orthodoxy are important and positive.[27] Angels, for instance, eat—in reality, not "in mist, the common gloss of theologians" (V, 435–36). Raphael makes the point that angelic digestion will probably be the model for fulfilled man: "time may come when men / With angels may participate" (V, 493–94).[28] So there is a transparadisal condition envisaged which is as superior to paradise as paradise theoretically should be to the fallen world.

At the conclusion of his discussion on love. Raphael hints at what this might be like. Adam asks if the angels make love:

> To whom the angel with a smile that glowed
> Celestial rosy red, love's proper hue,
> Answered. Let it suffice thee that thou know'st
> Us happy, and without love no happiness.   (VIII. 618–21)

Again the tone is uncertain. Is Raphael embarrassed? Or is red the color of passion kindling at the memory of angelic intercourse?[29] His answer is indirect but unequivocal, like an honest but inhibited parent refusing to put his/her child off with stories about birds or bees, but very uneasy nonetheless. Raphael continues:

> Whatever pure thou in the body enjoy'st
> (And pure thou wert created) we enjoy
> In eminence, and obstacle find none
> Of membrane, joint, or limb, exclusive bars:
> Easier than air with air, if spirits embrace,
> Total they mix.   (VIII, 622–27)

Behind this is a rejection of merely genital sexuality in favor of total orgasm, total union. Distinction of the sexes and associated contraries are superseded. And here it is important to register Milton's emphasis on the materiality of angels, for this explicitly makes them and their experience an extension of human potential, not a wholly other mode of existence. They become a way of expressing what it should be to be fully human, fully alive:

> All heart they live, all head, all eye, all ear,
> All intellect, all sense.   (VI, 350–51)

Angelic existence is a state of heightened sensuality, heightened feelings, coexisting with heightened intelligence. The angels represent a full spontaneous enjoyment, matter fully energized and humanized, a vision which was to be explored by Blake in *The Visions of the Daughters of Albion* and elsewhere.[30] It is a sad commentary on the evolution of western society that for even Milton angelology was his sole means of conceiving satisfactory human relations. All he could otherwise imagine and represent were deeply flawed and contradictory.

V

It is now time to ask, where is the male chauvinist so beloved of the neo-Christian critics? How do we take those passages which have given them so much satisfaction? And what is the significance of the Fall? What happens to the unerring discrimination between prelapsarian and postlapsarian love that was meant to shame us fallen readers?

The most famous, apparently the most unequivocal statement of the inequality of the sexes, is the introduction to Adam and Eve:

> Two of far nobler shape erect and tall,
> Godlike erect, with native honour clad
> In naked majesty seemed lords of all,
> And worthy seemed. (IV, 288–91)

This is how they appear to Satan; so "seemed" presumably places the judgment inside his consciousness. His initial judgment sees their undistinguished preeminance over all other creatures, their "empire." Then distinctions are made:

> though both
> Not equal, as their sex not equal seemed;
> For contemplation he and valour formed,
> For softness she and sweet attractive grace,
> He for God only, she for God in him:
> His fair large front and eye sublime declared
> Absolute rule. (IV, 295–301)

Does the "seemed" continue, placing this judgment as Satan's? Or has Milton forgotten Satan and become immersed in repressive seventeenth-century orthodox ideology? If he has, he has been reduced to repeating the contradictions of that ideology we discussed above. "Absolute rule" for instance: does Adam really have that? To the horror of the orothodox he does not claim it in the crucial exchange with Eve before the Fall. And in Eden all things are held in common (IV, 752), so what does "Absolute rule" mean? Then one might wonder whether "declared" (IV, 300) undercuts the whole speech on male rule since these signs may only "declare" absolute rule to the fallen Satan, who does not know what Raphael told Adam, "that great / Or bright infers not excellence" (VIII, 90–91). (Satan, after all, an automatic respecter of

visible hierarchies, landed on the sun first and had to be told by
Uriel that Eden was on earth.)

However, it must be said that these doubts or equivocations
are not dominant, and the passage basically supports a male supremacist reading. At a later stage it is easier to argue for Milton's
conscious control. This is the debate on love between Adam and
Raphael. Neo-Christian critics are so awed by authority that they
assume the archangel must be right, or more right than Adam.
Since Raphael argues a strict antifeminist line, which Adam resists, Milton must endorse Raphael and be dramatizing Adam's
fatal propensities to uxuriousness.[31]

However, this debate is preceded by Adam's reported debate
with God. (Or rather with someone he takes to be God: strictly it
is the Son, though he sounds like, and pretends to be, the Father
[cf. VII, 174–75; VIII, 356–451]. Adam is unaware of the distinction.) This deity clearly has no satisfactory relationship with
Adam, no meaningful friendship, in spite of Adam's later claims in
his fallen and nostalgic despair (X, 720–25; XI, 315–17). And he
lies. For instance, he claims that he is "alone from all eternity"
(VIII, 405–06). If this is the Son, he has never been alone, unless
the company of the Father constitutes loneliness; and he has not
existed from all eternity. If this is the Father, and strictly it isn't,
he seems not to be satisfied with the near equality of the Son, in
spite of the exaltation of the Son in Books III and V. Either way
the existential abyss and confusion is interesting. Furthermore, he
"seemed" (VIII, 376) to order Adam to live in solitude, whereas
he actually wanted Adam to disagree with him: "Thus far to try
thee, Adam, I was pleased" (VIII, 437). The conviction Adam
clings to is that he needs an equal:

> Among unequals what society
> Can sort, what harmony or true delight?
> Which must be mutual, in proportion due
> Given and received.   (VIII, 383–86)

Here Adam makes the equation Milton did not make in his prose
works, the crucial equation between mutuality, equality, and delight. This of course directly contradicts God's conception of
man's ideal existence (VIII, 374–75), but it turns out that God
wanted to be contradicted in precisely this way. And God, Milton
would have us know, outranks Raphael. So the effect of placing
the debate with God immediately before the debate with Raphael
is twofold. It gives divine sanction for Adam's view of marriage as

a mutual relationship between equals; and it gives a precedent for God's official spokesman giving out an inadequate ethic in order to "try" Adam, relying on Adam's man-centered ethic to prevail in argument.

The crucial debate between Adam and Raphael thus has a context that undercuts the authority of the angelic case. The traditional response to Adam's opening speech is given by Bush in his edition of Milton's poetry: "Adam's speech, which contains the seeds of catastrophe to come, is made a subtle revelation of mixed feelings, both right and wrong." Bush's comment on Adam's reply to Raphael is: "Though Adam now expresses a corrected view, he has revealed his instinctive weakness."[32] The "revelation" may be subtle but for the neo-Christian critic and literary scholar the difference between right and wrong is unmistakable. Raphael gives the correct view: whenever Adam deviates from a coldly pragmatic egoism, he is to be condemned. Bush spells it out: "neither intellectual pride nor human love should come between man and God—or man and his integrity." The alternative gloss here, replacing Milton's God by "integrity," is itself revealing about the values Bush sees Milton as reinforcing.

Whatever the judgment, Adam's speech is certainly an account of his experience of difficulties with the orthodox sexist view. Eve's beauty was undoubtedly disturbing to his cool egoism:

> in all enjoyment else
> Superior and unmoved, here only weak
> Against the charm of beauty's powerful glance.
>
> (VIII, 531–33)

In order to exorcise this (God-given) experience, he repeats the ideology of male supremacy:

> For well I understand in the prime end
> Of nature her the inferior, in the mind
> And inward faculties, which most excel.   (VIII, 540–42)

He then describes how inadequate this "understanding" is:

> yet when I approach
> Her loveliness, so absolute she seems
> And in her self complete, so well to know
> Her own, that what she wills to do or say,
> Seems wisest, virtuousest, discreetest, best.   (VIII, 546–50)

"Seems" is used twice here, matching the use of "seemed" in the introduction to Adam and Eve which we discussed above. To Satan, Eve "seemed" less than equal. To Adam she "seems" evidently superior, "absolute" (repeating Satan's word for Adam's own mode of rule [IV, 301]). Adam here is strenuously trying to distinguish appearance from reality, or trying to discredit the reality of how he feels by the qualifying "seems." But there is nothing evidently wrong with these appearances. "Absolute" is literally true of her; she has been "freed from" (*absoluta*) him; and metaphorically this is untrue of her to the same extent as it is untrue of him: neither is a self-sufficient individual. (Robinson Crusoe, we recall, is a mythological figure embodying many of the classic illusions of bourgeois individualism.)

Eve does indeed have a devastating effect on his earlier certainties:

> All higher knowledge in her presence falls
> Degraded, wisdom in discourse with her
> Looses discountenanced, and like folly shows.
>
> (VIII, 551–53)

Again he asserts that his knowledge is (as in the dominant ideology) superior to hers and is threatened by conversation with her. His judgment on this is severe, acting through "degraded," certainly a very harsh judgment on paradisal conversations. But the speech concludes like this:

> Authority and reason on her wait,
> As one intended first, not after made
> Occasionally; and to consummate all,
> Greatness of mind and nobleness their seat
> Build in her loveliest, and create an awe
> About her, as a guard angelic placed.   (VIII, 554–59)

No more "seems" here. He now repudiates his claim to "higher knowledge" and to power over her. Nor is he grudging and resentful about it. His praise is unqualified: "Greatness of mind and nobleness." His response does *not* show him "sunk in carnal pleasure" (VIII, 593) but is full of reverence, "awe." The basic premise that Eve was "not after made / Occasionally" (VIII, 555–56) is not wrong in terms of the poem. God himself had said:

> I, ere thou spakest,
> Knew it was not good for man to be alone.   (VIII, 444–45)

For neo-Christians Adam's statement is an unsubtle revelation of
wrong feeling. Certainly that is how Raphael reacts. With "con-
tracted brow" (VIII, 560) he condemns Adam's stance and opposes
it by a Neoplatonic asceticism, marked by the disjunction between
reason and feelings (so typical of "the Christian tradition") and an
insistence on the need for male domination.

At the center of the kind of love recommended by Raphael is
a simple egoism:

> weigh with her thyself;
> Then value: oft times nothing profits more
> Than self-esteem, grounded on just and right
> Well-managed.   (VIII, 570–3)

Adam's trouble has been that he cannot get this crude weighing
operation to come out right. It is certain that Milton would at one
time have totally endorsed Raphael here; in the *Apology* of 1642
he referred to his own "self-esteem either of what I was or what I
might be (which let envy call pride)" (YP, I, p. 890). Did he never
go beyond this? If he did not must we nonetheless admire the
doctrine? As even the younger Milton knew, there were those
(whom he accused of envy) who called this pride. And, in fact, our
discussion of his quest for marriage and woman, and of his dread
of loneliness, has suggested how he did come to find this inflated
individualism quite inadequate.

Raphael is contemptuous of what "transports" Adam so, "An
outside" (VIII, 568) he sneers. This is a profoundly ungenerous
response to Adam's celebration of Eve's loveliness, which troubled
him precisely because it did not remain simple and external. The
so-called love that Raphael advocates repudiates "the sense of
touch" (VIII, 579), equating it with the bestial, absolutely distinct
from "true love" (589). This too can be paralleled in Milton's prose,
in his rejection of "the mere notion of carnal lust, the mere goad of a
sensitive desire" as a motive to be considered in marriage.

The "corrected" Adam is only "half abashed" and retracts
nothing. When he says,

> Though higher of the genial bed by far,
> And with mysterious reverence I deem   (VIII, 598–99)

he implicitly corrects Raphael. "Higher" is ambiguous—higher
than "her outside" (596), or higher than Raphael deems, or both?
In any case he is rejecting the sterile egoism of Raphael's alleged
kind of love, with its dehumanised and rather hypocritical spiritu-
alism (cf. 618–27).

Where is Milton in all this? Insofar as Raphael repeats the papist "touch not," Milton early on, though with considerable difficulties, had repudiated that kind of "crabbed opinion." Furthermore, Raphael responds to Adam's refusal to be fully abashed with warm approval, a smile like God's when Adam passed his previous "trial." What Raphael then says of angelic love is partially aetherialized,[33] but otherwise, as we have seen, it is more intense, more mutual than "human" love and does not repudiate the physical.

So this exchange dramatizes a conflict between two conceptions of love. It is not clear that Milton is on the side of the angel (until the angel reveals he is on the side of man). If Adam's conception of love in Book VIII is closer to postlapsarian love and makes the Fall more likely (as it clearly does), then we may ask, with Empson and others, whether the fall itself may not have been fortunate and encouraged by the hidden God of *Paradise Lost* as an immediate and considerable improvement on his attempt to create a "prelapsarian" state.

Some natural modern responses to both unfallen and fallen sexuality would thus become legitimate. "Fallen readers" persist in finding "unfallen" sex unsatisfactory, and fallen sex not perfect but better. Here is Eve being charmingly submissive:

> So spake our general mother, and with eyes
> Of conjugal attraction unreproved,
> And meek surrender, half embracing leaned
> On our first father, half her swelling breast
> Naked met his under the flowing gold
> Of her loose tresses hid: he in delight
> Both of her beauty and submissive charms
> Smiled with superior love, as Jupiter
> On Juno smiles, when he impregns the clouds
> That shed May flowers; and pressed her matron lip
> With kisses pure. (IV, 492–502)

A sensuous and erotic description certainly, but one that has rarely received close scrutiny. There are, in fact, innumerable indications of tension. "Unreproved" for instance: who would think of "reproving" it we may ask—and Raphael could give the answer. "Meek surrender" sounds cloyingly abject and again raises a question: what battle has she lost? Why does she "half embracing" lean with only "half her swelling breast" meeting his? Female students usually find the reference to "superior love" rather absurd. It is worth pointing out here that Adam is delighted with his power, not his (or Eve's) wisdom: this is manipulative male love.

The kiss sounds rather gross: "pressed her matron lip / With kisses pure." Did she "press" back? The relationship is undoubtedly erotic and much superior to Satan's enforced and anguished celibacy (significantly, as Empson noticed, seen as one of the most fiendish of God's punishments) which frames the description. But this relationship feels intolerable in many ways, flawed with unacknowledged antagonisms, negative responses, manipulative, unfree and half-concealed sexuality.

Their first act of love after eating the fruit is undoubtedly guilt-ridden, hectic, and finally unfulfilling. But it is not necessarily less satisfying than prelapsarian sex. One of us had his education advanced immeasurably by a female student who cut throught layers of neo-Christian apologetics with "but I like it like that." She was, as the neo-Christians would gleefully retort, a very "fallen" reader indeed, and her insight was theoretically and existentially sound: Eve is *active* now as she never was in paradisal sexuality. Adam claims his senses are heightened, and though Eve is still external, something for him to "enjoy," to appropriate like the fruit, she is now a fully active partner:

> So said he, and forbore not glance or toy
> Of amorous intent, well understood
> Of Eve, whose eye darted contagious fire.   (IX, 1034–36)

At least it is she herself who consciously directs her sexual activity, not those detached, sublimating, fictitious "graces" (VIII, 60–63). Against this set the following description of paradisal love-making:

>   into their inmost bower
> Handed they went; and eased the putting off
> These troublesome disguises which we wear,
> Straight side by side were laid, nor turned I ween
> Adam from his fair spouse, nor Eve the rites
> Mysterious of connubial love refused.   (IV, 738–43)

Again, this is a much-admired passage whose language merits closer attention than it has received. The happy couple were "laid": who by? Adam is not seen to be doing anything, in this totally unfrank description. Eve does not "dart contagious fire": she just does not actually refuse. Does she lie there and think of England, as Victorian wives were supposed to do? Paradoxically the language here works strongly to draw attention to Milton's inability to be frank about their sexual union, at the very point where he is repudiating such mystification (IV, 740–47). "Mysterious" is the key word: why is he investing these "rites" with sacramental significance—the "mystery" he himself tried to *rescue* marriage from both in his published prose and his *Christian Doctrine*, a "mystery" which Blake so powerfully repudiates:

Embraces are Cominglings: from the Head even to the Feet;
And not a pompous High Priest entering by a Secret Place.

(*Jerusalem*, 69, 43–44)

Encouraged by Blake and many elements of his own work, we might be tempted to use Milton's own words against himself in this description of Adam and Eve—"austere hypocrite."

Nevertheless, we would be wrong to overlook the way Milton even here shows that he knows how inadequate prevailing sexual attitudes were. He also shows that either he knows about the inadequacies of Eden and its contradictions, or he is unable to free himself in practice of the very attitudes he is criticizing— perhaps there is a mixture of both. The underlying uncertainty is central to Milton's work and makes any final judgment on his "position" deeply problematic.

He seems to confront contemporary life with two versions of Utopia. One is the repository of his most important revolutionary ideals, an imagined condition in which all contradictions will be magically resolved, New Jerusalem. This acted as a critique not only of the fallen "state" but of Eden, the lesser Utopia, both politically and sexually. It was a visionary focus for a revolutionary egalitarian state which is also sexually radical. But the sexual critique is never fully articulated, and Milton gives great prominence to male supremacist stereotypes that at one level he knows must be superseded in the fourfold humanized world of the New Jerusalem. The radical Milton is pervasive but covert. He must have been conscious of holding many radical views, but he was unable, or unwilling, to express them and the confusions he was grappling with on the surface of his great poem. He may have meant the poem for a dimly envisaged "fit audience though few" of extreme radicals, with the dominant (orthodox) ideology displayed sufficiently to allay the suspicions of those many unfit conformists, whose heirs are Lewis, Fish, Patrides and others.[34] It is certainly unfair to abstract statements of a repressive sexual ethic in *Paradise Lost* and take them at their detached face value. Nor should we ignore his inevitable complicity with orthodox sexist ideology. His thought includes an immense, yet insecure, advance over the course of his life, but there are limits to how far even a heroic individual can transcend his background and education, in thought and practice.

University of East Anglia, England
Murdoch University, Australia

NOTES

1. Good examples of the kind of work we have in mind are: C. S. Lewis, *Preface to Paradise Lost* (Oxford, 1942); Stanley E. Fish, *Surprised by Sin* (Berkeley, 1967); C. A. Patrides, *Milton and the Christian Tradition* (Oxford, 1966), esp. pp. 165–86; J. Halkett, *Milton and the Idea of Matrimony* (New Haven, 1970), ch. 4; and most recently a typical expression by Barbara K. Lewalski, "Milton on Women—Yet Once More," in *Milton Studies*, VI, ed. James D. Simmonds (Pittsburgh, 1974), pp. 3–20, to which see Marcia Landy's most pertinent reply, "A Free and Open Encounter: Milton and the Modern Reader," in *Milton Studies*, VIII, ed. James D. Simmonds (Pittsburgh, 1976), pp. 3–36.

2. On this topic, excellent introductions are by B. Ollman, *Alienation* (Cambridge, 1971), and I. Mészáros, *Marx's Theory of Alienation* (London, 1970).

3. See: K. Thomas, "Women and the Civil War Sects," reprinted in *Crisis in Europe*, ed. T. Aston (London, 1965), pp. 317–40; P. Higgins, "The Reactions of Women," ch. 5 in *Politics, Religion and the English Civil War*, ed. B. Manning (London, 1973); W. Notestein, "The English Woman, 1580–1650," in *Studies in Social History*, ed. J. H. Plumb (London, 1955), pp. 69–107; L. Stone, *Crisis of the Aristocracy* (Oxford, 1966), ch. 11; also important suggestions in L. B. Wright, *Middle-Class Culture in Elizabethan England* (Chapel Hill, N.C., 1935), pp. 202–09 and 465–503, where he argues that changes in social organization, and a corresponding increase in "burgher writers," "had greatly increased women's liberties." This relevant area needs far more intensive research, and what has been done needs attention from literary critics. For the case that the overall position of women in the seventeenth century can actually be judged as deteriorating if compared with the position of women in the American colonies, see R. G. Thompson, *Women in Stuart England and America* (London, 1974).

4. R. Baxter, *A Christian Directory* (London, 1673), p. 529, spelling modernized.

5. J. Dod and R. Cleaver, *A Godly Forme of Household Government* (London, 1630), p. 1, spelling modernized.

6. Similarly William Gouge, in *Of Domestical Duties* (London, 1622), strongly discouraged any familiarity of speech between husband and wife, warning against the use of terms of affection or even letting the wife use the husband's Christian name. See Wright, *Middle-Class Culture*, p. 222.

7. See similar accounts, evidence, and references showing that women were normally and explicitly envisaged as commodities and useful property: Thompson, *Woman in Stuart England and America*, pp. 48–51, 116–22, 162–67; E. S. Morgan, *The Puritan Family* (1944), rpt. New York, 1966), pp. 38–54; Christopher Hill, *The World Turned Upside Down* (London, 1972), pp. 247–51; J. T. Johnson, *A Society*

Ordained by God: English Puritan Marriage Doctrine in the First Half of the Seventeenth Century (Nashville, 1970), pp. 23–24, 32–35. Since we first wrote this essay, L. Stone's monumental work has become available: *The Family and Marriage in England, 1500–1800* (London, 1977).

8. W. Haller and M. Haller, "The Puritan Art of Love," *Huntington Library Quarterly*, V (1941–42), 235–72.

9. We could follow Milton himself and add atheism. See *Complete Prose Works of John Milton*, ed. Don M. Wolfe et al. (New Haven, 1953–), vol. II, p. 269, etc. Of all the psychic consequences, perhaps the outstanding critique is contained in Blake's *Four Zoas*.

10. Max Weber, *The Protestant Ethic and the Spirit of Capitalism*, trans. T. Parsons (London, 1971), pp. 103–04. For a valuable commentary on the group organization and psychology of Puritans, see M. Walzer, *The Revolution of the Saints* (London, 1966), and on Puritanism and the family, pp. 183–98. Of course, Milton himself evolved a lucid critique of orthodox predestinarian ideology. See especially *Christian Doctrine* (YP, VI, pp. 153–202) and Maurice Kelley's introductory remarks (YP, VI, pp. 74–86).

11. For the economic basis and philosophical manifestations, see the outstanding study by C. B. Macpherson, *Possessive Individualism* (Oxford, 1962).

12. Like other militant Protestants, however, he could certainly see the relation between the traditional externalization and reification of grace and God in human institutions and the social realities involved here.

13. Compare Blake's continual emphasis that "all deities reside in the human breast" (*Marriage of Heaven and Hell*, plate 11). There are many examples of seventeenth-century versions of this position explored by Hill in *The World Turned Upside Down*, which includes an appendix on Milton and Bunyan.

14. Quotations of Milton's prose are from the Yale edition cited in note 9, hereafter given in the text as YP. We have modernized spelling. On the commonplace connection of family and state see, for example, Cleaver, *A Godly Forme;* Thompson, *Women in Stuart England and America*, ch. 7; Morgan, *The Puritan Family*, ch. 6; Christopher Hill, *Society and Puritanism* (London, 1964), ch. 13.

15. Another interesting effect is that in Milton's analogy "government," at least when it is resisted, does not include any people either—as though there is no *human* opposition to the revolutionary elite. Of course, as Marx noted, a revolutionary class, or dominant fraction of a class, must seem tò itself to represent the universal welfare of society.

16. In *The Ready and Easy Way*, see especially YP, VII, pp. 442–43, 458–59, where the revolutionary elite of the Saints is explicitly made into a traditional property elite.

17. See Thomas, "Women and the Civil War Sect."

18. Milton is obscure here, concealing his failure to deal with the problem of children by the vague gesture at the "ancient civil Law." It is clear that he only envisages upper-class marriages here (based on marriage contracts and transactions of property—see note 7 above) and fails to meet his "Answerer." See also G. E. Howard, *A History of Matrimonial Institutions* (1904; rpt. New York, 1964), II, 56–59, 71–96.

19. *Twelve Serious Questions* (1644), quoted in YP, II, p. 722, n. 5.

20. See David Masson, *The Life of John Milton* (London, 1859–80), III, 189–92; and references in William Riley Parker, *Milton*, 2 vols. (Oxford, 1968), II, 919–20, n. 6.

21. John Holland, *Smoke of the Bottomless Pit, or, A More True and fuller discovery of the Doctrine of those men which call themselves Ranters: or, The Mad Crew* (1651), quoted in N. Cohn, *The Pursuit of the Millenium* (London, 1970), p. 293. On the Ranters, see A. L. Morton, *The World of the Ranters* (London, 1970).

22. *A Single Eye All Light, no Darkness* . . . (1650), in Cohn, *Pursuit of the Millenium*, pp. 312–13.

23. *The Works of Gerrard Winstanley*, ed. G. Sabine (New York, 1965).

24. For the seventeenth century, see C. B. Macpherson, *Possessive Individualism* (Oxford, 1962). As the next paragraph notes, St. Augustine had an extremely pertinent comment on the aspect of Milton's argument which maintains that what he wants is an asexual companionship: "If it was company and good conversation that Adam needed it would have been much better arranged to have two men together, as friends equally, not a man and a woman." *De genesi ad litteram*, IX, 5.9 (*P. Lat.*, 34. 396). See also YP, II, p. 596, n. 26.

25. Poetry quoted from *The Poems of John Milton*, ed. J. Carey and A. Fowler (London, 1968).

26. Typological connections must not, of course, be confused with equations. It is also worth noticing how even in asserting Eve's *activity* Milton seems to dissociate the arrow-shooting from the subject, the woman (VIII, 60–63), by bringing in the graces; the syntax, however, does remain ambiguous.

27. On the subject of angelology see Robert H. West, *Milton and the Angels* (Athens, Ga., 1955), especially chs. 5–9.

28. On angelic eating, see West, *Milton and the Angels*, pp. 106, 138–40, 164–69. Empson makes an interesting connection between this half-promise and Satan's temptation to Eve in her dream (V, 79). See *Milton's God* (London, 1965), p. 150.

29. On angelic sex, see especially West, *Milton and the Angels*, pp. 169–74, 88–89, 106, 124. West himself treats Raphael's redness here as a sign his disclosure is "embarrassed" (pp. 171–72), though most commentators have simply accepted Milton's own gloss here, that red is "love's proper hue" (e.g., E. L. Marilla, "Milton on Conjugal Love Among the Heavenly Angels," *MLN*, LXVIII [1953], 485–86). It is also taken, in Fowler's words, as "the colour of angelic ardour" (gloss to VIII, 618–20, in the Carey and Fowler edition, n. 26), and West, *Milton and the Angels*, p. 146, links this passage with IV, 977 ff. Raphael is not red to represent the traditional cherubim since he is named as a seraph (V, 277), a virtue (V, 371) or an angel or archangel (see West, p. 134).

30. For all exegetes, and Hume editing *Paradise Lost* in 1695, the famous text on marriage in heaven at Matthew xxii, 30, settled any speculation about heavenly sex (West, *Milton and the Angels*, pp. 171–72). This reflects the traditional confusion of sexuality, procreation, and marriage (evidenced in the title of Marilla's article, n. 29 above). Milton's implicit approach to the text is fascinating: for him it seems to licence the fact that angelic sexuality is unfettered by any institutional restraints (such as conventional marriage and its market) and is the direct expression of spontaneous affection. This is a vision of liberated sexuality which transcends the socioeconomic and ethical nexus which had traditionally contained and controlled Eros. There is not space to develop this discussion at the present time, but there is suggestive material in Herbert Marcuse, *Eros and Civilization* (Boston, 1974). For Blake here, see D. Aers, "Blake and the Dialectics of Sex," *ELH*, XLIV (1977), 500–14.

31. For good measure, the reader's sympathies with Adam can be chastised as ghastly signs of his own corruption, out of which "Milton" is allegedly educating him into an uncritical orthodoxy. See, for example, Fish, *Surprised by Sin.* Contrast Peter Lindenbaum's discussion in "Lovemaking in Milton's Paradise," *Milton Studies,* VII, ed. James D. Simmonds (Pittsburgh, 1975), pp. 293–98, suggesting limitations in Raphael's views from a perspective different from our own.

32. Douglas Bush, ed., *The Complete Poetical Works of John Milton* (Boston, 1965), notes to VIII, 521–59, 596 ff.

33. John Carey unkindly calls it "gaseous love" in his *Milton* (London, 1969).

34. Since we first wrote this essay, Christopher Hill's study of Milton has been published: *Milton and the English Revolution* (London, 1977). Also relevant to these concluding remarks is R. I. V. Hodge, "Satan and the Revolution of the Saints," *Literature and History,* VII (1978), 23–33.

"IF SHAPE IT MIGHT BE CALL'D THAT SHAPE HAD NONE": ASPECTS OF DEATH IN MILTON

Cherrell Guilfoyle

DEATH, LIKE the Holy Spirit, has seemed to some of Milton's commentators a subject in which the poet found little interest and less inspiration. Saurat said that death to Milton was no more than "a cosmological incident." Another Frenchman, writing more than a century earlier, found Milton afraid to face death. Noting that Milton derided in *Eikonoklastes* each section of the *Eikon Basilike* except the last, "Meditations on Death," Chateaubriand wrote: "Que fait Milton? Il fuit devant ces méditations" ("What does Milton do, faced with these meditations? He runs away").[1]

In *Paradise Lost* the allegory of Sin and Death was to Dr. Johnson "one of the greatest faults in the poem," a confusion of real and figurative. Addison found the two characters out of place in the poem—"improper agents," not properly allegorical.[2] Milton was often ill at ease with allegory; he may have agreed with Luther that allegory was "the froth, as it were, of the Holy Scriptures," and Milton was determined to reveal and justify what lay beneath the froth.[3] His attitude to allegory was not that expressed by Tasso—"they drink deceived, and so deceived, they live";[4] he was at pains to make clear that the allegory was only one aspect of the reality, and the presentation of death in Adam's speeches in Book IX and in the "great review" of Books XI and XII of *Paradise Lost* is therefore nearer to the heart of Milton's thinking than the shapeless figure in hell and on the causeway. But, as St. Augustine wrote, "Death is a reality; and so troublesome a reality that it cannot be explained by any verbal formula, nor got rid of by any rational argument."[5] Milton certainly tried both verbal formulae and rational argument in *De Doctrina Christiana,* but the element of nameless horror in Augustine's troublesome reality he dealt with by allegory.

I

Death in person appears only twice in *Paradise Lost,* and apart from blackness (he is described by Raphael as Sin's "black attendant" [VII, 547]) he has no distinct physical characteristics— the shape "If shape it might be call'd that shape had none" (II, 667). In Book II, at the gate of hell, he confronts and then is recognized by Satan. In Book X he issues from the gate to build the causeway to Earth. Adam first mentions Death as "Som dreadful thing no doubt" (IV, 426), and the "thing" again appears in Satan's derisive reference to "the pain / Of Death denounc't, whatever thing Death be" (IX, 694–95). "The meager Shadow," "the grim Feature," "this vast unhide-bound Corps" (X, 264, 279, 601) has the terrifying quality of the dark unknown and undefined. Some of his accoutrements, however, are defined. On his first appearance, he wears the semblance of a kingly crown (II, 673), and on the second, he wields a "Mace petrific" (X, 274). He may lack shape, but he does not lack power.

In action, Death, the son of Sin, personifies first lust and then, more significantly, greed. According to Fox, Milton represents lust and gluttony released from the original sin of pride, just as Sin and Death are released from hell to invade the earth.[6] The connection between lust and death goes back to rabbinic tradition, in which the serpent poured lust over the forbidden fruit to get Eve to eat it; or, in other sources, seduced Eve and was the father of Cain, the first murderer.[7] Milton's pattern echoes James, i, 15: "Then when lust hath conceived, it bringeth forth sin; and sin, when it is finished, bringeth forth death." In *Paradise Lost,* Death enters the scene as the fruit of Satan's incestuous lust for his daughter, and, as his first action, rapes his mother, Sin (II, 777–802). Lust is also the "operation first displaid" by the forbidden fruit on Adam and Eve (IX, 1012)—the allegorical representation of Augustine's statement that "sensual desire arose in the disobedient bodies of the first human beings as a result of the sin of disobedience,"[8] expressed by Milton in *De Doctrina* as evil concupiscence (the lust to sin) being the sin of which Adam and Eve were first guilty (CM, XV, p. 193).

Greed, the intestinal appetite, is for Milton the sin that can best illustrate, and to some extent subsume, the other deathly appetite of lust. He noted in his Commonplace Book, "Tertullianus eleganter vocat homicidam gulam" ("Tertullian with nicety of phrase calls gluttony a murderer") (CM, XVIII, p. 131). The early poem *On Time* links time with death ("triumphing over Death, and Chance, and thee O Time"), and the phrases "glut thy self," "thy greedy self" link the ravages of time with greed, an image far more powerfully used when Death, "all nose," as Raleigh said, smells the feast of fallen man in *Paradise Lost.*[9] Satan had promised Sin and Death the Earth to prey upon—"there ye shall be fed and fill'd / Immeasurably" (II, 843–44). Death's hunger is insatiable, and the Almighty descends to some vigorous and earthy language in describing the "Hell-hounds" who must "lick up the draff and filth . . . till cramm'd and gorg'd, nigh burst / With suckt and glutted offal" (X, 630–33).

The description of Eve "eating Death" when she takes the forbidden fruit (IX, 792) expressed with Milton's peculiar succinctness the antithesis of the victim consuming the agent which will in turn consume him. Antithesis is also shown in the proximity of the two trees—"next to Life / Our Death" (IV, 220–21). But the most striking antithesis is that of the "unholy Trinity"; Satan the father, Sin the child (significantly perhaps a daughter and not a son), and Death the progeny of the last two. White has pointed out that this "repellent double incest" is an inversion of respectable Protestant theology, whereby the Father generates the Son, and together they generate the Holy Spirit, self-knowledge expressed in divine self-love.[10] With her black attendant, Sin looks toward Earth as a "happier Seat" (X, 237) provided for them by Satan, and this inversion of God sending the Son to Earth to redeem man is confirmed by Satan in his address to his offspring: "There dwell and Reign in bliss, thence on the Earth / Dominion exercise and in the Aire, / Chiefly on Man" (X, 399–401). Here the black shapeless monster opposes the indefinable light of the Holy Spirit; but it may be noted that in Book XI, when the figure of Death has left the stage, Milton uses the traditional typology of the figure of Christ opposing Death. Cain is the "sweatie Reaper," Death with his sickle; Abel, the "Shepherd . . . meek" (XI, 434–38).

II

In writing *Paradise Lost* Milton was, undoubtedly, trying to justify the ways of God to man; but also to justify Milton as an epic poet at previously unattempted heights. In *De Doctrina Christiana* he addressed "all the Churches of Christ" with his exposition of the "chief heads of Christian doctrine," and Death could not be left shapeless in the mists of allegory. Milton was concerned "in establishing my faith or assisting my memory . . . to have laid up for myself a treasure which would be a provision for my future life" (CM, XIV, pp. 3–9). In this work he used the "four degrees of death" to categorize his doctrinal beliefs on the subject. According to the Yale editor, Milton borrowed this concept from Johannes Wollebius, the Swiss theologian whose *Compendium Theologiae Christianae* was published in 1638 and translated into English in 1650.[11]

Primum est reatus. The first degree of death (*DDC*, CM, XV, pp. 203–04) is "all those evils which lead to death, and which it is agreed came into the world immediately upon the Fall of Man." "In the first place, guiltiness," followed by the terrors of conscience; by a diminution of the majesty of the human countenance; and by a conscious degradation of mind, whence arises total pollution and shame. The first degree of death is therefore, in essence, the Fall. Adam and Eve were "from that day mortal . . . expell'd . . . into a World / Of woe and sorrow" (*PL* VIII, 331–33)—*mundus reatus.* Milton's view of the progression of sin through to ultimate shame and degradation gives an answer to the problem argued at some length in *Paradise Lost:* why God's injunction "in that day thou diest" did not result in immediate physical dissolution. The initial act of disobedience or rebellion set in motion a progression of evil, the steps leading down to death.

Milton illustrated this in different ways through his works. In the Trinity MS. draft of *Paradise Lost* as a tragedy, Adam names the evils as they come into the world after the Fall, as he had previously named the animals at God's behest (CM, XVIII, p. 230); "sublime allégorie," according to Chateaubriand.[12] The first of these, interestingly enough, is labor; the last is death. In *Paradise Lost,* Adam finds "in our Faces evident the signes / Of foul concupiscence; whence evil store; / Even shame, the last of evils; of the first / Be sure then" (IX, 1077–80). Here, as in *De Doctrina,* shame comes last, after the initial guilt of the Fall. In his last prose tract, *Of True Religion,* Milton attacked the "pride, luxury, drunkenness, whoredomes, cursing, swearing, bold and open Atheism everywhere abounding" (CM, VI, p. 178), whereby the steps to the denial of God were those of intemperance. In *Defensio Secunda,* he warned against the "tyrant within," indeed the multiplication of tyrants "daily engendered in your own breasts"—"unless you banish avarice, ambition, luxury from your thoughts, and all excess even from your families" (CM, VIII, p. 241); again the downward ladder of intemperance, toward the lower stages of death. We are reminded of the spawning progeny of Death in the womb of Sin, as she writhes at the gate of hell (*PL* II, 636–39).

In this first stage there is one aspect which had a highly personal significance for Milton—the "diminution of the majesty of the human countenance." We have noted above that Adam found sin "in our Faces evident." In the Satan of *Paradise Lost*, the clouding of the archangel's face is a recurrent theme. In Book I, "his face / Deep scars of Thunder had intrencht, and care / Sat in his faded cheek" (600–02); in Book IV "each passion dimm'd his face" (114), his looks were "with passions foul obscur'd" (571), "His lustre visibly impar'd" (850). In Book X he ascends his throne "clad / With what permissive glory since his fall / Was left him, or false glitter" (450–52). What appears to be allegorical in the poem is, however, presented as a factual statement in *De Doctrina*, and there is evidence of Milton's concern that his own face should not lose its beauty. "[God] has instilled into me . . . a vehement love of the beautiful," he wrote in a letter to Diodati, and not least, it seems, of the physically beautiful (*Familiar Letters*, CM, XII, p. 27). In the aged Mansus he praised "the handsome features still intact."[13] In *Defensio Secunda*, at the age of forty-five, he described himself as past forty, but looking no more than thirty years old (CM, VIII, p. 61). In the same passage, and also in *Sonnet XXII*, he insists that his eyes, though sightless, are clear and unblemished. His dread of old age is shown in his description of blindness as an even worse affliction (*Letter to Oldenburg*, CM, XII, p. 65); and Haug has listed in the Yale edition the numerous instances of Milton backdating poems and referring to a youth he no longer had, the most famous of course being the phrase "E're half my days" in *Sonnet XIX*, probably written in 1652, when Milton was forty-three (YP, I, p. 806). Milton's fears were linked to a more serious danger, that of premature death; but both the treatment of Satan and the personal references show a concern for this physical aspect of the "prelude of death" beyond the purely doctrinal. It is not to be supposed that Milton inflated out of vanity the commonplace ravages of ugliness and old age; it is not likely that he mourned for the less than beautiful physiognomies of Socrates and Oliver Cromwell. But the derision he poured on the accusation of Salmasius, that blindness had been visited on him as a punishment, may have covered a deep disquiet (*Defensio Secunda*, CM, VIII, p. 21). Perhaps he had been accused nearer home and even fought back the suspicion in his own mind that his affliction was part of the pollution of the first degree; he needed his friends to assure him, three years after his blindness, that his eyes were "clear / To outward view of blemish or of Spot." As Leishman wrote, "a possibility had occurred which he had not contemplated when he wrote *Lycidas;* he had not, like King, been cut off by an early death, but his ability to use his talent had been destroyed"—or so he feared.[14]

III

The fear of fading beauty was perhaps itself a first stage in the fear of premature death which haunted Milton and inspired some of his most telling passages of poetry and prose. The death of the body was the third "degree of death," the loss or extinction of life that was part of the punishment for sin (for Adam's sin, let it be said, for no amount of virtue could circumvent it).[15] There is no reason to believe that Milton was "more afraid than became me of malice, or even of death," provided that he could survive to complete his life's work (*Defensio Secunda,* CM, VIII, p. 11). In the Greek epigram on the innocent philosopher condemned to death, and in *Sonnet VIII,* Milton exhorted authority to spare the life of the writer whose works can give reflected glory to the temporal rulers—the philosopher "so fam'd a champion of thy kingdom," the poet who "can spred thy Name o're Lands and Seas."

But it was not enough for Milton to be spared the executioner's ax or the soldier's fire. For him, fulfillment meant surviving into old age. Although in his youth he wrote fluently and memorably, he was highly conscious of being slow in reaching the heights to which he aspired. The sonnet "How soon hath Time" was accompanied by a letter in which Milton bewailed "my wasting youth" and referred to the parable of the talents, one of his recurrent themes.[16] After his visit to Italy, which did so much to give him the confidence and the recognition that he craved, he abandoned poetry for the prose writings, first in support of the rebels, and then as their employee; and well before the end of the Commonwealth, blindness descended on him. "O! should we freeze at noon," he had cried in the *Animadversions on the Remonstrant's Defence* (CM, III, p. 146). The irony of not dying young, but yet having one's maturity rendered impotent by blindness, showed in the echo of this phrase in Samson's despairing outburst, "O dark, dark, dark, amid the blaze of noon" (SA 80).

It is common for youth cut off by death to be symbolized in poetry by a fading flower—the flower containing the freshness of youth; its fading swift and, like death, irreversible. Almost the first two lines of verse written by Milton in his native tongue contain this image: "O fairest flower no sooner blown but blasted, / Soft silken Primrose fading timelesslie."[17] The death blast on the defenseless flower was used again in the quotation from Virgil prefacing the 1637 edition of *Comus:* "floribus austrum, perditus . . . [immisi]" ("distraught, I have let the south wind loose among the flowers"); frost on the flower in *Lycidas;* and the roses in Adam's hand fading on the instant when he hears of Eve's "fatal Trespass."[18]

How did Milton guard against the distraction of Virgil's careless shepherd? By his accounts in, for example, *The Reason of Church-government* (CM, III, pp. 234–41) and *Mansus* (95–96), it was by countering intemperance and greed with the discipline of study, and lust with the discipline of chastity. Yet even so, Milton could not fail to see, in the deaths of his friends, in the wars, and in the appalling mortality of the plagues, the nearness of premature death. In *Lycidas,* the greatest of his early poems, Milton was ostensibly writing on the premature death of one of his Cambridge friends, but it is his own "destin'd Urn," his eagerly sought "fair Guerdon" of fame which are the sources of the great lyric inspiration of the work. Six years earlier he had noted the swiftness of passing youth in "How soon hath time." When Edward King died, Milton was at Horton, preparing himself for his elected task of composing a truly great poem. The disappearance of a slightly younger contemporary, and the invitation to write on the event, spurred him to a formidable test of his technical and imaginative abilities. But through the "dense mass of echoes from previous literature" can be distinguished genuine concern and an affirmation of genuine belief.[19] By both classical and psychological means Milton confronted the threat of premature death. As Marcia Landy has pointed out, the process of mourning is reenacted in the poem, the procession of mourners progressively moving to a resolution of the theme.[20] The body, lost in the "bottom of the monstrous deep," is first resuscitated in the poet's mind to be strewn with the flowers of pastoral lament (158, 133–51).[21] This "false surmise" dismissed, the poet shows the true resurrection through baptism, using a range of water and resurrection imagery to make what Abrams calls "the leap from nature to revelation."[22] Mack has written of the triple significance of water in the poem— the impervious sea which can destroy; the fountains and springs of classical poetry leading, perhaps, to "false surmise"; and the waters of grace which give promise of resurrection.[23] The fear caused by "the wild incalculableness of this death at once early and by accident" is resolved, in Tillyard's phrase, into an exalted state of mental calm.[24] This calm, after the storm of Lycidas' drowning, figures faith in resurrection after the redeeming waters of baptism, the rise to grace after the descent into the waters of death.

Once the flowering of youth, with all Milton's prevarication, was definitely over, untimely death still haunted him, for his pen was used to the utmost as a sword in defense of England's liberty.[25] Undoubtedly he wanted to write his magnum opus under the reign of liberty—he regretted "an age too late" (PL IX, 44). But his time was fully occupied with pamphlets and the correspondence of office; and the third degree of death threatened, with ill health and, most of all, his blindness. "Adversa valetudo" was his "perpetua Adversatrix" (ill health his perpetual adversary)—the Satan that bedeviled the light of his genius (Letter to Mylius, CM, XIII, p. 53). He was oppressed "per valetudinem et hanc luminum orbitatem, omni senectute graviorem" ("by my health and my blindness, a worse affliction than old age") he wrote in 1654, the year of the great triumph of Defensio Secunda (Letter to Oldenburg, CM, XII, p. 65).

Light to the ancients was wisdom, and death extinguished the mortal world of light. In Lycidas, Milton used the word "blind" with contempt and horror—the "Blind mouthes" of the false shepherds, the "blind Fury" with the abhorred shears (119, 75). Adam explains the "Ministring light" of the stars as a protection "least total darkness should . . . extinguish life / In Nature and in all things" (PL IV, 665–67), and Milton compared "my own darkness" with "the darkness of death" in the letter to Philaras in which he praised God's grace for alleviating his own inner darkness, although, possibly, not the other (Letter 15, CM, XII, p. 71). Above all, in Samson Agonistes, when the Restoration had flung Milton, after his years of adulation and public office, right into the skin of his hero, "Blind among enemies, O worse than chains" (68), the cry is heard again and again of death inflicted through darkness—the dark amid the blaze of noon, "That these dark orbs no more shall treat with light, / Nor th'other light of life continue long" (591–92); the poem is "the cry of the chained Prometheus."[26] In the poem, the darkness is intensified, as Hyman has written, by Samson's sense of double betrayal, by Dalila on earth and by God in heaven.[27] As in Lycidas Milton had sought catharsis of his fear of premature death, so in Samson he sought it of the far more foreboding "double darkness" (593), the "Prison within Prison, / Inseparably dark" (153–54), of which the second curtain fell in 1660.

The loss or extinction of life first sinks into our consciousness through the loss of others. Milton's attitude toward bereavement is not as open as might appear from the number of early elegiac poems on the deaths of friends and acquaintances. He wrote fluently on the deaths of those for whom he cared little; the poem written after a really grievous loss, *Epitaphium Damonis*, is unhappily lacking both in the spontaneity of the Hobson poems and in the passion which informed *Lycidas*. We do not know what Milton felt about the death of his own fair infants, although perhaps the entries in the family Bible tell their own story (CM, XVIII, p. 274). What Milton felt about the death of his only son, and also about the impediments of his eldest daughter, could hardly be easily borne; but in his writing he is silent on these wounds. There is one interesting reference to the death of his mother in *Defensio Secunda*—"after the death of my mother," he wrote, "I travelled to Italy" (CM, VIII, p. 121). Parker has pointed out that the journey was not Milton's only activity soon after the bereavement.[28] Seven months after the death of Sara Milton, *Lycidas* was written, and the loss that the poet cited seventeen years later in connection with his decision to leave England for the first, and in the event the only, time may have contributed to the intensity of the inspiration in *Lycidas*.

In *Lycidas*, as has been noted above, the grief at death is objectified. In *Sonnet XXIII*, which, apart from *Epitaphium Damonis*, is the only direct expression of Milton's grief on bereavement, the poet's reaction is very different. The dream of the Alcestis-like figure fleeing before the day which "brought back my night" was echoed later in Book VIII of *Paradise Lost*, when Milton used the device of a dream to enable Adam to recount the creation of Eve. "She disappear'd, and left me dark" (VIII, 478) echoes more the tragedy of the poet than the temporary disappointment of Adam.[29] In the sonnet, the poet expresses the second of John Bowlby's three phases of mourning, quoted by Marcia Landy: the sense of loss, pain, and despair. He does not, as in *Lycidas*, proceed to the third phase, of reorientation.[30] But it is interesting that the imagery of the poem follows the same progression—pagan, Old Testament, New Testament—as in the earlier work. The truth is glimpsed in shadowy prefigurations before it is expressed in terms of Christian revelation. Milton may, as suggested in a much-quoted article by Spitzer, be striving for union with the Ideal, in heaven; but he seems conscious that he, unlike Admetus, cannot expect his love to return to him, and, for the present, he is unable to go to her.[31] Milton and King were contemporaries; when the poet's young wife died, he was middle-aged and blind. A sense of the great loneliness of bereavement pervades the description of his dream; as Daiches has said, the loss is expressed without self-pity, but also without immediate hope.[32] For the present the poet, like Adam, is "left dark." The striking difference in the endings of *Lycidas* and of *Sonnet XXIII* provides an interesting comparison with Wordsworth's opposing reactions to the death by drowning of his younger brother—a bereavement which combined features of both Milton's losses. "Not without hope we suffer and we mourn" echoes the resolution of *Lycidas;* but Wordsworth also wrote, "Oh do not Thou too fondly brood / Although deserving of all good / On any earthly hope, however pure"; this is the spirit of *Sonnet XXIII.*[33]

There is little to be gleaned of Milton's reactions to the deaths of those who were unimportant to him personally. In general he can deplore the waste of blood, the slaughter, of men at war; he showed amiable and quite appropriate detachment in the epitaphs on the university carrier, and contempt as far as his enemies were concerned. The death of Salmasius could hardly be expected to grieve him, but the references in *Defensio Secunda* (CM, VIII, pp. 5, 23) are completely callous (is it really just a pamphleteering point to have driven an enemy to his death?), and the virulence against More and the insistence on publishing even when Milton had been advised that his true adversary was not More have been attributed to the poet's chagrin that Salmasius' early death had cheated him of the opportunity for a renewed attack on his old enemy.[34] He cannot have been indifferent to the appalling torture at the execution of the regicides in 1660, but this is inference only, unless the hanging, drawing, and quartering were in his mind when writing of the "unsightly sufferings" and "inhuman pains" which shocked Adam into his apostrophe to "miserable Mankind," with its striking parody of *Nunc dimittis*—"Glad to be so dismist in peace" (*PL* XI, 500–14). Nevertheless it has to be remembered that modern sensibilities had not yet been awakened in the seventeenth century, and brutality was then a part of civilized life, as were the loss of tens of thousands in recurrent plagues, and the death of nine out of ten children in infancy.[35] And Milton's "divine Plato" had said that the good man should be sufficient for himself and his own happiness, so that bereavement should be less terrible for him than for other men.[36] In *Sonnet XVIII* Milton gave a clarion call for vengeance for the Christian martyrs in Piedmont; here he was, as Richmond somewhat slightingly remarked, "shouting at God, 'Do something about it, for heaven's sake!' " but in a very formal tone.[37]

What of Milton's attitude toward the most important physical death of all? In Tillyard's trenchant phrase, Milton "could have spared it [the Crucifixion] without inconvenience."[38] In his early poem *On the Circumcision*, Milton had adumbrated the "Huge pangs and strong" (27) which Christ was to suffer; in the Trinity MS. he listed *Cristus patiens* as a possible subject (CM, XVIII, p. 240). But the significance of the Crucifixion faded in Milton's growing independent Puritanism. Regeneration for Milton was not so much a matter of vicarious atonement as of the advent of Christ in man, the growth of Christ in the individual soul. For him the paradox of Christ vanquishing death on the cross was not a central issue; as Saurat said, the triumph of Christ according to Milton was not on the cross, but in the desert.[39] *Paradise Regained* ends with the angels' exhortation to Christ, "Queller of Satan, on thy glorious work / Now enter, and begin to save mankind" (*PR* IV, 634–35), from which it might well seem that in the progress from the beginning of Christ's ministry to the Last Judgment the Crucifixion was—shall we say—a theological incident.

It is noticeable also in *Samson Agonistes* that Milton plays down the element of sacrifice in Samson's final act. He does not see this in the more usual sense in which, for instance, Bunyan takes it ("Let me die, thought I, with the Philistines ... rather than deal corruptly with the blessed Word of God").[40] Milton describes Samson's fate in the *Argument* of the poem as "by accident" and in the text as "self-kill'd / Not willingly, but tangl'd in the fold / Of dire necessity" (1664–66). Milton seems to be following here in the steps of Augustine, who inveighed against the idea of death before dishonor in *The City of God*.[41] Life for Milton was to be lived for God, rather than laid down for him. In the more orthodox *Paradise Lost*, Christ's sacrifice is described in a metaphysical paean, first from the Son, and then from the Father; for man the Son will "lastly dye / Well pleas'd" and then rise to conquer death and Satan—"dying rise, and rising with him raise / His Brethren" (III, 227–65, 274–343). In the course of the second passage (292–98) the harrowing of hell and the second coming are telescoped to give a double force to the power of heavenly love over hellish hate.

This apocalyptic vision of Christ's victory reflects another aspect of Milton's mortal thoughts. "To die and to be with Christ," he wrote in *De Doctrina*, "will seem to take place at the same moment" (CM, XV, p. 241). This was the basis of the mortalist heresy—the soul would disappear or be dissolved with the body and both together be resurrected for final judgment. Belief in purgatory and in ghosts was offensive to most Protestants, and in particular to those of Puritan temper. But if the souls of the dead were not stored away in purgatory, nor in the environs of the earth, what were they doing? Calvin, with his usual caution, thought "over-curious enquiry . . . neither lawful nor useful."[42] The immortality of the soul was central to Christian doctrine, and no hint of the destruction of the soul, even pending resurrection, could be allowed.

But to many of those who, after the Reformation, veered away from what was considered the medieval concept of purgatory, the apostolic idea of the millenium gained ground. And if the second coming was imminent—and to many, including MIlton, it was— the question of immortality might be considered adiaphorous; and psychopannychism, the sleep of the soul after the death of the body, was a seductive theory.[43]

In his *Commentary on Ecclesiastes*, Luther wrote, "When they [the souls of the dead] are awakened, they shall seem to have slept scarce one minute . . . even as after the resurrection we shall be cleare from place and tyme."[44] Calvin saw clearly the danger of this to minds more literal than Luther's, and wrote a tract, *Psychopannychia* (1542), against the "soul-sleepers." In England, the heretical sects came up from underground in what was thought to be the free air of the Commonwealth, and the government legislated severely in its struggle to preserve immortality for the English Protestant soul. Milton had every reason to keep silent on the heresy in his published work. His old mentor Alexander Gill attacked "our late dreamers," as he called them, and Parliament later prescribed imprisonment for the mortalists.[45]

In *De Doctrina* Milton was categorical. Immortality was "a subject which may be discussed without endangering our faith or devotion." "I shall first show," he continued, "that the whole man dies, and secondly, that each component part suffers privation of life" (CM, XV, p. 219). But Milton's instincts, somewhat guarded when writing with "my left hand," were given freer rein in his poetry. Friedman writes of "that typical softening of focus that overtakes Milton's theological arguments as they move from *The*

Christian Doctrine to *Paradise Lost*."[46] Milton's God did indeed predict that at the Last Judgment ". . . forthwith the cited dead / Of all past Ages to the general Doom / Shall hasten, such a peal shall rouse thir sleep" (*PL* III, 327–29), but this, the common image of man summoned to appear before his Maker, would not get Milton imprisoned for heresy.

It is difficult to believe, however, that the "softening of focus" was primarily to protect Milton from pursuit by the authorities. Tillyard, comparing the prose works with *Paradise Lost*, observes that "only in the more emotional medium are we likely to get at the largest measure of unconscious truth."[47] One of the marvels of *Paradise Lost* is the keeping "cleare from place and tyme." Heaven and hell are at one moment defined and at the next wrapped in the mystery of Milton's resounding negatives; man's history flashes past Adam with Michael's commentary, the harrowing of hell and the Last Judgment appear to jostle one another. This is a superb poetic expression of Plato's "eternity is then only a single night,"[48] or of Psalm XC, 4, used as a text by the millenarians, "For a thousand years in thy sight are but as yesterday when it is past, and as a watch in the night." Similarly, the "death like sleep, / A gentle wafting to immortal Life" (*PL* XII, 434–35) can be taken as a figurative, not a literal, description. Sleep and death, in Milton as in the *Iliad*, are twin brothers—sleep, that is, and the third degree, physical death. The "real" death was the Second Death of *Revelation*, "eternal death to such as shall not believe" (*DDC*, CM XVI, p. 121), the fourth and last of the degrees of death.

IV

As might be expected, Milton deals with this with Olympian detachment; the Second Death was not for him. He promises in *De Doctrina* (Book I, chapter 13) to treat of the punishment of the damned in chapter 27, but in the event dismisses it there in a single paragraph. The earth, that world "under her own weight groaning" which Milton describes in disenchanted terms at the end of *Paradise Lost* (XII, 539), will be consumed by fire; hell, already occupied by Satan and the bad angels, will receive the damned. In the final chapter of Book I of *De Doctrina*, at the very end, he deals with the "General Conflagration," largely letting the biblical citations speak for themselves (CM, XVI, pp. 369–75). The very early poem *Naturam non pati senium* ends with the line "Ingentique rogo flagrabit machina mundi" ("and the frame of the

world blazes on one huge funeral pyre"). The conflagration occurs
again in *Paradise Lost* (III, 332–34): ". . . Hell, her numbers full, /
Thenceforth shall be for ever shut. Mean while / The World shall
burn."

A mighty and universal upheaval was postulated in Christian
theology at both the beginning and the end of man's history. It is
noticeable that Milton uses some of the images of Revelation, in
which the final cataclysm is described, in his description of the
first upheaval; the war in heaven, which was, as Saurat pointed
out, a civil war, has therefore overtones of the Last Judgment.[49]
And there, as far as specific description went, Milton left the
matter.

But in spiritual terms Milton sets the Second Death against
the second chance which man is given, through God's grace. In
the closing books of *Paradise Lost* he makes great use of biblical
typology, and the Last Judgment is foreshadowed by the story of
Noah and the deluge. Not only in Christian, but also in Judaic
tradition, the two catastrophes were linked, both resulting in the
destruction of the wicked and the rescue of the chosen few. Book
XI ends with God's rainbow covenant, and in the opening lines of
Book XII Michael tells Adam of the "second stock" (7), "This
second sours of Man" (13) which will rise from the eight survivors
in the ark, led and redeemed by Christ, the greater Noah. Earlier,
in Book III (287–89), God had foretold to the Son that "in thee /
As from a second root shall be restor'd / As many as are restor'd."
At first the fallen Adam had thought himself irretrievably lost—
"To Satan onely like both crime and doom" (X, 841)—but it is
Michael's task to show Adam that he may redeem his sin and not
share Satan's doom. The way has been prepared for this revelation
by the repentance of Adam and Eve—not canonical, but crucial to
the doctrine that Milton is expounding—which takes place when
they recover themselves after the waves of lust and anger which
sweep over them with the knowledge of evil. Book X ends with
the beautiful "double chord" of repentance—six lines repeated
almost word for word.[50] The First Death—or third degree—they
cannot escape, for it is now the lot of all men; the Second Death—
or fourth degree—can be annulled by Christ's sacrifice for repen-
tant sinners. The Second Death is "the death thou shouldst have
dy'd" (*PL* XII, 428), were not Christ ready to make the supreme
sacrifice, and this line most tellingly echoes and annuls Satan's
exultant call to his offspring "over Man / To rule, as over all he
should have rul'd" (X, 492–93).

V

The Second Death is annulled, but Adam and Eve still have their "long days dying" (X, 964) to augment their pain. This is the second "degree of death," between the attack of evil guilt and shame and the physical destruction of the body. The second degree is spiritual death, according to Milton the loss of divine grace and innate righteousness, the darkening of the understanding, the loss of right reason, the death of the will to do good (*DDC*, CM, XV, pp. 205–15). This is the degree of death that started immediately after the Fall, in which the whole force of the participle "dying" is evoked—"the slow-pac'd evill" (X, 963), "not one stroak, as I suppos'd . . . but endless miserie" (X, 809–10).

There is a poignant echo of the slow-paced evil in the title of *Samson Agonistes*—literally Samson the champion or contestant at the games;[51] but in the mid-seventeenth century the word *agonise* began to be used specifically for the struggle with death, and the action of the poem is indeed that of Samson dying.[52] Samson dies redeemed, but in another giant character of Milton's tragic poetry we are shown the full horror of spiritual dying.

In *Paradise Lost* Satan's "Empyreal form / Incapable of mortal injurie" (VI, 433–34) is nevertheless subject to the inevitable spiritual destruction which is the lot of "those who, when they may, accept not grace" (III, 302). The progress of Satan through the poem shows the soul "clotted by contagion . . . till she quite loose / The divine property of her first being," as described in the charming, divine Platonic philosophizing of the Elder Brother in the Ludlow *Masque* (466–68). As Satan is self-corrupted through making evil his good, he yearns to pass on his suffering through his self-generated daughter Sin and their joint offspring Death. This Milton describes in terms of Death's insatiable appetite, so that the "long days dying" becomes a process of "seasoning" man for the feast of Death: "His thoughts, his looks, words, actions all infect," Sin exhorts her son, "And season him thy last and sweetest prey" (X, 608–09). Satan's earlier instruction was "Him first make sure your thrall, and lastly kill" (X, 402), and the enthralling, the slavish subjection of man to sin and the devil, is the second degree of death. "Kill" is the last action of Death on man, after the rest of his devilish work is done; it is Milton's only use of the word in *Paradise Lost* (indeed, in this form, in all his poetry; "killed" he used three times, and "killing" once). There are no degrees of *kill* as there are of death; the second degree of death,

the "seasoning" and "infecting" is what we can *see* as death while
we are still living, whereas what happens afterward is swift and
inevitable, as was the south wind on the flowers in the Virgil
quotation, or in *Lycidas*, "as killing as the canker to the rose."[53]

The death that we can see in action—the living death—roused
Milton's imagination to some of his most powerful writing. Augustine defined the death of the soul as taking place when God aban-
dons it; the death of the body, when the soul departs.[54] It is therefore possible, he wrote, for a dead soul to subsist within a live
body. Dante, finally confronting his Satan, described the appalling
sensation of being neither dead nor living: "Io non mori, e non
rimasi vivo" ("I was not dead, nor was I still alive").[55] Experiencing both death and life, or deprived of both, man is facing the
depths of hell. The image of the dead soul in the live body was
used with violent antithesis by Milton in his second divorce tract,
in which he wrote of a living soul bound to a dead corpse.[56] Samson's agony is described in words similar to those used in Dante—
"Scarce half I seem to live, dead more than half" (*SA* 79), and he
laments:

> To live a life half dead, a living death,
> And buried; but O yet more miserable!
> My self, my Sepulcher, a moving Grave.   (100–02)

The fear in this last image is shown also by Adam who, once he
realizes that death is "not one stroak, as I suppos'd," finds that his
real fear is not of death as a finality, but as an endless state—"then
in the Grave . . . who knows / But I shall die a living Death?" (X,
786–88), and later "such acts / Of contumacie will provoke the
highest / To make death in us live" (X, 1026–28).

But perhaps the most striking evocation of spiritual death is in
Adam's description of the fallen Eve—"Defac't, deflourd, and now
to Death devote" (IX, 901). Milton made liberal use of alliteration
in his poetry, but never with greater technical audacity than here
(*d-f, d-f, d-th, d-v* in a single line). It is an unforgettable line, and
it encapsulates Milton's thinking on spiritual death. Eve is
doomed to death[57] and in this state appears defaced and de-
flowered. In immediate terms, her face has lost its innocence and
her flowers have faded, but in "defac't" we are taken back to the
first degree of death, the "diminution of the majesty of the human
countenance," and in "deflourd" is the equation of her sin with
the deadly sin of lust, the loss of virginity, like the cutting of the
flower, symbolizing a loss that cannot be retrieved.

The "loss of right reason" is an aspect of spiritual death which Milton uses in his "second" Satan—the hellish reasoner of *Paradise Regained.* In *Paradise Lost* Satan is the rebel, passing on his fatal sin of disobedience to God's creation, in an effort to make them share his fate. Milton here uses the Hebraic doctrine that obedience was the safeguard against sin, but he also embraced the Hellenic concept that reason is the weapon with which to combat sin. This concept informs the structure of *Paradise Regained,* in which Milton works out the distinction between "right reason" and the fallen reason which Satan deploys only to his own destruction. Thus the Satan of *Paradise Lost* illustrates, *inter alia,* one facet of the first degree of death, the "diminution of the majesty of the human countenance"; the Satan of *Paradise Regained* illustrates one facet of the second degree, the "loss of right reason."

It is not only Christ but also Milton who wins the battle against Satan in *Paradise Regained,* the third great victory over aspects of death in the text of Milton's poetry: in *Lycidas,* over the fear of premature death; in *Samson,* over the fear of blindness and the darkness of the understanding—a victory signaled by the *peripateia* of the final act, in which the Philistines, trying to destroy Samson, destroy themselves, ". . . with blindness internal struck" (*SA* 1686). In *Paradise Regained,* the victory is over the fear of the loss of right reason, for fear, in the words of *The Wisdom of Solomon* (XVII, 12) "is nothing else but a betraying of the succours which reason offereth." The tragedy of *Paradise Lost* resolves in the concluding books on an unmistakeable note of pessimism. Yet the greatest of Milton's poems ends with the key that finally robs death of its sting, and the grave of its victory, in the four words "and Providence thir guide" (XII, 647). It was eternal providence that Milton set out to assert, the "Just law indeed, but more exceeding love"[58] by which man by grace might overcome the last enemy.

VI

"Under the head of death, in Scripture," Milton wrote in *De Doctrina,* "all evils whatever, together with everything which in its consequence tends to death, must be understood as comprehended" (CM, XV, p. 203). This was Milton's doctrinal definition of the horrible allegorical being which in Book II of *Paradise Lost* "shape had none." But toward the end of his epic, Milton modifies this figure of shapelessness. Michael comforts Adam:

                                Death thou hast seen
        In his first shape of man; but many shapes
        Of Death, and many are the wayes that lead
        To his grim Cave, all dismal; yet to sense
        More terrible at th' entrance then within.   (XI, 466–70)

"In scripture," as Milton said, death is the wages of sin, but for the
righteous man there is a good death, a heaven-sent release. According to Plato, death "which men in their fear apprehend to be
the greatest evil, may . . . be the greatest good."[59] Augustine said
that death was good for the good, and bad for the bad; for the
good, "God has granted to faith so great a gift of grace that death,
which all agree to be the contrary of life, has become the means
by which men pass into life"[60]—in Milton's words, "to the faithful
Death the gate of Life" (PL XII, 571). With Milton's characteristic
direct and daring irony, Satan shows Eve a perversion of the end
of the righteous life, from which he is seducing her: "So ye shall
die perhaps, by putting off / Human, to put on Gods, death to be
wisht" (PL IX, 713–14). The terror of old age could be counter-
balanced by the grace of opportunity given by long years on earth.
Life was a blessed breathing-space in which man could grow into
faith, as Adam, unfallen, could have done among the flowers of
Eden.

        The distinction between the death analyzed in De Doctrina
and the "good" death within the grace of God is one which Milton
allows to speak for itself. The death provided by God, the "final
remedie" for man redeemed (PL XI, 62) is the good one; it is the
bad death from which Enoch is "exempt" (XI, 709). As his life
drew to its close, Milton was secure in the belief that he would
find the final remedy, "though the righteous be prevented with
death, yet shall he be in rest."[61] Milton had shown great understanding of the calm of quiet death in the early Hobson epitaphs
and in the closing lines of Mansus (before, of course, the blind
Fury started waving her shears at him). The Hobson poems were
youthful rhetorical exercises, but the exuberance is tempered by
sympathy in the comparison of life and death with motion and
inactivity, the old carrier being "newly gon to bed," and dying in
the "vacancy," when his cart was at a standstill.[62] The "hideous
roar" of Orpheus' death, which, as Daiches wrote, Milton found "a
peculiarly moving and somehow a very personal story,"[63] was described in Lycidas (61) and in Paradise Lost—"the savage clamor
dround / Both Harp and Voice" (VII, 36–37). Edwin Muir, in his
sonnet on Milton, wrote of "the steady clamour known too well /

On Saturday nights in every street in Hell"; the good death was in peace, in patience, and in quiet.[64] God's direction to Michael to "all terror hide" from Adam (*PL* XI, 111) leads to the resolution to "patiently attend / My dissolution" (XI, 551–52). Patience and calm are also in the resolution of *Samson*—"nothing but well and fair, / And what may quiet us in a death so noble" (*SA* 1723–24).

In Shelley's *Adonais*, Milton "went, unterrified, into the gulf of death" (34–35), a typical piece of romantic inversion of the figure of Satan, unterrified at the gates of hell (*PL* II, 707–08). There is another vision of Milton which perhaps is nearer home. Milton, poetically speaking, is not a "traveler," that is, he makes little if any use of the idea that life is a journey toward death, an idea so common that we dream of traveling to unknown destinations. The great narrative writings on man's condition, from the *Odyssey* to *The Pilgrim's Progress*, are founded on this idea. But if Milton, unlike most of us, did not see life as a journey, he saw its resolution in terms of other deep psychological images. The idea of death as a homecoming, into the arms of loving parents, occurs in *Samson* (1733) and also in Michael's laconic description of death in age "like ripe Fruit" dropping "Into thy Mothers lap" (*PL* XI, 535–36). The homecoming for the damned is into hell, described three times by Milton as a house—"this dark and dismal house of pain," "the house of woe and paine," "the house of woe" (*PL* II, 823; VI, 877; X, 465); we are reminded of the "dolorous mansions" of the Nativity ode (140).

Blondel described the death of Lycidas as "une progression, une ascension."[65] In life, Milton experienced isolation through blindness, through declining years under a hostile government (in Muir's words, "knowing that he and Paradise were lost / In separate desolation"),[66] but also through his unique calling. The inevitable isolation of death was for Milton an ascent. "His natural port," wrote Johnson, "is gigantic loftiness."[67] He saw man at the gates of death as abstracted from the world and looking down on his own history being enacted as in a play. Thus Michael takes Adam to a high place and shows him the grim pattern of what is to come of life on earth, and Milton likens this to Satan's action with "our second Adam in the Wilderness" (*PL* XI, 381–84), the subject later of *Paradise Regained*, when Satan takes Christ to the mountain and shows him on all sides the temptations of earthly life.[68] This was the death of Moses, high on the peak of Pisgah, looking down on the future lands of the children of Israel. In *Sonnet XVIII* Milton's diction, tone, and style were close to those of the

54 MILTON STUDIES

traditional Hebrew lament, and Mother Pecheux has noted how the last mourner in Lycidas can be seen as a composite of Moses, Peter and Christ.[69] The initial invocation in *Paradise Lost* is to the "Heav'nly Muse, that on the secret top / Of Oreb or of Sinai, didst inspire / That Shepherd, who first taught" (I, 6–8). In many ways Milton resembled the lonely figure of the first great prophet, secure in his personal relation with his God, destined not to see the fulfilment of his wishes on earth, and in the end mounted high like the young Lycidas, and taken, like the aged Samson, home to his father's house.

University of Western Australia

NOTES

The two main collections of Milton's Works, *The Works of John Milton*, ed. Frank Allen Patterson et al. (New York, 1931–38) and *Complete Prose Works of John Milton*, ed. Don M. Wolfe et al. (New Haven, 1953–) are cited here as CM and YP respectively. All quotations are from the Columbia edition. *De Doctrina Christiana* will be cited as *DDC*.

1. Denis Saurat, *Milton: Man and Thinker* (London, 1944), p. 167; F. de Chateaubriand, *Le Paradis Perdu; suivi de Essai sur la Littérature angloise* (Paris, n.d.), p. 415.
2. Samuel Johnson, *Lives of the English Poets*, (London, 1925), vol. I, p. 110; *The Spectator*, No. 357, April 19, 1712.
3. *Lectures on Genesis*, cited in Norman T. Burns, *Christian Mortalism from Tyndale to Milton* (Cambridge, Mass., 1972), p. 42.
4. *Gerusalemme Liberata*, in the Edward Fairfax translation (1600), bk. I, 24.
5. *The City of God*, trans. H. Bettenson (Harmondsworth, 1972), bk. XIII, chap. 11, p. 520. Milton may have borrowed his title from Augustine's *De Doctrina Christiana*, but according to Saurat, "of all his [Augustine's] works, Milton, like the whole of his century, knew chiefly *The City of God*" (*Milton*, p. 225).
6. Robert C. Fox, "The Allegory of Sin and Death in *Paradise Lost*," *MLQ*, XXIV (1963), p. 364.
7. See John Martin Evans, *"Paradise Lost" and the Genesis Tradition* (Oxford, 1968), ch. 2. The *Apocalypsis Moses* has the story of the serpent pouring lust on the fruit: the *Book of the Secrets of Enoch* the literal seduction of Eve by the serpent. See also the title of Milton's projected play on Sodom and Gomorrah, "Cupid's funeral pile" (Trinity MS., CM, XVIII, p. 233).
8. *The City of God*, bk. XIII, chap. 24, p. 546.
9. *PL* X, 279; Walter Raleigh, *Milton* (1900; rpt. New York, 1967), p. 240.
10. Robert B. White, Jr., "Milton's Allegory of Sin and Death: A Comment on Backgrounds," *MP*, LXX (1972–73), 337–41.

11. YP, VI, p. 393, gives the reference to the four degrees of death from the English translation *The Abridgment of Christian Divinitie*, I.XII, p. 69. The idea was not of course original to Wollebius, but was culled from the work of earlier theologians.

12. *Le Paradis Perdu*, p. 441.

13. *Mansus*, 76 (CM, I, p. 292): "Nondum deciduos servans tibi frontis hono-ris" (John Carey's translation). The phrase *frontis honor*, meaning physical beauty of face, is used by Valerius Flaccus (*Argonautica*, VI, 296).

14. J. B. Leishman, *Milton's Minor Poems* (London, 1969), p. 290.

15. *DDC*, CM, XV, pp. 215–51, "De Morte quae dicitur corporalis." I have dealt with the second degree of death last in this essay because it seems the most important from Milton's point of view.

16. *Letter to a friend*, CM, XII, p. 321. For the "talents" motif, see *Sonnet XIX; Reason of Church-government*, CM, III, pp. 229, 232; *Colasterion*, CM, IV, p. 272.

17. *On the death of a fair Infant*, 1–2 (CM, I, p. 15): written "anno aetatis 17," according to Milton.

18. Virgil, *Eclogue* II, 58–59; *Lycidas* 47; *PL* IX, 888–93.

19. Northrop Frye, "Literature as Context: Milton's *Lycidas*," in *Milton's "Lycidas": The Tradition and the Poem*, ed. C. A. Patrides (New York, 1961), p. 205.

20. "Language and Mourning in *Lycidas*," *American Imago*, 30 (1973), 294–312.

21. See A. S. P. Woodhouse and D. Bush, *A Variorum Commentary on the Poems of John Milton* (London, 1972), vol. II, pt. 2, p. 708.

22. M. H. Abrams, "Five Types of Lycidas," in Patrides, *Milton's "Lycidas*," p. 229.

23. M. Mack, *Milton*, quoted in Woodhouse and Bush, *Variorum Commentary*, p. 589.

24. Rosemond Tuve, *Images and Themes in Five Poems by Milton* (Cambridge, Mass., 1957), p. 93; E. M. W. Tillyard, *Milton*, rev. ed. (London, 1966) p. 72.

25. Milton's fears, according to his early biographer Jonathan Richardson, continued after the Restoration, when he was in terror of assassination (see Helen Darbishire, ed., *The Early Lives of Milton* [London, 1932], p. 276). If this was true, it is all the more curious that Christian von Boineburg should have written in 1662, when Milton was in the midst of writing *Paradise Lost* at last, that "Milton greatly laments that he is no longer allowed to write satire" (CM, XVIII, p. 371), although in the *Apology for Smectymnuus* Milton had compared satire with tragedy, in both of which the writer must "strike high, and adventure dangerously" (CM, III, p. 329).

26. W. Menzies, "Milton: The Last Poems," *Essays and Studies*, XXIV (1938), 81.

27. Lawrence W. Hyman, *The Quarrel Within* (New York, 1972), p. 105.

28. William Riley Parker, *Milton: A Biography* (Oxford, 1968), p. 157.

29. See John C. Ulreich, "Typological Symbolism in Milton's Sonnet XXIII," *Milton Quarterly*, VIII (March 1974), 8.

30. Landy, "Language and Mourning," p. 297.

31. Leo Spitzer, "Understanding Milton," *Hopkins Review*, IV (1950–51), 16–27. Cf. Dixon Fiske, "The Theme of Purification in Milton's *Sonnet XXIII*," *Milton Studies*, VIII, ed. James D. Simmonds (Pittsburgh, 1975), 158.

32. David Daiches, *Milton* (New York, 1966), p. 143.

33. William Wordsworth, *Elegiac Stanzas suggested by a picture of Peele Castle*, 60; *Elegiac Verses in Memory of my brother, John Wordsworth*, 68–70.

34. Parker, *Milton*, p. 433.

35. See ibid., p. 8.

36. *The Republic*, bk. III, 387 (*The Dialogues of Plato*, trans. B. Jowett [Oxford, 1892], vol. III, p. 70).

37. Hugh M. Richmond, *The Christian Revolutionary: John Milton* (Berkeley, 1974), p. 87.

38. Tillyard, *Milton*, p. 237.

39. Saurat, *Milton*, p. 143. In the eight-line reference to the crucifixion in Michael's narrative in *PL* XII the word "cross" is used twice (413, 415); the only other line of poetry in which Milton used the word was in the early Nativity ode (152).

40. *Grace Abounding to the Chief of Sinners*, ed. R. Sharrock (Oxford, 1962), p. 90.

41. Bk. I, ch. 17, pp. 26–27. See also The Wisdom of Solomon i, 12: "Seek not death in the error of your life; and pull not upon yourselves destruction with the works of your hands."

42. *Institutes of the Christian Religion*, bk. III, ch. XXV, sec. 6; see Burns, *Christian Mortalism*, pp. 26–27. See also Calvin's *Commentaries on Genesis*, ch. II, sec. 16, on the scriptural use of the word "death."

43. Mortalism is the belief that the soul does not exist apart from the body. On whether the soul "dies" or "sleeps" after the death of the body, "the psycho-pannychists believed that the immortal substance called soul literally slept until the resurrection of the body, the thnetopsychists, denying that the soul was an immortal substance, believed that the soul slept after death only in a figurative sense" (Burns, *Christian Mortalism*, p. 18). Milton is usually classified as a thnetopsychist, but stated in *DDC* (CM, XV, p. 341) that "the soul as well as the body sleeps till the day of resurrection." Cf. Chateaubriand, *Le Paradis Perdu*, p. 468: "Milton flottait entre mille systèmes."

44. *An exposition of Salomons Book, called Ecclesiastes or the Preacher*, trans. 1573, quoted in Burns, *Christian Mortalism*, p. 31.

45. Alexander Gill, *Sacred Philosophie of Holy Scripture* (1635); *An Ordinance for the punishing of blasphemies and heresies*, May 2, 1648.

46. Donald M. Friedman, *"Lycidas:* The Swain's Paideia," *Milton Studies*, III, ed. James D. Simmonds (Pittsburgh, 1971), p. 29.

47. Tillyard, *Milton*, p. 181.

48. *Apology*, in Jowett, *Dialogues*, vol. II, p. 134.

49. Saurat, *Milton*, p. 191. Cf. *PL* VI, 259: "Intestine War in Heav'n." Revelation xii, 7–12; xx, 1–2, 10–14.

50. F. T. Prince's phrase in "On the Last Two Books of *Paradise Lost*," *Essays and Studies*, 11 (n.s.) (1958), 38–52. The lines are *PL* X, 1087–92, 1099–1104.

51. An interesting variation of the *Samson Hybristes* of the Trinity MS. (CM, XVIII, p. 236).

52. *OED* gives the first reference as 1664 *Sylva* (J. Evelyn): "The Olive under which our blessed Saviour Agoniz'd."

53. Leishman, *Milton's Minor Poems*, p. 311, has a passage on this Shakespearean simile: as a symbol of a killer of innocent beauty the canker occurs thirty-three times in Shakespeare's plays.

54. *The City of God*, bk. XIII, ch. 2, p. 510.

55. *Inferno*, XXXIV, 25.

56. *The Doctrine and Discipline of Divorce*, CM, III, p. 478. Cf. Saurat, *Milton*, p. 130: "the abomination when man's inferior needs are satisfied without the participation of the higher desires. That is 'binding the living soul to the dead corpse'." Of course, it could also be said that this is binding the dying soul to the living body.

57. *Devote* (3): "to give over or consign to the powers of evil or destruction; to doom" (*OED*).

58. *Upon the Circumcision*, 16.

59. *Apology*, in Jowett, *Dialogues*, vol. II, p. 122.

60. *The City of God*, bk. XIII, ch. 2, p. 511; ch. 4, p. 514.

61. The Wisdom of Solomon iv, 7.

62. *On the University Carrier* (1), 18, and heading.

63. Daiches, *Milton*, p. 83.

64. Edwin Muir, "Milton," in *One Foot in Eden* (London, 1956), p. 15.

65. Jacques Blondel, "*Lycidas:* panorama critique et interprétation," *Etudes Anglaises*, XXV (1972), 115.

66. Muir, "Milton."

67. Samuel Johnson, *Lives of English Poets*, p. 104.

68. Waddington notes that of the five visions shown to Adam, four are concerned with death. R. B. Waddington, "The Death of Adam: Vision and Voice in Books XI–XII of *Paradise Lost*," *MP*, LXX (1972–73), 16.

69. Mother M. Christopher Pecheux, "The Dread Voice in *Lycidas*," *Milton Studies*, IX, ed. James D. Simmonds (Pittsburgh, 1976), 221–41.

FROM PASTORAL TO PROPHECY:
THE GENRES OF *LYCIDAS*

Joseph Wittreich

[A literary work] is a convergence of forms, and forms of disparate orders. It is the coincidence of forms that locks in the poem.

         —J. V. Cunningham

I N HIS life of Milton, Dr. Johnson presents a series of indictments against *Lycidas,* all of which reduce to his fundamental objection: written in the "form . . . of the pastoral," the poem is "easy, vulgar, and therefore disgusting."[1] Such an objection may have receded over the centuries, but even now it has not disappeared; rather, it reappears as an objection leveled not against *Lycidas* but against those critics of the poem, who, invoking pastoral to explain it, have produced a "scandal of literary scholarship": according to Louis Kampf, since Milton's use of the pastoral tradition "is a foolish irrelevance," that tradition "will hardly lead . . . to reflections on the meaning of death."[2] Sounding no less cranky than Dr. Johnson, Kampf, instead of dismissing *Lycidas* because it is a pastoral, dismisses pastoral because, for him, it is a tradition irrelevant to the meaning of Milton's poem. To his credit, Kampf would push us beyond pastoral, believing that *Lycidas* is first a response, a reaction, to death and not simply another rendering of the pastoral tradition; but he would do so without ever acknowledging: (1) that in its inception, pastoral was devised "to insinuate and glaunce at greater matters"; (2) that as a tradition, pastoral had become, during the 1630s, irrevocably bound to the problem of death through the "Et in Arcadia Ego" theme; (3) that since Theocritus, pastoral was continually reaching beyond itself, aspiring to be something other than itself; (4) that (and here Kampf is less culpable than Dr. Johnson) for purposes of initiation and discovery, pastoral—"the place of vision"—is also *the* place where "the Individual Talent is brought into confrontation with . . . Tradition."[3] However different their estimates of *Lycidas* may be then, both Johnson and Kampf reject pastoral and so reject the reason for which *Lycidas*, years before Johnson blasted it, had been praised.

Such praise came to *Lycidas*, in Milton's own century, through an anonymous commentary which describes the poem as "an Elegy . . . incomparable"[4] and, in the eighteenth century, through Thomas Purney's treatise on pastoral, one of whose objectives is to rescue pastoral from those who, defining it according to the rules, would isolate it from both epic and tragedy. If pastoral has become a problematical genre, says Purney, that is because too many poets have "gone in exactly the same Track, without endeavoring to raise [the genre] to a greater perfection"—without even recognizing that pastoral poetry, like epic and tragedy, can develop only if it engages poets in generic competition with their predecessors. Typically, the pastoral poet had relied on classical precedents. Thus Purney proposes that he turn from them to Scripture; that, recognizing the genre's potentiality for embracing a full range of human emotions, he remember his largest obligation, which is to "spread a Calm over the Mind." Milton, Purney concludes, is the great example of such a pastoral poet—of one who, ignoring classical precedents and established rules, grounds his poetry in Scripture.[5] And Purney might have continued, as Edward Tayler does, by asserting that in *Lycidas* "Milton has recapitulated the entire history of pastoral"—a history that, encompassing pastoral from its classical beginnings, through its Old Testament modifications, to its final development in the New Testament, is made to correspond with the three structural units that comprise Milton's poem. The form of the poem, Tayler remarks, imitates its theme; and its structure reflects its meaning,[6] showing Milton sinking into, then rising out of—Milton progressing beyond, then returning to—the pastoral tradition. The point of all this, of course, is that Milton is in the process of effecting one of the great revisions of the pastoral pattern: he explores its limits, as well as territory beyond, incorporating the pastoral pattern within the all-subsuming paradigm of prophecy. *Lycidas* is thus a classic example of a poem that, assuming a tradition, vaults beyond its limits.

The significance of Milton's turning from classical examples of pastoral to scriptural ones is suggested by Edwin Honig: the only way of keeping pastoral alive after its infection by "a literary plague"—once it becomes "broken and mute"—is to bring to pastoral "a strong sense of commitment to circumstances of living actuality" and, simultaneously, to create for pastoral "a new aesthetic."[7] The former Milton accomplishes by letting the bitter reality of Edward King's death shatter the pastoral world at the beginning of *Lycidas;* and the latter he does by becoming a biblical poet and cultivating a commentator's interest in the Bible—an interest that turned Milton to the prophets and that showed him how prophecy itself could be called upon to restore the atrophying form and fading dream of pastoral.

Lycidas is a triumph of the imagination; and its triumph, involving the transcendence and transformation of pastoral, occurs within the context of a tradition—"a continuing tradition"—whose unrealized potentiality Milton brings to fruition.[8] Pastoral is the tradition Milton receives; prophecy is the sometimes unseen presence in that tradition which, writing *Lycidas,* Milton makes manifest. Like so many of Milton's other poems, *Lycidas* is the decisive turning point in the history of a genre; and the turn it makes has its own history, which can be neither written nor understood apart from the long history it presumes. For our purposes, that history is especially worth recalling since, as Scott Elledge reminds us, "Milton knew well nearly all the poems of the genre, both classical and renaissance" and since, as Claudio Guillén observes, "the trajectory of a genre," especially pastoral, "constitutes some sort of historical series" and conditions and molds both literature and its history.[9] But Guillén also cautions that a poet, even one who invokes the whole history of a genre, may be more intent upon "the interaction between a contemporary model . . . and his own poetic efforts and gifts."[10] *Lycidas* asks to be viewed within the context of the whole pastoral tradition, but even more requires assessment in terms of Spenser's *The Shepheardes Calender* and *Astrophel*— poems that from Milton's perspective are the last great embodiments of the traditions of both pastoral and the pastoral elegy.

Pastoral is historically the oldest of the genres. The usual view is that Theocritus establishes the genre; nevertheless, Thomas Rosenmeyer has shown that Theocritus's real achievement is to have isolated pastoral elements in earlier literature, thereby creating a pure form. Theocritus is an "implementer," not the creator or "forerunner" of pastoral, a genre that before the Renaissance— from Aristotle onward—was regarded as sometimes a component, but more often as a type, of epic. Even when Renaissance critics determined that "pastoral was a genre in its own right," they were formulating a conclusion that some like Milton would have to revise and adopting an "exclusiveness," as Rosenmeyer remarks, that "was not destined to last."[11] Not an exclusive but an inclusive form, pastoral was by Theocritus extrapolated from epic to which Virgil returned it. The Virgilian combination had, however, been preceded by another: no sooner had Theocritus distilled a pure form than Bion and the poet who wrote Bion's lament began anew the process of assimilation, joining together pastoral and elegy. After Virgil—who, besides elevating pastoral to epic status, in his messianic eclogue combined pastoral and prophecy—the genre was allegorized and Christianized, and thereupon still other assimilations occurred, pastoral combining here with satire and invective, there with drama and romance.

In the last great pastoral before *Lycidas*, Spenser's *The Shepheardes Calender*, many of these same elements are evident. Within Spenser's microcosmic world, there are tragic movements and comedic ones, there is the satire of the May eclogue and the elegy of the November eclogue. The entire poem, moreover, is cast in the prophetic mode, though here, for political reasons, the prophetic element is muted. And *The Faerie Queene*, as Milton must have noticed, begins and ends in a pastoral world, Spenser in his greatest literary microcosm allowing pastoral to sit comfortably within a poem imbued with elements of romance, epic, and prophecy. In *The Shepheardes Calender*, Spenser may not radically alter the pastoral tradition he inherits; but here, and later in *The Faerie Queene*, he makes "pastoral a thing of significance for English writers" and so suggests the potentiality of the tradition of which *Lycidas* is an historic transformation.[12] Kathleen Williams puts it succinctly when she says that Spenser senses the limitations of the forms that Milton subjects to more radical criticism; and saying this, Williams explains that *Lycidas* is richer than the *Calender* because all that Milton's poems responds to is there in the earlier work: "Without it, *Lycidas* could not be what it is."[13] Nor probably would *Lycidas* be what it is without the model of generic confrontation provided by the juxtaposition of *Colin Clouts Come Home Againe* and *Astrophel* in a single volume. The first poem is a pure pastoral and the second, a notable example of the pastoral elegy.

Assimilation, then, describes the process by which pastoral, after Theocritus, aspires to a higher condition. That process is noted by Harold Toliver when he speaks of pastoral's "capacity to devour elegies, lyrics, plays, fairy tales, masques, odes, and even to gnaw ambitiously at romances, epics, and novels"; and the same process, Angus Fletcher has shown, is already operating in

Milton's poetry—in *Comus*—where Milton finds in the masque form "an unrivalled chance to mix all the modes already brought together" in other dramatic or quasi-dramatic genres.[14] An even greater opportunity for mixing the genres, and thus for not only rivaling but transcending this achievement in *Comus*, Milton found in prophecy—a form that more than any other is predicated upon assimilation and that, in this characteristic, of all the genres is most closely allied with epic.

The modern understanding is that epic, developing "from the older and commoner forms of poetry," is "the great matrix of all poetic genres"—that, in keeping with the requirements for encyclopedic quality and variety, it "is one of the most complex and comprehensive kinds of literature, in which most of the other kinds may be included."[15] Such an understanding of epic may be extended to pastoral; but it also accords perfectly with the Renaissance conception of prophecy. During this period, prophecy, even more than epic, is portrayed as the great encyclopedic form: it is *the* model for what Angus Fletcher calls "transcendental form" and for what E. H. Gombrich designates as "total form."[16] And *its* model, in turn, was commonly understood to be John of Patmos' Revelation.

The great example of prophecy, this book was said to be both an assimilation of all earlier prophecy and a compilation of all existing literary forms. "A posy of all flowers, a vision out of all visions," prophecy, as it is exemplified in Revelation, "takes all the eminent visions of the Old Testament, and makes use of them."[17] Everything coming before this scriptural book relates the history of the world from Creation through the First Coming; this book, however, in its very brief compass, completes that history, extending from the advent of the church and recounting its history until the Second Coming. Epic may reveal the destiny of a nation; but prophecy, according to these suppositions, was designed to reveal a "vision of the destiny of the world."[18] Prophecy was thus said to spread "infinitely farre and wide" and, like "the heaven it selfe," to contain "all things within the Circuit thereof."[19] Containing "all things," prophecy could be expected to encompass all the literary forms and all the styles deemed appropriate for each of them. In the words of Hugh Broughton, prophecy constructed according to the Revelation model represents a union of Aeschylean tragedy and Homeric epic, of lyrics and comedies, of history, philosophy, and oratory. In this regard, clearly, prophecy is like epic;[20] but to the extent that Christian forms now take precedence over classical ones, prophecy could be said to stand apart from and beyond epic in the generic hierarchy.

By virtue of their shared features, then, epic and prophecy were frequently paired as they are in both *The Faerie Queene* and *Paradise Lost;* yet their radically different traditions also tended to set these two genres, as they are in Milton's epics, on a collision course. Relevant here is Claudio Guillén's formulation of "the dialectics of genre and countergenre"—a process wherein "one genre is dialectically surpassed (and assimilated) by another" and one which testifies to genre's "ability to counter history."[21] Rosalie Colie, following Guillén, also speaks of generic "mixtures based on opposition"—of genres "twinned . . . yet opposite."[22] This spirit of contention generated by generic confrontations is evident in *Lycidas* itself, where not just epic and prophecy but other genres are competitively paired so as to pit world view against world view and, in this way, to symbolize a collision between two cultures.

Like most of his contemporaries, Milton subscribed to a hierarchy of genres, though he also seems inclined to exalt Christian over classical forms—the Christian hymn over the classical ode, biblical prophecy over classical epic. Or more exactly, Milton was inclined to view classical forms as perversions of their Christian models, which find their prototypes in Scripture. When Milton acknowledged epic to be at the apex of the secular genres, he did so not because he wished to acquiesce in critical commonplace, but because he believed that to be the proper position for a form that, because it was of the largest extent, subsumed all the others. He also recognized that the classical epic was a perversion of the Christian epic, whose true form was Scripture and whose true mode was prophecy. These suppositions have considerable bearing on *Lycidas*.

Wishing to burst the boundaries of pastoral in this poem, Milton allows *Lycidas* to climb the ladder of the genres, assimilating to itself various lyric forms like elegy, canzone, and madrigal, and various dramatic perspectives like tragedy, comedy, and satire, achieving dimensions that are epical and strains that are prophetic. The theme of generic progress first figured in *L'Allegro* and *Il Penseroso* is here in *Lycidas* set in motion again and reflected in a movement through lyric and dramatic to narrative forms. The aesthetic theory operative in *Lycidas* may have waited upon Stephen Dedalus for succinct formulation, but in *Lycidas* such a theory finds its most perfect poetic embodiment:

In literature, the highest and most spiritual art, the forms are often confused. The lyrical form is in fact the simplest verbal vesture of an instant of emotion, a rhythmical cry such as ages ago cheered on the man who pulled at the oar or dragged stones up a slope. He who utters it is more conscious of the instant of emotion than of himself as feeling emotion. The simplest epical form is seen emerging out of lyrical literature when the artist prolongs and broods upon himself as the center of an epical event and this form progresses till the centre of emotional gravity is equidistant from the artist himself and from others. The narrative is no longer purely personal. The personality of the artist passes into the narration itself, flowing round and round the persons and the action like a vital sea. . . . The dramatic form is reached when the vitality which has flowed and eddied round each person fills every person with such vital force that he or she assumes a proper and intangible esthetic life. The personality of the artist, at first a cry or a cadence or a mood and then a fluid and lambent narrative, finally refines itself out of existence, impersonalizes itself, so to speak. The esthetic image in the dramatic form is life purified in and reprojected from the human imagination.[23]

The deleted passage in that quotation is a single sentence: "This progress [from lyric to epic] you will see easily in that old English ballad *Turpin Hero* which begins in the first and ends in the third person." This same progress, Stephen might have continued, you will see in *Lycidas* which also begins in the first and ends in the third person; and here you will see even more: the passage from epic to dramatic, from epic to prophecy, the latter being the literary form in which narration and drama, visionary drama, meet. You will also see this progress, in these stages, as you move through Milton's canon—from the *Nativity Ode* (lyric) to *Paradise Lost* (epic) to *Samson Agonistes* (dramatic poem).

Forms within forms, visions within visions, each mediating the others—orbs within orbs, cycles and epicycles—*Lycidas* achieves what has recently been credited to Coleridge: the extension of pastoral to its outward bound, which is prophecy and which involves the exaltation of the visionary poet to the status of a cultural hero.[24] In the process, Milton demonstrates "the lowest of forms . . . to be capable of articulating the loftiest insights";[25] and part of that process involves Milton in the strategy of creating various and shifting perspectives, which, though they represent different angles of vision and also different attitudes toward the human condition, reflect a clash between different cultures, classical and Christian, and imply the triumph of the one over the other. In pastoral, as Milton inherited it, there is a perfect blending of the two cultures; but in pastoral, as Milton here uses it (in juxtaposition with prophecy), those two cultures are seen at odds. The crossing or mixing of the genres, Ernst Curtius has remarked, is part of the crossing of pagan and Christian canons; what Curtius does not say is that out of such crossings often arise confrontations.[26] A form here, and its perspective, may complement or augment—*or even conflict with*—a form there, and its very different perspective.

A series of perspectives and an aggregate of forms, *Lycidas* is also an assimilation of styles; yet between perspectives, forms, and styles there is also a contention which, enabling *Lycidas* to burst the boundaries of pastoral, "dilate's and widen's the Mind, and put's it upon the Stretch." In its various multiplicities, then, *Lycidas* "comprehends almost too big for it's Reach," exemplifying that kind of poetry, described by Thomas Purney, wherein "the Mind is most stretch'd."[27]

The occasion for *Lycidas,* one imagines, led Milton to position his poem within the pastoral tradition. Since the *Lament for Bion,* pastoral was understood to be the proper medium through which one poet could lament the death of another; and as recently as Spenser, it was the form chosen for such a purpose, Spenser in *Astrophel* lamenting, with others, the death of Sir Philip Sidney. Not only do the various poems accompanying *Astrophel* juxtapose pastoral and elegy, but the juxtaposition is accentuated by the fact that *Astrophel* is itself published in a volume along with *Colin Clouts Come Home Againe.* Here, forms themselves, elegy and pastoral, are set in opposition to accord with the belief that lamenting is altogether contrary to rejoicing. Moreover, as Octavio Paz has shown, elegy as a "collective" form reaches out to embrace tragedy, while, as Thomas McFarland has perceived, comedy finds one of its extensions in pastoral. The pastoral elegy, says McFarland, always strives to diminish, to soften, the fact of death. In any given elegy, tragedy may hold sway, but the possibility of a comedic triumph is always latent when pastoral and elegy are made to coexist in the same poem. Unlike Spenser's *Astrophel, Lycidas* makes explicit such a triumph: this poem, like its classical models and for that matter like Spenser's poem, "pastorally softens the meaning of death," but then it proceeds, "unlike those models, to an overt denial of death's reality. . . . In this version, the pastoral elegy becomes not only a lament for death, but the herald of a new life in paradise. This vision was always implicit in pastoral."[28] Only by Milton is it made explicit, and thus alone among pastoral elegies, Milton's poem can "burst smilingly." The juxtaposition of pastoral and elegy by Spenser and Milton, then, has literary precedents as well as theoretical justification; and these precedents, in an important way, are sanctioned by Scripture.

If the Bible contains multiple examples of pastoral, it also provides, through Jeremiah's *Lamentations*, examples of Christian elegy. Like pastoral, the elegy or lamentation is an important ingredient of prophetic poetry, complicating its artistry and universalizing its subject. As Bishop Lowth was to observe in the eighteenth century, an elegy like Jeremiah's, characterized by its rusticity of language, is full of abrupt, disconnected ruminations of the mind; and consequently it has no easy structure or arrangement, though it does possess a discernible, if difficult, order. Such an elegy fragments on its surface, says Lowth: apparent disorder is projected by combining short and long lines within stanzas and by multiplying the number of stanzas themselves. Yet these marks of irregularity gradually disappear as the underlying thematic divisions are perceived—divisions that find their continuity often in the theme of vengeance, of justice executed.[29] It would be difficult to find a more precise description of *Lycidas*, wherein the short-and-long-line canzone patterning is overwhelmed by the rhyme-weaving of madrigal patterning, wherein the verse-paragraph divisions, however conspicuous initially, are subdued within the poem's tripartite structure. The rough, fragmented appearance of *Lycidas* is achieved largely through revision subsequent to the poem's first printing, when the six verse paragraphs of 1637 become the eleven verse paragraphs of 1645 and 1673. In its original setting, we are most aware of pastoral triumphing over elegy; but in later settings we become aware of yet another generic competition, in which prophecy is seen subduing, then restoring, pastoral.

Pastoral universalizes in one way, usually by translating an historical into a mythological figure; elegy universalizes in still another way, by bewailing not just the death of a friend but, through that death, the condition of a whole nation. Elegy, as Lowth explains, reflects the "extreme anxiety of a mind" burdened by sorrow and "overcome by an accumulation of evils"; yet Christian elegy endeavors to resist, to overcome, those evils, "admitting, through the dark cloud of afflictions, a glimmering of hope and consolation." Milton surely realized, with Lowth, that "every species of poetry has . . . its peculiar mode of acting on the human feelings";[30] and by choosing to cast *Lycidas* as a prophecy, a mixture of species, he enabled himself to act—not just through pastoral and elegy, but through canzone and madrigal, comedy and tragedy, satire and epic—in different ways upon those "feelings," here storming the affections, there quietly insinuating himself into them.

Initially, Milton would have been drawn to pastoral because of its having both classical and Christian precedents and because many, during the Renaissance, regarded pastoral as a form discovered rather than invented—as a form deriving from man's experience in Eden before the fall and as therefore the oldest form of literary expression. Pastoral, Milton would also have noticed, combines forces with prophecy, indeed achieves its apotheosis, in that very scriptural book in which prophecy itself reaches its great culmination: the Apocalypse of St. John. Because of their classical and Christian precedents, Milton would also have been drawn to elegy and to prophecy—forms that are combined with one another by Jeremiah and that, even more pointedly than pastoral, speak to and of man in his fallen condition. Like pastoral, elegy (and prophecy too) drive the poet beyond the topical into the universal, prophecy itself effecting the turn from the dead to the living and thereby moving *Lycidas* beyond the grave. As Ruth Wallerstein explains, with specific reference to the juxtaposition of pastoral and elegy: "The pastoral gives voice to a universal rhythm of grief in a concentrated way paralleling the statement of it in the ritual and ceremony of funeral: the shock of death, the grief which must be realized, the stilling of that grief. The elegy . . . makes use of the power of ritual to absorb man into the experience of the race, to detach him from the desperation of the moment and draw him into that larger experience shared with all men."[31] The immediate subject, Edward King, is thus universalized by mythological identification into Lycidas; and Milton's immediate sorrow, in turn, is translated into world-sorrow, or world-weariness, Milton meditating not so much on King's death as on all the evidences of death he finds among those still living. In *Lycidas*, it is the living who cause Milton his greatest sorrow; and it is to the living that all prophecy is addressed.

Finally, committed as he was to the virtuoso performance, Milton would have been drawn to pastoral as a genre which, by mining its potentiality, he could transform. Historically, pastoral as it evolved reached out to embrace other forms; and elegy, along with pastoral, had in the Bible often been assimilated into prophecy. Indeed, the funeral elegy had been historically one of the favorite forms for prophesying. This same conjunction of forms occurs in *Lycidas*, and with this conjunction occurs a melding of styles. Forms, styles—in *Lycidas* both are powerful symbols, developing the paradox that while the exalted are humbled, the humble are exalted. In *Lycidas*, lowly pastoral and its mean style are transmuted into noble prophecy and its sublime style; simultaneously, Edward King, a lowly shepherd, becomes in the fiction of Milton's poem one with the King of Heaven; and in a parallel movement an uncouth swain becomes a mantle-bearing visionary.

Lycidas has always been thought a difficult poem, and much of its difficulty derives from the complexity emanating from this mixing of genres and from the multiple perspectives generated by that mixture. The poem's generic complexity may be both assessed and understood through distinctions devised by Kenneth Burke. He argues for a discrimination between forms of acceptance and rejection and then, comprehending the relative simplicity or complexity of the world view contained within any one genre, arranges them hierarchically.[32] The simplest forms of acceptance and rejection, according to Burke, are pastoral and elegy respectively. In the strict elegy, represented both by most of the poems in *Justa Edovardo King Naufrago* and by those accompanying *Astrophel*, the poet is at home in despair. Emphasizing the helplessness of man in a world where the issues of life and death are controlled from above, the elegist's vision of life is marked by a shallow pessimism. However, pure pastoral, which portrays God in his heaven and finds all right with the world, is no less simplistic, its vision of life being characterized by an easy optimism. *Lycidas* escapes the simplicity of either world view by subsuming both visions of life within the complicating perspectives of satire, tragedy, and comedy and the containing form of epic heightened to prophecy. Milton, therefore, sees beyond the literalism of Burke's poetic categories and so comprehends that whereas epic is the genre of experiential inclusiveness, subsuming all other genres horizontally because its expanse is so broad, pastoral is, at least in potentiality, like prophecy—a genre of transcendence, which subsumes both experience and the genres vertically and which then forms out of the resultant hierarchies a ladder of vision.

It has been said that the whole pastoral process involves "putting the complex into the simple."[33] Milton apparently thought differently; and so in his early companion poems, *L'Allegro* and *Il Penseroso*, and then again in *Lycidas*, he dichotomizes pure pastoral and pure vision, implying that pastoral poetry, so long as it is unassimilated, cannot be a vehicle of vision; rather, it depends upon the visionary mode of prophecy both to validate and to re-

deem it. Thus the process of simplification, here attributed to pastoral poetry, is one that Milton, writing *Lycidas*, would reverse;
and in the process, Milton, like Octavio Paz, seems to be proclaiming that "poetry opens up to us the possibility of being that is
intrinsic in every birth; it creates man and makes him assume his
true condition, which is not the dilemma: life or death, but a
totality: life and death in a single instant of incandescence."[34]

When pastoral and elegy combine, as they do in *Lycidas*, mis-
fortune becomes the basis for insight, the poet now being obliged
to mediate between acceptance and rejection—between elegy and
satire on the one hand, and pastoral and comedy, tragedy and epic
on the other. This Milton does by paradoxically finding a way of
accepting the universe, of reaffirming the principle of order that
seems to disappear with Edward King's death, while at the same
time symbolizing rejection and its attendant principle of chaos.

These contraries are mirrored by the pairing of genres like
pastoral and elegy and, more emphatically still, by the pairing of
verse forms—canzone and madrigal. As Thomas Greene explains,
to write in the canzone form is to encourage and evince fragmentation and division.[35] To write in the form of the madrigal, on the
other hand, is to reveal a rage for order amid all the apparent
chaos in the universe. Tied to the theme of order, as it expresses
itself in *Lycidas*, is, of course, the idea of justice. When seen as a
natural process, justice may seem capricious and disorderly; but,
viewed as a cosmic principle administered by God, justice becomes explicable in terms of providential design. Elegy, satire,
and tragedy tend to support the first proposition, while pastoral
and comedy, along with epic and prophecy, confirm the second.

As pastoral and elegy meet in *Lycidas*, the emphasis of each
form alters: each becomes more comprehensive and comprehending, encircling the good and the bad, the extremes of optimism and
pessimism, attitudes that in *Lycidas* are also beheld in the more
sophisticated perspectives of comedy and tragedy, epic and satire.
Milton knew, as Yeats did, that the poet is the servant of "mere
naked life, . . . of that life in its nobler forms, where joy and sorrow
are one."[36] The poet of *Lycidas* thus stands like Shakespeare's
Gloucester, "Twixt two extremes of passion, joy and grief" (*King
Lear* V.iii.198); but he also pushes beyond those extremes by introducing into his poem the cosmic dimensions of epic and prophecy.
In their very compositeness, these subsuming genres moderate between contending visions and philosophies of life.

"The lowly pastoral," says William Kerrigan, "is pregnant

with epic aspirations."[37] That Milton means us to see his poem opening into epic is suggested by various signatures written into *Lycidas*. This poem may not contain all the extravaganza of epic tradition, but its poet was aware of one fact to which Thomas Rosenmeyer has called our attention: "pastoral lyric was at first composed in the same verse form as epic, and remained faithful to the pattern for over 1700 years."[38] In keeping with this proposition, Milton employs certain devices that lodge his poem in epic tradition—especially the invocation of the muses, along with explicit reference to Calliope (the muse of epic poetry) and the *ottava rima* stanza (the verse form that during the Renaissance was acknowledged to be the proper one for epic poetry). These devices participate in the process whereby the epic kind is translated into a metaphor—as Rosalie Colie explains, not by reducing it so much as by compressing it into phrases, devices, and emblems "implying far more than they seem to hold."[39] Or as Northrop Frye writes, using *Lycidas* as his exemplum, lyric poetry sometimes "achieves a concentration that expands it into a miniature epic." Such poetry may not be exactly "the historical 'little epic' or epyllion" but is "something very like it generally"; it is, says Frye, like *Lycidas:* "a miniature scriptural epic extending over the whole range covered by *Paradise Lost*, the death of man and his redemption by Christ."[40]

With Virgil, pastoral had become a sort of miniature epic; and with Spenser it became once again an inextricable part of the epic poem. Epic poetry, of course, has a double purpose that pastoral, joining with it, comes to share. On the one hand, it lends dignity to human existence, ennobling those who prevail in it; on the other, through identification, the humble share in the worth of the hero—are made to do so by the process, operating in all epics, wherein heroes are humanized either by a flaw or by their predisposition to suffer. Pastoral like epic ennobles those who endure the necessities of human existence, but the process in pastoral is contrary to that in epic: rather than humanizing its hero, pastoral deifies him; both the dead man and his survivors experience an apotheosis. Epic thus converts downward, through a humbling process making men of gods; but pastoral, joining with epic, converts upward, through a deifying process making men into gods. No less celebratory than epic, pastoral simply selects a different segment of society to honor—not a social but a spiritual elite. The lowly, then, are portrayed as the bearers of true nobility as uncouth swains turn imperceptibly into kings and rulers, finding their ultimate identification in Christ. This pattern is wonderfully explicit in *Lycidas;* and when, in the New York Public Library copy of the 1645 *Poems,* Milton added the name of Edward King to his epigraph, he must have meant to make that pattern even more explicit (see CM, XVIII, p. 550). The stages of King's metamorphosis are carefully marked off in Milton's poem, first by the title that mythologizes King into Lycidas, then by a poem that, through analogies, associates Lycidas first with Orpheus, then with St. Peter, and finally with Christ the King, entertainer of Lycidas at the marriage feast in heaven.

As Lycidas undergoes metamorphosis, so too does his relationship with other men change. More like the rest of us in his death than in his life when he enjoyed a harmonious relationship with nature, King becomes like us when, defeated by nature, his relationship with her is broken. Yet by the end of Milton's poem, in the triumph over nature portrayed in the apotheosis passage, that harmony with nature is restored, King's resurrection being figured through the image of the sun that sinking into the western bay rises the next day to flame in the forehead of the morning sky, and King's resurrection being accomplished by the Son whose "blood streams in the firmament,"[41] is diffused through all nature, and sustains the whole universe.

> Weep no more, woful Shepherds weep no more,
> For *Lycidas* your sorrow is not dead,
> Sunk though he be beneath the watry floar,
> So sinks the day-star in the Ocean bed,
> And yet anon repairs his drooping head,
> And tricks his beams, and with new spangled Ore,
> Flames in the forehead of the morning sky:
> So *Lycidas* sunk low, but mounted high,
> Through the dear might of him that walk'd the waves
> Where other groves, and other streams along,
> With *Nectar* pure his oozy Lock's he laves,
> And hears the unexpressive nuptial Song,
> In the blest Kingdoms meek of joy and love.
> There entertain him all the Saints above,
> In solemn troops, and sweet Societies
> That sing, and singing in their glory move,
> And wipe the tears for ever from his eyes.   (165–81)

In this climactic moment, we discover that the dead man is truly alive—only to discover moments later that we too have been undergoing a metamorphosis, that King's resurrection is really a figure for the true subject of Milton's poem, the resurrection of the uncouth swain, the resurrection of us all, in this life. In this theme, pastoral and prophecy, as they are in Revelation, become wedded. Thus as the dead King rises up into new life in eternity, as the uncouth swain rises up into new life in this world, the natural man (Milton, his uncouth swain, and his readers) is transformed into a new spiritual man who will begin the work of reformation through which new harmonies will be established in the world, between man and both the natural and social worlds. Reformation, after all, is the note sounded as the poem gets underway; and prophecy, Milton well understood, is a vehicle for reform. Both concepts are thus combined in the epigraph to *Lycidas*, where the poet says that he will foretell (i.e., prophesy) "the ruin of our corrupted Clergy then in their height."

Milton, at least the early Milton, is often said to be the pastoral Milton; and accordingly, *Lycidas* has been described as "the most pastoral in form of all Milton's English poems, moreso considerably than the *Arcades* and *Comus*."[42] Yet this generalization, like so many others that have been used to explain the poet, oversimplifies and, oversimplifying, distorts the poems belonging to the period between 1629 and 1637. For all the pastoral elements in these poems, none is simply a pastoral, though they all exhibit Milton's sophisticated traffic with pastoral. This point is demonstrated most forcibly by turning to those poems that are most like pastoral. In *L'Allegro* and *Il Penseroso*, which have their pastoral moments, the poet moves beyond pastoral, reaching, in his own words, for the "Prophetic strain" (174). This same movement, this same reaching, the same impulse toward transcendence, is evident in *Lycidas*. That poem did not always appear in the same setting; but whatever its setting, *Lycidas* always marks a generic progress.

All the poems in the Edward King memorial volume are elegies; but *Lycidas* alone is a pastoral—and at that, a pastoral which, maturing into vision, moves on "the plane of . . . prophecy."[43] No less than *Justa Edovardo King Naufrago*, the 1645 *Poems* of Mr. John Milton has "an impressive and peculiar sense of wholeness," which, as Louis Martz has shown, derives from a purposeful "arrangement" that exhibits "the growing awareness of a guiding, central purpose."[44] Both *Justa Edovardo King Naufrago* and the 1645 *Poems*, then, possess integrity as volumes; and Milton's description of the latter volume, in the ode addressed to John Rouse, serves equally well as a description of the earlier one: each is a book in twin parts, "rejoicing in a single robe, yet with double leaves" (1–5); that is, each volume is divided into two sections—one of English, the other of Greek and Latin poems; and each of those sections has its own title page and pagination. In each volume, there is a sense of generic progress heightened by a parallel thematic movement. It is as if *Justa Edovardo King Naufrago* inspired both the physical layout and organizational plan of the 1645 *Poems.* In any event, the progression implicit in the earlier volume is made explicit, then is magnified, in the later one. Both volumes, carefully designed, are directed toward a common end—the representation of Milton as a "rising poet" and "predestined bard," as a poet who, though indebted to his English predecessors, is ready to move beyond them.[45]

Particularly noteworthy about the 1645 *Poems* is what Louis Martz calls "Milton's generic groupings."[46] The progress is portrayed initially in terms of a movement from ode (represented by Milton's Nativity poem) to hymn (represented by his paraphrase of two psalms). Within the volume, there is a sense of rising power as verse is lifted from the purely poetic to the prophetic and visionary; and that sense is augmented by an awareness of growing maturity, which involves the poet in a struggle that may be seen as the struggle of *L'Allegro* and *Il Penseroso* intensified and writ large. Not only do the first and last poems in the English section represent a generic progress, but so too do *Arcades* and *Comus*, the poems between which *Lycidas* is placed. Indeed, when Milton's elegy is reprinted in 1673, it is positioned not just between these poems but at the exact center of the English poems. Here the progress from ode to hymn is rendered even more emphatically; for the paraphrases of the psalms, which immediately follow the Nativity poem, are now supplemented by a group of translations that takes its place at the very end of the 1673 *Poems.* Now *A Mask* is integrated within the volume rather than presented as an appendage to it. And now *Lycidas* calls attention to itself, in "The Table of the *English* Poems," by the boldness of the typeface given this title. As the centerpiece of the English poems, *Lycidas* is also their epitome, portraying a generic progress from classical to Christian poetry, from Christian pastoral to biblical prophecy. "The habit of transcending and transforming genres," Isabel MacCaffrey remarks, "is most dazzlingly manifested, in the 1645 volume, in *Lycidas*"—a poem that, rendering "the fundamental pattern of Christian literature," also "reenacts . . . the immemorial journey of the maturing spirit."[47] That journey, the subject of

L'Allegro and *Il Penseroso* as well, is the master theme of the 1645 *Poems*. Because it is a kind of *summa, Lycidas* calls attention to itself; but in conjunction with *Arcades* and *Comus*, which like the elegy are each a "visionary ritual,"[48] *Lycidas* equally calls attention to the strong Spenserian element in all these poems—an element noted by Humphrey Moseley when, in a word to the reader, he praises Milton as Spenser's successor, one who not only "imitated" but "sweetly excelled" his precursor. Milton, it should be noted, never thought of Spenser as a "dangerous" poet, but instead turned to him as a creator whose genius was to expand, rather than restrict, the individuality of those who followed after him.[49] Yet, finally, even "Spenser must yield precedence" to the prophetic parts of Scripture, particularly to John's Apocalypse, various parts of which, as James Holly Hanford long ago noticed, became "the center of . . . [Milton's] imaginative activity."[50]

Profoundly Spenserian, the poems surrounding *Lycidas* are also poems that, like *Lycidas*, portray generic progress. Both *Arcades* and *Comus* have been called pastorals; but more precisely, *Arcades* commemorates one historic transformation of pastoral— the modification of classical into Christian pastoral, while *Lycidas* commemorates yet another—the transformation of pastoral into prophecy, a transformation that finds a precedent in John's Apocalypse and that, if not always accomplished in, is at least suggested by Spenser's poetry. The transformation is like the one achieved three years before, when writing *Comus* Milton gave to his pastoral masque visionary dimensions. In *Comus*, as in *Lycidas*, pastoral is harnessed to prophecy; and that harnessing is accomplished by Milton's allowing both poems to spring from Revelation, which itself yokes pastoral to prophecy and simultaneously, even as it interconnects the two forms, implies a progression from the one to the other.

Edward Tayler, we have said, acknowledges a progression that moves *Lycidas* beyond classical and Old Testament pastoral into the pastoralism of the New Testament; and, similarly, Louis Martz notices a generic progression in *Lycidas*, speaking of "the poem's movement beyond the limitations of pastoral elegy into the border reaches of the pastoral eclogue, with its awareness of the world of history."[51] Yet progression in *Lycidas* is most precisely marked by Stewart Baker, who describes the poem's process as a "mediation to prophecy," as a pressing beyond pastoral into the "apocalyptic prophecy" of St. Peter and then up "the mount of prophecy" whose pinnacle is reached in the tenth verse paragraph of Milton's poem.[52] Here, as both Thomas Warton and Henry John Todd perceived, is the place of *"great Vision"* where "the Apparition of St. Michael is said to have appeared" and from which the vision of Lycidas emanates.[53] This same progression is dramatized within Milton's poem by the constant pressing forward toward vision which, once achieved, seems to throw the poet back into the pastoral world, albeit with a different understanding of it. Three times the poet reaches "that fearsome crest of prophetic vision"; and each time, Martz observes, "the poem drops back to the mode of pastoral."[54] Milton's point is not to reject one mode, or one world, for another, but rather to assert the interconnection between them, to assert that through prophecy a new world, emblematized by the pastoral image, is to be born.

Pertinent here is William Empson's remark that pastoral is "a puzzling form which looks proletarian but isn't."[55] Pastoral is about the people, Empson concludes; but it is not, like proletarian literature, by and for the people. Milton knew, however, that "prophecy belongs not to the prophet but to the people";[56] and so, by joining pastoral to prophecy, he allows a form about the people to modulate into a form by and for the people. Just as the poet in *Lycidas* is at one with the prophet, the uncouth swain and the miscellaneous rabble are "one," and in their metamorphosis they become another "higher one." All the Lord's people, like the poet, are becoming prophets; and in the process, pastoral modulates into prophecy. The meaning of that modulation is grasped in the realization that "the art of pastoral is the art of the backward glance," the pastoral poet "revers[ing] the process (and the 'progress') of history."[57] The art of prophecy, in contrast, is the art of the forward gaze, and in consequence the process and progress of history are set in motion again: prophecy would thus move history to a last judgment, would bring history to its apotheosis.

For this reason, the pastoral world is a dominant but not an omnipresent image in Milton's poem: it is invoked in the opening lines of *Lycidas* only to be shattered by the knowledge that *"Lycidas* is dead, dead ere his prime" (8). Death shatters, disrupts everything in Milton's poem, as the world of experience invades the world of innocence; still, in the course of Milton's poem, the pastoral image obtrudes here and there only to be banished again and again until, in its epilogue, the pastoral world is reestablished. In the process, *Lycidas* shows how, through prophecy, the pastoral world can be reestablished in human history—how, through the agency of prophecy, the world is to be created anew. For a poet like Spenser, the pastoral world is finally relevant only as an image of life after death, as an emblem of immortality; for Milton, the pastoral world retains that symbolic significance but, equally, is a symbol for the world once all the Lord's people, having become prophets, establish the Lord's kingdom in history. If the pagan dies out of glory, the Christian dies into glory—not just at the end of time when the second resurrection occurs, but also within time, within history, where the first resurrection is accomplished. Time and history—both terms change in *Lycidas*. The present, the time of King's death and of universal corruption, is, in the poem's conclusion, displaced by "Tomorrow"—by "fresh Woods, and Pastures new" (193). But then such changes are the very essence of prophecy: its method is to invade history, its purpose being the transformation of history; its subject is the present, but its object is the future.

University of Maryland, College Park

NOTES

This essay expands upon principles that I have set forth in one section of a largely theoretical book, *Visionary Poetics: Milton's Tradition and His Legacy* (San Marino, 1979), p. 117–37. Within the essay, all quotations of Milton accord with *The Works of John Milton*, ed. Frank Allen Patterson et al. (New York, 1931–38), cited as CM parenthetically within the text. A grant from the National Endowment for the Humanities, awarded by the Henry E. Huntington Library and Art Gallery, enabled me to conduct and complete the research both for this essay and for the aforementioned book.

1. *Lives of the English Poets*, ed. George Birkbeck Hill, 3 vols. (Oxford, 1905), I, 163.
2. "The Scandal of Literary Scholarship," *Harper's Magazine*, CCXXXV (December, 1967), 90–91.
3. See George Puttenham, *The Arte of English Poesie* (London, 1807), p. 31; Erwin Panofsky, "*Et in Arcadia Ego*: Poussin and the Elegiac Tradition," in *Meaning in the Visual Arts* (Garden City, N.Y., 1955), pp. 295–320; and Peter V. Marinelli, *Pastoral* (London, 1971), pp. 47, 51.
4. John T. Shawcross, ed., *Milton: The Critical Heritage* (London, 1970), p. 98.
5. *A Full Enquiry into the True Nature of Pastoral* (London, 1717), pp. 9, 28, 57, 62.
6. "*Lycidas* Yet Once More," *Huntington Library Quarterly*, XLI (1978), 113.

7. See both E. K. Chambers, *English Pastorals* (London, 1895), p. xv; and Edwin Honig, *Dark Conceit: The Making of Allegory* (Cambridge: Walker-DeBerry, 1960), p. 164.

8. I borrow the phrase from Rosemond Tuve, "Theme, Pattern, and Imagery in *Lycidas*," in *Milton's "Lycidas": The Tradition and the Poem*, ed. C. A. Patrides (New York, 1961), p. 179.

9. Scott Elledge, ed., *Milton's "Lycidas"* (New York, 1966), p. xii, Claudio Guillén, *Literature as System: Essays Toward the Theory of Literary History* (Princeton, 1971), p. 51. Within this context, Balachandra Rajan observes that every point on the surface of *Lycidas* inherits a long tradition to which the poem "is competitively and creatively responsive" (*The Lofty Rhyme: A Study of Milton's Major Poetry* [Coral Cables, Fla., 1970], p. 55). The classic essay on *Lycidas* and the pastoral tradition is James Holly Hanford's "The Pastoral Elegy and Milton's *Lycidas*," in *Milton's "Lycidas*," ed. Patrides, pp. 27–55; but see also Edward W. Tayler, *Nature and Art in Renaissance Literature* (New York, 1964) and Renato Poggioli, *The Oaten Flute: Essays on Pastoral Poetry and the Pastoral Ideal* (Cambridge, Mass., 1975).

10. *Literature as System*, p. 130.

11. *The Green Cabinet: Theocritus and the European Pastoral Lyric* (Berkeley and Los Angeles, 1969), pp. 4, 5, 30.

12. Chambers, *English Pastorals*, p. xix. Maurice Evans comments similarly that *The Shepheardes Calender* "epitomizes all that the pastoral had done and heralds what it was to do during the next three decades. It is the first and also the last expression in English of the full range of the Renaissance pastoral, with the exception of *Lycidas* which crushes all the main pastoral themes into a single poem" (*English Poetry in the Sixteenth Century*, 2nd ed. [New York, 1967], p. 93).

13. "Milton, Greatest Spenserian," in *Milton and the Line of Vision*, ed. Joseph Anthony Wittreich, Jr. (Madison, 1975), p. 28. Previous to Williams, John Crowe Ransom had observed that "the enterprising Spenser paved the way for the daring Milton" ("A Poem Nearly Anonymous," in *Milton's "Lycidas*," ed. Patrides, p. 69); and Douglas Bush had acknowledged that "Spenser occupies a conspicuous place in the background of *Lycidas*" (*A Variorum Commentary on the Poems of John Milton*, ed. A. S. P. Woodhouse and Douglas Bush [London, 1970], vol. II, pt. 2, p. 560).

14. See Toliver's *Pastoral Forms and Attitudes* (Berkeley and Los Angeles, 1971), p. vii; and Fletcher's *The Transcendental Masque: An Essay on Milton's Comus* (Ithaca, 1971), p. 115.

15. Susanne Langer, *Feeling and Form: A Theory of Art* (New York, 1953), p. 304; W. P. Ker, *Epic and Romance: Essays on Medieval Literature* (London, 1897), p. 13.

16. Fletcher introduces his conception of "transcendental form" in *The Prophetic Moment: An Essay on Spenser* (Chicago, 1971), p. 301, and develops it in *The Transcendental Masque*, pp. 116–46; and E. H. Gombrich explains his idea of "total form" in *Norm and Form: Studies in the Art of the Renaissance*, 2nd ed. (London, 1971), esp. pp. 63, 73, 79. Both ideas derive ultimately from scriptural exegesis and are canonized as part of a critical idiom during the Romantic period. In his 1815 *Preface*, listing the various genres, Wordsworth acknowledges that some poets create a "composite order" from them; and Hazlitt, in *The Plain Speaker*, allows that the "productions" of Milton, more "multiform" even than Shakespeare's, "were of the *composite order*" and "sometimes even amount to

centos" (see *The Romantics on Milton: Formal Essays and Critical Asides*, ed. Joseph Anthony Wittreich, Jr. [Cleveland, 1970], pp. 128, 397).

Rosalie Colie's plea for "a good theoretical practicial article on *genera mixta*" is still awaiting a response. The point I make here, about prophecy as a mixed genre, in no way negates Colie's claim that "the pastoral mode is . . . particularly hospitable to different genres within it"; but my point is meant to modify her supposition that in the Renaissance "pastoral could be called *the* mixed genre, the only genre in which mixture was not only permissible but requisite" (see *"My Ecchoing Song": Andrew Marvell's Poetry of Criticism* [Princeton, 1970], p. 153.)

17. Thomas Goodwin, *The Exposition of the Revelation* (1639), in *The Works of Thomas Goodwin*, 12 vols. (London, 1861–66), V, 32, 33; Hugh Broughton, *A Revelation of the Holy Apocalpys* ([London], 1610), p. 70.

18. Morton Scott Enslin, *The Literature of the Christian Movement* (1938; rpt. New York, 1956), p. 355.

19. Thomas Brightman, *The Revelation of S. John* (Leyden, 1616), p. 212.

20. Broughton, *A Revelation of the Holy Apocalyps*, p. 70.

21. *Literature as System*, pp. 147, 155, 179.

22. *The Resources of Kind: Genre-Theory in the Renaissance*, ed. Barbara K. Lewalski (Berkeley and Los Angeles, 1973), pp. 33, 67.

23. James Joyce, *A Portrait of the Artist as a Young Man* (London, 1916), pp. 251–52.

24. See E. S. Shaffer, *Kubla Khan and the Fall of Jerusalem: The Mythological School in Biblical Criticism and Secular Literature, 1770–1800* (Cambridge, 1975), pp. 144, 183.

25. Isabel G. MacCaffrey, "*Lycidas:* The Poet in a Landscape," in *The Lyric and Dramatic Milton*, ed. Joseph H. Summers (New York, 1965), pp. 84, 91.

26. *European Literature and the Latin Middle Ages*, trans. Willard R. Trask (New York, 1953), p. 260.

27. Purney, *A Full Enquiry*, p. 35.

28. See Paz, *The Bow and the Lyre*, trans. Ruth L. C. Simms (New York, 1975), p. 184; and McFarland, *Shakespeare's Pastoral Comedy* (Chapel Hill, 1972), pp. 34–35.

29. *Lectures on the Sacred Poetry of the Hebrews*, trans. G. Gregory (Boston, 1815), pp. 43, 290, 317–20. Milton, of course, had Scaliger's *Poetics* to remind him of the association of elegy and lamentation with the prophets of Scripture (see *Milton's "Lycidas,"* ed. Elledge, p. 107).

30. *Lectures*, pp. 14–15, 322–25.

31. *Studies in Seventeenth-Century Poetic* (Madison, 1950), p. 109.

32. See *Attitudes Toward History*, 2 vols. (New York, 1937).

33. William Empson, *Some Versions of Pastoral* (London, 1950), p. 23.

34. *The Bow and the Lyre*, p. 139.

35. "Spenser and the Epithalamic Convention," in *The Prince of Poets: Essays on Edmund Spenser*, ed. John R. Elliott, Jr. (New York, 1968), p. 163.

36. *Essays and Introductions* (London, 1961), p. 260.

37. *The Prophetic Milton* (Charlottesville, 1974), p. 57.

38. *The Green Cabinet*, p. 14.

39. *The Resources of Kind*, p. 11.

40. *Anatomy of Criticism: Four Essays* (Princeton, 1957), p. 324. Such a perception has evidently led Irene Samuel to agree with Paul Elmer More, that *Lycidas* possesses "something like 'the mighty structure of Dante's *Paradiso*"

(Samuel, *Dante and Milton: The "Commedia" and "Paradise Lost"* [Ithaca, N.Y., 1966], p. 37).

41. See Empson's discussion of the implications of this phrase (quoted from a speech by Faustus) in *Some Versions of Pastoral*, p. 78.

42. *The Poetical Works of John Milton*, ed. David Masson, 3 vols. (London, 1882), I, 54.

43. MacCaffrey, *"Lycidas:* The Poet in a Landscape," p. 81.

44. "The Rising Poet, 1645," in *The Lyric and Dramatic Milton*, ed. Summers, p. 4.

45. Ibid., pp. 9, 12.

46. Ibid., p. 3.

47. *"Lycidas:* The Poet in a Landscape," pp. 77, 92.

48. Fletcher, *The Transcendental Masque*, p. 8. See also the passage on "the prophetic implications of the [masque] genre" (p. 25).

49. Harold Bloom, of course, thinks otherwise; see *A Map of Misreading* (New York, 1975), p. 126. For an intelligent rejoinder to Bloom's views, see Northrop Frye, "Expanding Eyes," *Critical Inquiry*, II (1975), 199–216.

50. *John Milton: Poet and Humanist*, ed. John S. Diekhoff (Cleveland, 1966), p. 62. On the indebtedness of *Comus* to Revelation, see Alice-Lyle Scoufos, "The Mysteries in Milton's *Masque*," *Milton Studies*, VI, ed. James D. Simmonds (Pittsburgh, 1974), 113–42; and for an introduction to the subject of the indebtedness of *Lycidas* to Revelation, see my own essay, " 'A Poet Amongst Poets': Milton and the Tradition of Prophecy," in *Milton and the Line of Vision*, ed. Wittreich, esp. pp. 111–29.

51. Tayler, *"Lycidas* Yet Once More," pp. 106–08; Louis Martz, "Who Is Lycidas?" *Yale French Studies*, XLVII (1972), 187. *Lycidas* "is only intermittently 'pastoral' ": the opening lines present an "incompletely realized pastoral landscape," alerting us to the fact, says Isabel MacCaffrey, that Milton could have, but did not, "take his bearings in the tradition of pastoral elegy" (*"Lycidas:* The Poet in a Landscape," pp. 67, 69, 71). Balanchandra Rajan describes *Lycidas* as a poem of "mergings," noting specifically its conflation of various kinds of pastoral (*The Lofty Rhyme*, p. 54).

52. "Milton's Uncouth Swain," *Milton Studies*, III, ed. James D. Simmonds (Pittsburgh, 1971), 51.

53. For Warton's note, and Todd's, see *The Poetical Works of John Milton*, ed. Henry John Todd, 3rd ed., 6 vols. (London, 1826), V, 9. For the tradition of St. Michael and the Mount of Vision, see A. B. Van Os, *Religious Visions: The Development of the Eschatological Elements in Medieval English Religious Literature* (Amsterdam, 1932), pp. 80–81.

54. "Who is Lycidas?" p. 184.

55. *Some Versions of Pastoral*, p. 6.

56. Shaffer, *Kubla Khan and the Fall of Jerusalem*, p. 155.

57. Marinelli, *Pastoral*, p. 9.

"DEARLY BOUGHT REVENGE": *SAMSON AGONISTES, HAMLET,* AND ELIZABETHAN REVENGE TRAGEDY

John F. Andrews

W HAT, IF ANYTHING, does *Samson Agonistes* have in common with *Hamlet*? Is there any reason, for example, to believe that *Hamlet* was one of the principal sources for *Samson Agonistes*? I'm not aware that anyone has ever suggested so, even though there are scattered lines in several of Milton's poems, including *Samson,* that some scholars have read as echoes of Shakespeare's most enigmatic tragedy.[1] I wouldn't dismiss the possibility that Milton was thinking of *Hamlet* now and then as he composed *Samson Agonistes,* but it is not my purpose here to prove any direct relationships. What I propose is something more modest and informal: a series of tentative probes into aspects of each work that seem to me to emerge with greater clarity when the two tragedies are examined side by side.

I

Let us begin with the later work. It has largely escaped critical notice, I think, that *Samson Agonistes* is, among other things, a species of revenge tragedy. Milton uses the word "revenge" six times in the poem, five of those times in the last 300 lines, as if to invite readers to compare *Samson Agonistes,* not merely with *Prometheus Bound* and *Oedipus at Colonus,* two Greek tragedies with which it has obvious and deep affinities, but also with such Elizabethan and Jacobean plays as *The Spanish Tragedy, Titus Andronicus, Hamlet,* and *Antonio's Revenge.*

Shortly after Samson has been led off to the temple of Dagon, his solicitous father returns from the city with the happy news that he has finally persuaded the Philistine lords to accept a ransom in exchange for the release of his son. "Some much averse I found and wondrous harsh," Manoa says, "Contemptuous, proud, set on revenge and spite"; but fortunately he has found others "More generous far and civil, who confess'd / They had enough reveng'd,

81

having reduc't / Thir foe to misery beneath thir fears" (1461–62, 1467–69). Before Manoa can finish telling the Israelite Chorus his welcome story, he hears a tumult from the city. Shortly thereafter, a messenger arrives to inform Manoa and his fellow Israelites that the "noise" and "shout" they heard was the "horrid spectacle" brought on by Samson when he pulled down the pillars of the "spacious Theater," killing thousands of Philistines, including all "thir choice nobility and flower"—and sacrificing his own life in the process (1508, 1510, 1542, 1605, 1654).

Hearing of this totally unanticipated development, which means that all his efforts on Samson's behalf have been in vain, Manoa is struck with dismay: "O lastly over-strong against thyself! / A dreadful way thou took'st to thy revenge" (1590–91). He fears that Samson has yielded to despair and brought shame upon himself by committing suicide. But as the messenger details the manner of the hero's death, it becomes clear that Samson's last "great act" (1389) has been an unblemished triumph. Whereupon the Chorus exclaims:

> O dearly bought revenge, yet glorious!
> Living or dying thou hast fulfill'd
> The work for which thou wast foretold
> To *Israel*, and now li'st victorious
> Among thy slain self-kill'd
> Not willingly, but tangl'd in the fold
> Of dire necessity, whose law in death conjoin'd
> Thee with thy slaughter'd foes in number more
> Than all thy life had slain before.   (1660–68)

A few lines later, Manoa himself expresses similar acceptance:

> Come, come, no time for lamentation now,
> Nor much more cause: *Samson* hath quit himself
> Like *Samson*, and heroicly hath finish'd
> A life Heroic, on his Enemies
> Fully reveng'd.   (1708–12)

It has always struck me as curious that the word "revenge" becomes important in *Samson Agonistes* only after the agent of revenge has departed and the poem is four-fifths complete, the protagonist himself having never used the word once. This, of course, is in sharp contrast to the usual revenge tragedy, in which the protagonist is preoccupied with revenge almost from the beginning of the drama. One possible interpretation of the contrast, certainly, is that it is a mistake to put too much emphasis on revenge as a theme in *Samson Agonistes*. Perhaps so; but I think it unlikely that Milton would have repeated the word "revenge" so many times in brief compass if he hadn't intended to summon up memories of the revenge motif in earlier Renaissance tragedies. What strikes me as the more plausible interpretation, then, is that Milton consciously modeled certain aspects of his poem on the structure of Elizabethan revenge tragedy—but did so in such a way as to comment on the substance of many of the works representative of the genre. Later I would like to propose that Milton's treatment of revenge tragedy amounts to something approximating a transformation of the genre—a transformation comparable to, though perhaps less radical than, his transformation of Greek epic in *Paradise Lost* and of Greek tragedy in *Samson Agonistes*.

Before considering any *transformation* of the genre, however, we must first outline some of the ways in which Milton *used* the traits of revenge tragedy as part of his artistic design in *Samson Agonistes*.

II

It is perhaps best to start with an examination of the central figure and his situation. The typical protagonist of a revenge tragedy is a man who, because of the distressing conditions in which he finds himself, is in an advanced state of melancholy.[2] Preoccupied with injustices and injuries that have disordered the past and blighted the present, he is pessimistic about the future and is given to mental disquiet, sleeplessness, world-weariness, impatience, and discontent.[3] He declines to take part in a society he regards as unjust and oppressive, and he expresses his contempt for its debased values by scorning norms and forms that others accept without question.[4] When prevailed upon to be present at ceremonial occasions, for example, he tends to isolate himself from the rest of the court by deliberately indecorous behavior, by ironic or seemingly foolish conversation, and by funereal or disheveled apparel.[5] While others are making merry with food, drink, and festive games, he stands on the peripheries, wearing black and playing the role of party-pooper, his refusal to join the fun serving as an implicit and often unnerving comment on the superficial, hedonistic, irresponsible escapism he judges so severely.[6] Much of his acerbic wit is directed at the foibles of women, whom he tends to regard as inherently weak-willed and deceitful; his disillusionment with womankind gives vent, at times, to sexual nausea, and it is not unusual to see him casting off a lover, a wife, or even a mother with bitter disgust.[7] When alone in soliloquy, or when in unguarded conversation with a confidant, the protagonist is given to deep, philosophical meditation, fearing that heaven, if it exists at all, has withdrawn its interest in, and influence on, human affairs, and pondering the nature of man in a world bereft of spiritual sustenance.[8] Feeling trapped in a profoundly unhealthy atmosphere, chained like a captive slave, the protagonist tends to view his state as a prison and himself as a tortured inmate, his moods alternating erratically between a will to break his bonds with wrathful violence and a will to end his troubles once and for all by taking his own life.[9] In his more hopeful, indignant moments, the protagonist meditates on vengeance, which he sees as the only way of liberating the present from a corrupt social and political order; but even in these moments, he tends to think of his imminent death, not as something to be feared and avoided, but as something to be welcomed, a relief from toil and trouble.[10] Understandably, the protagonist of the revenge tragedy is at times irrational, even neurotic, in his thoughts and actions, and it is not unusual for him to be regarded by others as mad or bordering on madness.[11] Frequently he has the wit to use this trait to his advantage, feigning an antic disposition to gain a degree of flexibility he would otherwise lack.[12]

Inasmuch as the protagonist is generally correct in his analysis of the ills and inequities of society, the audience is usually encouraged, at least at the outset, to respond to his anger sympathetically, to see much of his world through his eyes, so to speak, and therefore to be tolerant of his occasional excesses. This is particularly true when the protagonist has an unimpeachable case against his enemy or enemies—either through a reliable witness, such as a truthful ghost or a trustworthy friend, or through reliable evidence emerging from the events of the play, as happens, for example, when a suspected murderer tips his hand or attempts treachery against the protagonist. Sympathy for the protagonist is also encouraged by the frequency with which he is placed, dramaturgically, in an intimate relationship with the audience: on the stage alone in soliloquy, for example, or taking the audience into his confidence with asides or ironic innuendos not meant to be heard or understood by others on the stage.[13]

As anyone familiar with the history of *Hamlet* criticism knows, the plot of the typical revenge tragedy normally includes two basic ingredients: (1) a significant delay or hesitation between the moment when the protagonist knows his course and the moment in which he fulfills it;[14] and (2) a concluding confrontation in which a number of violent, bloody deaths occur, including that of the protagonist himself, either by his own hand or as a consequence of the means he employs to enact revenge on his enemy or enemies.[15] The delay or hesitation may have any of several causes, but its almost inevitable effect is to build suspense, allow for the development of a counterintrigue by the avenger's enemies, and put much of the focus on mental, as opposed to physical, conflict. The protagonist's interior psychomachia, in which he upbraids himself for his inability to take aggressive action, prepares the audience for the explosive release of energy that climaxes and concludes the drama.[16] When all is said and done, the audience is left with the sense that a sort of rough justice has been rendered; virtually every evildoer has paid the ultimate penalty for his crimes, and the avenger himself dies with the satisfaction that he has completed an appointed task. Just what attitude the audience will have toward the avenger at the end depends, in large measure, on the degree to which the avenger's motives and means have become tainted by the evils he has sought to eradicate. If he has clearly acted in terms of a divine mandate, so that it may credibly be affirmed that he has performed his vengeance as a minister of Providence, the audience will approve his actions as those of one of God's deputies. If, on the other hand, the avenger has acted more in terms of private motives, usurping from higher authorities the privilege of punishing crimes and righting wrongs, and using treacherous means to accomplish his revenge, the audience will normally be encouraged to judge him to be a reprobate scourge, a man who has been used by Providence to punish other evildoers, but a man who, once he has completed his role, is himself punished by divine vengeance.[17]

III

I doubt that anyone will need to be reminded that most of the foregoing characteristics of Elizabethan revenge tragedy are to be found in *Hamlet,* a play so well known and influential, in fact, that it has now become for many of us the very model of revenge tragedy. It may be of some interest, however, to observe how many of these features of the genre are also to be found, in one form or another, in *Samson Agonistes.*

When we first encounter Samson in Milton's poem, we discover that the prison imagery so prevalent in *Hamlet* is literally applicable to the man who, since his fall, has been chained to a

mill in a "common Prison" (6) where, in his blindness and servil-
ity, he is daily made "the scorn and gaze" (34) of his enemies.
Like Hamlet, he feels

> dark in light expos'd
> To daily fraud, contempt, abuse, and wrong,
> Within doors, or without, still as a fool,
> In power of others, never in my own.   (75–78)

"Retiring from the popular noise" (16) of the Philistines as they
celebrate "a solemn Feast . . . To *Dagon* thir Sea-Idol" (13), Samson is vaguely reminiscent of Hamlet in his disdain for the nightly
carousing of Claudius and his court, the "heavy-headed revel"
that Hamlet says has made the Danes proverbial for drunkenness,
"traduced and taxed of other nations" (*Ham.* I.iv.17–18). Like
Hamlet, Samson is tormented by

> restless thoughts, that like a deadly swarm
> Of hornets arm'd, no sooner found alone,
> But rush upon me thronging, and present
> Times past, what once I was, and what am now.   (19–22)

The Samson we see at the beginning of the poem cannot but
have "a will most incorrect to heaven" (*Ham.* I.ii.95–96), "a heart
unfortified, a mind impatient." For he is, as the Chorus notes
upon its entry,

> As one past hope, abandon'd,
> And by himself given over;
> In slavish habit, ill-fitted weeds
> O'erworn and soil'd.   (120–23)

As the Chorus bemoans the contrast between what Samson was
and what he now has fallen to—"The glory late of *Israel*, now the
grief" (179)—we may be reminded of Ophelia's reaction when she
witnesses Hamlet's apparently distracted state in act III, scene i of
Hamlet:

> O, what a noble mind is here o'erthrown!
> The courtier's, soldier's, scholar's, eye, tongue, sword,
> Th' expectancy and rose of the fair state,
> The glass of fashion and the mould of form,
> Th' observed of all observers, quite quite down!
>
> · · · · · · ·
>
>   O, woe is me
> T' have seen what I have seen, see what I see!
>
>   (*Ham.* III.i.146–57)

How parallel the situations are is a matter of interpretation, but the effect of the hero's downcast posture on those who wish him well is the same in both instances. And there can surely be no doubt that Samson's meditations prior to the entrance of the Israelite Chorus are tending toward the same kind of near-despair that marks Hamlet's "To be or not to be" soliloquy (III.i.56–88) just prior to the entrance of Ophelia. The man who should be guiding his people and delivering them from bondage is "Himself in bonds" (41), and that cannot but raise doubts about divine justice and providence, doubts that, in turn, prompt thoughts of easeful death.

With the coming of the Chorus, however, Samson's thoughts turn outward. He defends himself against the charge that his first mistake was in marrying the woman of Timna. What he "motion'd was of God" (222), he says, "by occasion hence" to "begin *Israel's* Deliverance" (224–25)—deliverance that was indeed "offer'd" by "great acts" (246, 243) of Samson's, but was not appropriated by "*Israel's* Governors, and Heads of Tribes" (242). Samson might, in other words, have accomplished his mission before his fall into the hands of Dalila, were it not for "Nations grown corrupt, / And by thir vices brought to servitude," loving "Bondage more than Liberty" (268–70).

When Manoa enters, blaming Samson's "miserable change" (340) on God rather than on Samson or on Israel's rulers, Samson's meditations shift inward once again. The ultimate blame for his captivity, Samson insists, is his own:

> Fearless of danger, like a petty God
> I walk'd about admir'd of all and dreaded
> On hostile ground, none daring my affront.
> Then swoll'n with pride into the snare I fell
> Of fair fallacious looks, venereal trains,
> Soft'n'd with pleasure and voluptuous life.   (529–34)

The more he reflects upon his past failures, the more Samson thinks his ills "remediless" (648). And by the end of this speech, he is all but overcome by a "sense of Heav'n's desertion" (632):

> So much I feel my genial spirits droop,
> My hopes all flat, nature within me seems
> In all her functions weary of herself;
> My race of glory run, and race of shame,
> And I shall shortly be with them that rest.   (594–98)

This meditation is so powerful in its effect that it leads the Chorus to the question implicit in all philosophical tragedy: "God of our Fathers, what is man!" (667).

The same question, of course, has been hinted at by Hamlet in his conversation with Rosencrantz and Guildenstern:

I have of late—but wherefore I know not—lost all my mirth, foregone all custom of exercises; and indeed it goes so heavily with my disposition, that this goodly frame the earth seems to me a sterile promontory, this most excellent canopy the air, look you, this brave o'er-hanging firmament, this majestical roof fretted with golden fire, why it appeareth nothing to me but a foul and pestilent congregation of vapors. What a piece of work is a man, how noble in reason, how infinite in faculties, in form and moving, how express and admirable in action, how like an angel in apprehension, how like a god: the beauty of the world, the paragon of animals. And yet to me, what is this quintessence of dust? (II.ii.285–96)

In this speech, in which man's high calling and lofty aspirations are viewed in bitterly ironic contrast to the human depravity to be seen on every hand, Hamlet expresses the world-weary pessimism that is characteristic of him following his mother's remarriage. Then, a few minutes later in the succeeding scene, Hamlet's general disillusionment becomes applicable to Ophelia. In one of the most painful encounters of the play, a moment that is usually acted in such a way that Hamlet's concluding words, "To a nunnery, go" (III.i.145), are spoken with as much anger as sadness, we see that Hamlet now believes he can place no more faith in Ophelia than in his mother: "Frailty, thy name is woman" (I.ii.146).

In similar vein, Samson responds to the visit of Dalila, an event that occurs immediately following *his* most grimly despondent meditation. Having been betrayed by her once, he is not about to let her get too close to him again:

> Out, out Hyaena; these are thy wonted arts.
> And arts of every woman false like thee,
> To break all faith, all vows, deceive, betray,
> Then as repentant to submit, beseech,
> And reconcilement move with feign'd remorse.   (748–52)

IV

Enough has now been said, I trust, to suggest that there are certain similarities between the situation and character of Hamlet and the situation and character of Samson. I'll be the first to admit that none of these similarities prove *Hamlet* a "source" for *Samson Agonistes*. I hope I have indicated, however, that there is some basis for fruitful comparison of the protagonists of the two tragedies. But does the same hold true for the plots involving the protagonists? I think so.

Both tragedies have been faulted for what some critics regard as structural weaknesses. Until relatively recently, for example, virtually every commentator on *Hamlet* has felt obliged to address the question, Why does Hamlet delay before carrying out the Ghost's command to kill Claudius? Since the question is one the protagonist himself was the first to ask, there can be no doubt that it is a legitimate inquiry. Answers to the question have varied so widely, however, that some critics—T. S. Eliot among them[18]—have seen in it an implicit indication that the playwright somehow lost control of his artistic design during the central portions of the play. Similarly, a good deal of the twentieth-century commentary on *Samson Agonistes* has been written directly or indirectly in response to Dr. Johnson's famous complaint that Milton's poem has a beginning and an end but no middle. In each instance, the critical problem has arisen because there is an expanse of time in which little or no overt action occurs to advance the plot in a traditionally Aristotelian sense. Rather than proceeding directly to the forceful deed the audience grows impatient to witness, the hero in each tragedy waits: reacting to external stimuli rather than initiating any motion of his own, coming to terms with himself and his situation before committing himself to a specific way of addressing his situation.

Once the decision to act does occur, one senses in each drama that the protagonist is conscious of taking a leap in the dark. Hamlet accepts an invitation to fence with Laertes even though he expresses some misgivings about it.

HOR. You will lose this wager, my lord.

HAM. I do not think so. Since he went into France I have been in continual practice. I shall win at the odds. But thou wouldst not think how ill all's here about my heart. But it is no matter.

HOR. Nay, good my lord—

HAM. It is but foolery, but it is such a kind of gaingiving as would perhaps trouble a woman.

HOR. If your mind dislike anything, obey it. I will forestall their repair hither, and say you are not fit.

HAM. Not a whit, we defy augury. There is special providence in the fall of a sparrow. If it be now, 'tis not to come; if it be not to come, it will be now; if it be not now, yet it will come. The readiness is all. Since no man of aught he leaves knows, what is't to leave betimes? Let be.

(V.ii.190–203)

Hamlet's concluding remarks in this exchange have usually been interpreted as a signal that the hero has overcome his earlier melancholy and near-despair and has now acquired a faith in divine guidance that will enable him to face with serenity whatever lies in store for him.

A few minutes later, Hamlet accomplishes the goal that has drawn him since the beginning of the play. He receives a death-wound from Laertes' poisoned sword, but before the poison takes its final effect he successfully retaliates against the agent ultimately responsible for the treachery—forcing the "incestuous, murd'rous, damned Dane" Claudius to "drink off" the "potion" intended for Hamlet (V.ii.310–11). As Hamlet then lies dying on the stage, young Fortinbras arrives with his Norwegian army to usher in a new era for the Danish throne. But not before Hamlet's loyal companion Horatio pronounces a touching benediction for the expiring hero:

> Now cracks a noble heart. Good night, sweet prince,
> And flights of angels sing thee to thy rest!   (V.ii.344–45)

The conclusion of *Samson Agonistes* is in some ways strikingly similar to the conclusion of *Hamlet*. Following Dalila's visit to the prison, which has had the effect of stirring Samson from his lethargy, the hero is taunted by the giant Harapha, strongest champion of the Philistines. After Harapha rouses Samson's anger to an even greater pitch than had Dalila, Samson challenges him to combat, not so much to vent personal animosity as to demonstrate "whose God is strongest" (1155). Harapha, a formidable warrior, is reduced by Samson's confidence to the condition of a "baffl'd coward" (1237) and slinks off ignominiously. Next comes an Officer, more dignified than Claudius' messenger Osric, to be sure, but commissioned to similar purpose. He says that the Philistine lords request the hero's presence at a "solemn feast" to Dagon—a celebration "with Sacrifices, Triumph, Pomp, and Games" in honor of the god who has delivered Samson into Philistine hands (1311–12). At first Samson refuses to accompany the Officer to Dagon's temple, saying

> Thou knowst I am an *Ebrew*, therefore tell them,
> Our Law forbids at thir Religious Rites
> My presence.   (1319–21)

He tells the Officer that the Philistines have enough "Jugglers and Dancers" to "make them sport" without further humiliating a man "over-labor'd at thir public Mill" (1325, 1328, 1327):

> Can they think me so broken, so debas'd
> With corporal servitude, that my mind ever
> Will condescend to such absurd commands?   (1335–38)

After considering the matter a few minutes, however, prompted by the Chorus, which, like the Officer and like Horatio in *Hamlet,* advises the hero to "regard" himself (1333), Samson changes his mind.

> Be of good courage, I begin to feel
> Some rousing motions in me which dispose
> To something extraordinary my thoughts.
> I with this Messenger will go along,
> Nothing to do, be sure, that may dishonor
> Our Law, or stain my vow of *Nazarite.*
> If there be aught of presage in the mind,
> This day will be remarkable in my life
> By some great act, or of my days the last.   (1381–89)

He then leaves with the Officer, not knowing exactly what the outcome will be but trusting in "the living God" (1140) to make provision for him. Shortly thereafter, we learn that Samson has performed his final victory and his greatest.

V

But this is where we came in, isn't it? Let us now pause and reflect on what we've seen. Thus far we have examined a few of the many ways in which *Samson Agonistes* and *Hamlet* are similar. Beginning with a general description of revenge tragedy, we have noted some of the characteristics of *Samson Agonistes* that resemble features of *Hamlet,* the most famous and certainly the most successful example of Elizabethan revenge tragedy.

Now let's reverse field and consider several ways in which *Samson Agonistes* may be seen to differ from *Hamlet* and most other revenge tragedies. For it is only when we are aware of the differences as well as the similarities that we can properly appreciate the relationship between *Samson Agonistes* and such revenge tragedies as *Hamlet.*

VI

While describing the general characteristics of Elizabethan revenge tragedy, I commented that the response of the audience to the protagonist and his actions is normally conditioned by the degree to which the protagonist is depicted as becoming tainted by the evil he is seeking to eradicate. If the play presents the protagonist as a good man who enacts vengeance in the name of divine justice and as a direct agent of God, the chances are that he will emerge more or less untainted by the evil he punishes; often, but not always, a "good" avenger, such as Macduff in *Macbeth*,[19] will survive the final holocaust. If, on the other hand, the play presents the protagonist as a man who enacts revenge out of personal malice rather than out of a concern for public good and divine justice, the chances are that he will forfeit the moral approval, if not the sympathy, of the audience as a man contaminated by the very evil he endeavors to remove.

The criterion that would have been most familiar to Elizabethan audiences was that found in St. Paul's Epistle to the Romans, where the Apostle reminds believers that it is un-Christian to return evil for evil and goes on to say that only God or his appointed ministers are permitted to punish injuries or crimes.

Dearly beloved, avenge not yourselves, but rather give place unto wrath: for it is written, Vengeance is mine; I will repay, saith the Lord. . . . Be not overcome of evil, but overcome evil with good. Let every soul be subject to the higher powers. For there is no power but of God . . . and they that resist shall receive to themselves damnation. . . . The ruler . . . beareth not the sword in vain: for he is the minister of God, a revenger to execute wrath upon him that doeth evil. (Romans xii,17–xiii,4)

As Fredson Bowers has pointed out in his pioneering study of *Elizabethan Revenge Tragedy*, most of the revenge tragedies performed between 1587 and 1642 present a protagonist who, for one reason or another, finds it necessary or desirable to take justice into his own hands. In most instances, the avenger is, at best, in a morally ambiguous position, and quite often he is presented as having ventured beyond the pale of legal, moral, and religious sanctions. Sometimes, indeed, he becomes a man so steeped in blood that he forgoes all sympathy, however just his original cause, his vengefulness having turned him into a reprobate scourge of God, doomed to perdition.[20] Despite the various legal, moral, and religious prohibitions against private vengeance, however, Bowers observes that dueling was not uncommon among Elizabethan and Jacobean noblemen seeking redress for slights or injuries, and that in the latter years of Elizabeth's reign "honor grew more valuable than life" for many courtiers.[21] "Such being the case," Bowers says, "the audience at the theatres seems to have made the customary compromise between a formal set of religious and moral ethics and an informal set of native convictions. Under these circumstances, ... the revenger of the drama started with the sympathy of the audience if his cause were good and if he acted according to the typically English notions of straightforward fair play. It was only, as with Hieronimo ..., when he turned to 'Machiavellian' treacherous intrigues that the audience began to veer against him."[22]

In a more recent study entitled *Hamlet and Revenge,* Eleanor Prosser has argued, persuasively in my opinion, that audiences and playwrights were generally less sympathetic to revenge than Bowers and his generation of scholars assumed. Prosser quotes from a variety of Elizabethan materials indicating that revenge was considered blasphemous (with the revenger, like Lucifer, seeking to rival God by usurping Christ's judicial office), rebellious (the private revenger seeking to subvert the authority of the magistrate, God's deputy for the rendering of justice in the state), and unhealthy (for both mind and body).[23]

Eternal damnation was not the only penalty for revenge. An age devoted to temporal pursuits was constantly warned that there were penalties in this world as well. The ravages of revenge appear most clearly in the deterioration of the mind. At first, the revenger becomes distracted, shutting everything but revenge out of his consciousness; he "mindeth none other thinge, which reason and experience doth wel declare." As he gives rein to his impatience, he "is therewith abstracte from reason and tourned in to a monstrous figure." "To be short, after that anger hath once got the bridle at will, the whole mind and judgement is so blinded & caried headlong, that an angry man thinkes of nothing but of revenge, insomuch that he forgetteth himselfe, and careth not what he doth, or what harm will light upon himselfe in so doing, so that he may be avenged.[24]

VII

Whether we accept Bowers' interpretation of the conventions of Elizabethan revenge tragedy (according to which audiences were expected to be sympathetic to a good number of revengers, even though their actions were difficult to reconcile with Christian religious and ethical principles) or Prosser's interpretation (according to which in all but a few isolated instances audiences were expected to disapprove of private revenge), we face a problem when we approach *Samson Agonistes.* For it is evident from all of Milton's writings that he regards private revenge in much the same way as do the moralists and theologians quoted in the citation from *Hamlet and Revenge.* For Milton, the only kind of revenge that is justifiable is that associated directly with divine vengeance. God and his ministers may execute vengeance, which thus becomes another term for divine justice; but private individuals who seek to usurp this judicial function do so at their peril. In *Paradise Lost*, Milton leaves no doubt that revenge apart from divine vengeance is unmistakably to be associated with Satanic rebellion. Satan is described in Book I as "Stirr'd up with Envy and Revenge" (I, 35); as studying "revenge, immortal hate, / And courage never to submit or yield" (I, 107–08); and as implacably harboring "considerate Pride / Waiting revenge" (I, 603–04). In Book II, Satan's "dire revenge" (II, 128) is associated not only with envy, hate, and pride, but also with cruelty, irrationality, and despair. And throughout *Paradise Lost*, revenge is synonymous with "falsehood," "deep malice to conceal" (IV, 122–23). Dame Helen Gardner has written an illuminating essay on "Milton's 'Satan' and the Theme of Damnation in Elizabethan Tragedy,"[25] but even so great a critic as she hasn't said all there is to be said about affinities between Milton's Satan and the avengers Milton would have found in many Elizabethan tragedies.

So how does this relate to *Samson Agonistes?* Is Samson an avenger in the tradition of the protagonist of the Elizabethan revenge tragedy? Is he in some ways similar to Satan? One recent commentator, Irene Samuel, has suggested so.[26] She is wrong, I think, in her argument that Milton disapproved of Samson's last "great act" of violence. And yet, in addition to the six references to revenge I cited at the beginning, there is another important reason for considering the possibility of such an interpretation. In the sixteenth chapter of Judges, the primary Biblical source for the Samson story, Milton would have found the following account of Samson's death.

Now the house was full of men and women; and all the lords of the Philistines were there; and there were upon the roof about three thousand men and women, that beheld while Samson made sport. And Samson called unto the LORD, and said O Lord GOD, remember me, I pray thee, only this once, O God, that I may be at once avenged of the Philistines for my two eyes. And Samson took hold of the two middle pillars upon which the house stood, and on which it was borne up, of the one with his right hand, and of the other with his left. And Samson said, Let me die with the Philistines. And he bowed himself with all his might; and the house fell upon the lords, and upon all the people that were therein. So the dead which he slew at his death were more than they which he slew in his life. (Judges xvi, 27–30)

As F. Michael Krouse[27] and other commentators have demonstrated, this was only one of several Biblical references to Samson that would have conditioned Milton's thinking about his heroic subject, and it was a passage that had been submitted to a wide variety of interpretations during the patristic and medieval periods—interpretations that usually elevated Samson's motivations and explained away the suggestion that he committed suicide while enacting a cruel personal vengeance on the Philistines for blinding him. Even so, however, this was, as Milton knew, the primary source of the Samson narrative, and there was no escaping the fact that there were certain affinities between its portrait of Samson and the image of the avenger made popular in dozens of Elizabethan revenge tragedies. How did Milton deal with this problem?

I'd like to suggest three ways. First, he faced the difficulty head-on, and, as we have seen, structured his tragedy in such a way as to echo the form, and thus the expectations, of the traditional Elizabethan revenge tragedy. Second, he included, as we have also seen, six references to revenge, strategically locating five of them near the end of the poem and taking care to have the word "revenge" employed only by characters—namely Manoa and the Israelite Chorus—who have been shown throughout the poem to be of limited understanding. Meanwhile, third, he presented the details of Samson's death in such a way to leave no doubt in the mind of the audience that the hero acted as an inspired minister of God rather than as a reprobate scourge.

Just before Samson leaves with the Officer, he says:

> Happ'n what may, of me expect to hear
> Nothing dishonorable, impure, unworthy
> Our God, our Law, my Nation, or myself;
> The last of me or no I cannot warrant.   (1423–26)

Like the hero of classical tradition, Samson is here presented as a man of high-minded self-assurance, concerned about honor and worthiness.[28] But a close examination of the speech will disclose that Samson invokes these traditional heroic concerns only to place their traditional locus in what Milton would have regarded as a properly subordinate position. For by this point in his life, Samson has learned that *personal* honor is of significance only if it is rightly related to higher values and loyalties. What we find in Samson's last speech, then, is the expression of a faithful champion's assured and unambiguous commitment to a perfectly aligned hierarchy of duties: first, to "Our God"; second, to "our Law"; third, to "my Nation"; and fourth, to "myself."[29]

The same unambiguous tone pervades the messenger's account of what happened once Samson arrived at the temple. "He patient but undaunted where they led him, / Came to the place" (1623–24).

> At length for intermission sake they led him
> Between the pillars; he his guide requested
> (For so from such as nearer stood we heard)
> As overtir'd to let him lean a while
> With both his arms on those two massy Pillars
> That to the arched roof gave main support.
> He unsuspicious led him; which when *Samson*
> Felt in his arms, with head a while inclin'd,
> And eyes fast fixt he stood, as one who pray'd,
> Or some great matter in his mind revolv'd.
> At last with head erect thus cried aloud,
> "Hitherto, Lords, what your commands impos'd
> I have perform'd, as reason was, obeying,
> Not without wonder or delight beheld.
> Now of my own accord such other trial
> I mean to show you of my strength, yet greater;
> As with amaze shall strike all who behold."   (1629–45)

As Anthony Low has noted, *this* Samson seems more like Isaiah's Suffering Servant in his passion than like the Samson of Judges begging revenge for the loss of his two eyes.[30] *This* Samson,

> though blind of sight,
> Despis'd and thought extinguish't quite,
> With inward eyes illuminated
> His fiery virtue rous'd
> From under ashes into sudden flame.   (1687–91)

As Manoa says, echoing our own "calm of mind, all passion spent" (1758),[31]

> Nothing is here for tears, nothing to wail
> Or knock the breast, no weakness, no contempt,
> Dispraise, or blame, nothing but well and fair,
> And what may quiet us in a death so noble.   (1720–24)

VIII

Most critics find similar "peace and consolation" (1757) in the manner of Hamlet's death, hearing Horatio's "flights of angels" benediction as Shakespeare's means of assuring us of the beatific destiny of Hamlet's soul. I must confess, however, that my confidence in Horatio as a spokesman for Shakespeare's view of Christian eschatology is severely limited—particularly in light of Horatio's immediately preceding speech in which he threatens to commit a Stoic-like suicide, describing himself as "more an antique Roman than a Dane" (V.ii.326).[32] I am similarly skeptical of the consolation many interpreters profess to find in the concluding remarks by Fortinbras:

> Let four captains
> Bear Hamlet like a soldier to the stage,
> For he was likely, had he been put on,
> To have proved most royal.   (V.ii.380–83)

This, after all, is the rhetoric of political transition; and there is no reason to assume that it is any more adequate to sum up Hamlet's career than Mark Antony's "This was the noblest Roman of them all" speech is adequate to sum up all that we have seen, heard, and inferred about Brutus during the course of Shakespeare's *Julius Caesar*. Like every so-called choral speech in Shakespeare, Fortinbras' eulogy for Hamlet must be considered in the context of the whole play. And no small part of that context is the fact that every time we have seen or heard about Fortinbras prior to this moment, he has been portrayed as an irresponsible young Hotspur eager to seize on any opportunity, however trifling, to advance his military honor. Can it augur well for the future of Denmark that "th' election lights / On Fortinbras" (V.ii.340–41)?[33] I seriously doubt that Milton would have considered such an outcome equivalent to the "occasion" for "honor" and "freedom" (1716, 1715) bequeathed to Israel by Samson's heroic death. Samson's death affords the opportunity for political liberation; Hamlet's death merely initiates a different kind of political subjugation.

But how might Milton have responded to the other aspects of *Hamlet*'s denouement? Would Milton have regarded Shakespeare's protagonist as an example of the way "rightly to be great" (IV.iv.53)? Unfortunately, we don't have any notes Milton may have made on *Hamlet*. We do have Milton's other writings, however, and it may not be altogether idle to extrapolate from them and speculate for a moment on how Milton might have interpreted *Hamlet*.

In view of Milton's treatment of the subject of revenge in *Paradise Lost* and in *Samson Agonistes*, it seems safe to infer that he would not have assumed, as many later readers have, that

Hamlet from the beginning of the play has a "sacred duty" to wipe everything from "the book and volume" of his "brain" except the Ghost's commandment to revenge the elder Hamlet's "foul and most unnatural murder" (I.v.103, 25). Milton would have examined the text closely to determine whether Hamlet's desire to kill the King is motivated primarily by a quest for private blood revenge or primarily by a quest to overthrow a tyrannous regime as a divine minister for the public good. Here and there Milton would have found hints that Hamlet does state his cause in political and theological terms,[34] but I think he would have been disturbed by the infrequency with which Hamlet suggests that his reasons go beyond a passionate desire to obtain a suitable personal revenge for the murder of his father. Milton would have been troubled, too, I think, by the strong indications in the text that the Ghost cannot be a "spirit of health" (I.iv.40).[35] And I suspect that he would have been just as alarmed as Horatio and the watch when Hamlet disregards their warnings and speaks to the Ghost without applying any of the traditional tests to prove that it is not a devil assuming the "pleasing shape" of Hamlet's father to "abuse" and "damn" the younger Hamlet (III.i.567, 570). It strikes me as likely that Milton would have regarded Hamlet, in the early portions of the play, as a "desperate" and "distracted" melancholic (I.iv.87; I.v.97), understandably aroused to a fever pitch of indignation at the suggestion that his beloved father was murdered by the slimy Claudius, but so emotionally overwrought that he is incapable of addressing the situation with rational judgment.

In this light, I suspect, Milton would have read many of Hamlet's soliloquies not merely as sincere disclosures of Hamlet's most intimate thoughts, but also as dramaturgical devices by means of which Shakespeare allows the audience to observe Hamlet's emotional, mental, and spiritual confusion at close range. Scrutiny of the celebrated "To be or not to be" soliloquy (III.i.56–88), for example, would have yielded three more or less distinct movements in Hamlet's thought processes. In the first movement (lines 56–65), Hamlet analyzes his situation as "an antique Roman" Stoic might, and thereby views suicide as an honorable and attractive option, given his "sea of troubles." In the second movement (65–82), Hamlet draws back in fear, recalling the Christian prohibition against suicide as a damnable sin. But in the third movement (83–88), as the soliloquy concludes, Hamlet's more habitual orientation toward the Renaissance code of honor drives

him on to upbraid "conscience" and accuse himself of cowardice
for allowing Christian ethical and eschatological considerations to
frustrate "the native hue of resolution." Here as elsewhere in the
play, Milton would have found a penetrating psychological exploration of a troubled man's consciousness, and one that would have
shown a "conscience" only intermittently aligned with what Milton—and I think Shakespeare—would have regarded as a proper
spiritual orientation. It seems possible, incidentally, that Milton
might have learned from these soliloquies a few of the techniques
by which he shows such characters as Satan and Adam agoniz-
ing—often with similarly convoluted expressions of confusion—in
Paradise Lost.[36]

But back to *Hamlet.* Would Milton have seen signs that Hamlet, like Adam in *Paradise Lost* and like Samson in *Samson Agonistes,* eventually emerges into a clearer perception of himself and
of the proper response to his situation? There are, of course, indications that Hamlet approaches his problems rather differently
toward the end of the play. As he tells Horatio of how he escaped
the plot Claudius laid for him by substituting a different commis-
sion for the one Rosencrantz and Guildenstern were bearing with
them aboard ship to England, Hamlet affirms belief in "a divinity
that shapes our ends, / Rough-hew them how we will" (V.ii.10–
11). This and two similar references to Providence in the final
scene of the play[37] have led many modern critics to the inference
that, however adrift he may have been earlier in the drama, Hamlet has now found his moorings. I'm bothered, however, as I think
Milton would have been, by counterindications suggesting that
Hamlet's spiritual perspective in act V is not much broader than it
was in act I.   /98 905

The "How all occasions do inform against me" soliloquy, near
the end of act IV, is even more tortuous in its "reasoning" than the
"To be or not to be" soliloquy, with Hamlet taking a negative
example—Fortinbras risking "two thousand souls" "to gain a
little patch of ground / That hath in it no profit but the name"—
and transforming it into a positive exhortation for Hamlet to prose-
cute his own cause: "O, from this time forth, / My thoughts be
bloody, or be nothing worth!" (IV.iv.32–66).

In similar fashion, following his return from the interrupted
voyage to England, Hamlet analyzes the folly of all worldly vanity
in his *memento mori* meditation in the graveyard (V.i.59–192)[38]
and then immediately reveals himself to be preoccupied with just
such worldly vanity in his altercation with Laertes at Ophelia's

grave (V.i.230–70). "Hamlet the Dane" is not to be "outfaced" by a brother leaping into the grave of his sister. Invoking the name of Mount Ossa—significantly, one of the mountains the Titans heaped on Olympus to scale heaven, and thus proverbial as a symbol of hubris—he flies into what he later acknowledges to have been a "towering passion" (V.ii.80).

But what about Hamlet's three references to Providence and his statement that it is "perfect conscience" to slay the murderous, incestuous, treacherous King (V.ii.63–70)? It seems to me that in each instance there is a qualifying context. The "perfect conscience" remarks occur immediately following Hamlet's gloating report about how he has dispatched Rosencrantz and Guildenstern "to sudden death, / Not shriving time allowed" (V.ii.46–47)—punishment that would have been unusually harsh even for convicted traitors, and punishment that seems all the more inhumane considering that the play provides no evidence that Hamlet's former schoolmates are at all aware of the treachery of the King they loyally serve. When Hamlet boasts that "They are not near my conscience" (V.ii.58), we are surely meant to wonder about the Prince's conscience—just as we will probably have been shocked earlier when Hamlet spares Claudius at prayer, not because Hamlet is too sensitive to "butcher a defenceless man,"[39] but because he wishes to await a moment when the King is unquestionably engaged in some activity that "has no relish of salvation in't" (III.iii.92), so that he will go straight to hell.

Hamlet's reference to Providence just before he enters the fatal fencing match occurs, we will recall, only after he has expressed some misgivings about participating in the wager. In view of Hamlet's knowledge that Claudius is not above treachery and that Laertes is eager to avenge the deaths of both Polonius and Ophelia, Hamlet's uneasiness is perfectly rational, a fact underscored by Horatio's reply: "If your mind dislike anything, obey it" (V.ii.197). Are we than to conclude that Hamlet is manifesting trust in Providence when he disregards such warnings and proceeds with the match anyway? Surely not. There is every indication that at this moment Hamlet is acting against his better judgment. We will do well to recall a sentence from the earlier Fortinbras soliloquy:

> Sure he that made us with such large discourse,
> Looking before and after, gave us not
> That capability and godlike reason
> To fust in us unused.   (IV.iv.36–39)

Prompted, no doubt, by the same pride that, according to Claudius, envenomed Hamlet with envy when a visiting young Frenchman gave a "masterly report" (IV.vii.94) concerning Laertes' skill with the rapier, Hamlet puts out of mind any need to take precautions. He is, in short, "remiss" (IV.vii.132) at this crucial moment, and his error costs him his life. The scene is not without parallels in *Julius Caesar*, a play Shakespeare probably composed only a few months earlier, and a play in which Caesar, similarly disregarding misgivings that "would perhaps trouble a woman" (*Ham.* V.ii.195–96), is led self-blinded to his assassination.[40]

Now, if Milton thought about this moment in *Hamlet* when he composed the ending of *Samson Agonistes*, we can be certain that he took great pains to make it apparent to his readers that the inner voice heeded by Samson is the voice of God, not the voice of misguided personal honor. For, despite superficial similarities, the concluding moments of *Samson Agonistes* are fundamentally different in their implications from the concluding moments of *Hamlet*. *Hamlet* may be described, in Horatio's words, as a tragedy of "purposes mistook / Fall'n on th' inventors' heads" (V.ii.369–70), and the protagonist himself is not exempt from the applicability of this judgment. *Samson Agonistes* also involves "purposes mistook / Fall'n on th' inventors' heads," of course, but in Milton's tragedy the irony is applicable only to the Philistines. There is no suggestion of "purposes mistook" in the protagonist's last great act.

In order to respond properly to *Hamlet*, the audience will need to have learned—or at least will need to have been powerfully led to recall—truths lost on the unwitting victims of "purposes mistook." In the process, perhaps, the "judicious" (III.ii.23) will have been reminded of the famous prayer of St. Augustine: "There, but for the grace of God, go I." For in *Hamlet*—as, I think, in other Shakespearean tragedies such as *Romeo and Juliet*, *Julius Caesar*, *Othello*, and *Macbeth*—"the pity of it" (*Othello* IV.i.192) is that the protagonist dies unprepared, in Christian terms, for his death. This, of course, is the usual pattern in religious tragedy, and certainly in Shakespearean tragedy.

But it is emphatically not the pattern in *Samson Agonistes* or in that play's chief classical prototype, *Oedipus at Colonus*, where the dramatist provides strong indications that the protagonist, far from dying unprepared, dies triumphantly and is received forthwith into the company of the blessed. In this kind of tragedy, which might almost be called a Divine Comedy, the hero grows in self-knowledge and humility as he profits from his suffering, and he dies purged of much of the pride and sinfulness that precipitated his earlier downfall. Among Shakespeare's tragedies, the only one that seems to me to approach this kind of pattern is *King Lear*, and there is enough ambiguity about *that* play's ending that some critics view it as the darkest of all of Shakespeare's tragedies.

With *Samson Agonistes*, I think, we are on surer ground. For by the conclusion of *this* tragedy there can be little doubt that the hero dies well, that he has been granted a degree of illumination that places him in a mysterious realm beyond the point where any member of the audience can go. We may not fully understand his fate, but we have faith that it is good.[41] For by the end of *his* life, Samson has attained, to appropriate a coda from T. S. Eliot's "Little Gidding":

> A condition of complete simplicity
> (Costing not less than everything).[42]

Folger Shakespeare Library

NOTES

This article is a slightly revised version of a lecture delivered at the Folger Shakespeare Library on April 25, 1977. All *Hamlet* quotations are cited from the Norton Critical Edition, ed. Cyrus Hoy (New York, 1963); other Shakespeare quotations are from *The Complete Pelican Shakespeare*, gen. ed. Alfred Harbage (Baltimore, 1969). Milton is quoted from *John Milton: Complete Poems and Major Prose*, ed. Merritt Y. Hughes (New York, 1957).

1. Frank Allen Patterson and French Rowe Fogle, in *An Index to the Columbia Edition of the Works of John Milton* (New York, 1940), list references to *Hamlet* in *Comus* (381, 431, 838), *Paradise Lost* (I, 91, 254; III, 231; IV, 79; VIII, 15; X, 718; XI, 15), and *Samson Agonistes* (1138).

2. Hieronimo in Kyd's *The Spanish Tragedy*, Titus in Shakespeare's *Titus Andronicus*, Malevole in Marston's *The Malcontent*, Antonio in Marston's *Antonio's Revenge*, and Vindice in Tourneur's *The Revenger's Tragedy* all suffer the psychological imbalance and philosophical disorientation characteristic of men placed in extreme situations, and all, at one point or another, experience severe melancholy.

3. In III.vii of *The Spanish Tragedy*, Heironimo describes himself with such terms as "wearied," "tormented," "restless," and "withered." Hamlet's every utterance is pregnant with world-weariness, from his first soliloquy in I.ii.129–59 ("How weary, stale, flat, and unprofitable / Seem to me all the uses of this world!") to the dying moments when he bids farewell to "this harsh world" (V.ii.333).

4. In *The Spanish Tragedy*, once aware that he cannot obtain justice from the king, Hieronimo becomes totally alienated from the court. Antonio in Marston's *Antonio's Revenge* appears in black, as do Hieronimo and Hamlet; like them, he also utters "wild and whirling words" (*Ham.* I.v.133) and on occasion behaves as a fool.

5. Hamlet's mocking asides and ironic sallies are almost as disturbing to Claudius as his "inky cloak" (I.ii.77); and the "antic disposition" (I.v.171) Hamlet adopts when dealing with Polonius is one of his most effective devices for misleading the court about his true mental state.

6. Though "to the manner born," Hamlet scorns the "heavy-headed revel" pervading Claudius' court; to him, it is "a custom / More honored in the breach than the observance" (I.iv.15–17).

7. Hamlet's obsession with his mother's incest poisons his relationship with Ophelia and leads him to a wholesale rejection of womankind ("Frailty, thy name is woman," I.ii.146) and of sexuality ("I say we will have no moe marriage," III.i.143). In later revenge tragedies, sexual depravity—adultery, incest, rape, prostitution—becomes an all-consuming preoccupation: e.g., Tourneur's *Revenger's Tragedy*, Webster's *The White Devil*, Middleton's *Women Beware Women*, and Middleton and Rowley's *The Changeling*.

8. Senecan revenge tragedy had abounded "in rhetorical reflections on life, death, and fate," and in this as in other respects it had established the genre as a vehicle for intellectual and spiritual deliberation. "The hero was set in a position which, as in *Hamlet*, wrenched his whole moral outlook. In *The Spanish Tragedy*, *Titus Andronicus*, and to an extent in *Antonio's Revenge*, tragedy came into the life of the hero with sufficient intensity to warp his character, drive him to insanity, and eventually to deal him ruin in victory" (Fredson Bowers, *Elizabethan Revenge Tragedy, 1587–1642* [Princeton, 1940], pp. 40, 154–55).

9. Hamlet tells Rosencrantz and Guildenstern that "Denmark's a prison" (II.ii.238), and much of the language and action of *Hamlet* substantiates this observation. The play is dominated by references to restraint and constraint, and the mobility and freedom of the protagonist are significantly limited by his environment.

10. Hamlet gives serious thought to suicide at several points in the play, beginning with his first soliloquy in I.ii.129–59 ("that the Everlasting had not fixed / His canon 'gainst self-slaughter") and culminating in his "To be or not to be" soliloquy (III.i.56–88); there remains an air of almost suicidal resignation even in his last meditative statement ("if it be not now, yet it will come," V.ii.201).

11. Madness is a motif in Senecan revenge tragedy (e.g., *Hercules Furens*) and in the Italian novelle that influenced English revenge tragedy, but of course its most celebrated pre-Shakespearean instance is Hieronimo's temporary insanity in *The Spanish Tragedy*.

12. As Fredson Bowers points out, Senecan revengers were "warned to conceal and dissemble revenge lest the chance for vengeance be lost" (*Elizabethan Revenge Tragedy*, p. 45). Hieronimo's revenge is accomplished by guile in *The Spanish Tragedy* (where, as later in *Hamlet*, a play-within-the-play figures in the revenger's tactics), as is Titus' in *Titus Andronicus*.

13. The protagonist's isolation predisposes a viewer to regard him sympathetically, especially when he is also a social critic and an ethical commentator—as with Hamlet—and when, through aside or soliloquy, he functions as a kind of mediator between the action of the play and the audience in the theater. In *Four*

Stages of Renaissance Style (Garden City, 1955), Wylie Sypher draws an interesting parallel between the soliloquy in *Hamlet* and the "Sprecher" (or "speaker") frequently found in Mannerist paintings—"a sharply accented foreground figure who faces outward toward the spectator, yet twirls inward, gesturing or glancing toward the action behind him" (pp. 143–44).

14. In *The Spanish Tragedy*, in many ways the prototype of Elizabethan revenge tragedy, Hieronimo delays, first, to be certain of the identities of his son's murderers and, second, to discover the most fitting way to accomplish his vengeance. Titus Andronicus delays for three and a half acts because he trusts the heavens to take up his cause; only when he concludes that justice has fled the earth does he take vengeance into his own hands. Amleth in Belleforest (and probably his counterpart in the Kydian *Ur-Hamlet* as well) delays only because he is powerless to act until the proper opportunity presents itself. Shakespeare's Hamlet, too, seems motivated primarily by a desire to await the first clear opportunity, but there are times when he offers plausible alternative motives: corroborating the testimony of the Ghost before concluding that Claudius has in fact committed fratricide and regicide (II.ii.565–72), and securing assurance that Claudius, when he dies, will be damned (III.iv.75–98).

15. The archetype of the vengeful holocaust in Western literature is the slaughter of the suitors by Odysseus upon his return to Ithaca in the *Odyssey*. But one finds the motif also in Greek tragedy (e.g., Clytemnestra's vengeance on her husband in Aeschylus' *Agamemnon*) and in Senecan tragedy (e.g., *Thyestes*, *Medea*), and it is basic to the structure of Elizabethan revenge tragedy from *The Spanish Tragedy* onward.

16. Wylie Sypher argues that in contrast to Mannerist art, which remains largely attenuated and unresolved at the close, Baroque art is characterized by a directional rhythm in which constriction of space and energy at the beginning propels the participant toward "complete release," "dynamic fulfillment," at the close (*Four Stages of Renaissance Style*, p. 204). Sypher quite rightly sees *Hamlet* as less "Baroque" in this sense than *Samson Agonistes*.

17. As Fredson Bowers has observed, in most of the early examples of Kydian revenge tragedy (e.g., *The Spanish Tragedy*, *Titus Andronicus*, *Hoffman*), an attractive, abused protagonist is presented sympathetically at first, then shown to be excessive and even at times villainous, so that by the time he completes his vengeance the audience sees him as deserving of death. In some plays, however, (e.g., Marston's *Antonio's Revenge*), the protagonist enacts his vengeance with cruelty and excessive zeal but nevertheless, apparently, retains the sympathy of the playwright and his audience. In others (e.g., Chettle's *Hoffman* and Marston's *Revenger's Tragedy*), the protagonist appears to have the playwright's approval until near the end of the play, only to forfeit it at the close. With Tourneur's *The Atheist's Tragedy*, a significant shift from tradition occurs: Charlemont is enjoined from revenge by the ghost of his murdered father, but eventually sees retribution visited on the villain D'Amville by a just heaven and learns that "Patience is the honest man's revenge." During the decade between 1610 and 1620 virtually every play dealing with revenge cast the revenger as a villain (e.g., Middleton's *Women Beware Women*, Beaumont and Fletcher's *The Maid's Tragedy*, Webster's *The White Devil*), thus implying ethical disapproval of revenge. And during the succeeding decade almost every revenge tragedy provided explicit and "absolute disapproval of revenge under any circumstances" (Bowers, *Elizabethan Revenge Tragedy*, p. 186).

18. In "Hamlet and His Problems"—first printed in *The Sacred Wood* (London, 1920)—Eliot argued that Shakespeare was simply unable to obtain complete control over his "intractable" source material, so that Hamlet's delay seems caused largely by a vague disgust for his mother that lacks an "objective correlative" sufficiently well defined to motivate a specific action in response.

19. "Sinful Macduff" (*Macbeth* IV.iii.224) is not a man entirely without fault, of course (he may be held responsible for the deaths of his wife and children, inasmuch as he left them defenseless), and his motives are private (to avenge the deaths of his slaughtered innocents) as well as public (to execute a king who has clearly become a tyrant); but there seems no doubt that Shakespeare expected his audience to view him as a divinely approved minister of the public good rather than as a reprobate scourge.

20. In a recent article in *Shakespeare Quarterly*, XXIX (1978), 82–84, R. W. Dent has pointed out that "scourge" and "minister" were not consistently used in Shakespeare's time—or Milton's—to indicate divine disapproval and approval, respectively, of an agent of vengeance. Both terms could be used more or less neutrally, or with implications opposite those assigned here. It remains convenient to distinguish between them, however, as a way of organizing and simplifying discourse about the various kinds of divine punishment. For a full discussion of the theological background of the two terms, see Fredson Bowers, "Hamlet as Minister and Scourge," *PMLA*, LXX (1955), 740–49 (reprinted in *Twentieth Century Interpretations of Hamlet*, ed. David Bevington [Englewood Cliffs, 1968], pp. 82–92); and two books by Roy W. Battenhouse: *Marlowe's Tamburlaine* (Nashville, 1941) and *Shakespearean Tragedy: Its Art and Its Christian Premises* (Bloomington, Ind., 1969). Bowers and Battenhouse both interpret Hamlet's reference to himself as heaven's "scourge and minister" (III.iv.179) as an indication that, having mistakenly slain Polonius, he expects some form of divine retribution to be visited upon him. Other statements in this speech, however, suggest that he regards Polonius' death as itself a punishment (both for Polonius, as a "rash, intruding fool" [III.iv.32], and for Hamlet, whose impulsive act may have put Claudius on guard and thereby forfeited an opportunity for revenge), but one for which Hamlet can and will "answer well" when called to account (III.iv.180). I also disagree with Bowers's view that Hamlet uses "scourge and minister" as contrasting terms here. Whether or not sophisticated members of the *audience* were expected to think of a "scourge" ("a man already damned for his sins") as different from a "minister" ("if a minister's duty is to exact God's punishment or retribution as an act of good, his hands will not be stained with crime"), as Bowers argues ("Hamlet as Minister and Scourge," pp. 743–44), the context suggests that Hamlet himself thinks of the terms as synonyms, or at least fails to discriminate between them with any theological precision. One may compare similar constructions elsewhere—e.g., "O all you host of heaven! O earth! What else? / And shall I couple hell?" (I.v. 92–93); "Prompted to my revenge by heaven and hell" (III.i.551)—in which Hamlet manifests a desire to reconcile the irreconcilable.

21. *Elizabethan Revenge Tragedy*, p. 30.

22. Ibid., p. 40.

23. Eleanor Prosser, *Hamlet and Revenge* (Stanford, 1967), pp. 3–13.

24. Ibid., p. 8.

25. *English Studies*, NS I (1948), 46–66; reprinted in *Milton: Modern Essays in Criticism*, ed. Arthur E. Barker (London, 1965), pp. 205–17.

26. "*Samson Agonistes* as Tragedy," in *Calm of Mind: Tercentenary Essays*

on *"Paradise Regained"* and *"Samson Agonistes"* in Honor of John S. Diekhoff, ed. Joseph Anthony Wittreich, Jr. (Cleveland, 1971), pp. 235–57.

27. *Milton's Samson and the Christian Tradition* (Princeton, 1949).

28. John M. Steadman discusses *megalopsychos* in his chapter, "The Critique of Magnanimity," in *Milton and the Renaissance Hero* (Oxford, 1967).

29. Irene Samuel ("*Samson Agonistes*," p. 246) writes: "The order of that penultimate line in Samson's final words on stage is revealing in its shift from 'our' to 'my' and in its climactic progress: *our* God, *our* Law, *my* Nation or *myself*. It is still something of a monomaniac who speaks, and the mania is still egomania—a not uncommon flaw in tragic agents." Here, of course, everything depends on whether one is reading up the scale of being or down; I think it perverse to interpret the line as a signal that Samson has inverted the accepted hierarchy of values.

30. *The Blaze of Noon: A Reading of "Samson Agonistes"* (New York, 1974), p. 176.

31. See Sherman Hawkins, "Samson's Catharsis," *Milton Studies*, II, ed. James D. Simmonds (Pittsburgh, 1970), 211–30, for a fine discussion of what these words are likely to have meant to Milton. For a discussion of catharsis in Shakespeare, see my article, "The Catharsis of *Romeo and Juliet*," in *Contributi dell' Istituto di filologia moderna*, ed. Sergio Rossi (Milan, 1974), pp. 142–75.

32. Battenhouse has interesting things to say about Horatio in *Shakespearean Tragedy* (pp. 259–60). For futher analyses of "Stoicism" as treated by Shakespeare, see John Anson, "*Julius Caesar:* The Politics of the Hardened Heart," *Shakespeare Studies*, II (1966), 11–33; and Marvin L. Vawter, " 'Division 'tween Our Souls': Shakespeare's Stoic Brutus," *Shakespeare Studies*, VII (1974), 173–95. Ruth M. Levitsky has analyzed Stoicism (along with "Renaissance Aristotelianism" and Christian ethics) in *Hamlet* in "Rightly to Be Great," *Shakespeare Studies*, I (1965), 142–67.

33. Battenhouse discusses this and several other points raised here in *Shakesperean Tragedy*; see esp. pp. 227–44.

34. The clearest instance occurs at V.ii.63–70:

> Does it not, think thee, stand me now upon—
> He that hath killed my king and whored my mother,
> Popped in between th' election and my hopes,
> Thrown out his angle for my proper life,
> And with such coz'nage—is't not perfect conscience
> To quit him with this arm? And is't not to be damned
> To let this canker of our nature come
> In further evil?

35. See Prosser, *Hamlet and Revenge*, pp. 97–142.

36. See, e.g., I, 242–63; IV, 32–113; IX, 896–959; and esp. X, 720–844.

37. V.ii.48; V.ii.199.

38. Harry Morris's useful article, "*Hamlet* as a *Memento Mori* Poem," *PMLA*, LXXXV (1970), 1035–40, is limited, I think, by his failure to take into account the contextual relevance of the graveyard scuffle.

39. In the introduction to his 1939 edition of *Hamlet*, G. L. Kittredge argued that Hamlet delays at this moment because he has an elevated "nature and education" at odds with the demands of a primitive, rigid revenge code, so that his cruel speech (which Dr. Johnson thought "too horrible to be read or to be uttered") is

"merely a pretext for delay" until a time when he will not be forced to "butcher a defenceless man" (reprinted in Irving Ribner's revised edition of Kittredge's edition of the *Complete Works* [Waltham, Mass., 1971], pp. 1044–45). Perhaps so; but I would find it easier to believe that "these diabolical sentiments are not Hamlet's sentiments" (p. 1045) if Hamlet did not elsewhere regard revenge as incomplete unless it includes damnation for the victim.

40. Caesar, too, is fatalistic ("What can be avoided / Whose end is purposed by the mighty gods?" II.ii.26–27), disdainful of augury (II.ii.37–43), and too much a "man" to yield to womanly "cowardice" (II.ii.41). "Seeing that death, a necessary end, / Will come when it will come" (II.ii.36–37; cf. *Ham.* V.ii.199–201); he disregards all portents, warnings, and misgivings and is led as a lamb to the slaughter. As Calphurnia says, "Alas, my lord, / Your wisdom is consumed in confidence" (II.ii.48–49); these words apply as aptly to Hamlet, I think, as to Caesar.

41. See Stanley Fish, "Question and Answer in *Samson Agonistes*," *Critical Quarterly*, II (1969), 237–64, for a brilliant analysis of the ambiguities—indeed, mysteries—that remain impenetrable in *Samson Agonistes*. A recent article by Thomas B. Stroup touches in passing on parallels between *Hamlet* and *Samson Agonistes* (see " 'All Comes Clear at Last,' but 'The Readiness is All' " in *Comparative Drama*, X [1976], 61–77); Stroup has nothing to say, however, about any significant differences between the two tragedies.

42. From *Four Quartets*. Reprinted by permission of the publishers: Harcourt Brace Jovanovich, Inc., New York; and Faber & Faber, Ltd., London.

SAMSON'S GOD: "BEASTLY HEBRAISM" AND "ASININE BIGOTRY"

Robert H. West

MOST CRITICS of Milton, even those who stress his faults, have agreed in principle that his commitment to Christianity ought not in itself to weigh against his poetry. Plainly, though, it has weighed against his poetry. What a dramatic or narrative poem says must always weigh against it with those who actively hate to hear it. Ezra Pound gave the classic capsule expression to the feelings of readers who ascribe to Milton "asinine bigotry" and "beastly Hebraism." Protesting that for the moment he wanted to disregard these monstrous traits, Pound made a technical point about the sonority of Milton's verse; but the self-evident fact is that Pound's characteristic response to Milton was "disgust with what he had to say."[1]

In spite of their disgust, neither Pound nor others who feel as he did suggest discarding Milton. The merit of the work is plain to them. Many critics incline, then, either to separate Milton's redeeming technical successes from a vital part of what he says or to reshape what he says to suit themselves. Some of the reshapers hold that much of what Milton says so powerfully is not really what readers have conventionally thought it, and others that regardless of how sound the conventional understanding may once have been, the passage of time has made it critically adjustable to "modern" values. Especially most of these critics shrink from Milton's God. Some apologize for him as unavoidably primitive in moral nature, others claim that his function in the work ought to be largely ignored, and still others hold that he functions strongly once we modify him to suit us.[2]

Most prominent among those disgusted with Milton's God yet asserting an effective place for him in the works is William Empson. Milton's God is, he says, so outrageous, so grotesque and horrible, that his very repulsiveness is a source of power in the fable, just as cruel lineaments are in Benin sculptures. In both *Paradise Lost* and *Samson Agonistes* Milton made cosmic power dramatic by ascribing to God abominable demands on his creatures. Less extreme is Lawrence W. Hyman's view that God's moral state should seem to readers now poignantly doubtful and that the force of the work depends on the force of the doubt.[3]

Of Milton's major works, the one that gives God most obscurely is *Samson Agonistes*. It is, perhaps, as Marjorie Nicolson said, "the least Christian."[4] It does not bring God or Christ on stage, nor any supernatural creature, and its time of action is Old Testament. It is free of direct reference to Christian doctrines such as that of the afterlife, and its characters are notably lacking in Christian traits like love for those who hate them. Dependence of human righteousness on God is emphatic, but it may seem rather in the spirit of Judges than of the Gospels. Undoubtedly Samson's God is a stern one, and sometimes the Jews speak of him as distant, unreliable, and fearsomely exacting.

Critical views about the moral nature of Samson's God should turn, of course, on what the tragedy can reasonably be supposed to convey about it. Inescapable is that in *Samson Agonistes* God chose and moved the protagonist. As Kenneth Burke puts it, Samson is "identified" with God.[5] The play has conventionally been supposed, too, to indicate that Samson is the virtuous champion of a God who is himself the supreme arbiter of virtue. If modern readers distrust the God that Samson testifies to because they see Samson as ferocious, hence an agent of ferocity, or if they trust Samson's hesitations about God more than his decision, or conclude simply that tragedy has no room for the near approach of an absolute and righteous deity, then they have radically reshaped the work.

Critics give, of course, many accounts of Samson's God, ranging from Empson's hostility to the piety of J. D. Ebbs.[6] They depend on background in theology, or on biography, or on sources and analogues. Here I shall have little space for such studies, but must depend instead on a straightforward reading of the text as it lays out the story of Samson. I take the characters to be understandable much as real persons are.[7] Such has, in fact, been the practice in most of the work that I shall cite. It is given chiefly to dealing with what Milton has to say, with characters and events and their meanings for the play world and its for them. It was such meanings, I take it, that disgusted Pound and that trouble those who want to put a new face on Samson's God.

I do not, though, contend that Milton was either "right" or "wrong" about God and the world and man. "If we take account of the diversity of impressive works of literary art we cannot suppose that there is some particular state-of-affairs that is *the* human condition, and that it is the task of literary artists to be correct about it."[8] I am concerned with what Milton seems to say in *Samson Agonistes* (with, if someone insists, the "surface meaning") and with that "modern" response which originates in it.

I

All the unarguable evidence of Samson's God is rather to his power than to his goodness. The miracles of Samson's dedicated birth, the monitions that move him to marry and to destroy, and most plainly his superhuman strength are undeniable as the text goes, and they may signify a finally righteous deity. But again, they may not. The insistence on faith and obedience in the speeches of Manoa, the Chorus, the Messenger, and, most important by far, of Samson himself, may express only the awe of the Hebrew tribesmen, whose piety is largely in submission. Even among them doubt of God's goodness is almost as prominent as devoutness, and their harsh motives and their jubilation at Philistine deaths may estrange us from them and from the God they profess to serve.

First, then, does Milton indicate that Samson's God is cruel and despotic by showing Samson as so savage that moderns must think him a demon worshipper?

Empson stresses the unlikeliness of Samson as a servant of beneficent deity. He is a vindictive ruffian, a false lover, a rejecter of all human reconciliation, a nihilist, an *agent provocateur,* a bloody avenger, an evident madman. If, as he claims, God does indeed move him, it is not to God's credit. At the best, both Samson and God are arrogant, bullying, and undemocratic. The fable endorses these traits in Samson and so in the God he testifies to. Dalila, on the other hand, Empson insists, is a woman who on the face of what she says and does is a very loving and worthy wife. Samson treats her churlishly, the Chorus defames her, and God is unjustly her enemy. She has as good a claim to her religion as Samson to his, and the fact that Dagon is no fair match for Jehovah is just a sign of the Jewish divinity's chauvinistic tribalism.[9]

Much of this attack is frivolous to aim at so lofty a work as *Samson.* But it does express a "relativistic" reading that has much appeal.[10] Samson unquestionably is a revolutionary and a terrorist. His ways are decided, abrasive, partisan, the ways of a committed activist. He is no more given to chivalry than a "Field Marshal" of the Symbionese Liberation Army is. Against the oppressive Philistine establishment he feels free to use any weapon that his inspiration shows him, including his shabby treatment of his Timnan wife. And he is, of course, careless of the blood of "innocent" enemies. Certainly these traits may displease readers who deplore all violence and trickery and those who insist on equal time for the point of view of the Philistines. Violence and trickery can, however, please those moderns who value them in a fighter for a righteous cause.

Can we now see Samson as such a fighter, or does he join Iago beyond our moral pale? Surely every postlapsarian time, including ours, has encouraged stern measures against evildoers—always allowing, of course, for redefinition of evildoing. The question becomes, Who does evil in *Samson* and what evil is it? Liberal moralists may think virtuous in African "freedom fighters" just such nationalistic motives and terroristic activities as they condemn in Samson. His submission to God they may liken to the submission to the C.I.A. attributed to South Vietnam's Thieu and other "colonial lackeys." But equally well, by the same principles, such submission could be likened admiringly to "party discipline" among socialist workers. Samson's intransigent speeches and deeds we can condemn as genocidal, or as easily praise as like those of heroic Israeli patriots (or Palestinian ones, if we prefer), and Samson's religion is hardly more severe than Malcolm X's—or perhaps Jimmy Carter's. In the light of many quite "modern" tastes and beliefs, what is often called *Samson Agonistes'* Old Testament "ferocity" need not automatically signify to us that Milton's worship and Samson's was demonolatry.[11]

Samson himself makes some point of being a legitimated activist. He waged, he says to Harapha, a war against his country's enemies that seemed private but was actually national, since the God of his enslaved people prompted him. And have not our own most principled warriors, especially our "soldiers of resistance," depended on some illumination of their private consciences, whether by Allah or Marcuse? Empson waves away this "rebel doctrine of the Inner Light" as Milton's political "encouragement to any self-righteous fanatic" and marvels that "critics in our very political age regard the matter so religiously." But, as Burke says, there is "an *objective* difference in motivation between an act conceived in the name of God and an act conceived in the name of godless nature."[12] Why should not a reader see Samson's ferocity as a terrible swift sword, like John Brown's? Such enmity as Danites felt against Philistines and seventeenth-century Protestants against the Piedmontese who massacred the Vaudois, Poles felt against Nazis and many Americans against the bombers of North Vietnam. That the feeling is political does not prevent it from sometimes being also religious, especially in literature that specifies its godliness.[13]

> O, how comely it is, and how reviving
> To spirits of just men long oppressed
> When God into the hands of their deliverer
> Puts invincible might,
> To quell the mighty of the earth, the oppressor.   (1268–72)

Here is an elevated expression of the delight that most men take in a champion (Huss, Cromwell, the Mahdi) of a furious religious cause in which they believe and for which they beseech a God of battles.

Plainly the world still has, as in Samson's time and in Milton's, some expression of moral principles by rage and turbulence. Decidedness and action, whether Samson's or Churchill's, do not necessarily seem evil to moderns. We have heroes yet who, single-minded in resistance, seek the good by just and self-sacrificing violence. And we are still capable of valuing such heroes in literature. (If not, we will indeed have to throw away much literature.) Though the corrupted creation in which Samson lives out his grim dedication is a very mixed one, our own time is not so unmixed nor our applauded acts all so mild that the God Samson testifies to must seem a devil to us.

II

But of course the mere feasibility of inverting Empson's articles of indictment need not make Samson's God seem good. Samson may be a champion whose fierce wrestle with the problem of evil can engage the sympathy of a modern reader and yet his pious sentiments be just self-encouragement. They may be finally ineffective for Samson and for us, so that, as Hyman insists, if Samson becomes a martyr it is an unwilling one, and if we accept his martyrdom as evidence of his God's justice we have deceived ourselves. Samson may end so riddled with doubt of divine benevolence that any sense of deity we get from his speeches rests on a favorable interpretation of what in itself is very ambiguous about the moral nature of the universe.

The tragedy's "greatness," Hyman says, "does not depend on the reconciliation of the hero or of the audience to the ways of God, but on its power to bring to the highest pitch the contradiction between human desires and divine purposes." Stress on this contradiction is not, perhaps, Milton's intention, Hyman admits, nor the original greatness of the work; but that is no matter. We are to read as suits our own time. The "imaginative experience" of the work "goes far beyond the official or ostensible morality that is embodied in it."[14] Hyman does not contend that the "experience" includes cosmic terror, as Empson asserts; it is simply of a rending dubiety. Samson, Manoa, and the Chorus ask again and again without satisfying answer how it can be that ruin descends on God's champion and God's people. How could Samson, given his suffering and his divine spurring to a self-destructive deed, believe in divine justice, and how can we?

What in fact is the "imaginative experience" that *Samson Agonistes* offers? Is it, as we must now receive it, finally alien to Judeo-Christian religious faith? I hold that Milton's religion and even Samson's is not necessarily so lost to us that in order to save the poem we must go in the face of what it says and at the end doubt Samson's God. The work overtly encourages us to take him finally as good. That encouragement still deserves respect.

As I have said, the unarguable evidence of God is rather to his power than to his goodness, and the testimony of the Jews has its questionable elements. But the prevalent devoutness of their meditations; the fact that the first of Samson's is soliloquy (considered particularly trustworthy in drama); and the general trend of the action, especially as Samson's inner state reflects it—all add up to reassurance of divine goodness. If, that is, we can indeed sufficiently reconcile all inspired deeds and motives with our sense of what is good.

One thing plain in Samson's meditations is honesty. Grant that he seeks comfort for the divided mind, some position of diminished unease. Still, he never denies his own responsibility for his troubles (though he does come near to blaming God in his last speech before Dalila's entry), and he always defies the physical costs yet imposable. Protagonists so far in doubt of the universe as to approach despair are likely to blame it rather than themselves (witness King Lear), and in their shaken spiritual state some of them yield, like Faustus, to bodily terrors. But Samson overcomes every impulse to blame God and to cherish his physical self.[15]

The faults that Samson honestly charges himself with are a different lot from those that Empson puts forward. Pride, sensuality, light-mindedness, and uxoriousness, all making for untrustworthiness in his high mission, seem slight to those now who do not value the mission and are tolerant of the traits. And indeed, some of these faults as Samson states them—"garrulity," for instance, and the rest of his weakness before Dalila's charms—may in themselves be humanly excusable. But Samson recognizes always (and we cannot doubt him) that they lead directly to a great fault: his disobedience, his profanation of God's mystery. Samson never scants the fact that divinely trusted he proved false. However vile his fallen state may be, he says to Manoa,

> As vile has been my folly, who have profaned
> The mystery of God, given me under pledge of
> Vow, and have betrayed it to a woman.   (376–79)

Such honesty quiets Samson's emotional suspicion that God has been unjust to him, for his case against God weakens every time he thinks of himself as sufficient to have stood had he willed to. The only way he could blame God for his suffering (or that we can) is to suppose himself defectively designed and made.

At the play's beginning, anyway, speculates John Huntley,[16] a depressed Samson was in fact wondering whether God had equipped him capriciously for the trials he was to undergo, and then in the midst of them deserted him to punishment through absurd physical vulnerabilities. "Why should he fight for a God who not only sent the ambivalent gift of strength, but betrayed him and was stupid" enough to confine the miracle of light to the frail eyeball? Was it "whimsy or malice" that "put sight and strength into eyes and hair?"

Certainly Samson does mourn the vulnerability of his eyes and hair in their high functions. But it is only a humbling puzzle to him. Perhaps, he speculates, God was just indicating how insignificant physical strength is. The terrible results of his shearing and blinding were no sign of God's whimsy, malice, or stupidity. The doubt that Samson expresses about God's part in his fall centers not on bodily deficiencies but on those of his decision-making faculties, equipment supposed not vulnerable. How could Samson's will have been weaker than a woman's? Was Samson in fact sufficient to have stood? In the light of his fall, either his will and judgment were poorly made for the trials they were put to or Samson himself misused them. Here is a rock on which moral speculation divides, a place at which everyone must make some affirmation, if only a tacit one, beyond any available evidence. Surely Samson makes his affirmation openly when he rejects Dalila's plea of weakness and his own with it.

All wickedness is weakness: that plea therefore
With God nor man will gain thee no remission.   (834–35)

So Samson answers, "though to his own condemnation," as Dalila notices, herself no more able than Shakespeare's Richard III (I.iii.183–92) to understand why a man might speak ill of himself. From his answer to her Samson never goes back.

Samson was, of course, spiritually vulnerable if the troubling of moral choice by human distractions is vulnerability. The play clearly conveys that though a dedicated hero of God, Samson was without privilege in nature except for his muscle. Like Edward King (and his elegist), like Adam and Eve, Samson was as fully human as a divinely appointed person could be.[17] He was exposed to temptation, perplexity, error, loss, death, and every other human darkness. Certainly such exposure did include for Samson doubt about God's relation to him, for after his fall Samson, like the rest of Milton's great sinners, was of a questioning spirit, as those who suffer are likely to be. But the indication is that Samson's doubt resembled Cromwell's in his dying days, that is, was more of his own deserts than of God's justice. In human meditation on evil these two doubts naturally coalesce; but however keenly Samson may have felt God's withdrawal from him, he always recognized his own previous withdrawal from God, and we have little option but to take his word for it.[18]

Samson's recovery is, of course, given as by God's favor at last.[19] The "rousing motions" that send him to the Philistine games make him sure again of what he should and can do, and after them we hear no more of moral doubt. Though exposed to error and pain, Samson is never an ordinary man; much less is he of that "common rout" the Chorus speaks of, "That wandering loose about / Grow up and perish as the summer fly." (675–76).[20] However humanly limited, he was still of those whom God had solemnly chosen with "gifts and graces eminently adorned / To some great work." But without reaching his firm conviction that God had made him with power of decision to do that work he could not have risen as he finally did above all worldly self-interest, including the distaste for martyrdom that Hyman asserts.

As Samson goes to the Philistine games he does not doubt his resumption of mission, nor can we doubt it. If he has still either any despairing wish for death or any troubling aversion to it, it appears only in such high gravity as we see also in Oedipus at Colonnus and Polyeucte and other redeemed protagonists with premonition of their ends. "This day will be remarkable in my life / By some great act or of my days the last." Samson does not speak here like one unwilling to be a martyr if that is called for.[21] Nor does he in the last words directly from his mouth:

> Happen what may, of me expect to hear
> Nothing dishonourable, impure, unworthy
> Our God, our law, my nation, or myself,
> The last of me or no I cannot warrant.   (1423–26)

This is all that Samson says about death (or martyrdom) after Harapha's departure except to insist that nothing which Harapha threatens can move him, since death itself would be a release. If Samson does have an intimation of mortality and is faintly melancholy at the prospect he still does not match the melancholy against his mission in a way to convey doubt of the mission's sponsor.

We can say, then, about Samson's doubt of God that it gives way totally at the end. Dubiety on the reader's part has to go against Samson's confirmed settling into faith, and against the rapt conviction of the other Jews. The mystery of God's purposes remains, of course, but that mystery is no longer in the "contradictions between human desires and divine purpose" which Hyman finds a source of *Samson Agonistes'* power, for plainly at the tragedy's end the desires of Samson draw mysteriously together with what he takes to be the purposes of God.[22]

III

And yet, can anyone now contemplate as wholesome mystery a culmination of grisly vengeance? Many critics, forceful though they find the tragedy, intensely dislike what they take to be its revenge theme.

One of the most troubled of them is ready, however, to forgive Milton "his fundmental fault" in "choice of material" on the ground that he achieved a "considerable emancipation from the fetters of the old tale" so that *Samson* occupies a "noble place in a long process" of exhausting the "possibilities of a story which lacks a mature teaching on the true way of dealing with one's enemies and renders imperative a recourse to a truly Christian subject."[23]

This backhanded compliment itself renders imperative a question: is *Samson Agonistes* a revenge tragedy? Empson says that it "in a sense completed the great series of Elizabethan Revenge Plays."[24] But is its theme really revenge at all? What does Samson revenge and on whom? The enslavement of his people on the Philistines? He is simply an inspired "freedom fighter" with a higher motive than national vengeance. Does he revenge his own betrayal, mutilation, and bondage on Dalila and her people? The Chorus and Manoa show some interest in retaliation for these inflictions, but Samson none as a personal enterprise. True his mission to be what Dalila calls a "fierce destroyer" is bloody. But he aims at no particular oppressor save Harapha and at him only because he is present and challenging. Vengeance is simply not in the play as Samson's motive. He acts as a warrior of God, with a sense of the retribution he brings on the wicked. Samson is surely a minister, not a scourge, and one even less infected with vindictiveness than Hamlet is, in both motive and execution. Admittedly Samson neither loves his enemies nor forgives them if forgiving means denying their faults, but he does seek and find a higher answer than just ferociously turning the tables.[25]

Has Samson some high motive even in his treatment of Dalila, whose overtures he rejects so unfeelingly as to make some readers flinch? A poignant fact about Samson's passage with Dalila is that even if she were as fine a woman as Empson makes her out, and all her excuses as humanly appealing as he thinks them, Samson could not in his state of dawning rededication receive her again. He has developed into something like the condition of Cato of Utica in the first canto of the *Purgatorio,* who as one of God's redeemed could no longer respond to the continued devotion of his wife in hell's first circle. When Virgil reports how Marcia's eyes pathetically pray that Cato will still hold her his, he answers curtly, "Now that beyond the accursed stream she dwells, / She may no longer move me, by that law / Which was ordain'd me, when I issued thence." Samson's implacability is like Cato's, though of course not the same.

Unlike Cato and Marcia, Samson and Dalila are still in this world, and their life together has not been exemplary. Further, their last parting follows a considerable face-to-face colloquy in which Samson, still full of hurt, is bitterly accusatory. Nevertheless, Samson, like Cato, rejects his wife with a removed fixity. His forgiveness for his own "folly" and for her "wicked deed" are, he says, "Impartial, self-severe, inexorable" (826–27), and beyond her acceptance. His certainty belongs not to resentment issuing in vengeful spite, as some critics see it (she was not, Samson insists, "the prime cause" of his trouble) but to his separation from her sinfulness as from his own. He and she are "long since twain" (929). Whether or not Dalila is a "specious monster," a "sorceress," and a "bosom snake," she and her pleas and protestations are pathetic in a way that Samson has about parted from forever. Many critics note that Milton gives full measure to Dalila's humanly appealing case, and we may agree that Dalila speaks "seriously."[26] But she cannot move Samson, "implacable, more deaf to prayers than winds and seas" (910–11), for he is turning from her passionate world toward Cato's impassable one.[27] Certainly Samson is not without passion when his "traitoress" first approaches him; and perhaps, as John Carey supposes, he fears, even as he dismisses her, that one touch would renew her erotic power over him. But he has a more absorbing motive now than retaliation or he might have jumped at the chance to "tear" her.[28]

If Samson's motive in rejecting Dalila and in collapsing the Philistine theater is God-centered, not vengeful, what of his God's motive? Samson plainly does not, like Hamlet, suspect any taint in the violence that he practices as God's agent. Must we, nevertheless, acknowledge such taint in the story's putative lack of a "mature teaching on the true way of dealing with one's enemies"? To be mature must a treatment of any story dealing with enemies be one divested of vigorous retribution for wrongdoing?

Milton's "teaching," if we must call it that, is theistic Christianity's: defects in human conduct bring penalties not explicable as divine injustice. The moral decidedness in God's rule is largely divine respect for the freedom of the rational creature to sin and so to incure sin's consequences.[29]

Those with a distaste for Christianity reply, of course, that the freedom is illusory, and those with a kindred distaste for what Milton has to say assert that Samson's God, going beyond permissive respect for his creatures' freedom to sin, does himself promote sin, which he then punishes. Samson, they specify, holds that God moved him to marry the woman of Timna the better to afflict her people, and that God sent Dalila at last to "debase" him and "aggravate" his folly. The Chorus supposes that God a "spirit of frenzy sent" among the Philistines to make them run on destruction.

In this dispute we have one of those divisions that depend for resolution more on will than on reason, since evidence fails. So far as *Samson Agonistes* is concerned, even if we acknowledge as exact every ascription to God of entrance into the affairs of Jews and Philistines, the divine action still need not be held morally objectionable. God did not make Samson fail his temptation by

Dalila, and he did not smite the Philistines without reason. Stein says that "God's 'motives' are, we may guess, those of the moral drama"; and so, evidently, they are as far as they are guessable. The play gives us no reason to suppose that God is playing cat and mouse with Samson or with the Philistines. As the author shows the Philistines, some of them, anyway, are indeed wicked: in enslaving the Chosen People, in "chanting their idol," and in the unjust use of Samson's wife to ruin him, "against the law of nature, law of nations" (890).[30]

When their spirit of frenzy moves the Philistine rulers vaingloriously to send for Samson, they have already courted their madness. God did not himself ready them for it any more than he readied Samson for despair. The "spirit of frenzy," says Frye, was their faith that Dagon could contain Samson's strength "within limits convenient to them."[31] Those who persist in sin will "their own ruin on themselves invite." Such seems God's purpose as far as it is not dark to us. Obviously Samson himself had a very close call. But these consequences of unregenerate wrongdoing cannot be named vengeance in the petty way that inimical critics assert. The Chorus does, of course, speak of "wrath divine," and Milton's time did not hesitate to apply the word *vengeance* to God's way with sinners. The meaning, though, was rather the relentless progress of the sinner's way with himself than any squaring of accounts such as the Ghost urges upon Hamlet. Milton does not, as Fell claims, "retain the primitive conception of the divine nature as vengeful."[32]

IV

A final distress of the modern reader with Samson's God, one close kin to those already noticed, is that his favoring of the Jews offends against egalitarian justice. Milton does not give Dagon and the Philistines equal treatment with God and the Jews. This, our moralists may indicate, is an ethical flaw in the tragedy. Because of it we must either condemn *Samson* or reinterpret it as itself covertly condemning massive unfairness in God himself. Empson snorts that Dalila plainly had as much right to her opinion and her religion as Samson to his and that God seemed to need human help as much as Dagon did. Carey wants us to remember the point of view of the Philistines. Moral authority is very hard for us to accept now, even that of a divinity in a play who has the author's backing for it, if it goes against our confidence that one being should have one vote.[33]

This democratic notion does not, of course, express very successfully the moral nature of things. It is simply the best that a secular age can do to give political recognition to the dogma that all men are created equal. From it we seem to conclude that men's gods are equal too, or at least that literature may not successfully portray one god as supreme. Just here, then, comes the central difficulty of *Samson Agonistes* for moderns: to feel Samson's God as the inscrutable arbiter of truth and goodness. We may simply recoil from a literary "character" to whom we can impute no moral weakness, with whom we can at last compare no being within our normal experience and ready conception. For an Olympian, hard-pressed by fate or his peers, we can make allowances, and we tend automatically to make them for Dagon and those other Philistine gods whom Samson contemptuously writes off as no gods because they fall to ungodlike expedients (896–97). We incline often to embrace moral weakness, even in gods, for it lends comprehensibility. As Dalila pleads, such weakness binds us all kin. When we condemn terrible acts—those, say, of interrogators in the Gulag Archipelago—we still feel, as Solzhenitsyn notes, some human companionability with their human openness to error.[34] We can summon such commonness with Dagon, but not with Samson's God. If we level him with Dagon we must do it by reducing him and interpreting him some other way than as the tragedy gives him. To find a "reason" for the Philistines' harsh fate we will look for a creaturely hatefulness in God. Naturally, if we succeed in seeing him with it, he is not clothed in majesty.

Samson Agonistes advertises no hatefulness or other weakness in God and eliminates suggestion of it as thoroughly as is possible in fiction that has his unbalancing hand in the world's affairs. Little in the tragedy justifies critical reduction of God, and nothing compels it. That Samson serves God can, granted, be read to mean that God must have his service. That Samson's service is destructive and that he suffers in his role as divine agent can be taken, perversely, to mean that God is vicious. But as I have argued, the text makes neither of these interpretations mandatory. What it is plainly intended to say, and does say to the willing reader even yet, is that God's being and purposes and relation to man are finally an awesome but reassuring mystery.

Most of what Milton proffers about this mystery is describable as Hebraism, for Milton does, of course, keep quite reasonably close to the Old Testament in both story and meaning. A modern authority on the Bible says that to the "Hebrew mind . . . knowledge of God comes not by contemplating his being and attributes [in the Greek manner] but by obeying his commandments, and the OT knows nothing of a 'theoretical' or even mystical vision of God." In doing God's will one comes to "know" him by "entering into subjective relations as between person and person—relations of trust, obedience, respect, worship, love, fear, and so on."[35] And so in *Samson* God's "dispose" is "unsearchable" though the Jews grow to "knowledge" in contemplation of Samson's final overwhelming obedience, a deed spectacular enough to convince them past question. The Graeco-Christian speculation that ascribes to God the attributes of infinite power, goodness, and so on, the tragedy certainly implies to the reader who is aware of Christian doctrine and theology. But to the Jews of the play God's mystery is nearer, though less penetrable. They see his miracles and sense his will. And so it is that the drawing together at last in the tragedy of man's desires and God's purposes is a "great event" of human closeness to transcendence.

Are these mysteries, whether of Hebraism or Christianism, "beastly"? Not unless the reader is so hostile toward devotion to a "true" God that he will not tolerate it even in literature. If we can read of Samson's God magnanimously, putting aside our tendency to huddle together in suspicion of weakness and meanness, then we may accept his goodness both in principle and in feeling, and do it with a gladness something like Milton's.

V

I have here still what may seem a large "if." Many modern readers will be reluctant to give up any of their sympathy for weakness in the face of an inexorable universe and will prefer to a sense of divine transcendence their scepticism about the moral nature of a "jealous" God. Against such preference the tragedy must, I concede, make its own way. What it has to say will at last sway the reader to God's party or it won't. To sway him it must have a force beyond that of arguments and descriptions sketched, like most of the Chorus' and many of mine (and of Empson's) from the face of events.[36] Inference and description are not what establish cosmic mystery in literature. Simply, the "imaginative experience" of it must open out numinously in appropriate language. The best we can do at last is to recognize it for what it is and let it work.

The detractors of Samson's God have small respect for the working of the lines that convey his majesty and his mystery, holding them all naive at best. Thus the mystery that Samson laments profaning is obviously just the occult link between his strength and his hair and so may seem absurdly disproportionate to supposed divine energies. But must not divine energies portrayed in mundane action necessarily seem disproportionate to their results as we perceive them? Miracles especially are by definition thus disproportionate to nature in one way or another. The specific application of God's power to human sexuality in Samson's conception is out of scale with anything asserted in ontogeny, and the angelic prophecy to Manoa is much beyond obstetrics. Like the seating of Samson's strength in his hair, they are, of course, entirely arbitrary. But surely the arbitrary is part of active mystery.

These physical marvels are relatively unimportant as shapers of our sense of mystery in *Samson Agonistes*. "Mere miracles," as Jung says, cannot "demonstrate the reality of the spirit or *meaning* that underlies them."[37] When the Jews of the Chorus speculate about the meaning they are not very successful. Manoa muses fruitlessly on the irony that joy at God's answer to his prayer for issue should turn into misery at the sight of his fallen son, and later he guesses that since Samson's strength has returned, his physical sight will return too. The Chorus exclaims at God's "contrarious" hand toward man, the erratic tempering of providence for even the dedicated. It wavers from its earlier assertion that God's ways are just and justifiable. Certainly no voice in the play ever contents us dialectically about that assertion.

What does content us is not dialectic but passion. In their search for God all of the Jews are moved and moving according to their several capacities, until Samson goes in complete conviction to fulfill his dedication, leaving the others to contemplate their "true experience" in a way both serene and intense, however undiagrammatic. Our sense of Samson's approach to mystery and our recognition of its absorbing vastness in both troubling and contenting him is the work largely of the tragic conclusion. Like the Danites, we sense God's "uncontrollable intent." Speculation fades into the intuitive confidence of the rhymed lines of the close: "All is best"; though God often seems to hide his face, he unexpectedly returns and

> His servants he with new acquist
> Of true experience from this great event
> With peace and consolation has dismissed
> And calm of mind all passion spent.

Yet however contributory to the Jews' catharsis and to ours, the words of exultation at the "great event" are less explanatory of God's "intent" than the speakers think. In spite of their passionate conviction Manoa and the Chorus do not accept all the clues to the mystery that the tragedy offers the reader. Especially they think Samson and God alike to be narrowly partisan. But the reader may suspect a current the Danites do not notice.

In his masterful article Stanley Fish discusses the gap between "two plots" of *Samson:* "an 'outer' or 'public' plot, with its denouement in the temple scene, and an 'inner' plot which has run its course by line 1377" when Samson realizes that God may dispense with observance of the law that forbids attending "idolatrous rites." The gap between the plots, Fish thinks, is logically unbridgeable. In the outer one we naturally feel a causation that the incomprehensibility of God's reasons and even of man's disables. Samson's submission to Dalila and his recovery from it Fish finds alike inexplicable, and so does he Dalila's betrayal of Samson and her return to him. As for God's reasons, neither the Chorus and Manoa nor we can puzzle them out to a finish. Progress, then, in the public plot to an exultant culmination in Samson's "dearly bought revenge" is in a way a fiction of Manoa and the Chorus and of literalistic critics. In making his point Fish notices our "humanitarian reservations" about violent retribution, not simply to praise them on behalf of modern sensibilities but to suggest how dark to us God's purposes remain, and, in the light of his purposes, our desires. We may feel troubled that many of the Philistines whom Samson slew were good persons, as Milton makes appear in Manoa's account of the civil and generous lords willing to accept ransom and in the kindliness of the Public Officer and of the guide who "unsuspicious led" Samson to the pillars. The fact of their goodness, Fish holds, just may indicate that the indiscriminate slaughter of them with the rest was no sign of God's disfavor to them. We cannot after all conclude as the Chorus seems to that God urged all Philistines "on with mad desire / To call in haste for their destroyer." "We do not know what the event means *sub specie aeternitatis*"—that is, in the inner plot—Fish says.[38]

I agree that we do not know in whole, any more than the Chorus does. But unlike the Chorus, we know that we don't know. When the Messenger calls the overthrow of the Philistines "sad," Manoa assents with less conviction of the sadness than pleasure in the event. Samson's mission, we could suppose, is against only that "impious crew" he speaks of that was "conspiring to uphold their state / By worse than hostile deeds" (891–93). The Chorus' jubilation at the "great event" gives no grasp of why with this evil "crew" the others had to suffer, any more than the earlier life of Dalila discloses fully the springs of human conduct that led her to humble herself to Samson or whether her humanly appealing speeches were heartfelt or guileful.

These and other obscurities help shape the "imaginative experience" of mystery for us. As Fish indicates, the mystery of God's purpose behind human suffering and death (often of those who seem blameless in the main action, anyway) does run through the tragedy, and equally the mystery of how man's desires respond to divine purpose. The only motive wholly lucid in Samson is his last one. Like Fish, I hold that the combined plots make clear the rightness of Samson's peace with his dedication and the conformity to it of his final act.[39] Although we cannot penetrate to a definitive understanding of either Samson or his God, still what we see and what we sense behind it may reassure us about them both.[40] Certainly the Jews' "living dread" suggests little that is expressly Christian and nothing of softer Christian sentiment. But God as "dread" is majesty, not blood. His mystery is in the awful concentration and inclusiveness of divine being and purpose poetically conveyed. The very fact that God's actions always, and his free creatures' often, are inexplicable to us is, as in most tragedy touching on deity, a necessary dignifying element.

Carey urges us not to swallow some "objectionable moral" that depends on " 'faith in the ultimate manifestation of God's will,' " and I must agree that a piously complacent measurement of God's will belittles the tragedy.[41] But so does Carey's evident assumption that a humanistic moralist can so keep track of that will that he himself may confidently recognize its "ultimate manifestation" and be rightly offended if it does not suit every particular of his humanistic morals. When the reader loses track, as he must, of God's deeds and justice it is in glimpses of depths not merely contrived and frustrating but moving and spirit-nourishing. The mysteries of iniquity and of godliness (of moral strength and weakness, that is), and of divine purpose and being are not, as Milton offers them, just pious cover-ups for an obvious hostility between man and his universe, but a poetic clothing of the great Judeo-Christian conviction of God's concern with man. Upon recognition of deity's passionless veil may attend those quieting positive choices in moral life that require decision beyond the available evidence. The force of the interminability of Samson's God resides for us finally in a sense of

son Agonistes," SP, LXVII (1970), 89–102, for straightforward declarative accounts. For more reserved remarks see Northrop Frye, "Agon and Logos: Revolution and Revelation," in The Prison and the Pinnacle, ed. Balachandra Rajan (Toronto, 1973), pp. 135–63; Joseph H. Summers, "The Movements of the Drama," in The Lyric and Dramatic Milton, ed. Joseph H. Summers (New York, 1965), pp. 153–76; Arnold Stein, Heroic Knowledge (Minneapolis, 1957), pp. 137–202; and Stanley Fish, "Question and Answer in Samson Agonistes," Critical Quarterly, XI (1969), 239–64. Anthony Low's The Blaze of Noon: A Reading of Samson Agonistes (New York, 1974) is finely inclusive in consideration of questions about Samson's God.

7. See Stanley Cavell, "The Avoidance of Love: A Reading of King Lear," in Must We Mean What We Say? (1969; rpt. New York, 1976), pp. 268–70, for a spirited defense of such readings of literary characters by an aesthetician and linguistic philosopher. I am not so confident of my applications of "psychology" as Cavell seems to be of his, but I do hold it reasonable to speak of characters and their actions as though one in some sense "knows" them, so long as one remembers to stick to the text and not press unreasonably. In some obvious ways fictitious persons do differ sharply from real-life ones. But if these differences defeat our grasp of them as persons they hurt the author sooner than the critic and worse.

8. Dorothy Walsh, Literature and Knowledge (Middletown, Conn., 1966), p. 133.

9. Empson's chapter on Samson is titled "Dalilah," but it is an integral part of his case against Milton's God.

10. See Mollenkott, "Relativism," pp. 89–93.

11. Burke, "The Imagery of Killing," p. 152; E. M. W. Tillyard, Milton, (London, 1946), p. 333; Isabel MacCaffrey, "Samson Agonistes" and the Poems of Milton (New York, 1967), p. xxxvi.

12. Empson, Milton's God, p. 217; Burke, "The Imagery of Killing," p. 155.

13. See Low, The Blaze of Noon, p. 84, on how Milton makes meeting force with force acceptable.

14. The Quarrel Within, pp. 113, 93.

15. See E. M. W. Tillyard, The Miltonic Setting (London, 1947), p. 79, on Samson's acceptance of responsibility. Fish, "Question and Answer," p. 249, thinks Samson presumptuous in self-blame. Undoubtedly, as Fish indicates, the balance between presumption of God's wrath and presumption of his mercy is a ticklish one. Samson does sink toward despair as he talks to Manoa of his sense of "Heaven's desertion." But he also says "His pardon I implore" (591), and he remains confident that "Dagon must stoop" (468).

16. "A Revaluation of the Chorus's Role," p. 134.

17. See Summers, "The Movements of the Drama," p. 156; and Barbara K. Lewalski, "Samson Agonistes and the 'Tragedy' of the Apocalypse," PMLA, LXXXV (1970), 1062.

18. See Fish, "Question and Answer," p. 249.

19. See Low, The Blaze of Noon, p. 183.

20. See Frye, "Agon and Logos," p. 141.

21. Stein calls Samson here "detached and calm." Heroic Knowledge, p. 184.

22. See ibid., p. 202; and Martin Mueller, "Pathos and Katharsis in Samson Agonistes," Critical Essays on Milton from ELH (Baltimore, 1969), p. 237.

23. Fell, "From Myth to Martyrdom," p. 145.

24. Milton's God, p. 213. See Sir Herbert Grierson, "Milton and Liberty," MLR, XXXIX (1944), p. 106: "Revenge is the dominant note of Milton's last poem."

Many writers refer to Samson's "revenge" as though it were as plain to see as Hieronimo's.

25. Frye, "Agon and Logos," p. 153, notices that Milton "suppressed" the statement in Judges that Samson prayed for private revenge; and Fish, "Question and Answer," p. 256, insists on the difference between Milton's Samson and the Samson of Judges: "Whatever Milton's Samson asks for, it is not vengeance." Louis L. Martz, "Chorus and Character in *Samson Agonistes*," *Milton Studies*, I, ed. James D. Simmonds (Pittsburgh, 1969), p. 132, stresses the difference between Samson's view of his last bloody act and the Chorus's, as does Low, *The Blaze of Noon*, p. 187.

26. Allen, *The Harmonious Vision*, p. 88.

27. A. B. Chambers, "Wisdom and Fortitude in *Samson Agonistes*," *PMLA*, LXXVIII (1963), 319, holds that Samson's anger is with Dalila's sin, not with her, and Hugh M. Richmond, *The Christian Revolutionary: John Milton* (Berkeley, 1974), p. 183, that Samson's last speech to Dalila has "an explicit mercifulness at the core of its abuse." Mollenkott's article is largely on the human touchingness and reasonableness of Dalila's appeal and the impossibility that it can move Samson on the plane that Milton wants to raise him to. Frye, "Agon and Logos," p. 160, and others notice the human sympathy that we are bound to feel for Dalila. Many critics, Low most effectively (*The Blaze of Noon*, pp. 148–51) have analyzed Dalila's speeches to her disadvantage.

28. John Carey, introduction to *Samson Agonistes*, in *The Poems of John Milton*, ed. John Carey and Alastair Fowler (London, 1968), p. 335. Cf. Low, *The Blaze of Noon*, p. 156.

29. Richmond, *The Christian Revolutionary*, p. 182, comments on Milton's firmness in recognizing the "range and illogicality of human suffering" and a "universe frequently unresponsive to conventional human expectations of reward."

30. Stein, *Heroic Knowledge*, p. 176. See Low, *The Blaze of Noon*, pp. 118–19, on good and evil as "given" in the play and on the deeper reasons it provides for us to accept God's goodness, and p. 202 on the sins of the Philistines.

31. "Agon and Logos," p. 143.

32. "From Myth to Martyrdom," p. 149.

33. Empson, *Milton's God*, pp. 215–21; Carey, introduction, p. 335.

34. Aleksandr I. Solzhenitsyn, *The Gulag Archipelago: 1918–1956*, trans. Thomas P. Whitney (New York, 1974), I, 168–75.

35. Allan Richardson, *An Introduction to the Theology of the New Testament* (New York, 1958), pp. 39–40.

36. See, for instance, Martz, "Chorus and Character," pp. 119–22 on the flatness of the Chorus' arguments and verse. Irene Samuel, "*Samson Agonistes* as Tragedy," in *Calm of Mind*, ed. J. A. Wittreich (Cleveland, 1971), p. 250, is convincing about the Chorus' deficiencies of understanding. R. W. Condee, *Structure in Milton's Poetry* (University Part, Pa., 1974), pp. 146–48 doubts some elements of her case.

37. C. G. Jung, *Answer to Job*, trans. R. F. C. Hull (1960; rpt. New York, 1965), pp. 14–15.

38. "Question and Answer," p. 259–61.

39. Mueller, "*Pathos*," p. 252.

40. See Low, *The Blaze of Noon*, p. 92.

41. Carey, introduction, p. 335. The "objectionable moral" he cites is in an article by J. D. Ebbs, *MLQ*, XXII (1961), 377–89.

MILTON AND
THE JONSONIAN PLAIN STYLE

A. H. Tricomi

<hr/>

B EN JONSON'S reputation as the most learned of poets in
James' reign could not have been without attraction to the
young Milton, nor could the fact that Jonson chose throughout his
life to defend the poetic muse against her detractors. His immense
influence in England, his avowed Horatian commitment to the
instructive purposes of poetry, and his insistence upon the importance of learning, classical culture, and craft made him a figure of
sufficient standing that no poet aspiring as Milton did to assimilate
the masters of English poetry could have ignored this "tun of
man."

The extent of Jonson's influence on Milton is, however, difficult to gauge because it comprehends the larger issue of the development, in Milton's poetry, of "the plain style" which is so
closely associated with Jonson.[1] Part of the problem is that our
ability to cite numerous echoes of Jonson in Milton's work does
not answer the broader need to understand the development of
Milton's plain style. On the other hand, previous attempts to describe the more enduring aspects of Jonson's influence have resulted in the inadequate but familiar generalization that Jonson
provided Milton with "a model of classical restraint."[2] Our failure
to define satisfactorily the nature of this influence is, however,
understandable, since many models of the plain style beside Jonson's were available to Milton in Martial's poetry, that of the Neo-
Latin epigrammatists, and the contributors to the Greek Anthology, to say nothing of Jonson's own contemporaries.

In addressing this problem, I propose to distinguish sharply
between the influence of specific Jonson poems on Milton, which
can be known only in a narrow way, and the more comprehensive
development of Milton's plain style. The application of this method involves several steps. In order to show the distinctiveness of
the plain style in Milton's poetry, it will be useful to compare it to
the extremely ornamented "Spenserian" verse that dominates his
earlier work. Next, by putting into a coherent pattern certain bio-

graphical and historical data relating to the composition of *On Shakespeare* in 1630, it will be possible to identify the circumstances that excited Milton's interest in Ben Jonson as a poet and literary figure in the court of Charles I. From this date begins the period of Milton's experimentations in a broad humanizing conception of epigram that harks back to the Greek Anthology and to a style that we have come to call "Jonsonian" because Jonson was its most distinguished English practitioner. Among the poems of this period, *An Epitaph on the Marchioness of Winchester* reveals Milton's intimate knowledge of Jonson's epigrams on persons who died young and of the plain style generally. Far from being a wholly derivative exercise, however, the Winchester epitaph seeks to integrate the slender lyricism of the plain style into a richer, more mythological one. The mixture of these "Miltonic" and Jonsonian elements in the Winchester epitaph will prepare us to examine the verse of *L'Allegro* and *Il Penseroso,* in which Milton leaves behind the genre of the elegiac epigram. Although these companion poems display a playful, sometimes florid bent for description, I propose to show that these first fruits of Milton's maturity are nevertheless written from the perspective of a sterner, less ostentatious plain style.

I

Set beside the simplicity of the Jonsonian model, Milton's "Spenserian" style, as it is usually called, is all that the other is not. Lush pictorial descriptions laden with adjectives, compound epithets, and highly decorated phrasing endow this poetry with vivid imagistic effects such as Jonson deliberately eschewed in his epigrammatic verse. The scene-painting that is the natural product of such a style is generally supported by vivid allegorical or mythological descriptions, usually Ovidian, that in turn include elements from the pastoral elegy, ode, or eclogue. As the *Fair Infant Dying of a Cough* and the Nativity ode both illustrate, Milton integrates pagan motifs into an explicitly Christian setting, heightened and dramatized by elements we associate with chivalric romance.

The more technical appurtenances of this rich Spenserian style include elaborate stanzaic patterns derived from the Italian *canzone* as well as from Spenser,[3] frequent disyllabic and polysyllabic expressions, and the preference for rhetorical devices that include compound epithets—"green-ey'd *Neptune*" (*Vacation Exercise,* 43), "Swift-rushing black perdition" (*Fair Infant,* 67), "sable-stoled Sorcerers" (Nativity ode, 220); catachrestic or transferred epithets—"Unweeting hand" (*Fair Infant*, 23), "willing chains" (*Vacation Exercise*, 52), "melodious time" (Nativity ode, 129); and, of course, an irrepressible love of alliteration.[4] Other more widely appreciated indicators of the style include a devotion to archaic words and prefixes, inversions of the normal order of the adjective before the noun, and that most distinctive Spenserian practice of employing an Alexandrine at the end of a stanza. Throughout these early poems, the style is discursive and full of embellishments; the Spartan virtues of the plain style—brevity, clarity, simplicity of diction and syntax, and a scrupulously controlled unity of tone—all expressed in rhyming tetrameter or pentameter couplets—are largely absent.

If this highly restrained style is lacking in Milton's earliest poems, *On Shakespeare* (1630)[5] signifies the genesis, not yet of the plain style, but of the initial influence of Ben Jonson on the young Milton. Some critics have claimed, of course, that the influence is readily discernible. The technical similarities Milton's poem shares with Jonson's own, *To the Memory of My Beloved, . . . Mr. William Shakespeare*—both elegies written in iambic pentameter couplets on the Horatian topos, "Exegi monumentum aere perennius" ("I have built a monument more lasting than bronze")—have been widely observed. Heinrich Mutschman finds, in fact, eleven identical minor verbal items in the two poems.[6] The intimate tone of direct address and the reverential elevation of the subject, both characteristic of Jonson's elegiac practice, show less commonly recognized similarities. However, they do not necessarily prove Milton's indebtedness to Jonson since the occasional subject matter and the Horatian topos in both poems illustrate the common classical heritage to which each poet had access.

Even if Jonson's particular influence could be demonstrated beyond doubt, it would be less significant than the circumstances surrounding the publication of Milton's elegy in the second Shakespeare Folio. These circumstances appear to have aroused Milton's interest in the kinds of elegiac epigram that Jonson practiced. Henry Lawes, Milton's close friend, was the man who arranged for the publication of Milton's epigram through his friendship with William Herbert, the earl of Pembroke.[7] In this carefully made, second edition of Shakespeare's works, Milton's elegy was prepared to appear beside the already famous tribute of Ben Jonson— by that time England's first genuine laureate. Much of the impetus for Milton's study of Jonson's epigrams and of the elegiac epitaph in general appears to have been sparked by this rare opportunity Lawes provided. Little recognized, however, is that Milton's awareness of Jonson as a living figure in Charles' court dates in all probability from these events in which Lawes figures so prominently.

Lawes knew Jonson well—perhaps as well as he knew Pembroke. They were all very much in the same world of the court and had personal dealing with one another. When Jonson was imprisoned with Chapman in the *Eastward Ho* affair, he had, for example, addressed a letter of distress to Pembroke and to him had dedicated his *Catiline* as well as his *Epigrammes* of 1616.[8] Pembroke, for his part, had not only acted in *The Hue and Cry after Cupid*, but had also sent a gift of twenty pounds each year to Jonson so that he might buy books.[9] Not commonly known is that Henry Lawes acted in Jonson's *Chloridia* in 1630—just the year in which Milton's Shakespeare epigram was written—and had actually set three of Jonson's lyrics to music. Equally certain is that Lawes was at court in 1630 during the preparation of the first major masque presented after Charles I had ascended to the throne, Jonson's *Love's Triumph*. This was, of course, precisely the year that Lawes was negotiating with Pembroke about the publication of Milton's poem. Even more striking is that Lawes was made a member of the King's Private Musicke on the same day that Jonson's masque was performed.[10] It thus appears that Lawes composed the music for Jonson's masque and may have consulted with the old poet who had been confined to his apartment for the most part since his disabling stroke of 1628. This structure of personal and literary relationships surrounding Milton's *On Shakespeare* strongly indicates that Milton's knowledge of Ben Jonson was not limited to the latter's purely literary achievement. By 1630, it seems clear, Milton, through his friendship with the increasingly successful Lawes, knew of Ben Jonson as a personality, poet, and masque writer in Charles' court. Through that same friendship arose Milton's own connection with the writing of court masques which, again, curiously touches Jonson. The text of *Comus* (1634), whose music was composed by Lawes, bears notable associations with Jonson's own masques, as does *Arcades* (1633?).[11] These years between 1630, when Lawes arranged for the publication of Milton's Shakespeare elegy beside Jonson's own, and 1633–34, when Milton worked with Lawes, as Jonson had, to present his masques before the nobility, thus delimit the period of Milton's most intense interest in Ben Jonson as a famous personality and model for his own poetry.

II

If ever the young Milton were to absorb himself in the epi-grammatic tradition that Jonson had labored in with such distinc-tion, the period following his first publication, *On Shakespeare* in 1630, ought to have been the time. And so it turns out to have been. The inspiration for the poems that immediately followed this event cannot, however, be attributed exclusively to the influ-ence of this or that Jonson poem *per se*. More readily ascertainable is Milton's sustained interest in writing an unexpected variety of epigrams, each of which demonstrates his increasing mastery of the plain style. With the important exception of the Trinity manu-script poems, the English poetry that Milton composed between 1630 and 1632 is written in decasyllabic couplets or rhyming te-trameters, the two verse forms in which Jonson wrote virtually all his nondramatic poetry.[12] The first four poems of this period—*On Shakespeare* (1630), *On the University Carrier* (1631), *Another on the Same* (1631), and *An Epitaph on the Marchioness of Win-chester* (1631)—are all examples of epigrams written in commemo-ration of the dead. In their variety these poems reflect an enlarged conception of the epigram that has its precedent in the example of the Greek Anthology, to which Milton had direct access.[13] Jonson, however, in his *Epigrammes* (1616), was a prime mover in revital-izing this conception of the epigram. Following the precedent of the Anthology, he took the humble genre of the epigram that had come to signify a satirical or cynical indictment and enlarged its scope to include elegiac epitaphs and humorous elegiac epigrams. The distance between this enlarged conception of the epigram and the narrower one than current in English poetry may be mea-sured, for example, against the immensely popular anecdotal and satiric *Epigrams* of Sir John Harington (1616), which takes only the slightest notice of the epigrammatic epitaph.[14]

Since Milton's Hobson poems are so frequently seen as depar-tures from the main current of Milton's "serious" poetic develop-ment, it is important to remember their generic relationship to an epigrammatic tradition that includes the Shakespeare elegy and *An Epitaph on the Marchioness of Winchester* as well. Compared with the conceited metaphysicality of *On Shakespeare*, Milton's Hobson poems—themselves often perceived as "metaphysical"—show, moreover, a definite movement toward a plainer style, which is in keeping with their unexalted subject. Despite their farfetched and sometimes adolescent fancifulness, these poems exhibit a diction that is native and pithy rather than polysyllabic and Latinate. They are also prosaic rather than imagistic or decorated, and possess a syntax (molded by its end-stop couplets) that regularly excludes complex sentence patterns. In their witty demonstrations of irony and paradox in couplet after self-sustained couplet (cf. Jonson's *On English Monsieur*), these poems also display a notable movement toward the plain style. However, in contrast to the Winchester epitaph, the Hobson epigrams do not express, nor do they strive to achieve, the pellucid grace and understatement of Jonson's lyric epitaphs. Their irreverence and mock solemnity show, naturally, that they belong more to that group of epigrams Milton's Cambridge classmates produced on the occasion of the university carrier's death—the models for which may lie as much in the flourishing practice of Neo-Latin epigrams as in any native English models.[15] Nevertheless, insofar as Milton's Hobson epigrams are not satires but inscriptions intended to memorialize, however humorously, the most memorable features of a man's life or situation, they belong to the broader, humanizing conception of the epigram that Jonson, bucking the main current, had championed some fifteen years earlier.

III

Whereas the Hobson poems fall under the broad spectrum of the witty epigram, *An Epitaph on the Marchioness of Winchester*, written several months later, bears a direct relationship to the narrower, more distinctive subgenre of the lyric epitaph that Jonson had perfected. As Michael Moloney observes: "From Jonson the 17th century learned the secret of stateliness in the four-stress line. In his regular octosyllabics but especially in his heptasyllables he had demonstrated to his contemporaries its full potentiality for solemn effect."[16] Not only did Jonson retard the inherent racing movement of these meters through a heavy caesura, but he achieved a stately monosyllabic diction that allowed him to introduce as many as three poetic words to a single seven-syllable line. This he achieved without ever losing the formal simplicity and grace that marks his lyrical plain style.

The verses in *An Epitaph on the Marchioness of Winchester*, like Jonson's, average only one polysyllable per line, employ a heavy caesura, show relatively simple syntactic structures, and achieve dignified solemnity.[17] No other poem by Milton expresses as fully as this epitaph so many formal similarities to Jonson's own epitaph style. Although he had never submitted himself to the four-stress line (except in his translation of Psalm cxxxvi) and although he had never before experimented in mixing, as Jonson had done in *On Margaret Ratcliffe*, octosyllabic lines with heptasyllabic ones, *The Marchioness* is Milton's effort to master on the first attempt the technical virtuosity and understated delicacy of Jonson's most famous lyric epitaphs.

This conclusion does not rest on stylistic inference alone; the poem is saturated with phrases and imagistic motifs that appear in Jonson's epitaphs on persons who died young. For example, the opening verses of *The Marchioness*,

> This rich Marble doth inter
> The honor'd Wife of *Winchester,*
> A Viscount's daughter, an Earl's heir,
> Beside what her virtues fair,
> Added to her noble birth,
> More than she could own from Earth,   (1–6)

bear an intimate relationship to Jonson's beloved *Epitaph on Elizabeth, L. H.:*

> Under-neath this stone doth lye
>   As much beautie, as could dye:
> Which in life did harbour give
>   To more vertue, then doth live.   (3–6)

The verse patterns of the two poems are remarkably similar, mixing hepta- and octosyllabic lines in tetrameter couplets. The accents of the two poems, blending as they do regular iambs with frequent trochaic lines, are almost identical. Regarded more closely, Milton's first, fourth, and fifth lines, with their variant trochaic meters and their catalectic final syllable, employ the same metrical variations that Jonson does in the third and fifth lines of his epigram. The poems, in fact, echo each other, not only in technique but in poetic idea. The gentle compliment of Milton's epitaph, that the Lady Pawlet possessed more virtue than this earth affords, and the subtle hyperbole behind the compliment that her virtue is not sublunary but divine—this poetic notion in all its conventional gracefulness receives comparable expression in Jonson's own inscription to Elizabeth, L. H.

Similarly, when Milton sports with the irony that the Fates, perhaps mistakenly, took Lady Pawlet's life (25–28), his wit, as J. B. Leishman has discovered, follows closely Jonson's conceit in the *Epitaph on S. [alomon] P. [avy]*, A Child of Q. El. Chappel:

> Yet three fill'd *Zodiackes* had he beene
>   The stages jewell;
> And did act (what now we mone)
>   Old men so duely,
> As, sooth, the *Parcae* thought him one,
>   He plai'd so truely.   (11–16)[18]

Woodhouse and Bush also emphasize the derivativeness of the Winchester epitaph in remarking that the opening verses of the poem "remind us at once of William Browne's poem on the Countess of Pembroke," whose opening verses they quote:

> UNDERNEATH this sable herse
> Lies the subject of all verse:
> Sidney's sister, Pembroke's mother.[19]

Browne's third line recalling the countess' pedigree matches functionally and syntactically the third verse of Milton's epitaph which informs us that Lady Jane is "A Viscount's daughter, an Earl's heir." Then too, as Leishman notices, Milton's epitaph sports with the irony of the "womb" becoming a "tomb" (33–34), as does Browne's epitaph *On an Infant Unborn and the Mother Dying in Travail* (1–2).[20]

In view of Milton's annotations of Browne's *Brittannia's Pastorals,* the possibility of his indebtedness to Browne's epigrammatic poetry as well cannot be ignored.[21] Nevertheless, it is important to emphasize that these conceits are Renaissance commonplaces and that the plain style is itself highly conventionalized. The fact, moreover, that Browne was a friend of Jonson's and a notable practitioner of the plain style in his own right shows that the lines of potential influence are too numerous to isolate.[22] By the same token, however, the formal similarities between the Winchester epitaph and those of Browne and Jonson do demonstrate how fully Milton's poem participates in the conventions of the elegiac epigram and, more pointedly, in the self-conscious practice of the plain style.

Despite the widely recognized Jonsonian characteristics of the Winchester epitaph, they reveal only one aspect of Milton's experimentation with the plain style. The distinctiveness of Milton's maturing poetic voice, which seems so derivative at first, needs to be more fully appreciated. Although the epitaph reveals much of Jonson's metrical virtuosity, it resists the utter starkness of his vocabulary. The diction is undoubtedly like Jonson's, but with a difference. Jonson impresses upon us the cold fact of death, "Underneath this stone doth lye" (3); Milton emphasizes "This rich Marble" (1), drawing attention to the opulence and social standing of Lady Pawlet's family. Jonson informs us that Elizabeth "lies"; Milton chooses the more distinctive and less expected term "inter" to describe the placement of the body. The very kinship between the two styles highlights their dissimilarities. While Milton submits himself on the one hand to the formal restraints of the plain style, his predilection on the other for imaginative descriptions actually strives with the epigrammatic form of the epitaph because it continually seeks variety rather than Jonson's intensity of effect. In fact, when Milton is most himself in the poem, he breaks down the formal limitations to which he initially commits himself. In contrast to Jonson's epitaphs, rarely more than twenty-five lines in length, the seventy-five line length of Milton's epitaph on the Marchioness is indicative of more substantive differences between these poets. Particularly notable is that Milton's bent for dramatic narrative and multiple effects induces him even here, in the midst of a strictly disciplined Jonsonian form, to pursue extended mythological and Christian parallels that cast the central subject into sharp relief. In a luxurious blend of pagan and Christian story, Milton recreates (from lines 15 through 34) Lady Jane's marriage feast, the birth of her first son, and the ensuing death of Lady Jane with her yet unborn child. A variety of emotional effects necessarily results.

So too, while Milton employs the same witty conceit as Jonson does in his *Epitaph on S. P.*—that Atropos, not the Goddess of Childbirth, mistakenly attended Lady Jane—the overall effect of the two passages is decidedly dissimilar. In Jonson the single ironic conceit governs the entire epitaph; in Milton that same conceit takes its place as one in a flock. Through the use of simile, Milton pauses to retell the story of Lady Jane in the sweet pathos of Virgilian pastoral (35–46), and then, in an extended metaphor drawn from the Bible, compares Lady Jane's personal history to that of Rachel, who died while giving birth to Benjamin. The very multiplicity of Milton's poetic conceits and borrowings thus creates a variety of emotional responses that necessarily alters the slender Jonsonian unity of effect.

Despite these discursive elements, however, Milton always returns to Lady Jane and the immediacy of the funeral occasion. When he does so, his direct address to the deceased woman is unembroidered by fanciful speculation or mythological analogies. Graceful, delicate, and tastefully restrained, he strikes an unmistakably Jonsonian accent:

Gentle Lady, may thy grave
Peace and quiet ever have:
After this thy travail sore
Sweet rest seize thee evermore,
That to give the world increase,
Short'ned hast thy own life's lease.   (47–52)

By the end of the poem, it is true, Milton envisions in a way that Jonson seldom does that final triumph in which the soul, clothed in the radiant robes of beatitude, conquers death forever. *An Epitaph on the Marchioness of Winchester* thus transcends the Jonsonian poignancy of the "Gentle" mother's "travail sore"; yet the gentleness of Milton's address to this young woman makes it one of the most affecting sections in the poem, precisely because of its noble discipline and restraint.

IV

Now restrained, now discursive, *An Epitaph on the Marchioness of Winchester* reveals Milton's uncertain attempt to assimilate the plain style into his characteristically richer poetic practice. For Milton the task that awaited mastery was to speak with assurance in his own voice while working within the formal constraints imposed by the plain style. In the lyrics of *L'Allegro* and *Il Penseroso*, written at the beginning of the Horton period in 1632 or slightly before, Milton perfects the formal beauties of this lyric art even as he achieves a confident and distinctive poetic voice.

L'Allegro and *Il Penseroso* reveal certain departures from the plain style. Milton's fondness for pastoral settings and romantic lore remains strong in these poems, as does his continued Spenserian use of archaic verb forms—"In Heav'n yclep'd *Euphrosyne*" (*L'Allegro*, 12); his love of anaphora—"And the Milkmaid singeth blithe, / And the Mower whets his scythe, / And every Shepherd tells his tale" (*L'Allegro*, 65–67); his preference for having adjectives follow their nouns—"Daisies pied" (*L'Allegro*, 75), "enchantments drear" (*Il Penseroso*, 119); or, more elaborately, for making one adjective precede and one follow its noun—"native Wood-notes wild" (*L'Allegro*, 134) and 'Russet Lawns and Fallows Gray" (*L'Allegro*, 71); his predilection for extended rhetorical periods; and his frequent use of feminine endings. All these usages, quite rare in Jonson's plain style, are characteristic of Milton's, not only in these companion poems but in Milton's poetry generally.

Despite these stylistic features, *L'Allegro* and *Il Penseroso* display a lyrical plain style that we very properly associate with Jonson's own. For one thing, Jonson's voice can be heard through a host of echoes and minor literary allusions. More significant than these particular repetitions of phrase, however, is Milton's assimilation of the plain style. In order to appreciate the scale of this stylistic achievement, we need to peruse the first ten lines of *L'Allegro*, which define, by antithesis as it were, the elaborate kind of verse Milton had by now learned to eschew:

> Hence Loathed Melancholy
>   Of *Cerberus* and blackest midnight born,
> In *Stygian* Cave forlorn
>   'Mongst horrid shapes, and shrieks, and sight unholy,
> Find out some uncouth cell,
>   Where brooding darkness spreads his jealous wings,
> And the night-Raven sings;
>   There under *Ebon* shades, the low-brow'd Rocks,
> As ragged as thy Locks,
>   In dark *Cimmerian* desert ever dwell.   (1–10)

The observation of E. M. W. Tillyard, that students who knew their Ovid "with his endless mythology" would appreciate this vigorous burlesque of his style, seems to me right.[23] Less obvious, however, is that the lines resurrect the earlier style Milton had employed before he began his experiments in writing elegiac epitaphs. Tillyard does not go far enough when he fixes the burlesque in the first Prolusion with its reference to "Cimmerian darkness."[24] Nearly all of Milton's earliest poetry in English partakes of this exuberant style which the poet now employs as a preface to the more restrained Jonson-like measures that dominate the rest of the poem. The juxtaposition of this florid opening and the more sober tetrameters in the body of the poem confidently announces Milton's self-conscious mastery of each style. In fact, the distance between the inflated rhetoric of the prologue and the restrained measures in the body of *L'Allegro* illustrates Milton's mastery of a more disciplined craftsmanship that would not have been possible without his prior apprenticeship to the plain style.

Among Milton's earliest poems, many would reveal the stylistic prototype of the flamboyant opening lines in *L'Allegro*, but none exemplifies the point so well as the Nativity ode (1629). Two stanzas in particular demonstrate the stylistic paternity of the opening verses from *L'Allegro*:

With such a horrid clang
As on mount *Sinai* rang
  While the red fire, and smold'ring clouds outbrake:
The Aged Earth aghast
With terror of that blast,
  Shall from the surface to the center shake,

     . . . .

The Oracles are dumb,
No voice or hideous hum
  Runs through the arched roof in words deceiving.
Apollo from his shrine
Can no more divine,
  With hollow shriek the steep of *Delphos* leaving.
No nightly trance, or breathed spell,
Inspires the pale-ey'd Priest from the prophetic cell.
                    (157–62, 173–80)

In *L'Allegro* the rhetorical exaggeration of such phrases as "horrid
shapes, and shrieks, and sight unholy" (4), finds its melodramatic
parallel in the "horrid clang" (157), the "hollow shriek" (178), and
the "hideous hum" (174) of the Nativity ode. The "brooding darkness" with its "jealous wings" (6) and the "night-Raven['s]" song
(7) are similarly matched by the obtrusive use of pathetic fallacy in
the Nativity ode, as in "The aged Earth aghast / With terror of that
blast" (160–61). Even the horrific Senecan evocations of darkness
and fear in *L'Allegro* find their counterparts in the eerie sounds
and images of the ode where neither "nightly trance" nor
"breathed spell" can hearten "the pale-ey'd Priest" of Delphos
(179–80). The strange polysyllabic expressions in both pieces,
their heavy mythological allusiveness, their emphatic alliterations
(cf. *L'Allegro*'s tenth line, "In dark *Cimmerian* desert ever dwell,"
with line 180 in the Nativity ode, "Inspires the pale-ey'd Priest
from the prophetic cell"), even the mixture of three-stress and
five-stress lines, demonstrate the kinship of Milton's early verse to
these opening lines from *L'Allegro,* now artfully counterpoised
against the poem's dominant tetrameter rhythms.

    Milton's confinement of the earlier exaggerated style to the
opening lines of *L'Allegro* is, of course, one measure of the control
that is the boast of the remainder of the poem. A second measure
of this control in *L'Allegro* and *Il Penseroso* is Milton's exploration
of the range of potentialities contained in the four-stress couplet—
the form he had earlier assayed with mixed results in the epitaph
on the Marchioness. Considered now as two aspects of the same

form, *L'Allegro* and *Il Penseroso* define more completely than Jonson's poetry ever did the variety of effects that could be wrought from the seven- and eight-syllable couplet. In the famous seven-syllabled trochee of the invocation to Euphrosyne—"Come, and trip it as ye go / On the light fantastic toe" (33–34)—and in the disyllabic, heavily caesured invocation to Melancholy—"Come pensive Nun, devout and pure, / Sober, steadfast, and demure" (31–32)—Milton deftly depicts the movements of each goddess, which in turn embody the dominant rhythms of the two poems.[25]

There is no danger, of course, of our forgetting the variety of these metrical accomplishments—they have become cliches of criticism—but there is some need of our realizing that *L'Allegro* and *Il Penseroso* are the culmination of Milton's apprenticeship to the plain style. Whereas *L'Allegro,* by the nature of its subject, displays a more varied use of the tetrameter line than Jonson had attempted in his tetrameter epitaphs, *Il Penseroso* shows most clearly Milton's mastery of the formal discipline demanded by the plain style. The same "dancing" meters of *L'Allegro* are summoned in *Il Penseroso* to appear as slow and as stately as any in Jonson's epitaphs. In accomplishing these ends in *Il Penseroso,* Milton employs a larger number of octosyllabic lines than in *L'Allegro,* largely avoids the truncation of the first unaccented syllable, and relies more heavily upon an iambic rather than a sprightly trochaic meter. Additionally, he returns to the weighted internal pause of *The Marchioness,* employing prolonged nasals and double endings in iambic lines to enhance the sense of regal solemnity. As the following passage illustrates, Milton is in complete possession of his *own* plain style:

> And join with thee calm Peace and Quiet,
> Spare Fast, that oft with gods doth diet,
> And hears the Muses in a ring
> Aye round about *Jove's* Altar sing.
> And add to these retired Leisure,
> That in trim Gardens takes his pleasure.   (45–50)

To these achievements Milton adds another—a characteristic Jonsonian unity of tone that he maintains for over one hundred fifty lines in both poems, an achievement that contrasts strikingly with the infirm control of tone in the earlier *An Epitaph on the Marchioness of Winchester.* Gone too in *L'Allegro* and *Il Penseroso* are the expansive, digressive similes of *The Marchioness.* In their stead Milton conjures up a host of activities that are controlled by the unities of tone and emotional effect, the hallmarks of the classical plain style. This achievement Milton reveals in a style that had been limited in Jonson's own poetry to the lyric epitaph. In this sense too Milton's companion poems announce their freedom from the dominant but limited generic forms in which the plain style had been practiced in sixteenth-century England.

Thus, in what is really a brief season of apprenticeship, roughly from 1630 to 1632—the period that begins with the publication of *On Shakespeare* and which includes the two Hobson epigrams, *An Epitaph on the Marchioness of Winchester*, *L'Allegro*, and *Il Penseroso*—Milton began to assimilate into his own ever more distinctive style the virtues of lucidity, simplicity, understatement, unity of tone, and clarity of emotional response. In his earliest exercises, it is true, Milton had demonstrated his preference, which was never fully to leave him, for poetic exuberance and complexity of statement; nevertheless, the poet needed to submit himself to a stricter regimen of form and diction. This the practice of the Jonsonian plain style helped to provide. Brief then as this period of experimentation was, the plain style had an enduring effect upon Milton's developing art, for it gave to the young poet a new mastery over language and meter that were preconditions to the achievement of the symphonic art that is the glory of *Lycidas* and the great poems of Milton's maturity.

State University of New York at Binghamton

NOTES

1. The phrase derives from the subtitle of Wesley Trimpi's book, *Ben Jonson's Poems* (Stanford, 1962).

2. Characteristic of this generalized understanding of Jonson's influence is James Holly Hanford's *A Milton Handbook*, 4th ed. (New York, 1946), which makes repeated appeals to Jonson's "classical lyric style," e.g., pp. 143, 146, 148.

3. F. T. Prince, *The Italian Element in Milton's Verse* (Oxford, 1954), pp. 60–61.

4. All citations of Milton's poetry refer to the modern-spelling edition of Merritt Y. Hughes, *John Milton: Complete Poems and Major Prose* (New York, 1957).

5. J. Milton French, ed., *The Life Records of John Milton* (New Brunswick, N.J., 1949), I, 215. Unless otherwise noted, the chronology of Milton's poems is from French. The notion that Jonson's influence upon Milton predates 1630 is

plausible. Prince (*Italian Element*, p. 59) and Hanford (*Milton Handbook*, pp. 140–41) indicate that Jonson's influence reveals itself as early as 1628 with the heroic couplets of *At a Vacation Exercise*, but the looseness of this imputation is evident, and Milton's continued infatuation with pastoral romance and high-flown diction points decidedly in the other direction.

6. *Further Studies Concerning the Origin of "Paradise Lost"* (Tarte, 1934), pp. 48–49.

7. Morris Freedman, "Milton's 'On Shakespeare' and Henry Lawes," *SQ*, XIV (1963), 280–81.

8. For the commendatory dedication of Jonson's *Epigrammes*, see William B. Hunter, ed., *The Complete Poetry of Ben Jonson* (New York, 1963), pp. 3–4. All citations of Jonson's poems refer to this edition. For Jonson's dedication of *Catiline* to the earl, see C. H. Herford and Percy and Evelyn Simpson, *Ben Jonson*, 11 vols. (Oxford, 1925–52), V, 431. On Jonson's letter to Pembroke, see Herford and Simpson, I, 199–200. All references to Jonson's plays and masques are from this standard edition.

9. E. K. Chambers, *The Elizabethan Stage* (Oxford, 1923; corrections, 1951), III, 377, 382. Also, Herford and Simpson, *Ben Jonson*, I, 141.

10. On Lawes's activities at court, I am indebted throughout the paragraph to Willa M. Evans, *Henry Lawes: Musician and Friend of Poets* (New York, 1941), pp. 47–57.

11. The subject of Jonson's influence on Milton's masques is beyond the scope of this essay, which limits itself to the influence of Jonson's nondramatic poetry on Milton's English verse. However, for Jonson's influence on *Arcades*, see Douglas Bush, *English Literature in the Earlier Seventeenth Century: 1600–1660*, 2nd ed., rev. (Oxford, 1966), pp. 382–83). The date of *Arcades* is uncertain, but on the slender basis offered by John Carey and Alastair Fowler, eds., *The Poems of John Milton* (New York, 1968), p. 155, I follow their date of "1633?" For Jonson's influence on *Comus*, see ibid., p. 171, where the editors note seven echoes of Jonson in Milton's masque.

12. If French (*Life Records*, pp. 278–79) is right in thinking that the Trinity manuscript poems—which include *At A Solemn Music*, *The Circumcision*, and the two sonnets on time—were composed in 1633, then they postdate those Milton poems that show Jonson's influence most strongly.

13. On Jonson's extension of the epigram, see Hoyt Hopewell Hudson, *The Epigram in the English Renaissance* (Princeton, 1947), pp. 5–7. However, T. K. Whipple, "Martial and the English Epigram from Sir Thomas Wyatt to Ben Jonson," *University of California Publications in Modern Philology*, X (1925), 386–404, emphasizes that the bulk of Jonson's epigrams do have "point" (*acclamatio*), and that most derive from Martial. He contentiously disputes the influence of the Greek Anthology on Jonson (pp. 386–87) and largely ignores Jonson's inscriptional epitaphs, which do not support his thesis.

14. Published in the Norman Egbert McClure edition (Philadelphia, 1926). Along with Harington's *Epigrams*, which were printed in 1613, 1615, 1618, 1628, and 1633, the satiric epigrams of Parrot and Owen were most popular in Milton's youth. As the *STC* and the British Museum Catalogue illustrate, Parrot's *Epigrammata* was printed in 1608, 1615, 1626, and 1629, and versions of Owen's epigrams appeared in 1607, 1619, 1628, and 1633. See Henry Parrot, *Cures for the Itch: Characters, Epigrams, Epitaphs* (1626), STC 19328; and John Owen, *Epigrammata* (1618, 1619), STC 18993.

15. Most of the existing Hobson poems are collected by G. Blakemore Evans in "Milton and the Hobson Poems," *MLQ*, IV (1943), 281–90, and "Some More Hobson Verses," *MLQ*, IX (1948), 10.

16. "The Prosody of Milton's 'Epitaph', 'L'Allegro,' and 'Il Penseroso,'" *MLN*, LXXII (1957), 176.

17. Jonson too wrote an epitaph on the Marchioness of Winchester, or in Jonson's rendering, to "Lady Jane Pawlet Marchion: of Winton." Despite the identity of subject, Milton's poem was written independently of Jonson's and appears to owe nothing whatever to it.

18. *Milton's Minor Poems* (Oxford, 1969), pp. 87–88.

19. A. S. P. Woodhouse and Douglas Bush, *Variorum Commentary on . . . John Milton: The Minor Poems*, II, (New York, 1972), p. 193.

20. *Milton's Minor Poems*, pp. 88–89.

21. See the introduction by A. H. Bullen in *The Poems of William Browne of Tavistock*, ed. Gordon Goodwin (London, 1894), I, xxx.

22. Frederic W. Moorman, *William Browne* (Strassburg, 1897), pp. 4–9.

23. "Milton: 'L'Allegro' and 'Il Penseroso,'" *English Association Pamphlet*, LXXXII (Oxford, 1932), 16.

24. Ibid., pp. 13–14.

25. For percentages of trochaic and iambic lines in Milton's early poetry, see S. Ernest Sprott, *Milton's Art of Prosody* (Oxford, 1953), p. 19; and Ants Oras, "Metre and Chronology in Milton's 'Epitaph on the Marchioness of Winchester,' 'L'Allegro,' and 'Il Penseroso,'" *N&Q*, CXCVIII (1953), 332.

"AMBIGUOUS WORDS AND JEALOUSIES": A SECULAR READING OF *PARADISE LOST*

John R. Mulder

*P*ARADISE LOST is a difficult poem, and we should therefore resist the casual Voltairean manner of finding fault with Milton for the defects of logic in his justification of God's ways. Modern readers who can easily detect flaws in the poem's intellectual argument ought to remember that Milton, himself no mean theologian, probably could have raised the same rationalist objections. If we find the thought of *Paradise Lost* problematical, we should accept this as a characteristic feature of the poem and not treat it condescendingly as evidence of the limitations of Milton's intellect.[1] Similarly, if the plotting of this poem amuses us, because it is so obviously manipulated, we should resist the easy argument that this is due to Milton's inexperience in narrative art; rather, we ought to accept the looped and windowed raggedness of the plot as part of the poem's ostensible design and thus as something to be accounted for.

Many readers have tried to account for the peculiarities of *Paradise Lost* by tracing the causes of them in past habits of thought and expression. This approach requires that we surrender our judgment altogether and become believers; we assume that what seems problematic, or inartistic, or ethically dubious to us *now* was accepted as truth, beauty, and goodness *then*. Such a reading is likely to become academic, for we will find ourselves constantly pulling back from our private reactions to the poem and exchanging them for something borrowed from books. Whether we play the rationalist or the believer, we will in each case fail to account for some notable features of the text, for we will have dismissed them either by imposing our own judgment or by casting aside our own experience.

The alternative to the stances of the rationalist and the believer is that we put no prior limitations on the originality of the mind that produced *Paradise Lost*. The selection of this third stance means that we must deal with the text as we find it, exhaustively searching through all its stylistic details. Such an undertaking is obviously so large that any single reader can offer no more than an hypothesis. The first part of my essay gives therefore an outline of my approach, with the considerations of theory and method that govern me; the second part is an analysis of the invocation of Book VII and illustrates one kind of attention we might give to the text; the third and final section is a preliminary examination of what I call the duplicity of *Paradise Lost*, instanced in the poem's rendering of Adam and Eve.

I

My reading of *Paradise Lost* is contrived as an experiment; its intention is to raise questions concerning the criteria for distinguishing, at our distance, the conscious intention of an author from the involuntary intentions of his text. To that end, I shall be pursuing the somewhat unusual hypothesis that the narrative voice of the poem is not identical with Milton but is rather the voice of a persona who illustrates the loss of paradise in his inspirations, his motives, his reasoning, and his counsel. So viewed, *Paradise Lost* is only incidentally a theological poem. In it Milton uses certain clichés of theological, philosophical, and moral thought as instruments in the characterization of his narrator.

The interpreter who argues for the presence of a persona proceeds upon an inference; strictly speaking, the reader of *Paradise Lost* encounters only an arrangement of words. This arrangement has two aspects: sequence and structure. The sequence is the shape the poem assumes for us as we read it. Every stage of that sequence is the result of choice; the poem resonates against unwritten alternatives. The sequence is therefore determined by the choices made in the selection and combination of its parts, and the motives that govern the poet's choices are the structuring principles of the poem. Sequence and structure are thus inseparable: sequence illustrates structure, and structure is known only through its effects in the sequence. In other words, we must work back from the shape of the poem as we find it in order to uncover the structuring motives that account for that shape. I argue that the unstated idea or pattern—what Sidney called the "foreconceit"—reflected in the sequence of *Paradise Lost* is the delineation of a character, an imitation of a particular kind of human nature. The disparate parts of the poem are unified by Milton's conception and execution of a special narrative voice, as distinctive as any of Swift's personae.

It is therefore fruitless to debate whether *Paradise Lost* is ill or well made unless we first perceive that the shape of the poem is itself symbolic. There is no need to ridicule or defend Milton against the charges of defective logic and cavalier plotting; *Paradise Lost* is illogical and fragmented because Milton designed it to illustrate an experience of unreason and fragmentation. The characterization of the persona is the result of the selection and combination of details, and the reader's response derives both from what is and from what is not included. The reader's perception of a narrating persona at work is the result of the reader's intuition, progressively shaped by the sequence of the text.

This theoretical distinction between sequence and structure enables us to distinguish between two points of view or intentions to be found in the text: one is the narrator's, the other is Milton's. The point of view of the narrator is made known sequentially; that of Milton is apprehended in the way in which Milton has structured the narrator's perspective. The poem is therefore consistently duplicitous, or, borrowing one of Milton's famous metaphors, we might call it a two-handed engine. This complex view of *Paradise Lost* is the unavoidable consequence of my earlier contention: once the shape of the poem is regarded as symbolic, it acquires the peculiar characteristic of all figurative expression, ambiguity.

Our perception of the structure—and therefore Milton's intention in the disposition of his material—is the result of the gradual accumulation of our responses to the details of the text. Our interpretation is therefore inevitably subjective, but it is never merely personal. The experience engendered in us has an artificial cause, since it is shaped by the artifice of the poem's rhetoric. The latter can be described, and it is therefore our necessary focus.

In the textbooks of rhetoric of Milton's day the first two steps in the art of composition were invention and judgment. Invention was the systematic discovery of whatever arguments may be brought to bear upon a topic; judgment was the arrangement of the selected arguments in a fitting order, the fitness depending on the author's purpose for the whole composition. In traditional rhetoric, as in the stylistics of our own day, the sequence of a work is therefore of utmost importance; ancient rhetoric and modern stylistics alike forbid commentaries in which selected passages are newly interwoven, and they alike require that we aim for an interpretation that leaves the sequence of the poem as we find it. We are bidden to discover a reading in which all the parts of the poem

are interrelated, verse by verse, and word by word, without in-
terfering with the sequence on the page.

Regard for sequence means that we should grant no prior
advantage to any part or party in the poem. As we follow the
narrative voice from hell to heaven, and from heaven to earth, we
may be tempted to play the believer and think that the heavenly
perspective is the one we should adopt: the Satan who looks so
tragic in hell, so terrifying when viewed from earth, appears comic
in the divine overview. Readers who give in to the temptation and
identify with the god-in-the-poem will find that they can make the
divine view prevail only by discounting recorded human experience—evil and consequent suffering are not, after all, cause for
laughter—and by sheltering the poem from any direct response
on their part. Any time they find the divine management of affairs
problematical, they will have to use the argument that the problems are inherent in Milton's subject matter, because for them as
believers the poem will deal for nine books with things that are,
paradoxically, real but not known: the circumstances of "life" in
hell, paradise, and heaven. These places are not within human
ken and thus human judgment and experience are preempted.

The temptation to play God can be resisted by adhering to
literary criteria; meaning must be read out of the interrelation-
ships between parts, and no part takes precedence over the whole.
In practice this means that we may avoid giving undue weight to
the council in heaven of Book III by observing its position in the
sequence of the poem. In the order of the narrator's justification of
God's ways, that council is a brief interruption in the narrative
account of Satan's rising and quest. Books I and II, filled with
awful intimations of the evil and suffering that will visit the earth,
prompt the question why God should let all hell break loose on
the world. Book III opens with a prayer that expresses the need
for help on the part of the narrator, who describes himself now as
an old man in a new season, alone and in the dark. If we observe
from the outside what happens in the poem, instead of merely
obeying the I-eye of the blind narrator inside it, the brief shift to
the perspective of heaven seems prompted by the obvious need
for a rationale. We note then also a peculiar irony in the rationale
that is offered. The heavenly council of Book III is a discourse on
providence, foreknowledge, will, and fate, which is the sort of
undertaking that was condemned as fruitless in the hell of Book II
(555–61). The same enterprise that was called confusion in hell is

praised as orderly light in heaven. If we are to live by reason, must we not make a choice and deny the narrative voice the privilege of having it both ways?

The reader must in any case decide whether Milton or a persona is divided against himself on this and other issues. Either Milton or a persona fails to see that the fiction of being present at the council in heaven constitutes the very thing that he ridicules shortly thereafter in the paradise of fools: the inane anticipation of immortality. Either Milton or a persona lays down as a rule, in Book I, that pagan gods are devils by another name, and then scatters pagan references throughout the poem, likening Adam and Eve to Jupiter and Juno, and Raphael to Hermes.

We should not simply believe what is said in the poem, nor should we indulge in the merely rationalist critique of it. Both the believer and the rationalist assume that the poem deals with what, for Milton at least, constituted a reality. Both parties assume that the god-in-the-poem is the best picture Milton could contrive of his own concept of deity. Both parties rearrange the text to their own liking by arguing that modern literary criteria cannot furnish a norm, because Milton's genius had not the benefit of recent advances in technical virtuosity.

I recommend the opposite: if we apply modern criteria—which are the result of the advance of the discipline of criticism as a gradual structure of knowledge—we will enlarge our view of the power of a poet such as Milton (or Dante) to forge language into a sophisticated instrument for transmitting his personal and individual insight, to develop a poem that is a delicately balanced artifact, a verbal heterocosm, a symbolic word-world order, with a guilty narrator, and hence with multiple levels of irony.

If we apply literary criteria first, *Paradise Lost* will become a verbal event, and the narrator changes into a fabricated character: a blind man who affects an inner eye, who claims to have microscopic, telescopic, panoramic sight, the perfect camera eye for technicolor Panavision. The narrative voice of *Paradise Lost* is that of a man who makes an immodest proposal: he wishes to justify the course of everyone and everything. He is thus a character who acts in ignorance of his own condition, since the latter renders him decisively incapable of what he attempts. Milton appears to be saying, among other things, that the inability to accept the human condition leads to the extravagance of human claims, that the belief in those claims in turn makes us more miserable, and that we are thus tossed from joy to misery and back again, till we arrive at the paroxysm of finding grandeur in misery—an unearthly mix of heaven and hell.

If we follow the literary method we cannot rely on sources external to the poem to furnish us with a norm. We must instead make a judgment from the very first: how are we to respond to a voice that presumes to translate for us the mind of God? Milton surely did not attempt such an act of hybris, because he believed that the light of God is unavailable to mortals except in the oracle that is Christ. Rather, Milton lights up in *Paradise Lost* the inevitability of misery whenever self-righteousness parades as righteousness. The voice of the poem acts out the fallen condition.

Examined as verbal event, *Paradise Lost* reveals its motive power inside itself, and the poem becomes, not a resolution for the metaphysically perplexed, but an appeal to more comprehensive human experience and to abiding aspects of human nature. It is not a discourse on ideas but an illustration of behavior and is designed to throw into relief those traits that are typically human, rather than typically Protestant, or even typically Christian. If we consider *Paradise Lost* in this modern literary light, we will find that it conforms to some very ancient tenets of literary theory: it is a speaking picture (the speech constituting the picture), it feigns a notable image, and it imitates human nature. A literary scholar avoids having to search for correspondence between *Paradise Lost* and Milton's *Christian Doctrine*, for it follows from his literary assumptions that the poem was not meant to fit the treatise. They are works of different kinds, different structures for different purposes.

It is undeniable that the explicit rationale of the justification executed by the narrative voice echoes the Christian tradition, but it does not follow that the received prelatical interpretation of that tradition can provide us with the criteria for judging artistic function. The latter can only be examined in the poem's verbal arrangement—again we come back to the study of the way the text is designed.

For the analysis of literary design there is a precept, akin to a rule, which says that deviations are stylistically more significant than the norm: in meter, diction, order, image, and idea, the deviation from the norm catches the reader's attention and provides him with clues to the artist's shaping of the material. The extent to which the reader apprehends Milton's structuring of the sequence of the text (and therefore the principles by which Milton makes his choices) thus depends on the reader's ability to be surprised.

That ability in turn depends on the expectations with which he comes to the poem. Hence the literary study of the text cannot proceed if we take away the reader's capacity for surprise. This is precisely what happens when we assume beforehand that our own responses are inappropriately modern and that we must adjust our expectations to traditions and conventions of which we have no sympathetic understanding.

That we need a knowledge of traditions and conventions is obvious, for they are inherent in Milton's language, but gaining that knowledge does not tell us how to use it in the study of Milton's poems. When the divine father's speeches in Book III echo the patristic exposition of the problem of foreknowledge versus free will, it does not follow that the function of these discourses in the design of *Paradise Lost* is merely Milton's reassertion of patristic verities. Deviation (and therefore the element of surprise) need not be purely verbal but may also result from context (i.e., the reverberation of details in the sequence of the poem), as in the contrast between the dismissal of metaphysical speculation in Book II and the grand display of the same in Book III.

We can look at everything in *Paradise Lost* in terms of tradition or in terms of deviation. The angelology of the poem furnishes a provocative example, for it endows angels with digestive systems, a feature that is traditional only in the sense that it repeatedly occurs in medieval treatises. The belief in this peculiar corporeality of angels had become a deviation in the seventeenth century, and it is therefore surprising that Milton retained it.[2] Do we conclude then that Milton wished to revive the medieval picture because he believed in it? Or does this detail function to make us aware of the crude literal-mindedness of the poem's narrative voice? Whatever our verdict, it obviously makes a considerable difference whether or not we are biased (or think that our author is biased) in favor of the received interpretation, the convention, and the cliché.

II

A just documentation of the literary approach to *Paradise Lost* requires the extensive description of all the features of the text, both in their immediate surroundings and in the effects of their gradual accumulation in the poem's sequence. I can only begin to illustrate the kind of effort involved in this large undertaking by providing a commentary on the rhetoric of the invocation of Book VII.

The patterning of this invocation illustrates how the intensification of need goes paired with increasing megalomania and blindness to the causes of that need. The more information the narrator gives us about what he does, the more uncertain his undertaking becomes. As the evidence he gives about himself accumulates, we become aware that his station, motive, and condition work in counterpoint to what he presumes to argue. By the end of the invocation, uncertainty has grown into anxiety.

> Descend from Heav'n *Urania*, by that name
> If rightly thou art call'd, whose Voice divine
> Following, above th' *Olympian* Hill I soar,
> Above the flight of *Pegasean* wing.

(1) The name Urania is questioned as soon as it is uttered; the uncertainty is thrown into relief by the inversion of the word order, so that "name" and "If," forming a run-on line, occupy positions of rhythmical stress. (2) "Whose Voice divine / Following" is an instance of amphibology (or ambiguity resulting from the order of the words); the meaning hovers between "I follow thy divine voice" and "thy divine voice follows me." (3) The repetition of "above" stresses a motif that is repeated throughout the poem: whatever the narrator does is superlative and far exceeds anything accomplished by others before him. (4) The line that begins with "Following" ends with an emphasis on self-propulsion in "I soar."

> The meaning, not the Name I call: for thou
> Nor of the Muses nine, nor on the top
> Of old *Olympus* dwell'st, but Heav'nlie born,
> Before the Hills appeerd, or Fountain flow'd.

(1) In his attempt to authenticate the source of his inspiration, the speaker reaches the limits of language and must define himself by contrast. Although he alleges that his work is greater than any that have come down from antiquity, he is confined to the language of the ancients and can only say that, in *his* use of it, the language does not mean the same thing. (2) The repetition "Nor . . . nor" stresses that the speaker must follow a *via negativa* to affirm what he cannot express. (3) Being without a vocabulary of his own, the speaker translates the name *Urania* and applies it to a heaven antecedent to that of the ancients, before there were either hills or fountains sacred to the muses. (4) Since the literary method of studying *Paradise Lost* differs from other approaches in its first assumption (concerning the relationship between Milton and his text), that assumption reveals itself in all subsidiary con-

clusions. It leads eventually to the reexamination of the peculiarities of Milton's orthography, in which he took care to be exact. Is
"Heav'nlie" not only "of heaven" but a "heavenly lie" as well?

> Thou with Eternal wisdom didst converse,
> Wisdom thy Sister, and with her didst play
> In presence of th' Almightie Father, pleas'd
> With thy Celestial Song.

(1) Having dismissed as inferior the mythos of the ancients,
who only had eyes for the visible heavens, the voice shadows its
own inspiration in a new mythos in which Urania is fathered along
with her sister, Wisdom. (2) "Converse" means that Urania lives
with her sister, that they make verses together, and that they trade
places (*converse* once meant turning around into an opposite or
contrary direction). (3) The repeated emphasis in "didst converse" and "didst play" suggests that Urania uses Wisdom not as
partner but as instrument; the outcome is Urania's doing, not that
of Wisdom, for the father is pleased with "*thy* Celestial Song"
(emphasis mine). (4) This passage may serve as one example of
Milton's constant double entendre. The lines characterize the narrator's ambition (for his reach far exceeds his grasp), but they also
describe the method in the apparent madness of the poem: wisdom and absurdity are playfully turned around and upside down,
and the father (Milton) who begot this combination is pleased by
the effect.

> Up led by thee
> Into the Heav'n of Heav'ns I have presum'd,
> An Earthlie Guest, and drawn Empyreal Air,
> Thy tempring; with like safetie guided down
> Return me to my Native Element.

(1) "Presum'd" is ironic: the narrator believes that he is permitted to go where no other human being may claim to enter. He
excuses the presumption in "Up led by thee." The phrasing images his ambivalence: had he been truly led, there would be no
need for saying "presum'd." The meaning hovers therefore between an indictment and a validation; the narrator says simultaneously that "you did it" and "I did it." The language here repeats
the equivocation implicit in the amphibology of "Voice divine /
Following." (2) In *Paradise Lost*, the language of a speaker ignorant of his own condition comments ironically on the speaker himself. This happens noticeably in "An Earthlie Guest, and drawn
Empyreal Air." The metrical and grammatical balance of the

line—adjective, noun, verb, adjective, noun—points up a rhetorical antithesis that illustrates presumption: although "Earthlie" the
speaker has "drawn Empyreal Air." He has breathed in the air of
the heaven above the heavens, and he has also drawn a picture of
the Empyreal-Imperial manner, explicitly in his portrait of deity
and, unwittingly, in the airs he has given himself. "Empyreal,"
from the Greek "in the fire," allows also for the inference that the
persona has been breathing fire. (3) The description of presumption begins and ends with a transfer of responsibility: "Up led by
thee / . . . presum'd / Thy tempring"; "thee" and "Thy" receive
particular stress because of their location. (4) "Tempring" sprouts
many meanings: mixing elements, preparing colors, assuaging, re-
straining, moistening, melting, tuning and attuning; hard steel is
tempered or made resilient, by immersing it, while hot, in cold
water. All these meanings can be applied. The word signals the
structural change from the first to the second part of the invocation, from exultation over exploits to a complaint of misery; the
first part ends with the suggestion of fear in the brief reference to
Bellerophon's presumption, the second closes with implied terror
in the extended recall of the cruel death of Orpheus; the first part
invokes the muse, the second implores her. (5) "Tempring," like
"converse," allows us to perceive the double pattern of *Paradise
Lost:* it illustrates the narrator at his self-portraiture, but it also
reflects another power that tempers him, that mixes his (rhetorical)
colors, and immerses him, hot from the fire of heaven, in the cold
element of earth, of which the narrator is about to give a sad
description in the second half of his invocation. (6) Located at the
end of the line, "down" may go with both "guided" and "Return."
The narrator is both led down to earth and returned down to (i.e.,
changed back into) his earthly self.

> Least from this flying Steed unrein'd (as once
> *Bellerophon*, though from a lower Clime),
> Dismounted, on th' *Aleian* Field I fall
> Erroneous there to wander and forlorn.

(1) "Least": the narrator shows himself aware of danger.
(2) "Unrein'd" is another amphibology: does it qualify "I" or
"Steed"? Again the meaning hovers: does the narrator lose (or
loose) the reins, or does the horse run out of control? The language is chosen so as to reverberate against the story of Bellerophon. Both Bellerophon and the narrator are horsed by a higher
aegis: Bellerophon received a magical bridle from Athena, and the

narrator both rides and soars by a power that he can only qualify as "*Urania* . . . Celestial . . . Heav'nlie"; Bellerophon was presumptuous in exploring the visible heavens, and the narrator half admits that he has been more so in flying up to an invisible spacetime. (3) "Dismounted" equivocates on whether the rider steps down or is thrown off. Bellerophon was thrown off, but the narrator ignores any likeness and, characteristically, stresses his own superior achievement: Bellerophon fell from a lower clime-climb. (4) "Fall" receives emphasis through alliteration, rhythm, and placement. (5) Because of its location, "Erroneous" may be read with "I fall" and "wander." To wander means that one is in error or that one has lost one's way; in this line, the voice places the verb midway between "Erroneous" and "forlorn," again equivocating on the meaning to be assigned to "wander."

> Half yet remains unsung but narrower bound
> Within the visible Diurnal Sphear;
> Standing on Earth, not rapt above the Pole,
> More safe I sing with mortal voice, unchang'd
> To hoarce or mute, though fall'n on evil dayes,
> On evil dayes though fall'n, and evil tongues;
> In darkness, and with dangers compast round.

(1) This passage begins the second part of the invocation, the description of the narrator's present condition. The language is consistently ironic for the outside observer. The speaker is "narrower bound / Within the visible Diurnal Sphear," which is, however, invisible to him, since he has earlier admitted his blindness; here he allows only that he lives "In darkness, and with dangers compast ['compassed' and 'compost'] round." The circular movement around the chiasmus of "though fall'n on evil dayes / On evil dayes though fall'n" verbally illustrates a life in bondage. The emphatic "Standing" contrasts with the earlier "I fall" and the subsequently repeated "fall'n." In view of what the narrator admits about himself, it is a grim paradox that it should make him "More safe": here is a man who can make the worse appear the better reason. (2) Homer says of Bellerophon that "he wandered alone, eating his heart out, far from the roads of men" (*Iliad*, VI, 201–02). The narrator who has cast himself as greater than Bellerophon denies the evidence that he has, like Bellerophon, become a vagabond among men. Although he admits that he has fallen, he is not aware of any responsibility for this decline; he attributes it to the malice of fortune and society, "evil dayes" and "evil tongues." He acts in igno-

rance of his own condition, even though his language reveals what
his condition is. (3) "Unchang'd to hoarce or mute" allows us to see
a pun on "hoarse" and "horse." The equivocation that embraces all
the other equivocations in the narrator's performance is the uncertainty about whether he knows himself to be horse or rider in his
soaring up to the secret mounts of heaven and paradise, leaving not
only the mounts of Olympus and Parnassus but also those of Oreb
and Sinai far behind—not to mention the hill of Sion with its special christological significance.

> with dangers compast round,
> And solitude; yet not alone, while thou
> Visit'st my slumbers Nightly, or when Morn
> Purples the East: still govern thou my Song,
> Urania, and fit audience find, though few.

(1) Again the voice equivocates: it is alone and not alone; it is
sometimes visited by something called "heav'nlie." (2) How can a
blind man tell when the morning "Purples the East"? Although
the narrator is blind, he is "Unchang'd to hoarce or mute"—he is
not deaf and dumb and hears what is said around him by "evil
tongues." The nightly visitations of his unmentionable muse are
interrupted when the sounds of the new day intrude on him,
another evil day with evil tongues, and he "sees red" at the
thought that few may hear his voice among those noises.

> But drive farr off the barbarous dissonance
> Of Bacchus and his revellers, the Race
> Of that wild Rout that tore the Thracian Bard
> In Rhodope, where Woods and Rocks had Eares
> To rapture, till the savage clamor dround
> Both Harp and Voice; nor could the Muse defend
> Her Son. So fail not thou, who thee implores:
> For thou art Heav'nlie, shee an empty dream.

(1) This passage continues the references to sound and hearing. In the stillness of the night, the narrator may fancy that the
whole creation attends to him as it attended to Orpheus, all ear to
be enraptured, but in the morning a "barbarous dissonance," the
sound of human voices, wakes him and he drowns. He first admits
that few will listen to him, but his version of the death of Orpheus
reflects his fear that he too may be drowned out. (2) The elabo-
rated recall of the murder of Orpheus illustrates how the narrator
comes to suffer from a symbolizing imagination. He fails to see
what his language half admits: that he is an aging, blind man,

excluded from participation in life. He manages instead to cover his frailty with grandeur. His gradual awakening to the world, reflected in the sequence of this invocation, is transformed into a reenactment of a great mythical archetype. The narrator becomes another Orpheus, and those whom he hears but cannot see are made over into a murderous rout, victimizing the sacred son of a sacred muse. He cries out for help: "So fail not thou." (3) The last line of the invocation is arranged so as to lead one to expect an antithesis. If the true "thou" is "heav'nlie," would not the deluding "shee" be either infernal or earthly? "Shee" however is neutralized as an "empty dream"; yet the narrator's own use of dreams (in Books V and VIII) argues that there are no empty dreams.

The stylistic examination of the opening of Book VII reveals in the conduct of the narrative voice two features that characterize it at this point in *Paradise Lost.* The narrator consistently equivocates on the source of, and the responsibility for, his interpretation of divine will, and he transforms his own fall—in spite of "I soar," the sequence of the invocation is decidedly a comedown—into the descent of Urania. Urania is his own experience projected onto a limitless canvas; it is an illustration of idol worship, for the narrator begets his own goddess; he fathers a parody of wisdom. After the opening invocation of Book I, the narrative voice began: "Say first"; now it intones: "Say goddess." There is a notable contrast between the frequent and explicit biblical references in the first invocation and the absence of them in the second. (Although the lyrical beginning of Book III is sometimes called an invocation, its rhetorical form is that of a prayer; there are only two invocations proper in *Paradise Lost.*) In the second invocation the explicit references are pagan, but the narrator only half perceives their instructive content. His recall of Bellerophon and Orpheus betrays his fear, but his conclusions show that he triumphs over his own fear by fearlessly presuming a greater privilege. Orpheus had long been recognized as one of the masks of God and therefore as a type of Christ, but the mythical poet-prophet-priest becomes, like Bellerophon, merely a negative example, a poet with an empty dream.

By tracing a few comparisons between the first and second invocation, I have already passed on to the question that must follow upon the analysis of the style of the passage itself: since both the first invocation and the prayer of Book III invoke a "Heav'nly muse" without further circumscription, why this wandering in search of name and meaning now, at this place in the poem's sequence? My (tentative) answer is that the narrator grows more helpless as his song proceeds. Although his justification fits what he alleges to be the facts, he cannot make the latter fit any demonstrable pattern of wisdom; the consequences of his justifying tale prove always problematic, because they are begot upon his own arrogant assumptions. The second invocation records the halfway mark in a process of deterioration. Trying to sketch the grounds for this interpretation of the narrator's sequential development, we must begin with the first invocation. Foregoing a detailed rhetorical analysis of the opening of *Paradise Lost*, we merely observe again how the conduct of the narrative voice reveals a condition.

> Of Mans First Disobedience, and the Fruit
> Of that Forbidden Tree, whose mortal tast
> Brought Death into the World, and all our woe,
> With loss of *Eden*, till one greater Man
> Restore us, and regain the blissful Seat.

The trailing order of the clauses unfolds, out of the first act of disobedience, the present consequences of death, woe, loss, and longing for restoration. Strictly considered, the tense of "Restore" implies that this work has not yet been accomplished. The rhythm of the voice, moving first down, then up, reflects the struggle against misery and the search for deliverance.

> Sing Heav'nly Muse, that on the secret top
> Of *Oreb*, or of *Sinai*, didst inspire
> That Shepherd, who first taught the chosen Seed,
> In the Beginning, how the Heav'ns and Earth
> Rose out of *Chaos:* Or if *Sion* Hill
> Delight thee more, and *Siloa's* Brook that flow'd
> Fast by the Oracle of God; I thence
> Invoke thy aid to my adventrous Song.

Although a human being does the singing, he alleges in "Sing Heav'nly Muse" that his voice is not his own: "I am another." Immediately there emerges the problem of authenticating the source of this infusion. He adduces a precedent in the first revealer of secrets, Moses, the shepherd elected to instruct a "chosen Seed" about the origin of creation. Yet the narrative voice cannot locate the origin of the secret inspiration of Moses: is it Oreb, or Sinai, or some later place of Old Testament revelation such as Sion's hill and Siloa's brook? Without knowledge of the source, the narrator's song must necessarily be "adventrous." He would like to make a beginning but he does not know how; he decides to fly:

> That with no middle flight intends to soar
> Above th' *Aonian* Mount, while it pursues
> Things unattempted yet in Prose or Rime.

The voice knows what it would like to accomplish: scorning, like the fateful Icarus, the middle way, he intends to soar above Helicon or Parnassus, in pursuit of what no other song has yet attempted.[3] The narrator needs therefore something other than an Old Testament source that he cannot name, and he begins again, now using New Testament language:

> And chiefly Thou O Spirit, that dost prefer
> Before all Temples th' upright heart and pure,
> Instruct me, for Thou know'st; Thou from the first
> Wast present, and with mighty wings outspread
> Dove-like satst brooding on the vast Abyss
> And mad'st it pregnant: What in me is dark
> Illumin, what is low raise and support.

The clause "that dost prefer" introduces an ambiguity, for it fails to make clear whether the Spirit is invoked *because* the narrator knows his heart to be upright and pure. The speaker has reason to feel ambivalent, for he admits that he confronts within himself that which is dark and low. The moral meaning of "low" ("vile") is carefully edited out by the development of the architectural meaning of "low" into a metaphor—"low . . . raise . . . support . . . highth":

> That to the highth of this great Argument
> I may assert Eternal Providence
> And justifie the wayes of God to men.

The spirit that informed the chaos of the abyss may also bring forth light and order from the as yet chaotic condition in the narrator's self. The authenticity of his song will not derive from the Old Testament temple but from his own heart, preferred by a new spirit to become the latest oracle of God.

The ostentatiousness of this invocation is without precedent in epic. The claim that this kind of justifying undertaking has not yet been attempted is a violation of Christian doctrine, because the Bible is the authoritative record of providential design. The one true oracle of divinity is its manifestation in Christ. Although

Christ is shadowed in the typological references to Moses and the Old Testament places of revelation, the narrator's song flows fast by Christ, the Savior. Although Christ is the antitypical temple of the New Testament, the narrator looks upon his own heart as God's sacred precinct. Although Milton himself declares that the kingdom of heaven is at hand through Christ's redemption,[4] the voice of this poem is still longing for a restoration. Although Luther, Calvin, and Trent are in accord on the principle that Christ is the only justifier, the narrator arrogates that role to himself.[5] As soon as he mentions the first disobedience, he commits it. His insane pride keeps him from acknowledging where his salvation lies. Without a savior, he is lost; without seeing Christ in the center of God's providential design, he must henceforth reel and stagger to the circumference, without ever finding rest there.

The narrator's behavior toward God-in-Christ illumines his darkness. To the outside observer it illustrates that the narrator is in the dark; to the narrator himself, however, his being in the dark is no evidence of his wrongdoing. He sees it instead as a God-given darkness out of which he must mediate a design; he regards his feelings as inspirations and, instead of reading them as a warning to himself, he translates them into a judgment on the world. He flees his chaos.

There are hence two reasons why the narration begins with Satan in hell. One is academic: epics conventionally begin *in medias res*. The other is artistic: the narrator begins with Satan in hell, because he is himself in misery. The speaker's vision of hell is the projection of his own condition. Milton manipulates verb tenses in order to indicate the narrator's changeable disposition toward the details he narrates. In the first description of Satan in hell, the lyrical evocation of horror, torment, despair, and torture uses the present tense, and the extended pathos of the rendering draws us in . Then comes a sudden reversal; rhythm, syntax, and tenses change as the speaker finds the principle that, for him, clarifies a dire situation:

> Regions of sorrow, doleful shades, where peace
> And rest can never dwell, hope never comes
> That comes to all; but torture without end
> Still urges, and a fiery Deluge, fed
> With ever-burning Sulphur unconsum'd:
> Such place Eternal Justice had prepar'd
> For those rebellious, here thir Prison ordain'd
> In utter darkness, and thir portion set.   (I, 65–72)

This divided response—at once sympathetic and cruel—to the plight of Satan is not in Milton's mind but is contrived by Milton as a feature of the narrator's divided self. Unable to see the import of his inspirations, the narrator is engaged in an enterprise akin to that of Pangloss in *Candide:* to show how everything that seems wrong can be made to seem right. The first and fatal principle of this justifier is "Eternal Justice," a human notion enlarged into an attribute of an anthropomorphic divinity. As the narrator's inspirations furnish him with more matter, things happen in hell: Satan rears his head—which the narrator alternately describes as monstrous (I, 192–202) and noble (I, 589–600)—and moves. These actions contradict the earlier statement that Satan's fate is fixed and require therefore a new editorial, in which God is said to leave Satan "at large to his own dark designs" (I, 213). Does "his" refer to the designs of Satan or of God? Paradoxically, God has a hand in Satan's designs, and the narrator alleges that events will show that God ultimately turns Satan's evil to God's own good. It is somewhat unsatisfactory—to say the least—that the visible consequences of what the narrator alleges to be God's design are so palpably miserable in their effects on mankind, whereas the benefits of Providence remain hidden in a secret and invisible space-time, to which only the privileged narrator has access.

After he has disclosed, in Books I and II, the "just" horrors of hell, and has presaged their manifestations on earth, the narrator fleshes out his image of divinity, in Book III, with another attribute: mercy. This God becomes the very picture of a king, invested with the imperial virtues that allow for unlimited and willful power: *justitia* and *clementia.*[6] This combination, theoretically alluring, is problematic in practice; just how problematic may be seen in the conduct of Shakespeare's kings. The monarch who lays down the law by virtue of the first attribute may also undo it by virtue of the second. Oblivious to the human contradiction in his deity, the narrator will turn wisdom inside out and upside down in order to make his idea of divine right prevail. He is continually discomfited by the consequences of its application, and he must continually make things up.

Refusing to see any connection between his misery and his moral conduct, the narrator regards his woe as symbolic of the fall of mankind. To justify that fall he begins by reaching back beyond time to the fall of Satan. The farther his plot proceeds, the farther he has to reach back to explore the causes of it. This explains why the Son's election is given in reverse order, his sacrifice (in Book

III) preceding his begetting (in Book V): having introduced Satan as a cause, the narrator must eventually find a cause for Satan's fall. This maneuvering does not, however, explain anything. The tale of Satan illustrates merely the triumph of superior power: omnipotent justice is compelled by its own principles to ruin but keep alive the creature of its own making. When Satan is thrown from heaven in Book VI, the tale comes full circle, and we are back where it began: with Satan, in the fire. The only point demonstrably clear is that the de facto illustration of divine right is might. The literary analysis of Milton's text confirms Shelley's verdict that the God in *Paradise Lost* enjoys no moral advantage over Satan; it also confirms Shelley's contention that Milton used conventional religion as a cover for his own judgment.[7]

The narrator reveals the problems he encounters whenever he tries his best to escape from them. Every digression from the story proper—invocations, prayers, apostrophes, explanations both short ("fondly overcome with Femal charm" [IX, 999]) and long (the discourse between Raphael and Adam)—is an attempt to cover one or another difficulty.[8] After the council in heaven provides a rationale for letting Satan loose on the world, the digression on hypocrisy at the end of Book III (691–98) draws attention to the narrator's manipulation: Uriel, expressly placed in the sun to keep an eye out for Satan, fails to recognize him. At this point the narrator enters upon a condemnation of hypocrisy as the only evil that walks invisible, except to God. Once he has found this excuse for a defense, the narrator can let Satan roam at will, and hence Gabriel's angelic squadron twice fail to see Satan enter the garden. The opening apostrophe of Book IV, "O for that warning voice," shows the narrator in need of further justifying reasons. When Satan makes directly for Eve, the narrator executes a balancing act with the scales of Libra to get him off the stage (IV, 995–1015), and he brings in Raphael as the warning voice in Book V. After Adam has been instructed, Satan is again set upon Eve, this time by means of a dive in a river (IX, 70–75). In his prologue of Book IX, at precisely the point at which his plot becomes inexplicable, the narrator glories in the superiority of his enterprise over all other poems.

The style of the last few books grows cold, flat, and increasingly pedantic. Here, as everywhere in *Paradise Lost*, a change in style reflects a change in the narrator; in Books XI and XII the voice becomes that of the hardened stoic. Instead of the argument that the later style of *Paradise Lost* fits the content—for which argument we need to invoke preconceived attitudes towards that content—I hold that the style conveys an attitude toward the subject matter. The later style is the result of an evolving disposition: an increasingly stoic mien is forced on the narrator by the gruesome consequences of his principles. The last time the narrator intrudes directly in the story is his commiserating address to Adam, when Adam, in tears, beholds a vision of the flood that washes his paradise away: "How didst thou grieve then, *Adam*, to behold / The end of all thy Ofspring, end so sad" (XI, 754–55). At this point the narrator cannot keep his own feelings back, because Adam suffers the grief from which his maker, the narrator, also suffers: "O Visions ill forseen! better had I / Liv'd ignorant of future" (763).

From the study of *Paradise Lost* as a notable feigned image, we must conclude that Milton's psychological insight was not limited to the usual commonplaces of his age, and that we must abide by the hypothesis that his understanding may have been more comprehensive than ours. The narrator of *Paradise Lost,* as contrived by Milton, is a man who makes up for the painful deficiencies of his daily life in compensating fantasies; yet, since these fantasies also remind him of what he does not have, he is driven to unmake them. He is thus divided against himself. The discord between his heaven and hell, his God and Satan, cannot be resolved, because both parties in the conflict derive from the divided narrator and embody the aspects of his nature that feed one another: the misery of his condition and the splendor of his fantasies. His God and Satan, his Adam and Eve, are "cumjustled . . . *isce et ille,* equals of opposites, evolved by a onesame power of nature or of spirit, *iste,* as the sole condition and means of its himundher manifestation and polarized for reunion by the symphysis of their antipathies."⁹

III

My introductory remarks announced that the third part of my essay would illustrate the duplicity of *Paradise Lost* in its rendering of Adam and Eve. No longer sure whether I am horse or rider in this undertaking, I cannot, in either case, dismount, and I must therefore proceed on the grounds that were laid down in the first part and amplified in the second. The literary method enables us to distinguish between the conduct of the narrative voice of *Paradise Lost* and Milton's management or execution of that voice. The text is a manipulation that simultaneously conveys both the attitude of a narrator and a commentary on that attitude. Duplicity is characteristic of the Miltonic style, and we are forced to recognize it whenever we encounter a deviation or, in other words, whenever we come upon something that surprises us. The complications that arise in the practice of the literary method—as in the instance of the poem's angelology—argue the need for scholarship. Yet scholarship is ancillary to criticism; it precedes a critical judgment but it follows upon a critical attitude. The literary method requires that we adopt, as critical attitude, the stance of the observer who looks at what happens in the text, and that we call on scholarship to guide us in drawing inferences from our observations.

By way of illustration, I focus on a decision announced early in *Paradise Lost*. When the voice mentions the abominations for which Belial will be responsible on earth, it brings in evidence:

> And when Night
> Darkens the Streets, then wander forth the Sons
> Of *Belial*, flown with insolence and wine.
> Witness the Streets of *Sodom*, and that night
> In *Gibeah*, when th' hospitable door
> Expos'd a Matron to avoid worse rape.   (I, 500–05)

"Matron" catches the attention: it particularizes the act. Striking also is the tragic paradox that a "hospitable" door casts her out. The paradox necessitates the editorial explanation: "to avoid worse rape." The violation of the woman is the price that must be paid for the safety of the man. By what criterion? That is left unsaid; only the conclusion is given. What are we to make of this?

In the biblical passage which we are explicitly invited to witness, Judges xix, the narrator's "matron" is a "concubine" who "played the whore against" her lord, a Levite, and runs away from him to her father's house. The Levite goes to seek her and obtains her again. On the return journey he and his party must spend the night in Gibeah, a city of the Benjamites. Refused hospitality by the natives of the place, they find shelter with an old man who is not a Benjamite. During the night "certain sons of Belial" surround the old man's house and demand that he deliver to them the Levite for the purpose "that we may know him." The host tries to dissuade them from doing "so vile a thing" and offers them instead the use of his own daughter and the Levite's concubine. The offer is refused. Thereupon the Levite personally throws his woman out of doors, and "they abused her all the night until the morning; and when the day began to spring, they let her go."

Then came the woman in the dawning of the day, and fell down at the door of the man's house where her lord was, till it was light. And her lord rose up in the morning, and opened the doors of the house, and went out to go his way; and, behold, the woman his concubine was fallen down at the door of the house, and her hands were upon the threshold. And he said unto her, Up, and let us be going. But none answered. Then the man took her up upon an ass, and the man rose up, and got him unto his place. And when he was come into his house, he took a knife, and laid hold on his concubine, and divided her, together with her bones, into twelve pieces, and sent her into all the coasts of Israel. And it was so, that all that saw it said, There was no such deed done nor seen from the day that the children of Israel came up out of the land of Egypt unto this day: consider of it, take advice, and speak your minds. (Judges xix, 26–30)

Throughout the chapter, the woman is silent. We are not even sure when she dies, an uncertainty that allows us to see that the story aims, not at narrative accuracy, but at the delineation of a response, or disposition. The act of hacking the woman up repeats the act of casting her out. The Levite, the host, and the sons of Belial are alike in using the woman as the dumb instrument for their satisfaction. This disposition, or moral choice, is a motif in the closing chapters of Judges. When the Levite is called to account before the congregation of Israel, he keeps his guilty secret; his accusation that the men of Gibeah "thought to have slain me" clearly falsifies the words of the sons of Belial in xix, 22: "that we may know him."

The Levite's misrepresentation of facts and motives starts a war against the Benjamites that very nearly kills off that tribe: only six hundred fighting men survive. The congregation of the elders of Israel now faces a dilemma: either the tribe of Benjamin dies out or the other tribes must go back on their oath that said: "Cursed be he that giveth a wife to Benjamin" (xxi, 18). The oath again uses women as instruments and the Israelites cannot give up that practice. Instead, they are driven to further rape by devastating Jabesh-gilead, the only camp that has abstained from the war. Its entire population is slain, except for four hundred virgins, who are then given to the Benjamite men. Since this fails to provide a woman for every one of the six hundred Benjamites, the elders next arrange for the hunt and capture of the daughters of Shiloh at the feast of the Lord in the vineyards of that place. The counsel of the elders, when they set the Benjamites upon the daughters of Shiloh, illustrates that the elders, like the Levite, knowingly deceive themselves:

And it shall be, when their fathers or their brethren come unto us to complain, that we will say unto them, Be favorable unto them for our sakes: because we reserved not to each man his wife in the war: for ye did not give unto them at this time, that ye should be guilty. (xx, 22)

The pretext of applying only the letter of the oath ("cursed be he that *giveth* a wife") confirms the spirit behind the oath; the conduct of the elders illustrates that the women are theirs to be used.

The elders are deceived in their reasoning that there shall be no need for rape if every male is provided with a female for his use. The original cause of the war, the rape of the woman as substitute for the rape of the male, remains hidden. Yet the guilt of the elders is the same as that of the Levite. If the sons of Belial are guilty of preferring their own sex, are not the host and the Levite sons of Belial? Are not the elders of Israel also sons of Belial? The Book of Judges starkly illustrates the male abuse of power. In *Paradise Lost* the narrator's "to avoid worse rape" is equally brutal. This editorial is his portrait: he too is a son of Belial. His use of the events in Gibeah as witness announces a bias against women that is consistently maintained: his account of the fall puts Eve to shame in order to avoid putting Adam to shame. This bias can be observed at work in his first introduction of Adam and Eve (IV, 288–318):

> Two of far nobler shape erect and tall,
> Godlike erect, with native Honour clad
> In naked Majestie seemd Lords of all,
> And worthie seemd, for in thir looks Divine
> The image of thir glorious Maker shon,
> Truth, Wisdom, Sanctitude severe and pure,
> Severe, but in true filial freedom plac't:
> Whence true autoritie in men.

The solemnity of the high style is a cloak for all manner of subterfuge. In the description of the first human pair, this style is suffused with irony at the expense of the narrator, who clothes simple nakedness in so many grand words, and who will have us believe that unadorned human nakedness is the image of the glorious majesty of God. The divine image that shines in Adam and Eve is "Severe, but in true filial freedom plac't." We encounter here another paradox: the freedom of children must coexist with obedience to paternal authority. One may, of course, choose to see in this comment Milton pointing to a mystery of life, but I see at this point another muddle in the narration, especially since the para-

dox is the source of "true autoritie in *men*." The narrator, as I will
show, solves the problem inherent in the paradox by assigning
authority or "autoritie" (self-will?) to the male and filial obedience
to the female.

> though both
> Not equal, as thir sex not equal seemd;
> For contemplation hee, and valour formd,
> For softness shee and sweet attractive Grace,
> Hee for God only, shee for God in him.

Note that a mere difference in sex is silently taken for an inequality, and that this inequality is in turn deduced merely from a
general description of the appearance of Adam and Eve: he is
formed for contemplation and valor, she for sweetness and grace.
This leads in turn to the definition of their relationship: "Hee for
God only, shee for God in him." This line is ambiguous, but it
clearly allows us to read that Eve is to Adam as Adam is to God.
This is, in fact, the horrendous assumption on which both the
narrator and Adam operate. Adam consistently behaves as Eve's
"Author and Disposer" (IV, 635); although he makes her his wife,
his dream of her birth (VIII, 452–90) shows that he first regards
her as his daughter, sprung (like daughter Sin from father Satan)
from Adam's left. This is why Adam assumes authority-autoritie
over Eve and puts her in the paradoxical position of being both
free and dependent. Inevitably Adam confronts in Eve the same
dilemma as the god-in-the-poem faces but cannot solve in the
creatures of his making. As the narrator's God rules over creatures
but cannot rule them against their will, so Adam has, theoretically,
the power to make Eve stay with him on the morning of the fall in
Book IX, but he cannot enforce that authority without Eve's consent. As there is no conclusion to the heavenly debate on right and
might, so is there no conclusion to the postlapsarian debates between Adam and Eve on who is responsible for the tragic outcome
of events in paradise (Book X). In paradise, as in heaven, the
arguments are circular and inconclusive because they proceed
from an error, or sin, in the first assumption.

> His fair large Front and Eye sublime declar'd
> Absolute rule; and Hyacinthin locks
> Round from his parted forelock manly hung
> Clustring, but not beneath his shoulders broad:
> Shee as a vail down to the slender waste
> Her unadorned golden tresses wore

> Dissheveld, but in wanton ringlets wav'd
> As the Vine curls her tendrils, which impli'd
> Subjection, but requir'd with gentle sway,
> And by her yielded, by him best receiv'd,
> Yielded with coy submission, modest pride,
> And sweet reluctant amorous delay.

The conclusion about the stature and relationship of Adam and Eve has been reached before we are given the evidence on which it rests. Adam's "absolute rule" is declared by what is visible in his appearance. The notable contrast between his looks and those of Eve is that in him everything is visible; his hair is short, so that his eyes, face, and broad shoulders can be seen. Eve, however, is veiled in her hair; only that and her sex are visible. Sexual organs and coiffure are therefore the only features available for comparison. The difference in the sex has already been interpreted as an inequality. Next the voice interprets the coiffure, which is, except for length, alike in both: the hair of Adam and Eve is all curls. The hair of Adam is "Hyacinthin" and, like the blossoms of that flower, "clust'ring." The bias of the narrator is evident in his calling Eve's hair "waved" in "wanton ringlets" and in his applying to it the simile "As the Vine curls her tendrils." This image, left implicit in the "clustring" of Adam's hair, is made explicit in the case of Eve. What this image means is next alleged in an editorial addition: it "impli'd / Subjection"—it might also imply the need for support, but the narrator's judgment rules out that possibility. The narrator avoids the logical implication of his portrayal: if Adam's rule is absolute, the submission of Eve must be equally absolute. On this issue, however, the voice equivocates and ends inevitably in a tangle of paradoxes: Eve's submission requires "gentle sway" and is "Yielded with coy submission, modest pride, / And sweet reluctant amorous delay."

> Nor those mysterious parts were then conceald,
> Then was not guiltie shame, dishonest shame
> Of natures works, honor dishonorable,
> Sin-bred, how have ye troubl'd all mankind
> With shews instead, meer shews of seeming pure,
> And banisht from mans life his happiest life,
> Simplicitie and spotless innocence.

In his introduction of the first parents, the narrator began by describing them at a distance, declaring that God's image shines in them both. As he brings them nearer (i.e., as he examines them more closely), the image of God resides more in Adam than in Eve, but the differentiation between the two begins and ends with a focus on their sexuality. His performance illustrates how much he is himself "troubl'd" by the "meer shews" of sex; again he plays the hypocrite: he merely seems pure. The conclusion that he reaches in this first rendering of Adam and Eve determines his justification of the subsequent events in paradise. He is biased in favor of Adam from the very beginning; his rationale for Adam's fall is a foregone conclusion, a circle of vicious reasoning.

The same bias is evident in the narrator's hymn in praise of connubial bliss, a long digression that he offers as substitute for the description of the sexual intercourse between Adam and Eve (IV, 744–75). It proclaims wedded love as the source of "all the Charities / Of Father, Son, and Brother" (756–57). What has happened to Wife, Mother, Daughter, Sister? Is not this distinct preference for the male, this exclusion of the female in a hymn that celebrates the male-female relationship, a very odd phenomenon? Do we ascribe such an act of casting the woman out to the blind Milton, who depended for every comfort of his daily life on the sustenance of his wife and daughters? May this be a signature by which we are meant to recognize the narrator as a son of Belial? Does the text comment on the origin and consequences of selecting maleness—one-half of life's inevitable duality—as a symbol for the indivisible God of life? How ironic is Milton, throughout his poem, about the exclusively male pantheon of the heaven designed by his enemy, prelatical episcopacy? To Belial

> no Temple stood
> Or Altar smoak'd; Yet who more oft then hee
> In Temples and at Altars, when the Priest
> Turns Atheist, as did Ely's Sons, who fill'd
> With lust and violence the house of God.   (I, 492–96)

Given the way in which the narrator of *Paradise Lost* rigs the situation in the garden, it is unavoidable that Satan (who is like any other figure in the poem made and moved about by the narrator) makes directly for Eve. The narrator's portrait of Adam and Eve has already shown on which point, in his view, Adam is vulnerable. The woman is a liability to Adam, who must still learn how to handle her. The narrator has thus created an embarrassing situation for himself. He knows what Adam does not yet know. Satan is therefore removed from the scene by a curious balancing act with the scales of Libra at the end of Book IV, and another nonbiblical element is introduced into the plot: Adam is to be instructed, during the next four books, by a heavenly messenger. The long discourse between Raphael and Adam makes explicit what was left implicit in the first description of Adam and Eve: the woman is subject to the man, and the rule of the man is absolute. Consider this question: What would have happened if the allegedly Edenic situation had got permanently stuck at the point reached at the end of Book VIII? Adam would have been like the narrator's god-in-heaven, sitting on top of his lookout over all his sons spread out on the plains below, and shouting, "Thou shalt not eat of the tree." But what has that command become at the end of Book VIII? It has changed into "Thou shalt keep the woman under submission."

There are two versions of a fall in *Paradise Lost.* One version is officially designated as *the* fall in Book IX. It is a tragic rendering, arranged in five acts, the narrator providing prologue, choric commentary, and stage directions. In this dramatization of the myth of paradise, Eve is blamed for eating of the fruit. But the discourse that precedes this high tragedy—the conversation between Raphael and Adam from Books V to VIII—is also about eating. It begins with a luncheon and continues with what is to Adam a far more excellent food, that of knowledge. Adam too indulges a taste for the fruit of knowledge, yet Adam is not blamed. Adam's temptation develops as follows.

Raphael, who is a hermetic figure—"Like *Maia's* son" (V, 285)—answers Adam's every inquiry, but the answer always contains a warning that Adam should beware of further searching. Although Raphael enlarges Adam's knowledge on every step of Adam's ladder to heaven, each answer also imposes new bounds. The trouble with boundaries is that they necessarily imply that there is something beyond them. Hence every piece of additional information received by Adam prompts another question in him, and he keeps on asking questions till Raphael's powers run out: "But I can now no more" (VIII, 630).

If we continue to apply the literary method that permits us to distinguish the voice of the narrator from Milton's intention, we observe a number of ironies that would otherwise escape our attention. One of the motifs of Book VIII is the repetition of solemn injunctions about humility and lowliness. Raphael's instruction that God has placed heaven so high "that earthly sight / If it presume, might err in things too high" (120–21) is one example, his warning "Dream not of other Worlds" (175) is another. This pose is underscored by Adam's confession that everything is "fond impertinence" (195) except the knowledge of "That which before us lies in daily life" (193) and by his repetition that man ought not "with perplexing thoughts to interrupt the sweet of Life" (183–84). The passages that embody this motif are sonorous and quotable, but they are also, in view of the tradition they continue, mere clichés. This is not to say that Milton did not believe them; on the contrary, Milton believed that we must perforce abide by the recognition of our creatureliness. Milton's originality, artistry, and insight cannot be found, however, in those ideas themselves, but in his manipulation of them. In the design of the poem, these clichés of thought function to illustrate how the behavior of Adam reflects that of his maker, the narrator. What Adam does is also at variance with what Adam professes. He pontificates about the vanity of knowledge, yet he wishes to know more and more, indulging in an endless longing:

> For while I sit with thee, I seem in Heav'n,
> And sweeter thy discourse is to my ear
> Then Fruits of Palm-tree pleasantest to thirst
> And hunger both, from labour, at the hour
> Of sweet repast; they satiate, and soon fill,
> Though pleasant, but thy words with Grace Divine
> Imbu'd, bring to thir sweetness no satietie.   (210–16)

If we practice literary analysis, we are allowed to speculate on a pun on "lies" in the lines "to know / That which before us lies in daily life, / Is the prime Wisdom" (192–94), so that a cliché begins to sparkle with wit. The whole poem is an illustration of the causes and consequences of the falsification of experience; the narrator is the most obvious example of this, and the narrator's sin is repeated in his Adam. This reduplication of error in Adam's behavior can be observed in Book VIII.

The discourse of Book VIII is divided into two parts, the first dealing with Adam's view of the heavens, the second with Adam's view of himself. The problem Adam tries to solve in both parts is the same problem of disproportion: the greater seem to serve the lesser. The discourse gradually focuses on the real issue, which is that, at some point of touch, Eve vanquishes Adam's self-esteem (521–33). Adam's questioning begins, however, at considerable distance from himself. He starts with the heavens and, reasoning from a primitive world view, asks why the greater heaven serves the lesser earth, which effortlessly receives the tribute of heaven's

restless revolution (15–38). At this very moment Eve's action illustrates Adam's distinction between greater and lesser. Perceiving
that Adam's thoughts restlessly move in heaven, she leaves him to
his revolutions and moves within her own compass as she visits
with the fruits and flowers of the earth, her nursery (39–47). The
event of her leaving requires a lengthy editorial:

> Yet went she not, as not with such discourse
> Delighted, or not capable her ear
> Of what was high: such pleasure she reserv'd,
> *Adam* relating, she sole Auditress;
> Her Husband the Relater she preferr'd
> Before the Angel, and of him to ask
> Chose rather; hee, she knew would intermix
> Grateful digressions, and solve high dispute
> With conjugal Caresses, from his Lip
> Not words alone pleas'd her. O when meet now
> Such pairs, in Love and mutual Honour joyn'd?   (48–58)

The narrator gives us a strange picture of the conversation of
our first parents; it is a mix of sporting and philosophizing. The
wife much prefers the sporting to the philosophizing, and the conclusion ("solve high dispute / With conjugal Caresses") proves
that she wins her husband over. The narrator's editorial foreshadows the problem that Adam will make explicit, for Adam will in
the end admit to Raphael that he feels sexually subjected. (This is
the inevitable result of the prior assumption that he is superior.)

A notable feature of Eve's leave-taking is that, both at the
beginning and the end of his description, the narrator says that all
who saw her wished that she would stay (43, 62–63). Yet he also
says that Eve "sat retir'd in sight" (41). Since neither Raphael nor
Adam bid her stay, they do not notice her leaving. Who sees her
then? Who but the narrator who claims to have so many visions?
We observe again how the narrator's comments draw attention to
himself. There are the usual contradictions: his protestation that
he would like her to stay is denied by the fact that he makes her
leave; he indulges, moreover, in a hypocritical paean to the union
between Adam and Eve on the very occasion that he separates
them. He illustrates that, given the choice, he too would rather
sport than philosophize, but, like his Adam, he is not ready yet.
He still has to finish his rationale for the free use of the woman.
The conflict that the narrator here undergoes is one that he will
project onto Satan in Book IX, when the latter is driven to ruin
what he most desires, the peace of paradise and the beauty of Eve:

> the more I see
> Pleasures about me, so much more I feel
> Torment within me, as from the hateful siege
> Of contraries.   (IX, 119–22)

As he plots his justification, the narrator moves Eve about in the same way Adam manages Eve in the plot of the story (the story is only part of the narrator's justification). Adam tells Eve only what he thinks she should know. The narrator deals with her after the same fashion; by removing her now, he decides that Eve is not to hear Adam's *confessio amantis*, addressed to Raphael, and she is not to know of the power that she has over Adam. The poem also gives us here a view of Eve in tragic innocence. She suspects no ill where no ill seems; she trusts Adam. She is not troubled by any question concerning disproportion, about the greater serving the lesser; she herself serves the plants of her garden that "toucht by her fair tendance gladlier grew" (47).

It is Adam who has a problem with the consequences of distinctions between greater and lesser. He raises his dilemma first apropos of the heavens. Raphael disputes with him and concludes that Adam may not reason from analogy to the heavens, because Adam does not know how the heavens work. Instead: "joy thou / In what he gives to thee, this Paradise / And thy fair *Eve*" (170–72). Adam, retreating to "That which before us lies in daily life," tells the story of the making and mating of himself and Eve. The mating, please note, is the end of his account, since it is "the sum of earthly bliss / Which I enjoy" (522–23).

Reading the poem in sequence, we now recall that Eve has also given a version of her first encounter with Adam. In her story, Adam claimed and seized her (IV, 481–91). In Adam's version to Raphael, he led her because "she what was Honour knew" (508). Did she know the honorable thing to do? Or: did she know that Adam did her an honor by approaching her? The equivocation on this point hides Adam's lie, but we can tell the lie by the paradox to which Adam must resort in order to leave shreds of dignity to the woman whom he caused to submit to him: "she what was Honour knew, / And with obsequious Majestie approv'd / My pleaded reason." Words are mere counters and can be forged into artificial combinations, but what kind of deportment can possibly express both obsequiousness and majesty?

Throughout the discourse of Book VIII, Adam's superiority as image and representative of God is taken for granted. Near the end Adam openly admits that he knows himself superior in inward and outward faculties. He looks, as male, more like God than Eve does, for the simplistic reason that he is more powerful, a better expression of "The character of that Dominion giv'n / O're other Creatures" (544–45). The dilemma engendered by this self-regard emerges immediately thereafter: if the attributes of *his* sex single him out for rule, how can the attributes of *her* sex overpower him so? When Raphael replies that Adam ought not to be governed by a mere procreative urge common to all animals, Adam "half-abash't" beats a retreat and changes his position. The mating, which he has earlier called "the sum of earthly bliss" is now put below the sweetness and amiability of Eve's daily conduct. But Adam adds: "Yet these subject not" (607). It is not the social harmony but that other part of their union, the mating, that conquers Adam's sense of self. Why should the sense of touch transport him so? Adam finally starts to question the expertise of his instructor and wishes to know from Raphael if angels make love and, if so, how? Do they perhaps make "touch"?

> Bear with me then, if lawful what I ask;
> Love not the heav'nly Spirits, and how thir Love
> Express they, by looks onely, or do they mix
> Irradiance, virtual or immediate touch?   (614–17)

This question, at which Raphael sees red, is embarrassing and apparently not lawful: angelic love is mysterious beyond human comprehension. In both parts of the discourse of Book VIII, Adam's search for a resolution of his dilemma meets with the same answer: since you do not know heaven, you may not reason from analogies to heaven. Raphael, who "can now no more," leaves Adam in "the thick shade" (653) with the consequences of Adam's own assumptions. Adam's pride is a *pre*sumption; its consistent application by Adam (and the narrator) promotes the evil inherent in it.

Deviation in the sequence of the poem, I have argued, is an index to the author's structure. Yet, since *Paradise Lost* offers very many surprises, we may not rush to inferences. We ought at least to find evidence that an element of surprise and the deviation that causes it are repeated in such a way that their cumulative effects force us to an inference or choice. As an example of such a repetition I reintroduce a topic mentioned before: the internal contradiction in the god-in-the-poem, who knowingly mounts an ineffective guard against his enemy. None of his appointed guardians—Uriel, Gabriel, and Raphael—can prevent the advance of Satan,

Sin, and Death. We have noted the excuse the narrator provides on the occasion of Satan's slipping by Uriel: hypocrisy is visible only to an invisible god. Raphael advances a like excuse when he explains why he knows nothing of Adam's creation. He was, at the time of that event, stationed elsewhere to keep Satan in hell. That mission obviously proved a failure, and Raphael adds, by way of apology, that his god does not have to depend on his angels because this deity has other, private and secret, methods. The ineffectiveness of all the angel-eyes of the god-in-the-poem is again and again defended by resorting to a paradox. This god needs no eyes for he can see without them: "from within the golden Lamps that burn / Nightly before him, *saw without thir light* / Rebellion rising" (V, 713–15, emphasis mine). The narrator escapes from the contradiction implicit in his god's ineffective guardianship—a god who winks an eye at evil—by appealing to mystery: an invisible god who sees things in the dark. The narrator's ultimate appeal is his own confusion deified: "There is a Cave / Within the Mount of God, fast by his Throne, / Where light and darkness in perpetual round / Lodge and dislodge by turns" (VI, 4–7).

The principle that Satan advances by hypocrisy is also consistently applied. Uriel is taken in by Satan's expressed desire to know of God's glory through knowledge of God's creation. Uriel finds this reason commendable and enlarges on his own knowledge of divine works (III, 694–735). Raphael's behavior repeats that of Uriel, for Adam takes in Raphael under the same pretext that Satan offered to Uriel: the desire to know in order to glorify God. The patient (Adam) and the doctor (Raphael) suffer from the same disease. Both Raphael and Adam are the narrator's fabrications and are formed to conform to his rationale. At the end of Book IV the narrator is on the horns of a dilemma: the man in his own image, the Adam of his story, is already in trouble because of that mysterious woman in his presence. If Adam were to fall unforewarned, there would be no way for the narrator to allocate responsibility. Hence Adam must be instructed that "thine and of all thy Sons / The weal or woe in thee is plac't" (VIII, 637–38). The Raphael of the story is the embodiment of the narrator's own teaching. Both Raphael and Adam are split off from the same character, the narrator, and illustrate the latter's divided self.[10] Raphael can no more see into Adam's heart than the narrator can see into his own. Note, however, a singular surprise in a pattern of deviations: no one is blamed for not detecting Satan because Satan is a hypocrite, but when Satan plays the hypocrite with Eve, she is blamed for being taken in.

The foregoing observations amount to a mere sketch of the double structure of *Paradise Lost* that emerges when we play off the narrator's sequential rendering against those correspondences and contrasts that come into view if we observe rather than believe what happens in the text. I add one last touch and point to the particular ironies in the contradiction between Adam's stated reason for a companion and the actual place assigned to her. Adam argues that perfect equality is needed for a harmonious relationship; otherwise inequality will soon make companionship "tedious" (see VIII, 383–89). Yet throughout his other arguments, Adam assumes that his companion is not equal. This paradox in Adam may explain why he is, in contrast to Eve, so eager to talk to Raphael: Adam has not had a chance to exercise his intellectual power with his inferior, Eve. It may also explain why Eve chooses to be alone and indulges in Book IX in a "Desire of wandring" that Adam calls "strange" (IX, 1135–36). It is not so strange, if we remember that Eve had been left to wander the day before, during Adam's quest for knowledge.

Eve does not eat of the tree until events have prompted her. She is effectively on her own at the end of Book VIII. She has heard the angel's parting words to Adam: "thine and of all thy Sons / The weal or woe in thee is plac't." Eve and her daughters have become the instrument for, not a part of, Adam's scheme of things. It is Adam's conduct that infects Eve, and I believe Milton meant to annotate this when the voice compares the serpent of the garden to the serpentine changes of Hermione and Cadmus (IX, 505–06). In that mythological tale, the husband becomes a serpent first and effects the same transformation in his wife by embracing her. Adam abuses the power of knowing; when Eve tries to match him, Adam subjects her. The fall in Book IX does not change love into lust; it reveals what love has been all along—a lust that begets the divided god of love and power, whose "higher" knowledge begets those concepts of justice and mercy that make his strength seem lawful. The son of Belial divides strength from beauty in order that strength can suborn beauty; he cannot accept beauty in his own being, for the fear of not-being drives him to the desire of having.

IV

In a deceiving poem that illustrates deception as self-deception we should heed the mention of clouds, coverts, bowers, shades, and mists. Milton as author is the "sovran Planter" of the poem-garden, who "fram'd / All things to mans delightful use." He wanted us to be free in it, so that we may-must choose. His description of the "blissful Bower" (IV, 690–719) is especially duplicitous. It is a place "wrought / Mosaic," of "rich inlay / Broiderd, . . . more colour'd then with stone / Of costliest Emblem." Hidden sexuality is hinted at in the reference to Apollo's laurel and the myrtle of Aphrodite: "the roof / Of thickest covert was inwoven shade / Laurel and Mirtle";

> In shadier Bower
> More sacred and sequesterd, though but feign'd,
> *Pan* or *Silvanus* never slept, nor Nymph,
> Nor *Faunus* haunted.

The next allusion anticipates (1) the snare in the advice that Raphael gives Adam, (2) Adam's folly in solving rather than revering the riddle in his image of Eve, and (3) Eve's revenge on Adam's presumption of authority:

> the genial angel to our Sire
> Brought her in naked beauty more adorn'd,
> More lovely than *Pandora*, whom the Gods
> Endowd with all thir gifts, and O too like
> In sad event, when to th' unwiser Son
> Of *Japhet* brought by *Hermes*, she ensnar'd
> Mankind with her fair looks, to be aveng'd
> On him who had stole *Joves* authentic fire.   (712–19)

The consideration of the poem as verbal heterocosm turns it into an arcanum that invites us to apply the alchemist's motto, *Solve et Coagula.* The study of the blind poet's monument asks that we consider its orthography, the multiple possibilities in its latinate or unusual grammar and syntax, and the interplay of its patterns of biblical, historical, cosmological, and mythological allusions. The narrator is the hero-anti-hero of *Paradise Lost*, that is, the "foreconceited" narrative voice is the device by which the action of the poem unfolds; the conflicts between heaven and hell, Adam and Eve, are the symbolic reenactments of the struggle within the narrator. The poem has therefore two plots: one is the narrator's explicit plotting, his way of telling the story; the other is Milton's plotting of the narrator's performance. Milton has plotted a rich inlay of structures: his poem is the verbal reconstruction of a blind man's experience through the seasons of the year, the days of the week, and the hours of the day.

Paradise Lost is Milton's judgment on his contemporaries and his message for aftertimes. Through his poem Milton executes the roles of poet, prophet, and priest; his poem is the mediatorial sacrifice in which he has effaced himself. Invisible behind his poem, Milton, by means of his chosen narrator, tempts us in order that we may taste the fruit and know good by evil. *Paradise Lost* is a strategically arranged device. And it may be said of Milton's way with the reader what Milton said of God's way with man: he does not make "that will evil which was before good, but the will being already in a state of perversion, he influences it in such a manner, that out of its own wickedness it either operates good for others, or punishment for itself, though unknowingly, and with the intention of producing a very different result."[11]

Now that my argument has reached so egregious a summit, I must repeat that it is contrived and implies, at every twist and turn, the counterarguments by which it may be dismantled. Yet it manages perhaps to set off the duplicity of the text as well as our inability to draw a sure line between Milton's conscious intention and involuntary purpose. The case I have presented is a written approximation of a technique used in teaching students to whom the usual identification of Milton with the voice of *Paradise Lost* seems altogether obvious. The method sometimes helps them to care for the details of the text, to experience afresh the provocations of the poem, and to see how remarkably it coheres as the developing portrait and performance of its narrator, who exists only in a manner of speaking.

Drew University

NOTES

I am indebted to Peter M. Wetherill's discussion of sequence and deviation in *The Literary Text* (Berkeley, 1974). Quotations from *Paradise Lost* follow the text as edited by John T. Shawcross in *The Complete English Poetry of John Milton* (New York, 1963). I owe a special debt to Joseph A. Wittreich, Jr., for restoring a neglected portrait of Milton through *The Romantics on Milton* (Cleveland, 1970).

1. Some notable readers of Milton have found it problematical. Shelley observes: "Milton so far violated all that part of the popular creed which is susceptible of being preached and defended in argument, as to allege no superiority in moral virtue to his God over his Devil" (Wittreich, *Romantics on Milton*, p. 535). James Holly Hanford finds in *Paradise Lost* "unresolved contradictions . . . which have persistently suggested that he [Milton] was divided against himself on the

fundamental issues which the poem presents." *John Milton, Englishman* (New York, 1949), p. 174.

2. Robert H. West, *Milton and the Angels* (Athens, Ga., 1955), pp. 38–42, 175–85.

3. "Th' *Aonian* Mount" alludes to both Mount Helicon and the horse Pegasus, who stamped his foot there and so created the Hippocrene spring. After Pegasus threw off Bellerophon, the horse flew on to Olympus and there carried the thunderbolts for Zeus. Cf. VII, 3–4: "above th' *Olympian* Hill I soar, / Above the flight of *Pegasean* wing."

4. Cf. *Christian Doctrine*, in *The Works of John Milton,* ed. Frank Allen Patterson et al. (New York, 1931–38), vol. XV, pp. 300–01. Hereafter cited as CM.

5. Hans Küng, *Justification,* trans. Thomas Collins, Edmund E. Tolk, and David Granskou (New York: Nelson, 1964), p. 262.

6. Cf. Frances A. Yates, "Queen Elizabeth as Astrea," *Journal of the Warburg and Courtauld Institute,* X (1947), 67.

7. Shelley: "The distorted notions of invisible things which Dante and his rival Milton have idealised, are merely the mask and mantle in which these great poets walk through eternity enveloped and disguised" (Wittreich, *Romantics on Milton,* p. 537).

8. The verses following IX, 999, introduce a new millenium: "Earth trembl'd from her entrails, as again / In pangs, and Nature gave a second groan."

9. James Joyce, *Finnegans Wake* (New York, 1939), p. 92.

10. The splitting up of a self-divided will into separate characters is repeated in the interplay between Michael and Adam in Books XI and XII. The same feature also accounts for the conflict in heaven. The Father is the projection or image of the narrator's starting point: will amid primordial confusion. This image explodes into two mirrors: the Son and Satan. The Son is one-half of the Father's self-image, crystallized at that moment when the Father's determination makes darkness visible by calling up Light. Satan and the Son are thus twinned images of the Father. The Son reflects the Father's (and the narrator's) ideal image of control: harmony between freedom and authority; Satan reflects the real consequences of that image: tyranny that leaves no freedom but to break one's bonds. This vicious cycle cannot be broken by any instrument devised by the narrator's logic. The key is in that Word which the narrator consistently denies by proclaiming his own word as oracle; the key is Christ, whose name is never once voiced throughout Milton's poem.

11. *Christian Doctrine,* CM, XV, pp. 72–73.

THE HEBRAIC INFLUENCE UPON
THE CREATION OF EVE
IN *PARADISE LOST*

Cheryl H. Fresch

SCHOLARS FREQUENTLY question Milton's ability as a Hebraist. The conclusions reached by Harris Francis Fletcher,
the first major researcher of Milton's Hebrew studies, continue to
be scrutinized.[1] Kitty Cohen opened her recent study of Milton's
Hebraism (*The Throne and the Chariot,* 1975) by agreeing with
Fletcher's major conclusions: "The question of Milton's knowledge of Hebrew and usage of Buxtorf's Rabbinical Bible is no
longer controversial.... He certainly was a hebraist in the old
sense, that is, a Hebrew scholar."[2] More recently, however, Leon-
ard Mendelsohn has been able to reach a different conclusion:
"Although some of his material was ultimately from rabbinic
sources, Milton did not, and in all likelihood could not, read the
rabbinic commentators."[3]

What Mendelsohn and Cohen and others concerned with Milton's Hebrew learning also disagree about, therefore, is the source
of the poet's knowledge. Mendelsohn, for example, wondered if
the "phrase books and lexicons and glossaries" Milton accused
Salmasius of using could have been among Milton's own sources.[4]
Controversial as these questions about Milton's Hebrew sources
and his scholarship are, not to be disputed is the fact that Hebrew
phrases, attitudes, themes, and motifs abound in his poetry and
prose.

As to the actual effect and overall significance of this Hebraic
influence even upon the major poem, *Paradise Lost,* scholars have
not yet agreed. Sister Mary Irma Corcoran (*Milton's Paradise with
Reference to the Hexameral Background,* 1945) minimized the
importance of the Hebraic influence upon *Paradise Lost.* She
stressed that Milton "rejected much Jewish exegesis," and concluded that when he did incorporate Hebraic elements into the
epic, these elements were merely "dissociated bits of narrative"
used for "amplification" of the Genesis story.[5] And although

181

Cohen insisted upon the importance of recognizing the Hebraic element in the sensuous love shared by Adam and Eve, she nonetheless maintained that Milton's Hebraism is more evident in his concern with "the description of the moral forces underlying man's soul" than with psychological realism in characterization.[6]

Cohen explained that her interpretation of the effect and significance of the Hebraic influence upon the presentation of Adam and Eve in *Paradise Lost* is opposed to the view J. M. Evans had advanced (*"Paradise Lost" and the Genesis Tradition*, 1968). In independent studies published in the late sixties, both Evans and Harold Fisch endeavored to describe the basic difference between Christian and Hebrew exegesis of Genesis, and their conclusions were very similar. Evans claimed that "while the Christian Fathers were generally more interested in interpretative questions, the Rabbis . . . tended to concentrate more on . . . narrative problems." In his chapter "The Jewish Interpretation" he insisted that "it is obvious that the literal meaning of the Biblical text took pride of place, and that as a result the story's narrative problems received more attention than its interpretative or metaphysical difficulties."[7] Fisch's essay ("Hebraic Style and Motifs in *Paradise Lost,*" 1967) stressed the very same point: "While the hexameral tradition represented by DuBartas, Pererius, and a host of Christian authorities early and late had emphasized the metahistorical region of theogony and eschatology, the Hebraic tradition had emphasized the quotidian, the concrete, and the historically visualizable aspects of the story."[8]

Among the most "concrete" and "historically visualizable aspects" of the Genesis story is the creation of Eve. The following study of three specific events in Milton's version of the creation of Eve, in relationship to relevant passages in the writings of the three major theological traditions, supports the distinctions formulated by Fisch and Evans. More importantly, however, it indicates that the humanizing effect of the Hebraic influence upon *Paradise Lost* is assuredly of more than minor significance. The three incidents to be examined are Adam's request for a mate (VIII, 357–436), his sleep during the creation of Eve (VIII, 452–77), and his first words at the presentation of Eve, "This turn hath made amends" (VIII, 491).[9]

I

The motif of the request, as J. M. Evans noted, was "first put forward by the Rabbis and Dracontius," and it is of central importance in the popular Hebrew exegesis of Genesis.[10] The midrash on Genesis ii, 18, reads, "Said he [Adam], 'Every one has a partner, yet I have none': thus, *But for Adam there was not found a help meet* for *him!*"[11] Rashi, the eleventh-century rabbi who continues to be acknowledged as the "commentator *par excellence* of both the Bible and the Talmud,"[12] incorporated that comment into his annotation on the same verse: "When He brought them, He brought them before him male and female of each and every kind. Thereupon he said: all these have a mate, but I have no mate!"[13] Milton's Adam may not address his God as indignantly as did the Adam of the Hebrew tradition, but the same motive prompted both men to speak. Adam asks for Eve because he is lonely and because his lonelines prevents his happiness and his contentment: "In solitude / What happiness, who can enjoy alone, / Or all enjoying, what contentment find?" (VIII, 364–66).

Milton's sensitive concern with the psychological bond between a man and a woman is seldom to be found in the remarks of any Christian theologians. It is, instead, in the Zohar that it is written, "The blessing of the Lord is found only when there is a happy communion of man and woman." Similar aphorisms are scattered throughout the writings of the Hebrews: "A wife is the joy of a man's heart." "Whatever blessing dwells in the house comes from her."[14]

Corcoran supplied yet another important midrashic remark on Genesis ii, 18, which also contributes to a sharper understanding of the Hebrew attitude toward the marriage of Adam and Eve: "*It is not good.* It was taught: He who has no wife dwells without good, without help, without joy, without blessing and without atonement."[15] But the importance of this interpretation is diminished in Corcoran's presentation because it is inserted between two highly theoretical ones by Philo and St. Thomas Aquinas about the metaphysical necessity of the creation of Eve, as if all exerted equal control over Milton's account of the request for Eve. It is true, of course, that Milton's Adam argues, as did Philo and St. Thomas, that God is perfect and is therefore one, but because man is not perfect, he needs to "solace his defects" by associating with other humans (415–26). Milton's Adam, however, is not so much a philosopher or a theologian as he is a lonely man, a much more intelligent lonely man than was Rashi's Adam, but still a lonely man.

It is appropriate to note in passing that, in this conversation between God and Adam, Milton's characterization of God also appears to have been influenced by Hebrew legends attending the Genesis narrative. Yahweh, who was said by the Hebrews to have laughed heartily at the sight of Sammael riding upon a cam- el, now smiles at the nervous effrontery of Milton's Adam and teasingly encourages his extended rationalization of his desire for a companion.

The midrash in which the lonely Adam confronts God with his displeasure, "Every one has a partner, yet I have none," con- tinues, "And why did He not create her for him at the begin- ning? Because the Holy One, blessed be He, foresaw that he would bring charges against her, therefore He did not create her until he expressly demanded her."[16] God, being omniscient, knew Adam would accept the forbidden fruit from Eve and knew Eve would therefore be involved in Adam's sin. If God had pre- vented Adam's loneliness by bestowing Eve upon him immedi- ately, God could have been accused of ultimate responsibility for the Fall.

Without referring to this midrashic account, Leon Howard and Dennis Burden have studied the logical necessity of Adam's re- quest for Eve in *Paradise Lost.* Howard's essay established paral- lels between Milton's *Artis logicae* and the epic:

God made Adam

just and right,
Sufficient to have stood, though free to fall;   [III, 98–99]

and in this freedom lay the chief difference between man and the Creator in whose image he had been formed. Adam himself identified it through his own self-knowledge as a "deficience" (VIII, 416) in his nature and was praised by God for recognizing it (VIII, 437 ff.). Briefly, it was an inability to be satisfied by himself, a lack of self-sufficiency as Tillyard has aptly called it, which was

the cause of his desire
By conversation with his like to help
Or solace his defects.   [VIII, 417–19]

It was this lack of self-sufficiency, this need for companionship, which led to the creation of Eve, who, in turn, provided the "procatarctic" cause (operating from without) or "occasion" for the fall.[17]

Dennis Burden's more generalized remarks about the logical imperative directing much Biblical exegesis are as applicable to the above remark from the midrash as to the request passage in *Paradise Lost:*

The Bible was Christian history and so was necessarily rational because
God was rational . . . and so any snags or difficulties that the Bible narrative provided had to be smoothed out into reason and system. This was
indeed where the opportunity and skill of much Biblical commentary
lay. The commentary was often enough logical in essence since the
concern was with the rationality of the book and with the purposes of
God. The Bible had to be saved on occasion from apparent inconsistency
and self-contradiction in order to save God from apparent arbitrariness
and absurdity.[18]

Behind the charming external similarity between the God of the
Hebrews, who laughed at Sammael, and Milton's God during the
dialogue with Adam in Book VIII, then, there is an essential identity—the need to be just and inculpable—which explains more
than just a deity with a sense of humor. Adam's request accomplished the same two purposes for Milton and the Hebrews: it
humanized Adam and glorified God.

Catholic exegetes never adopted the Hebrew tale in which
Adam asks for a mate. Ambrose's reaction to Genesis ii, 18, indicates the direction in which the early Fathers moved in their
quest to make Genesis reasonable: "If, therefore, the woman is
responsible for the sin, how than can her accession be considered
a good? But, if you consider that the universe is in the care of God,
then you will discover this fact, namely, that the Lord must have
gained more pleasure for Himself in being responsible for all creation than condemnation from us for providing the basis for sin.
Accordingly, the Lord declared that it was not good for man to be
alone, because the human race could not have been propagated
from man alone. God preferred the existence of more than one
whom He would be able to save than to have to confine this
possibility to one man who was free from error."[19]

Like the Hebrews, Christian commentators such as Ambrose
also pondered the connection between the naming of the animals
and the creation of Eve. Ambrose concluded that the animals were
brought to Adam so "he would be able to see that nature in every
aspect is constituted of two sexes: male and female. Following
these observations, he would become aware that association with
a woman was a necessity of his lot."[20]

In *De Genesi ad litteram* Augustine made explicit the hint of
rancor that had lurked within Ambrose's explanation of the necessity for the creation of Eve. Augustine hypothesized that if woman
had not been necessary for reproduction, it would have been
much better if Eve had never been created: "Qunto enim congru-

entius ad convivendum et conloquendum duo amici pariter quam
vir et mulier habitarent?" ("Indeed how much more suitable for
living and conversing could two friends have dwelled together
than a man and a woman").[21]

Centuries later, Aquinas' consideration of the creation of Eve
in *Summa theologica* reveals how influential the opinions of Ambrose and Augustine had been in establishing the traditional Catholic understanding of the reason for the creation of Eve. The precise issue on which Aquinas was deliberating was "whether the
woman should have been made in the first production of things":

God foresaw that the woman would be an occasion of sin to man. Therefore He should not have made woman.
    On the contrary, It is written (Gen. ii. 18): *It is not good for man to
be alone; let us make him a helper like to himself.*
    I answer that, It was necessary for woman to be made, as the Scrip-
ture says, as *a helper* to man; not, indeed, as a helpmate in other works, as
some say, since man can be more efficiently helped by another man in
other works; but as a helper in the work of generation.[22]

Obviously, in the Catholic hexameral tradition the creation of
Eve was regarded as a matter of destiny—not desire. She supplied a
means of reproduction for Adam; she did not satisfy a psychological
need. Adam, who had not asked for her, was obliged to accept her.
Speaking as a Protestant, Milton attacked these views; the interpretation of Genesis ii, 18, argued in the *Tetrachordon* anticipates
Milton's dramatization of the "married state" in *Paradise Lost:*

Som would have the sense heerof to be in respect of procreation only:
and *Austin* contests that manly friendship in all other regards had bin a
more becomming solace for *Adam*, than to spend so many secret years in
an empty world with one woman. But our Writers deservedly reject this
crabbed opinion; and defend that there is a peculiar comfort in the married state besides the genial bed, which no other society affords.[23]

Although most of Milton's Protestant peers probably did reject
Augustine's "crabbed opinion," their glosses on Genesis ii, 18–20,
reveal a somewhat unsettled understanding of Adam's need for
Eve. In *The Instruction of a Christian Woman* Vives argued that
Adam's psychological welfare prompted God to declare it was not
good for him to be alone: "After that God the Prince and maker of
this excellent worke, had brought man into this worlde, he
thought it unconvenient to leave him all alone and so joined to
him a living creature, moste like unto him of minde shape: with
whose conversation and compenable wordes, he might sweetly

spende his time, and also because of generation, if it pleased him. And indeed wedlock was not ordained so much for generation, as for certain company of life, and continual fellowship."[24] But Vives' emphasis upon Adam's emotional need for Eve is not typical of the Protestant glosses on this passage.

Some Protestant exegetes could be accused of hedging in their annotations on Genesis ii, 18–20. In the 1651 *Annotations Upon All the Books of the Old And New Testament,* the gloss on "It is not good" is a list: "That is, first, not so profitable for increase: Secondly, not so comfortable for a man's self. . . . Thirdly, not so conformable to the community of living creatures, who as male and female sort together for the increase of their kind: Fourthly, not so honourable for the Creator" The emphasis upon procreation is lost, however, when "help meet for him" is considered: "As graceful in his sight above other creatures, and grateful to him both as a companion in the comforts of life, and as a partner for the propagation and increase of mankind."[25]

Weemse's explanatory notes on the same passages create a similar problem: "It is good for man not be alone, for the propation of mankinde: but it is good for man to be alone, in respect of that, *quod bonum utilie vocamus*, that is, when hee hath the gift of God to abstaine, for the kingdome of God, *Matth.* 19. that he may the more exercise himselfe in these holy duties of prayer, and other religious exercises." "The woman was made a helper to the man. This helpe stands in three things. First, in *religion*, I Pet. 3. 7. *Take heed that yee jarre not, lest Satan hinder your prayers*, he is speaking to the man and wife here: such a helper was *Priscilla* to *Aquila, Acts* 18."[26]

As might be expected, however, the majority of the Protestant exegetes simply accepted the views of Calvin and Luther. The misogynistic passages so frequent in the hexaemeral writings of the Catholic Fathers are absent from the Protestant examinations of Genesis, but the majority of the Christians agreed that Eve was created not because Adam needed a solace for his loneliness, but because the world needed to be peopled. On Genesis ii, 18, Calvin commented, "Moses now explains the design of God in creating the woman; namely, that there should be human beings on the earth who might cultivate mutual society between themselves. . . . The commencement, therefore, involves a general principle, that man was formed to be a social animal."[27] Calvin's "mutual society" permits an emotional dimension to the relationship between Adam and Eve, but it was to develop *subsequent* to the creation of

Eve—Adam's need for "mutual society" did not precede the creation of Eve.

Discussing the meaning of Genesis ii, 18, in his *Lectures on Genesis*, Luther made no allowance for the development of an emotional bond between Adam and Eve. He insisted that Adam had no personal need for Eve:

My answer is that God is speaking of the common good or that of the species, not of personal good. The personal good is the fact that Adam had innocence. But he was not yet in possession of the common good which the rest of the living beings who propagated their kind through procreation had. For so far Adam was alone; he still had no partner for that magnificent work of begetting and preserving his kind. Therefore good in this passage denotes the increase of the human race.[28]

From the pulpits of the most illustrious seventeenth-century English preachers echoed that basic interpretation of the first marriage, of Adam's need for Eve, which had been set forth by Luther and Calvin. Jeremy Taylor proclaimed, "The preservation of a family, the production of children, the avoiding fornication, the refreshment of our sorrows by the comforts of society; all these are fair ends of marriage and hallow the entrance.... But of all these the noblest end is the multiplying children."[29]

When Donne spoke on Genesis ii, 18, he too was the voice of orthodoxy:

For, upon the first, will be grounded this consideration, that in regard of the *publique* good, God pretermits *private*, and particular respects; for, God doth not say, *Non bonum homini*, it is not good for man to be alone, man might have done well enough so; nor God does not say, *non bonum hunc hominem*, it is not good for *this*, or that *particular* man to be alone; but *non bonum, Hominem,* it is not good in the *generall,* for the *whole frame of the world,* that *man should be alone,* because then both Gods purposes had been frustrated, of being glorified by man here, in this world, and of glorifying man, in the world to come; for neither of these could have been done, without a succession, and propagation of man; and therefore, *non bonum hominem,* it was *not good, that man should be alone.*[30]

John Halkett's analysis of the Protestant concept of marriage in *Milton and the Idea of Matrimony* offers support for the judgment, based on the foregoing explications of Genesis ii, 18–20, that in the Protestant tradition it was generally agreed that Eve was created for the sake of procreation. Halkett's thesis refutes the conclusions William and Malleville Haller had presented over thirty years ago:

For it is not accurate to assert [as did the Hallers] that the primary end of matrimony according to the Puritans was the consolation of loneliness. . . . as a matter of fact there is evidence not only that the Puritans held otherwise, but also that there was little distinction between Puritan and Anglican on this point. Puritan preachers saw matrimonial ends in very much the same light as Anglican preachers. The objects presented were inevitably the same. . . . The objects were procreation, the avoidance of vice and mutual solace.[31]

Certainly, no major Protestant exegete can be found who believed that Adam requested or, as the Hebrews would have it, demanded a companion. Joseph Hall, familiar with Hebrew, was, in fact, very outspoken in his objection to the popular Hebrew gloss, and few of his fellow Christians would have disagreed with him:

I do not find, that man, thus framed, found the want of a helper. His fruition of God gave him fulness of contentment; the sweetness which he found in the contemplation of the new workmanship, and the glory of the Author, did so take him up, tht he had neither leisure nor cause of complaint. If man had craved a helper, he had grudged at the condition of his creation, and had questioned that which he had: perfection of being.[32]

A specie is defined or identified by noting its similarities to and differences from other species. The specie can be biological or literary; the process of identification is no different. When Milton's lonely Adam explains to God his need for "fellowship . . . fit to participate / All rational delight," he provides the evidence needed for identifying the nature of his being. In this passage Adam strongly evinces the direct and powerful influence the most fundamental Hebrew reading of Genesis had upon Milton. Furthermore, and in a larger sense, it was the basic and common urge toward demystification, toward realization of the human aspects of Biblical history, that established this sympathetic link between *Paradise Lost* and the popular Hebrew understanding of Genesis.

II

A reconsideration of Adam's sleep (VIII, 452–77) against the background of the three major hexaemeral traditions again discloses the ultimate importance of the standard Hebrew explanation of Genesis, to which, of course, many knowledgeable Christian scholars felt obliged to respond. The pattern of relationships that appears, however, is unlike that which evolved during the study of Adam's request. Although Milton's version of the sleep of

Adam again establishes an emphasis not typical of Christian exegesis, it endeavors, perhaps more vigorously, to contradict the
main tenet of the Hebraic exegesis of Genesis ii, 21.

In the gloss on Genesis ii, 18, in Andrew Willet's very popular
Hexapla, Adam is said to have "slept, and thought nothing" while
Eve was created, but very shortly thereafter Willet also explains
that although Adam was unconscious during the creation of Eve,
he was able to understand her origin in him. Adam's sleep was an
ecstasy during which divine knowledge was instilled into him:
"We doe think, that as this was a sound, heavie, or deep sleepe of
the bodie, or the soule of Adam was in an *ecstasis* or trance,
beeing illuminated by God, as it may appeare by this, that when
he awaked, he knew that the woman was taken out of him."[33]

Primarily because they need to explain how Adam knew Eve
had derived from him, many Catholics and Protestants emphasized,
as Willet had, the extraordinary nature of Adam's sleep. Calvin
avoided a detailed discussion of the manner in which the information was conveyed to Adam, but stressed the fact that Adam was
made to understand:

It is demanded whence Adam derived this knowledge, since he was at
that time buried in deep sleep. If we say that his quickness of perception
was then such as to enable him by conjecture to form a judgment, the
solution would be weak. But we ought not to doubt that God would make
the whole course of the affair manifest to him, either by secret revelation
or by his word. . . . Moses does not indeed explain by what means God
gave them this information; yet; unless we would make the work of God
superfluous, we must conclude that its Author revealed both the fact itself
and the method and design of its accomplishment.[34]

In his explanation that Adam's sleep was an ecstasy, Augustine used metaphor to steer through the deep waters Calvin would
later shun. According to Augustine, Adam's mind, once ecstati-
cally freed from his body, left the scene of the creation of Eve,
and, as it were, entered the divine presence. When Adam awakened, the prophetic wisdom he had so effortlessly assimilated
streamed forth almost autonomously:

Ac per hoc etiam illa extasis, quam deus inmisit in Adam, ut soporatus .
obdormiret, recte intellegitur ad hoc inmissa, ut et ipsius mens per extasin
particeps fieret tamquam angelicae curiae et intrans in sanctuarium dei
intellegeret in novissima. Denique evigilans tamquam prophetia plenus,
cum ad se adductam mulierem suam videret, eructuavit continuo, quod
magnum sacramentum commendat apostalus: *hoc nunc os ex ossibus.*

[Therefore for this reason that ecstasy, which God sent into Adam, so that drowsy he might fall asleep, is correctly understood as sent for this purpose—that his mind through ecstasy might as it were participate in the angelic company and entering into the sanctuary of God it might understand the latest things. At last awaking, as it were, full of prophecy, when he saw his wife coming to him, he immediately spoke forth that great mystery the apostle records: *this now is bone of my bone*.][35]

With a footnote reference to these passages from Augustine and Willet, as well as from Cornelius à Lapide to be examined shortly, Corcoran stated, "many authorities, prompted perhaps by the Greek use of the word ἔκστασις to designate the sleep of Adam, construed this slumber as an ecstasy in which Adam witnessed the making of Eve."[36] This statement is simply not true. To be mysteriously filled with the knowledge of the creation of Eve is not to witness that creation, and the difference is a crucial one. To witness the creation of Eve is to see a wound in Adam's side, to see blood streaming from that wound, and to see a bone slowly reshaped by the hands of God into the loveliest creature in Eden. Milton's Adam reports that he saw

> the shape
> Still glorious before whom awake I stood;
> Who stooping op'n'd my left side, and took
> From thence a Rib, with cordial spirits warm,
> And Life-blood streaming fresh: wide was the wound,
> But suddenly with flesh fill'd up and heal'd;
> The Rib he form'd and fashion'd with his hands;
> Under his forming hands a Creature grew,
> Manlike, but different sex, so lovely fair,
> That what seem'd fair in all the World, seem'd now
> Mean.   (VIII, 462–73)

The uniqueness of Adam's vision of the creation of Eve in *Paradise Lost* must not be disregarded. Adam's "Cell of Fancy," his "internal sight" does not figuratively slip away to some otherworldly place, nor is it mysteriously illuminated so Adam can be made to understand Eve's birth. Heaven is too high for Milton's Adam; on earth he and his internal sight remain. Adam is permitted to see the vividly literal creation of Eve, and understanding follows, as does also love.

To be sure, Cornelius à Lapide, unlike Willet, Calvin, and Augustine, did indeed argue that Adam's "mind's eye" *witnessed* the creation of Eve ("ut videret ea quae gerebantur"), but he also accorded equal importance to the role of the prophetic spirit that permitted Adam's divinely elevated mind to know the significance of the mystery he had witnessed ("et spiritu prophetico cognosceret mysterium per ea significatum"):

Pro *soporem* hebraice est חרדמה *tardema*, id est gravem et profundum somnum, quem Symmachus χαρον, LXX. melius ἐκστασιν vertunt, unde patet, non tantum somnum hic Adae immissum esse ad hoc, ne sentiret costam sibi detrahi, itaque exhorresceret et doleret; sed etiam simul cum somno eum raptum esse in ecstasim mentis, que mens eius non tantum naturali modo soluta et libera erat a corporis et sensuum functionibus, sed et divinitus ita elevabatur, ut videret ea quae gerebantur, et spiritu prophetico cognosceret mysterium per ea significatum: videret, inquam, mentis oculis costam sibi eximi, et ex ea Evam formari: atque per hoc significari matrimonium, tum suum naturale cum Eve, tum mysticum Christi cum ecclesia.

[The Hebrew for sleep is חרדמה *tardema*; it is a deep and heavy sleep, which Symmachus translated χαρον, the Seventy better translated ἐκστασιν; whence it is clear, not only was sleep sent upon Adam at this time so that he would not feel the rib withdrawn from his side, and therefore not be terrified and suffer pain, but also at the same time with sleep he was taken into an ecstasy of mind and his mind not only was released from its natural limit and freed from the functions of body and senses but it also was lifted up by God so that it might see what was being done and could understand by prophetic spirit the mystery thereby signified: so that he might see, I say, with the eyes of the mind the rib being removed from him and Eve being formed from it: and by this marriage is signified, first his natural marriage with Eve, then the mystical marriage of Christ with the Church.][37]

It is true that Milton's Adam does more than observe and therefore understand. If it is a prophetic spirit that permits Cornelius à Lapide's Adam to understand the natural and mysterious marriages presaged by Eve's creation, it is a prophetic spirit that speaks in Milton's Adam: "for this cause he shall forgo / Father and Mother, and to his Wife adhere" (VIII, 497–98). But, it must be noted, Genesis was the only sacred source Milton recognized, and in Genesis ii, 24, Adam prophesies. Moreover, in these accounts of Adam's experience by Milton and Cornelius à Lapide, the emphases are exactly reversed. What Milton's Adam prophesies is of secondary importance in the narrative compared to what sparks the prophecy and what Adam's emotional reaction is to the newly created Eve. Milton's foremost concern in this sequence, as in the request sequence, was to demystify and to humanize the Genesis narrative.

A certain concern with the concrete and literal details of the creation of Eve is nevertheless evident in Cornelius à Lapide's gloss. Adam's sleep was not only ecstatic but anesthetic; the sleep was induced to prevent pain and fear which naturally would accompany the removal of a rib. Such references to this anesthetic aspect of Adam's sleep are frequent.[38] Willet's comment on Genesis ii, 21, for example, continues, "And this was done (Adam sleeping rather than waking) both that neither Adam's sight might be offended, in seeing his side to be opened, and a ribbe taken forth, nor yet his sense of feeling oppressed, with the griefe thereof, which was not only by sleepe mitigated, but by the power of God concurring with the ordinary meanes."[39] In John Swan's *Speculum mundi* Willet's explanation is quoted almost verbatim.[40] So too, Bishop Hall concluded that "the Lord God had cast man into a deep sleep or ecstasy, that he might not be sensible of what he suffered."[41] Indeed, one wonders why Hall even mentioned ecstasy for he insisted, "As man knew not while he was made, so shall he not know while his other self is made out him: that the comfort might be greater, which was seen before it was expected." Hall went on to disclose an unexpected concern for the emotional relationship between Eve and her future husband that is not present in any of the above remarks on Adam's sleep: "If the woman should have been made, not without pain, or will of the man, she might have been upbraided with her dependence and obligations. Now she owes nothing but to her Creator: the rib of Adam sleeping, can challenge no more of her than the earth can of him."[42]

Calvin considered the anesthetic purpose of Adam's sleep by immediately dismissing a somewhat similar psychological consideration: "The deep sleep was sent upon Adam, not to hide from him the origin of his wife, but to exempt him from pain and trouble."[43] Endeavoring to explain the purpose of Adam's sleep, Calvin began, as did many Biblical commentators, by rejecting the erroneous interpretations of earlier theologians. It was a standard Hebrew gloss of Genesis ii, 21, to which Calvin was alluding when he argued that the deep sleep had not been sent "to hide from him the origin of his wife." The Hebrew story also illuminates Hall's analysis of Adam's sleep.

In the midrash a conversation between a matron and Rabbi Jose is reported. The woman explained to the Rabbi that she "wished to understand . . . why Adam had to be asleep when Eve was created. Surely God's action would not have brought him pain."

"The reason was," said the Rabbi, "that had Adam seen the woman in a state of incompletion, he would have been displeased with her."

"You are quite right," said the matron. "And furthermore it required a surprise to call forth his love for her. I once cherished the hope that I might marry the brother of my mother, but he went away and married a woman said to be less charming. Doubtlesse he knew me too well."[44]

This explanation of Adam's sleep also appears in Rashi's commentary: "*And He Closed Up* the place where it was cut. *And He Slept And* then *He Took* in order that he should not see the piece of flesh out of which she was created for she might be despised by him."[45]

At this point Dennis Burden's observation about the logical imperative controlling biblical commentary is again helpful. Applied to the results of this survey of the Hebraic, Catholic, Protestant, and Miltonic interpretations of Adam's sleep, the demand to make the Bible reasonable or to "justify the ways of God to men" appears to have sent most interpreters in one of two directions. (1) The sleep was a surgical anesthesia that made Adam insensible to bodily pain, but it was also an ecstasy that permitted his soul to be divinely illuminated and prophetically inspired. (2) The sleep was a surgical anesthesia that made Adam insensible to bodily pain, but it was also an emotional anesthesia that prevented Adam from being repelled by Eve because of her humble origin and offensive birth. Hence, Adam was either an extraordinary man granted prophetic power by divine influence, or he was an ordinary man with a queasy stomach and an equally sensitive view of romantic love.

It is Milton's Adam, however, who demands that new categories be devised. Milton minimized the mystery of Adam's prophecy only to emphasize the details of his visual experience during Eve's creation: his interpretation coincides with neither the traditional Hebrew nor the traditional Christian readings. Yet, without the Hebrew explanation of Adam's sleep as a foil, the important uniqueness of Milton's achievement would be but dimly visible.

Referring to the jealousy which prompts both Rashi's Eve and Milton's Eve to give the apple to Adam, Harold Fisch pointed out "the emphasis is all on realistic human motivation."[46] This very same emphasis dominates the Hebraic and Miltonic elaborations of Adam's sleep, but after considering Genesis ii, 21, with the same criterion in mind, they arrived at different conclusions. Milton's Adam witnesses the creation of Eve, and he finds it awesome and wonderful. He sees a bloody bone reshaped into Eve, and he loves her. The Hebrews, on the other hand, insisted that had Adam seen the gory birth of Eve, it would have destroyed the possibility of love. The final difference in their accounts develops simply because Milton believed a philosophical notion could be as powerful a determinant of human behavior as was a nervous stomach:

> O *Adam*, one Almighty is, from whom
> All things proceed, and up to him return,
> If not deprav'd from good, created all
> Such to perfection, one first matter all,
> Indu'd with various forms, various degrees
> Of substance, and in things that live, of life.   (V, 469–74)

III

The final point in this consideration of the Hebraic influence upon the creation of Eve in *Paradise Lost* is Adam's first statement to God upon awakening: "This turn hath made amends" (VIII, 491). Corcoran pointed out that the remark "corresponds to the apparently similar interpretation of *hac vice*" in the *Quaestiones celeberrimae in Genesim* of a seventeenth-century French monk, Marin Mersenne. This particular correspondence, Corcoran suggested, was only one point of contact establishing a larger connection between Milton and Mersenne: "In these lines [VIII, 491–99], Milton used the device of Mersenne in casting the ecstatic delight of Adam upon his reception of Eve into the form of a greeting to his first human companion. Although both writers used key phrases from Genesis, they also have other phrases in common, the 'part of my soul' of Milton's Adam echoing the *pars mea* of Mersenne, and the 'this turn hath made amends' by which the Adam of *Paradise Lost* signified his satisfaction at the gift he had received in place of the rib taken from his side corresponds to the apparently similar interpretation of *hac vice* by the commentator."[47]

It should be noted, however, that fifty years before Mersenne's commentary appeared, another Frenchman had similarly described Adam's first response to Eve:

> . Now, after this profound and pleasing Traunce,
> No sooner Adams ravisht eyes did glaunce
> On the rare beauties of his new-come Halfe,
> But in his heart he gan to leape and laugh,
> Kissing her kindly, calling her his Life,
> His Love, his Stay, his Rest, his Weale, his Wife,
> His other-Selfe, his Helpe (him to refresh)
> Bone of his Bone, Flesh of his very Flesh.[48]

Nevertheless, one would be wise to avoid hastily concluding that the greeting was original with DuBartas for, as Frank Robbins cautioned, "imitation is commoner in this branch of literature [hexaemeral writings] than in almost any other, and the majority of the Hexaemera are consequently lacking in originality."[49]

When Milton's Adam assures God, "This turn hath made amends," he does indeed recall the *hac vice* in Mersenne's commentary. The French monk's phrase, however, is merely a vestige of a traditional Hebrew gloss on the story of the creation of Eve. The midrash on Genesis ii, 21, begins when the woman questioning Rabbi Jose about the creation of Eve asks,

"Why did God find it necessary to send a deep sleep upon Adam and remove his rib by stealth to create woman?"

"Do you call it stealth," asked the Rabbi, "when one takes away an ounce and returns a pound?"[50]

The echo of this interview is but momentary and muted in Book VIII of *Paradise Lost,* and perhaps it lacks the larger significance of the other two incidents studied in this essay. But it appears that Milton was as aware of the anecdote as were some other Protestant leaders who were acquainted with the Hebrew readings of Genesis. After discounting one of Rabbi Jose's answers to the matron, Calvin revealed his sympathy with the other: "The deep sleep was set upon Adam, not to hide from him the origin of his wife, but to exempt him from pain and trouble, until he should receive a compensation so excellent for the loss of his rib."[51] Bishop Hall concluded his consideration of the creation of Eve with a prayer of thanksgiving that also more than slightly recalls Rabbi Jose's reply to the inquisitive matron: "O God, we can never be losers by thy changes, we have nothing but what is thine: take from us thine own, when thou wilt, we are sure thou canst not but give us better."[52]

IV

It therefore appears that when the standard Hebrew interpretations touched Milton's version of the creation of Eve, the effect was a consistent impulse toward the humanization of Adam and Eve. This accords with Harold Fisch's explanation that the Hebrew influence upon *Paradise Lost* is revealed in the "domestic" narrative, as opposed to the epic narrative, and that this low style is marked by "quotidian realism."[53] To associate this low style exclusively with the description of postlapsarian human weakness, as Cohen has, is to miss the major significance of Milton's achievement in the presentation of Adam and Eve.[54] He, and the Rabbis before him, sought to demonstrate the kinship between ordinary humanity and those first two people in the garden. Milton and the Rabbis believed loneliness and the love that ends loneliness have always remained very much what they were even in Eden. This similarity does not corrupt prelapsarian love any more than the humanization of Adam and Eve taints their prelapsarian purity. The similarity quite simply implies that humanity is not always as far from paradise as it seems and furthermore that the way back may very well be through love.

University of New Mexico

NOTES

1. Harris Francis Fletcher, *Milton's Semitic Studies and Some Manifestations of Them in His Poetry* (Chicago, 1926) and *Milton's Rabbinical Readings* (Urbana, 1930). Cf. George N. Conklin, *Biblical Criticism and Heresy in Milton* (New York, 1949); Robert M. Adams, *Ikon: John Milton and the Modern Critics* (Ithaca, 1955).

2. (The Hague, 1975), pp. 2–3.

3. "Milton and the Rabbis: A Later Inquiry," *SEL*, XVIII (1978), 125.

4. Ibid., p. 134.

5. (Washington, 1945), p. 126.

6. Cohen, *The Throne and the Chariot*, p. 5.

7. (Oxford, 1968), pp. 22, 48.

8. In *Language and Style in Milton*, ed. Ronald David Emma and John T. Shawcross (New York, 1967), p. 41.

9. *Paradise Lost*, in *Complete Poems and Major Prose*, ed. Merritt Y. Hughes (New York, 1957). All subsequent quotations from *Paradise Lost* are from this edition.

10. Evans, *"Paradise Lost,"* p. 259.

11. *Midrash Rabbah*, ed. Rabbi Dr. H. Freedman and Maurice Simon (London, 1939), p. 136. Hereafter cited as *Midrash*.

12. Fisch, "Hebraic Style," p. 35.

13. *Pentateuch with Targum Onkelos, Haphtaroth and Prayers for Sabbath and Rashi's Commentary*, trans. Rev. M. Rosenbaum and Dr. A. M. Silbermann in collaboration with A. Blashki and L. Joseph (London, 1946), pp. 11–12.

14. *The Talmudic Anthology*, ed. Louis Newman (New York, 1947), p. 539.

15. Corcoran, *Milton's Paradise*, p. 60; *Midrash*, p. 132.

16. *Midrash*, p. 136.

17. " 'The Invention' of Milton's 'Great Argument': A Study of the Logic of 'God's Ways to Men,' " *Huntington Library Quarterly*, IX (1945), 160.

18. *The Logical Epic: A Study of the Argument of "Paradise Lost"* (Cambridge, 1967), pp. 3–4.

19. *Paradise*, trans. John J. Savage (New York, 1961), p. 326.
20. Ibid., p. 328.
21. *De Genesi ad litteram libri duodecim*, bk. 9, pt. 5, ed. Josephus Zycha, in *Corpus scriptorum ecclesiasticorum Latinorum*, XXVIII (Prague, 1894), p. 273.
22. *Summa theologica*, quest. 92, article 1, object. 2, trans. Fathers of the English Dominican Province (London, 1922), pp. 274–75.
23. *Tetrachordon*, in *Complete Prose Works of John Milton*, ed. Don M. Wolfe et al. (New Haven, 1953–), vol. II, p. 596.
24. *A Very Fruitfull and Pleasant Booke Called the Instruction of a Christian Woman*, trans. Richard Hyrde (London, 1585), pp. 180–81.
25. *Annotations Upon All the Books of the Old and New Testament*, 2d. ed. (London, 1651). The annotations on the Pentateuch were prepared by John Ley.
26. John Weemse, *The Portraiture of the Image of God in Man*, 2d. ed. (London, 1632), pp. 280–81, 178.
27. *Commentaries on The First Book of Moses Called Genesis*, trans. Rev. John King (Edinburgh, 1847), vol. I, pp. 128–29.
28. *Lectures on Genesis*, in *Luther's Works*, ed. Jaroslav Pelikan (Saint Louis, 1958), vol. IV, pp. 115–16.
29. Sermon XVII, "The Marriage Ring," in *The Whole Works*, ed. Reginald Heber, rev. Charles Page Eden (1847–1854; rpt. New York, 1970), vol. IV, p. 215.
30. Sermon XVII, in *The Sermons of John Donne*, vol. II, ed. George Potter and Evelyn Simpson (Berkeley, 1955), pp. 336–37.
31. (New Haven, 1970), pp. 13–14.
32. *Contemplations upon the Principal Passages in the Holy Story*, in *Works of Joseph Hall*, ed. Philip Wynter (1863; rpt. New York, 1969), vol. I, pp. 12–13.
33. *Hexapla in Genesis* (London, 1605), p. 37.
34. Calvin, *Commentaries*, p. 133.
35. *De Genesi*, bk. 9, pt. 19 (p. 294).
36. Corcoran, *Milton's Paradise*, p. 61. Corcoran also refers to Moses Barcephas, a ninth-century Syrian bishop whose works I have been unable to examine.
37. *Commentarii in Sacram Scripturam* (London, 1865).
38. Corcoran, *Milton's Paradise*, p. 61.
39. Willet, *Hexapla*, p. 37.
40. *Speculum mundi*, 4th ed. (London, 1698), pp. 451–52.
41. *A Paraphrase upon the Hard Texts of the Whole Divine Scripture*, in *Works*, ed. Philip Wynter, III, 10.
42. *Contemplations*, p. 13.
43. *Commentaries*, p. 133.
44. *Talmudic Anthology*, pp. 264–65.
45. *Pentateuch*, p. 12.
46. Fisch, "Hebraic Style," p. 58. J. M. Evans has also commented on the jealousy motivating Eve: "There can be no doubt that this shrewd insight into her character is ultimately of Jewish origin" (*"Paradise Lost,"* p. 281).
47. Corcoran, *Milton's Paradise*, pp. 73–74. The phrase "part of my soul" is not found in Adam's initial greeting to Eve. It is found in Eve's version of Adam's speech as he pursued her through Eden (IV, 498).
48. DuBartas, *Bartas: His Devine Weekes and Workes*, trans. Joshua Sylvester, intro. Francis C. Haber (1605; facsimile rpt. Gainsville, Florida, 1965), p. 226.

49. *The Hexaemeral Literature: A Study of the Greek and Latin Commentaries on Genesis* (Chicago, 1912), p. 2.

50. *Talmudic Anthology*, pp. 264–65.

51. *Commentaries, p. 133.*

52. *Contemplations, p. 13.*

53. Fisch, "Hebraic Style," p. 56. Also see Harold E. Toliver, "Milton's Household Epic," in *Milton Studies*, IX, ed. James D. Simmonds (Pittsburgh, 1976), 105–20. Toliver argues that the importance accorded the human story of Adam and Eve "is part of Milton's conscious resistance to chivalric epic on behalf of Puritan and domestic values" (p. 105).

54. Cohen, *The Throne and the Chariot*, p. 96.

DRAMATIC STRUCTURE AND
EMOTIVE PATTERN IN THE FALL:
PARADISE LOST IX

rising emotion

Marshall Grossman

THE OPENING lines of *Paradise Lost* IX warn us that the curve of action is now to turn downward, that we have reached the dramatic climax promised in the poem's opening proclamation of a tragic and then a restorative movement.[1] Close examination of Book IX shows that its "tragic notes" are projected in various ways. Besides the narrator's explicit proclamations and the surface story he tells, we have the deeper psychological movement—the poetically controlled alteration of Adam's and Eve's perception of Eden. This perception is at first one of fecund harmony, as expressed by Eve:

> This Garden, still to tend Plant, Herb and Flour.
> Our pleasant task enjoyn'd, but till more hands
> Aid us, the work under our labour grows,
> Luxurious by restraint; what we by day
> Lop overgrown, or prune, or prop, or bind,
> One night or two with wanton growth derides
> Tending to wilde. (IX, 206–12)[2]

But Eden becomes what Adam calls "these wilde Woods forlorn" (IX, 910), an alien place in which to hide from heavenly presences:

> O might I here
> In solitude live savage, in some glade
> Obscur'd, where highest Woods impenetrable
> To Starr or Sun-light, spread thir umbrage broad,
> And brown as Evening: Cover me ye Pines,
> Ye Cedars, with innumerable boughs
> Hide me, where I may never see them more. (1084–90)

The distance which the poetry of Book IX must cover is not between the abstract concepts of innocence and guilt; it is the distance between the feelings presented in these opposed perceptions of Eden, or in Adam's and Eve's terms, "the world." Focusing attention on several representative passages will make it possible

201

to trace the curve of this movement from happiness to sorrow, from fertility to barrenness, and to illustrate the emotive values that give the narrative its poetic validity. An understanding of the emotive strategies employed in Book IX should in turn provide some insight into Milton's method of characterization and his elaboration of the narrative throughout the poem.

I

The decorum of Book IX is distinctly dramatic. The action is confined to Eden from beginning to end. On this stage we find three characters in four combinations: Satan alone, Adam with Eve, Satan with Eve, and Eve alone. The narrative action comprises a narrator's prologue (1–47), Satan's entrance and soliloquy (48–191), a domestic agon between Adam and Eve (205–411), the temptation of Eve by the serpent and her soliloquy (471–833), the temptation of Adam by Eve (834–1045), and an open-ended agon between the now fallen Adam and Eve (1046–1189). The narrator appears throughout these scenes providing choral comment and stage directions. The book can be seen as a "closet drama" in which the unities are observed. The restriction of the action to such well-defined segments in time, all occurring in the same place and among the limited number of characters, contributes to the tense atmosphere of tragic inevitability. In this respect Book IX stands in sharp contrast to the rest of *Paradise Lost*, which "soar[s] above the Aeonian mount," traversing cosmic distances in short poetic spaces. The classic five-act structure operates in two specific ways: it associates itself with the reader's memory of classical drama, its heroes and themes; and it makes available to Milton the strategies and techniques for dramatic representation that the ancients developed within the form. In effect it provides a style answerable to the poem's needs.

One of the major themes of *Paradise Lost* is certainly that of human limitation. The Fall itself embodies our first parents' unfortunate attempt to transcend their merely human understanding. The poem is precise about the nature of human knowledge and its limitations: Adam and Eve are empiricists. Lacking the intuitive intellection of the angels, they know only what they can deduce or infer from direct observation and divine revelation. Their happiness in the garden depends upon their faith in revelation. To remain happy, they must refrain from any attempt to test revelation empirically, to bring it within their specifically human precincts. Adam's empiricism and its limitations are made clear to him (and the reader) in Book VIII when Raphael rebukes him for his astronomical speculations. The angel warns Adam not to confuse appearance and essence: "That Great / Or Bright inferrs not Excellence" (VIII, 90–91). Adam is to use his empirical wisdom, "for Heav'n / Is as the Book of God before thee set, / Wherin to read his wondrous Works" (VIII, 66–68), but he must remember that, despite its efficacy when properly used to interpret Adam's earthly kingdom, his wisdom will prove ineffective in probing what "the great Architect / Did wisely to conceal" (VIII, 72–73). Any attempt to constrain the divine will, or its revelations, within human conceptual range might well be answered with the words Abdiel uses to answer Satan's arguments: "Shalt thou give Law to God, shalt thou dispute / With him the points of libertie, who made / Thee what thou art" (V, 822–24).

When Adam and Eve eat the forbidden fruit, they expect to be released from their temporal limitations and to know good and evil essentially, as the angels know it. (Though the vagueness of Eve's understanding leads her to confuse the acquisition of knowledge with the acquisition of power—a confusion common among gnostics). Of course the knowledge actually conferred upon them by the fruit is empirical and appropriate to the intellectual constitution God had chosen for them. Thus the Father explains the irony:

> O Sons, like one of us is Man become
> To know both Good and Evil, since his taste
> Of that defended Fruit; but let him boast
> His knowledge of Good lost, and Evil got,
> Happier, had it suffic'd him to have known
> Good by itself, and Evil not at all.   (XI, 84–89)

Adam and Eve know evil by doing it, and learn that it is simply the negation of good.

Adam and Eve fall because they forget the divine world of essences that informs this temporal world of appearances. The dramatic structure of Book IX invites the reader's participation in a similar forgetting. We know that Adam and Eve will fall on this day, just as we know that Oedipus will encounter his father on the road to Thebes. Yet we wish for a warning voice as the narrator did when Satan entered the garden (IV, 1). We concentrate our attention on the human act "That brought into this World a world of woe" (IX, 11), and, perhaps, we forget that Adam and Eve are not alone and helpless—that there is recourse beyond their strained intellects—and thus we repeat the tragedy of man.

The stage of Book IX is walked by man and the devil. Even before the Fall, it is quite like our world. Adam and Eve appear domestic; the angels retire from the scene. When man and devil meet, "this world of woe" is formed. This is the narrative action that Milton dramatizes. The dramatic structure translates this action into an emotive pattern. The specific details of this pattern and its interaction with the discursive narrative surface will become apparent as each "act" of the "drama" is examined.

II

The narrative action begins with the fiend's entrance into Eden. The narrator stresses the physical reality of Eden by offering geographical details about the river Tigris and locating the Tree of Life.[3] Satan emerges from a fountain near the Tree of Life, "involv'd in rising Mist" (75). The wreaker of destruction, then, makes a shrouded entrance into human life at its very root. "Involv'd" was and is a word rich with connotations, most of which are relevant in this context. Its contemporary definitions included "to wind a spiral form or in a series of curves, coils, or folds; to wreathe, coil, entwine," and "to roll up within itself, to envelop and take in; to overwhelm and swallow up."[4] Thus this simple word evokes images of the movement of the snake (see Satan's description of the snake climbing the Tree of Knowledge, IX, 589–93), self-absorption, and Satan's dual nature as a villain destined to be his own downfall.

The sexual connotations of Satan's entrance at the root of the Tree of Life fit the conceptual scheme of pollution of the generative process and enable the reader to relate the devil's activity in the garden to the felt experiences of his own life. Jackson Cope's suggestion, that "the choice of sexuality as the chief image of evil at crucial points in *Paradise Lost* was no personal or merely traditional accident, but perhaps the most important single stroke of unifying genius in the epic," is well taken as regards the frank phallicism of Satan's appearance in Book IX.[5] Previously, we have heard Adam speak of his passion for Eve and we have heard the narrator's celebration of the prelapsarian expression of physical love. The sensual pleasure of sexuality has been linked with the spiritual values of procreation and completion (VIII, 419–27), but the eroticism that attends Satan in Book IX, even before his incarnation in the traditionally phallic snake, foreshadows the degeneration of love into lust that will follow the Fall. We have seen lust earlier in the epic in the parodic Sin and Death episode where the shrill drama of seduction and abandonment deflates Satan's heroic pretensions. Here, however, the effect is more sinister because it links the fallen reader with the devil and anticipates the tragedy that befalls us as it overtakes Adam and Eve. The reader recognizes Satan's sensuality as simultaneously consistent with the reader's fallen experience, yet obscene and alien in the prelapsarian garden. He observes the intrusion of his world into the better one he has lost.

Satan's role as an instrument of nongeneration is antithetical to that of Adam and Eve as progenitors of their species (and of course to God's infinite creativity). Satan himself substantiates the narrator on this point:

> For onely in destroying I finde ease
> To my relentless thoughts; and him destroyd,
> Or won to what may work his utter loss,
> For whom all this was made, all this will soon
> Follow, as to him linkt in weal or woe,
> In wo then; that destruction wide may range.   (129–34)

Similarly, Adam and Eve frequently refer to their expectation of "more hands" and the narrator describes Satan, in the snake, seeking "where likliest he might finde / The onely two of Mankinde, but in them / The whole included Race, his purposd prey" (414–16). Thus, the imagery of Satan's entrance into Eden reflects the great clash of creative and destructive principles underlying the entire poem. The final lines of the verse paragraph introduce Satan's soliloquy and continue the metaphoric realization of Satan as a negative correlative to procreation. "Thus he resolv'd, but first from inward griefe / His bursting passions into plaints thus pour'd" (96–97). The culmination of his passion, following his penetration at the root of the Tree of Life, is a painful implosion.

When Satan speaks we see some of the points in the narrator's introduction dramatized. The narrator indicates that Satan is "irresolute" (87) at times and grief stricken. When the fiend speaks for himself the reader is able to discern his inner state more precisely. Satan's position in the cosmos of *Paradise Lost* is unique. He is an archangel who has rejected the telos represented by the Godhead. Now he exists as a creature who retains much of his former awareness, but lacks rational control over his passions. He is, in effect, condemned to be their slave and to possess an exquisite awareness of his enslavement. Having rejected the order of Divine Providence, Satan constantly projects alternate realities out of his own desires; these he sees through almost as he creates them. His processes of thought and abstraction are shaped by his commitment to subjectivity.[6] In his soliloquy Satan runs through a series of impressions of Eden, quickly rejecting each one and replacing it with an alternative impression. Thus he exults in the beauty of Eden, "O Earth, how like to Heav'n, if not preferr'd" (99), only to wear himself down to the despair and degradation objectified in the shape and behavior of the snake (163–77). The shaping factor that moves Satan's language along this path is a series of suppositional statements structured "if . . . but."

After his initial exultation at seeing God's work in the garden, Satan remembers his mission and, trapped in his infernal nature, soon drifts off into "what might have been":

> If I could joy in aught, sweet interchange
> Of Hill and Vallie, Rivers, Woods and Plaines,
> Now Land, now Sea, & Shores with Forrest crownd,
> Rocks, Dens, and Caves; but I in none of these
> Find place or refuge; and the more I see
> Pleasures about me, so much more I feel
> Torment within me, as from the hateful seige
> Of contraries; all good to me becomes
> Bane, and in Heav'n much worse would be my state. (115–23)

He is far too aware, however, to resist the despairing "but" that cancels his hopes. This is one of the points that differentiates degrees of fallenness in *Paradise Lost*. Satan often sees through his own rationalizations and gets at the truth while less expert sinners only replace one rationalization with another.[7]

The syntactic shape of Satan's speech reflects his consciousness, as well as his place in the conceptual framework of the narrative. The conditional mode of thought ascribed to Satan is generally shared by postlapsarian human beings. Thus the reader recognizes his own fallen uncertainties in the thought patterns of the devil.

These thought patterns can be related to the conceptual and epistemological constraints of the fallen state. When Satan denied the supremacy of God, he denied reality. The objective power and goodness of the deity is overthrown not in heaven but in the fallen sensibility, which must replace it with fantasy. The fantasies of the fallen mind are unstable, however, persisting only until reason or the evidence of the senses undermines them. Without recourse to objective fact, which Satan has negated at the nihilistic insistence of pride, he is doomed to oscillate forever between the "ifs"

and "buts" of his profligate fancy. The pattern is poignantly established by Satan's first words in the poem, when his recognition of
Beelzebub is tempered by his recognition of their fall: "If thou
beest he; But O how fall'n!" (I, 84).[8] Moreover, the pattern of
restless dissatisfaction resulting in the multiplication of fanciful
hypotheses that comprises Satan's soliloquy may be correlated
with the experience of most readers who, at one time or another,
find themselves similarly testing and rejecting their interpretations of reality. Indeed the inability of the human mind to come to
rest is part of the universal experience which fall myths are intended to explain. Thus the fiction begins with observed human
experience and points to its origins in the consequences of the
Fall. To make that fall credible, the consequences that we associate with it are shown operating in its original victim.

In making this point I am simply restating the ancient definition of art as a mimesis of life.[9] Yet we may perhaps understand, in
this light, Millicent Bell's conviction that Adam and Eve do not
really fall in the dramatic climax of *Paradise Lost*. Bell feels that
Milton does not present a "prime cause" to motivate the Fall and
that therefore, "instead of asking what caused the Fall, Milton was
preoccupied . . . in employing the somewhat intractable legend to
characterize the state of fallen Man—Man as he knew him."[10] Bell
is referring to Adam's and Eve's act of disobedience rather than to
Satan's fallen condition. But in both the presentation of the fallen
state and the motivation of man's first disobedience, it is difficult
to see how the poem could be based on anything other than observation of fallen man. Yet it is, like all great art, also projective,
metaphoric in the sense that it extends outward from a known
term (human experience) to suggest the outlines of an unknown
term (prelapsarian existence). By making our present subjectivity
contiguous with Satan's past, Milton interprets human experience
using the materials at hand. Any understanding of the Fall, or
justification of God's ways to man, that is credible in emotional
terms must begin with a close study of man in the fallen condition.
Answering the question of why man fell, insofar as it can be
answered, must start with the fact that man fell. From the experience of fallen man Milton deduced that Satan fell because he
misunderstood his relationship to God, because he believed that
the absolute could be approached by aggregating increments of
power, and because he confused appearance and essence. Once
he rebelled, these errors became intrinsic to his fallen state. Divorced from God's "correction," Satan was doomed to be no better

than he was. The Fall of Man, as we shall see, is similar. In other words, the conditions observable after the Fall are the institutionalization of the error made before it—that man or angel can stand alone; the cause is deduced from its effect.

What should be understood with respect to the so-called antecedents of the Fall is that they serve dramatically to emphasize the presence of the contingent. As J. B. Savage has shown, Adam and Eve "maintain their freedom by ensuring the conditions on which it depends, by resisting the possibilities that are inimical to it."[11] The errors or near errors that they blunder into, while remaining on the better side of sin, give point to the seriousness of the divine charge; they indicate how the inaction of remaining obedient can, of itself, refine their natures until they are "improv'd by tract of time" (V, 498). The risk of error is a necessary part of the education of Adam and Eve. By approaching, yet resisting sin, they grow into greater spirituality; however, their prelapsarian errors necessarily appear simple to postlapsarian readers: "The Fall must have the effect of revising our notion of the events preceding it, of causing us to see them in relation to itself, of making us aware for the first time of the essential historicity of things."[12]

The relationship of the explicit theme and the implicit characterization we find in *Paradise Lost* is, I think, that suggested by Susanne Langer in her remarks on the achievement of "organic form" in the drama:

It is true that tragedy usually—perhaps even always—presents a moral struggle, and that comedy very commonly castigates foibles and vices. But neither a great moral issue, nor folly inviting embarrassment and laughter, in itself furnishes an artistic principle; neither ethics nor common sense produces any image of organic form. Drama, however, always exhibits such form, it does so by creating the semblance of a history, and composing its elements into a rhythmic single structure. The moral content is thematic material, which, like everything that enters into a work of art, has to serve to make the primary illusion and articulate the pattern of "felt life" the artist intends.[13]

Although Langer is writing of stage drama, I see no reason why her argument should not apply to *Paradise Lost* IX as well. In choosing the highly dramatic structure he used in this book, Milton perhaps exhibited considerably more wisdom than those critics who attempt to reduce this poem to theological statement imposed upon a mechanical style.

The conclusion of Satan's soliloquy draws together many of the motives that adhere to the fiend:

> O foul descent! that I who erst contended
> With Gods to sit the highest, am now constraind
> Into a Beast, and mixt with bestial slime,
> This essence to incarnate and imbrute,
> That to the hight of Deitie aspir'd. (163–67)

The relationship between Satan and the snake is clearly realized; his incarnation suffers from the inevitable comparison with the nobler incarnation depicted in Book XII. Although Satan considers his entry into the snake a foul descent, we may remember that he has risen quite laboriously from hell to execute his mission. His entry into man's world will pull man down along the poem's narrative axis and necessitate the incarnation of the Son which raises man up the higher. Satan's image of revenge that "Bitter ere long back on itself recoiles" (172) foreshadows this event, draws together the shape of the snake and the motion of Satan's "if . . . but" logic, and recalls the narrator's characterization of the soliloquy as an inverted orgasm "but first from inward griefe / His bursting passion into plaints thus pour'd" (97–98). Knowing that he will ultimately suffer the more himself, Satan still attempts to transfer his self-hatred onto the unoffending Adam, "on him who next / Provokes my envie" (174–75). Although the Fall of Man is ultimately a human act, Satan's role as tempter is recognized as significant by the Father (III, 129–31) and must be taken seriously by the reader. The fact that Adam is, for Satan, merely a target of opportunity contributes to the tragic effect of the presentation. As the fatal confrontation of man and devil draws near, the events that mesh to bring them together promote an atmosphere of inevitability that works with the reader's prior knowledge of the plot to involve him emotionally in the approaching climax. Yet at the same time there is a strong element of the accidental or the contingent in the Fall—the motivelessness of Satan's envy, the time of day, Eve's hunger. The effect is simultaneously to invest each act with meaning while maintaining that except for the eating of the fruit the events of Adam's and Eve's day are routine. Perhaps this can best be approached if we consider that Satan had limitless time to effect the temptation. Adam and Eve, though tempted on the particular day depicted in Book IX, were subject, as we are, to continual temptation. Obedience is an act of will; as a pledge of faith, they would have had to uphold it eternally. As the war in heaven of Book VI shows, even had they ascended the scale of nature to become angels, they would still have remained subject to temptation. Thus the tragedy of the Fall, as presented, is a mixture of the inevitable and the coincidental which, like the syntax of Satan's soliloquy, finds its ultimate credibility in the fact that it accords with our experience of life.

III

After Satan enters the snake, the scene shifts to the newly awakened Adam and Eve as the second "act" of the drama begins. In their domestic quarrel, our first parents emerge as clearly recognizable human beings who bear a severe responsibility. As Satan points out, Adam is "though of terrestrial mould / Foe not informidable, exempt from wound, / I not" (485–87).

Adam and Eve reflect this stature by beginning their dispute on a high level, addressing each other with ceremony and debating theological issues intelligently (235–376). But the ideational development of the argument is paralleled by the poetic realization of a man and wife for whom the ideas are secondary to the emotional interaction; Eve, by valuing efficiency over the "looks" and "smiles" she shares with Adam (220–25), challenges the importance of the very thing he considers essential to his existence.[14] As the separation issue becomes a test of their relationship, they become more interested in their effect upon one another than in the substance of the argument (Eve's "I expected not to hear" at line 281 brings this sharply into focus). This does not happen because they are imperfect or somehow already fallen, but because the substance of the dispute is on the level of their emotions. Adam and Eve are not concerned with efficiency, but rather use that issue to explore their love, about which they are experiencing some uncertainty.

The interaction between Adam and Eve overwhelms "right reason" but the ascension of passion over reason occurs by degrees in the course of the dispute, with issues close to the core of their existence at stake. An analogy may be made between Adam's lapse in the separation and the descent of the good angels into militarism during the war in heaven. In both cases there is no sin against God, but there is error in judgment brought about by difficult contexts of decision. Milton gives the argument between Adam and Eve the emotional tension and movement of an incipient domestic quarrel. Along with the ideational context, he provides the tonal movements of exasperation, competitiveness, manipulativeness, and emotional hurt that would usually underlie this sort of confrontation. Adam is more concerned with his relationship to Eve than with their obligation to God.[15] But the error

he makes, and Eve's provocation, fall short of a prematurely fallen
state. They allow passion to overcome reason, but until they act
against God's commandment they are simply wrong, not sinful.
The intellectual equipment God gives them to discern right from
wrong is sufficient. When Adam falls it will be knowingly. But
sufficiency is not a guarantee, and the error of separation allows
the Fall to occur, though it in no way necessitates it. Thus when
Raphael chides Adam for his astronomical speculations, he first
makes clear that the exercise of intellect is not, in itself, wrongful:
"To ask or search I blame thee not" (VIII, 66). The angel warns
Adam against speculation for its own sake, but Adam's concern
with his relationship to Eve obeys Raphael's injunction to "be
Lowlie wise: / Think onely what concernes thee and thy being"
(VIII, 173–74). As empirical creatures Adam and Eve learn by
experience. They are created not immutable, but capable of developing within the context of their situation. The freedom necessary
for this process is the same freedom which permits the error of
separation. In dramatic terms, the fatality of this error is not in the
quarrel but in the reader's apprehension. Like most of us, Adam
and Eve must work at their marriage, even before the Fall.

Eve is created a more sensual creature than Adam. She is
used to observing details and then referring them to him for interpretation, and in the separation scene Adam argues the importance of this collaboration (309–17). When Satan returns to the
stage, he uses his sensual rhetoric to exploit Eve's proper nature.
In the temptation, argument is supplemented by sensual description. The fruit is of "fairest colours mixt, / Ruddie and Gold" (577–
78); the serpent is first attracted by "a savorie odour blow'n, /
Grateful to appetite" (579–80); hunger and thirst are "powerful
persuaders" which "quick'nd at the scent / Of that alluring fruit"
(587–88). Thus the serpent gives the appearance of engaging
Eve's reason with promises of the fruit's magic powers, but first
engages her senses, her appetite, her curiosity to see this beautiful
and savory food and to learn how a snake came to speak. The
superficial appeal to reasoned argument serves only to dramatize
the conflict of reason and passion at the heart of the scene.[16]

Satan's argument begins with the proposition that what works
for a serpent would work for man (691–92). Eve errs in assuming
that she is speaking with a serpent when in fact the words only
appear to issue from the snake. From this deception, Satan begins
to speculate on God's intentions (692–715). The proper response
is, of course, Abdiel's "Shalt thou give Law to God" (V, 822), but

Eve is too absorbed in the curious phenomenon of the talking snake and its flattery to go beyond her habitual empiricism.[17] She forgets that the appearance of a thing may not reveal its essence, and she fails to distinguish nature, which is subject to her inductive logic, from divine command, which is not; but Satan's manipulation is not confined to simple flattering. He uses the conversation he overheard in Book IV (411–39) by paraphrasing Adam's "what ere Death is" (IV, 425) as "what ever thing Death be" (695); thus he puts her off guard by sounding like Adam, as he had previously done in her dream. According to Kathleen Swaim, "Eve's nature is sensual, vain, and submissive but also imitative," and it is true that in her meditation on Satan's argument, Eve repeats his specious syllogisms (747–79).[18] But it should be noted that Satan fashions her sensual, vain, submissive, and imitative responses. Of these characteristics only vanity could be construed as pejorative, and she is vain principally in wanting to be as smart as Adam is, to discourse with superior minds as she has seen Adam do. In sum, Eve's nature is subverted by Satan; as the Father attests, she is deceived but not "self-deprav'd" (III, 129–31). Her fall is presented as believably growing out of her nature, and her error; it presupposes no prior sin or depravity. To attribute Eve's fall simply to a prideful susceptibility to flattery would require a willful abstraction of the temptation scene and a blindness not only to the expertise of her tempter but to the confusions and mitigations, emotional as well as intellectual, which the dramatic presentation draws into a "pattern of 'felt life.' "

Once Eve eats the fatal fruit, the serpent withdraws, leaving her an empty stage on which to soliloquize.[19] The language and structure of Eve's speech are as revealing as were those of Satan's soliloquy. In fact the differences between the two distinguish the sophisticated sinner from the novice and imply a standard by which degrees of "fallenness" may be measured. Like Satan, the newly fallen Eve is alienated from the divine order. She seeks to affirm the empiricism that contributed to her fall by trying to form a new world order based, not on God and faith, but on the tree (i.e. knowledge) and experience (807–17). The thought processes represented in her soliloquy differ markedly from those of the prelapsarian Eve; she envisions herself as an initiate of a new gnostic order. The pattern of participation and interaction upon which divine creation was based is now replaced by a political structure of power and manipulation. For the first time Eve objectifies herself. She plans her appearance and calculates the effect she will promote (816–30). Thus she is separated not only from providential order, but from herself.

Eve's earlier speeches were logically ordered; her soliloquy is moved by free association. She flies from "though secret she retire," referring to wisdom, to "And I perhaps am secret" (810–11), a rationalization aimed at avoiding punishment. Before the Fall, language had been one of the prime factors distinguishing bestial from human life. The now fallen Eve is closer to the brutal state in that her language is no longer the servant of her reason but its master.[20] The change in the structure of Eve's thoughts reflects an acute observation on human life; yet it is made so quietly that the reader is more likely to feel it than to think about it. In this same passage we also see the use of the "fallen" conditional case. The thought that she is "perhaps secret" sends Eve off on a series of fantastic suppositions. But, where Satan's fantasies and rationalizations are stopped by his dismal awareness, Eve's speculations are curtailed by a survival of love:

> Confirm'd then I resolve,
> *Adam* shall share with me in bliss or woe:
> So dear I love him, that with him all deaths
> I could endure, without him live no life.   (830–33)

The lyric close of the soliloquy prevents the reader from becoming completely alienated by Eve's scheming in the lines directly preceding it. Thus Milton maintains a high degree of identification, never letting the reader get too far from his filial relationship to Eve. Eve forgets Adam when she falls, but remembers him immediately after. Even though she considers manipulating him and resolves to bring about his fall, her inability to forget him more than momentarily keeps her from completely falling away from Providence. It is significant that while Eve echoes Satan earlier in the soliloquy, her final lines echo Adam (cf. lines 831 and 269). Her imitation of Satan is a tragic departure, but after her fall she returns as best she can to her original teacher. Had love not stopped Eve's rationalizations and reconnected her with external reality (i.e. Adam), she might presumably have gone on forever in a state of paralyzed fantasy-making. This is the situation after Adam's fall and prior to the intercession of the Son. The dramatic presentation of Eve's temptation and fall thus distinguishes precisely between Satan's "self-depravity" and the increments of error which lead Eve to sin. The careful modulations of rhythm, vocabulary, and syntactic

structure militate against any abstracted or reductive reading of
these events. The poem's effect is to demonstrate the danger of a
quick slide into error, not the willful propensity to sin.

This third "act" of Book IX ends with Eve seeking Adam and
with the Fall of Man well under way. The fourth "act" includes
Eve's confrontation with Adam, his fall, and the redefinition of
their relationship when both are lost.

IV

We know from as early as line 269 ("or with her the worst
endures") that Adam will not let Eve fall alone. The narrator's
preface to Adam's response to her disobedience highlights Adam's
predicament, "First to himself he inward silence broke" (895).
With Eve lost, the still innocent Adam has no one with whom to
interact in the old way. The narrator places him in a poignant
position, at once with his beloved and alone. His words to Eve
place him in a sympathetic light:

> I with thee have fixt my Lot,
> Certain to undergo like doom, if Death
> Consort with thee, Death is to mee as Life;
> So forcible within my heart I feel
> The Bond of Nature draw me to my owne,
> My own in thee, for what thou art is mine;
> Our State cannot be severd, we are one,
> One Flesh; to loose thee were to loose myself.   (952–59)

The plentiful monosyllables and heavy intralinear stops give
the passage a measured pace which emphasizes that Adam, unlike
Eve, falls with considerable appreciation of what he is doing and
why; "he scrupl'd not to eat / Against his better knowledge, not
deceav'd, / But fondly overcome with Femal charm" (997–99).
The emotive value of Adam's fall is complex. We are attracted to
his apparent nobility but we must reject his action. Aristotle pre-
scribes that the hero of a tragedy should suffer not for depravity of
character but rather for a grave error in judgment.[21] If the audience is to feel pity and fear it must first care about the hero.
Milton's presentation is consistent with Aristotelian doctrine.

Arthur Barker correctly locates the error that leads to Adam's
fall not in uxoriousness, but in his failure of faith, "his failure to
believe that Satan can no more win on earth than in heaven."[22]
Yet Adam errs in a dramatic situation that presents him with a
difficult choice in a highly emotional moment. The pattern of a

proper response to that moment can be found in the behavior of the Son who, in Book III, responds to Adam's fall by interceding with the Father.[23] Adam, horrified at the thought of losing Eve, forgets all he knows of the Father's infinite goodness, forgets even that the Father gave him Eve. The reader is left wondering what might have resulted if Adam, instead of joining with Eve in disobedience, had called on the Father to forgive her, acknowledged his responsibility for her action and asked for mercy. At the same time, the reader can see that the Fall arises not from depravity but from error, that Adam's position in its dramatic context is one in which any individual might have fallen. Indeed, the dramatic structure Milton presents answers the argument he proposes: Adam is sufficient to have stood, yet free to fall.

Moreover, Adam's failure is best understood in context with the Son's success. The reader knows that the first Adam's error will be redeemed by the second Adam's sacrifice. Christ's love will provide fallen man with the exemplar through which he may understand and correct Adam's error. The narrative of God's entry into time will thus provide an eternal context within which Christian man can understand the dramatic working out of his everyday life.

Once the Fall is completed, the garden is transformed; Paradise becomes "these wilde woods forlorn." The interaction between Adam and Eve, which had been love, is now transformed to lust:

> For never did thy Beautie since the day
> I saw thee first and wedded thee, adorn'd
> With all perfections, so enflame my sense
> With ardor to enjoy thee, fairer now
> Then ever, bountie of this vertuous Tree.   (1029–33)[24]

Adam's reference to "all perfections" emphasizes the loss of those perfections as sense conquers spirit and right reason and the garden becomes the world. Adam unknowingly poses an opposition between the day he first saw Eve—that is, the day she was created by God—and this tragic day when she is uncreated by the "bountie of this vertuous Tree," and the human drama ensues.

V

In the fifth and final "act" of the drama, Adam and Eve awake after having spent their carnal desires to find themselves trapped in their new consciousness. Before the Fall, Adam and Eve were busy in their garden, preparing for the ultimate ascent described by Raphael. Their mission was to obey and to multiply: "But Man by number is to manifest / His single imperfection, and beget / Like of his like, his Image multipli'd, / In unitie defective" (VIII, 422–25). Now they find themselves without purpose:

> Cover'd, but not at rest or ease of Mind,
> They sate them down to weep, nor onely Teares
> Raind at thir Eyes, but high Winds worse within
> Began to rise, high Passions, Anger, Hate,
> Mistrust, Suspicion, Discord, and shook sore
> Thir inward State of Mind, calme Region once
> And full of Peace, now tost and turbulent:
> For Understanding rul'd not, and the Will
> Heard not her lore, both in subjection now
> To sensual Appetite, who from beneathe
> Usurping over sovran Reason claimd
> Superior sway.   (1120–31)

Their "State of Mind" now resembles the physical conditions of chaos, "tost and turbulent," restlessly subject to contesting passions. The narrator's summary of the internal changes in the pair follows the orthodox theological interpretation of the Fall: reason now serves the appetites instead of the will reason. But even here, the allusion to Psalm cxxxvii (1121), the lament of the exiles from Zion, adds an important nondiscursive note which returns us to the first line of Book IX, where the exile of Adam and Eve is anticipated.

The book ends with Adam and Eve trapped in an agon which cannot be resolved in a world suddenly without objective reality:

> Thus they in mutual accusation spent
> The fruitless hours, but neither self-condemning:
> And of thir vain contest appeer'd no end.   (1187–89)

Since right and wrong are no longer apprehensible to them, and their reason is beclouded by "high winds" of passion, anger, and hate, Adam and Eve will need divine help, prevenient grace (XI, 3), to emerge from their wretched state. Their recognition of this need initiates the cycle of regeneration that completes the epic.

VI

Milton calls upon the holy spirit for inspiration, "What in me is dark / Illumine, what is low raise and support" (I, 22–23), and he asks "Celestial light" to "Purge and disperse" all mists that he "may see and tell / Of things invisible to mortal sight" (III, 54–55), but in the composition of his great epic he does what we all must do; he observes carefully the world about him and he *infers* its causes. His master stroke in characterization is a psychological one: he realizes the intimate connection between one's interpretation of sense data and the internal organization of one's personality. Thus he infers Satan's neurotic personality from his deeds and constructs the theater in which the devil acts from the materials available to his personality. The poem's dramatic structure captures the intricate rhythm of human perception and presents it bare, stripped to its essentials so that it may send the attentive reader back again to St. Paul's assertion of the fallibility of human knowledge, reminding him that "we see through a glass darkly."

The Christian universe Milton portrays is deeply paradoxical. We live in history, yet eternally. Our acts determine the course of history, yet history itself will be abrogated when "The World shall burn, and from her ashes spring / New Heav'n and Earth, wherein the just shall dwell" (III, 334–35). The Fall of Man is tragic, yet it is the *felix culpa* that brings eternity into the temporal world, incarnate as a man among men, and seals the covenant of love which assures the ultimate unity of essence and appearance.

Milton borrows the form of classic drama because he borrows its theme—the strange mixture of accident and fate that seems to direct and shape our lives. But he encloses this tragic form in the atemporal, essentially comic, Christian view of history. To do this Milton must tell us that we are relatively insignificant yet that our acts are crucially important, that our enemy, the devil, is formidable, deadly, yet helpless, doomed to torment and defeat. He can do this because his art is mimetic, drawing its validity from the rhythm of "felt life." He warns us to keep separate the two contexts we live in—human history and Christian eternity—by showing us how we depend on dramatic context, on our immediate situation, when we construct the world we see.

Blackburn College

NOTES

1. Christopher Ricks discusses the significant echoes of the invocation to Book I in the opening lines of Book IX in *Milton's Grand Style* (Oxford, 1963), p. 69.

2. All citations of *Paradise Lost* refer to F. A. Patterson, ed., *The Student's Milton*, rev. ed. (New York, 1946).

3. *PL* IX, 69–76. This motif continues through the verse paragraph which includes references to Maeotis, Ob, the Antarctic, Darien, Orontes, Ganges, Indus, etc. These references establish the large scale of Satan's travels as well as the historical continuity of pre- and postlapsarian earth.

4. *OED*, "involve," 2 and 7.

5. Jackson I. Cope, *The Metaphoric Structure of "Paradise Lost"* (Baltimore, 1962), p. 80.

6. Lee A. Jacobus places Satan's unstable subjectivity within the context of Calvinist dependence on self-knowledge. To know oneself it is necessary to know God; Satan, by denying God, denies himself. See "Self-Knowledge in *Paradise Lost*," *Milton Studies*, III, ed. James D. Simmonds (Pittsburgh, 1971), 104–07; and Calvin, *Institutes of the Christian Religion*, bk. I, ch. 1, par. ii. My purpose here is more concerned with the emotionally credible realization of the doctrine in dramatic poetry, the technique that makes the reader feel the truth by concretizing Calvin's abstraction.

7. On the rationalizations in *Paradise Lost* see Northrop Frye, *The Return of Eden* (Toronto, 1965), pp. 97–98.

8. See Jack Foley, " 'Sin Not Time': Satan's First Speech in *Paradise Lost*," *ELH*, XXXVII (1970), 38.

9. The mimetic basis of Milton's epic is noted by Irene Samuel, "The Development of Milton's Poetics," *PMLA*, XCII (1977), 231–40.

10. "The Fallacy of the Fall in *Paradise Lost*," *PMLA*, LXVIII (1953), 864–65. See also the exchange between Bell and Wayne Shumaker, *PMLA*, LXX (1955), 1185–1203; and A. J. A. Waldock, *"Paradise Lost" and Its Critics* (New York, 1947), p. 40.

11. "Freedom and Necessity in *Paradise Lost*," *ELH*, XLIV (1977), 299.

12. Ibid., p. 300.

13. Susanne K. Langer, *Feeling and Form* (New York, 1953), p. 326.

14. See Arnold Stein, *Answerable Style: Essays on "Paradise Lost"* (Minneapolis, 1953), p. 95. Cf. Dianne Kelsey McColley, "Free Will and Obedience in the Separation Scene of *Paradise Lost*," *SEL*, XII (1972), 104–20. McColley's contention that the separation is a positive step in Adam's and Eve's developing understanding of their relationship and their respective roles is attractive and logically argued, but it seems to me that it ignores the emotions underlying the scene. The reader, knowing what the result of the separation will be, can hardly urge Eve on in her assertion of independence. Further, as I have argued, the tone, diction, and pacing of the dialogue are easily associated with the reader's experience of marital discord in the fallen world. The existence of a strong defense for Eve's behavior, such as that advanced by McColley, strengthens the effect of apprehension by keeping Eve more securely within the reader's sympathetic grasp, but the dramatic context of the argument (and it is an argument) cannot be ignored.

15. See Joseph Summers, *The Muse's Method: An Introduction to "Paradise Lost"* (Cambridge, Mass., 1970), p. 174. On the question of force and its relationship to command, see Anthony Low, "The Parting in the Garden in *Paradise Lost*," *PQ*, XLVII (1968), 30–35.

16. See Kathleen M. Swaim, "The Art of the Maze in Book IX of *Paradise Lost*," *SEL*, XII (1972), 138.

17. Stanley E. Fish, *Surprised by Sin: The Reader in "Paradise Lost"* (New York, 1967), pp. 253–54; and Lee A. Jacobus, *Sudden Apprehension: Aspects of Knowledge in "Paradise Lost"* (The Hague, 1976), pp. 144–66.

18. Swaim, "The Art of the Maze," p. 139.

19. See Jun Harada, "Self and Language in the Fall," *Milton Studies,* V, ed. James D. Simmonds (Pittsburgh, 1973), 215–19.

20. See Fish, *Surprised by Sin,* p. 95.

21. *Poetics,* 1453a. The distinction between depravity and error is maintained in the presentation of Eve as well as Adam.

22. "Structural and Doctrinal Patterns in Milton's Later Poems," in *Essays in English Literature from the Renaissance to the Victorian Age Presented to A. S. P. Woodhouse* (Toronto, 1964), p. 191. See also, H. V. S. Ogden, "The Crises of *Paradise Lost* Reconsidered," *PQ,* XXXVI (1957), 14.

23. See Anthony Low, *The Blaze of Noon: A Reading of "Samson Agonistes"* (New York, 1974), pp. 23–24, 30–31.

24. See Cleanth Brooks, "Eve's Awakening," in *Essays in Honor of Walter Clyde Curry* (Nashville, 1954), p. 295.

OSIRIS AND URANIA

B. Rajan

WHEN RAPHAEL expounds the scale of nature to Adam he
assures him of the possibility of body working up to spirit
in the movement of creative change in paradise. That possibility is
linked to a condition:

> If ye be found obedient, and retain
> Unalterably firm his love entire
> Whose progenie you are.   (V, 501–03)[1]

Adam expresses some surprise at the possibility of disobedience
and of deserting that love which he is counseled to "retain" in
unalterable firmness. Raphael then advises him that God made
him perfect rather than immutable, that obedience lies within the
area of free choice, and that there have already been certain cases
of disobedience. Adam, whose "constant thoughts" continue to
assure him of his commitment to love and obedience, now asks to
hear "The full relation, which must needs be strange" (V, 556).
Raphael then begins his account of the battle in heaven, prefacing
it by the following words:

> High matter thou injoinst me, O prime of men,
> Sad task and hard, for how shall I relate
> To human sense th' invisible exploits
> Of warring Spirits; how without remorse
> The ruin of so many glorious once
> And perfet while they stood; how last unfould
> The secrets of another world, perhaps
> Not lawful to reveal? yet for thy good
> This is dispenc't, and what surmounts the reach
> Of human sense, I shall delineate so,
> By lik'ning spiritual to corporal forms,
> As may express them best, though what if Earth
> Be but the shaddow of Heav'n and therein,
> Each to other like, more than on earth is thought?
>   (V, 563–76)

These lines do not overwhelm one by their poetic power, and
comment upon them has been less than lavish. Hughes and

Fowler, following Newton, cite the beginning of Aeneas' narration to Dido in connection with Raphael's opening phrases. But it is the reference to earth as the shadow of heaven which has attracted the bulk of comment. Fowler's citation is of *Republic*, Book X. Hughes refers us to the *Timaeus* and to Plato's "doctrine of the universe as formed on a divine and eternal model," a doctrine evoked explicitly by Milton in Book VII, lines 555–57. Cicero's interpretation of Plato, which Hughes also quotes, implies that "the world which we see is a simulacrum of an eternal one." Jon S. Lawry, whose book on Milton bears the title *The Shadow of Heaven*, suggests that Raphael's lines contain "an anagogic myth for the existence and meaning of all man's spiritual experience and contemplation. . . . man's individual experience can be seen within the stories of election, fall and creation."[2] The shadow here becomes a shadowing forth.

One does not need to read the passage very searchingly to become aware of the prevarications in it. Raphael first points to the difficulty of making the "invisible" accessible to "human sense." He wonders about the extent to which it is lawful to "unfould / The secrets of another world." The doctrine of forbidden knowledge touched on here is touched on more emphatically in Book VII, lines 167–78. Nevertheless Raphael undertakes to delineate what surmounts the reach of human sense by likening spiritual forms to those corporeal forms which express them best. So far the weight of misgiving is sufficient to suggest that the "likenings" may be less than satisfactory and that their pertinence may be restricted to the injunctions they are designed to exemplify. But then Raphael turns the other way by suggesting not simply that earth may be the "simulacrum" of heaven but also that the likeness between earth and heaven may be greater than terrestrial experience might suggest. It is true that the suggestion ends with a question mark but we need to ask ourselves about the weight of this device. In particular as we look back on Adam's education so far, we need to remember that the final possibility is firmly supported by Raphael's previous description of the scale of nature and more specifically by his account of intuitive and discursive reason as differing in degree rather than in kind and as being the dominant rather than the exclusive characteristic of angels and men respectively.

The simplest explanation will be offered first and for the sake of comfort we shall call it generic. All storytellers indulge in standard flourishes. The task is always hard and language is always inadequate to the event. Nevertheless the task will be undertaken, and as the storyteller commits himself to his enterprise, he begins to think that he may do better at it than his initial cautions suggested. So he poses that possibility, undercutting it prudently by a rhetorical question mark.

Such an explanation is acceptable as far as it goes but few students of Milton will feel that it goes far enough. We can expect the initiating gestures to be in the right style; but we also expect them to direct our attention to something beyond the gestures. Perhaps at this stage we can take up the view that Raphael is something of a fumbler and ask ourselves whether his prevarications put us on notice about his future fumbling. More charitably we can look at the dramatic situation. Raphael has been asked to bring on discourse (V, 233), and his remark about previous disobedience brings it on with a rapidity that finds him unprepared. His reaction is typical of beings other than angels—to say as much as possible while giving away as little as he can. He is uncertain about the extent of his mandate. He wonders if his tactics have not committed him to more disclosure than is really necessary. So he puts it to Adam that the account will be metaphorical, while remaining carefully ambiguous about the eventual status of his metaphors.

In this essay it is proposed to investigate what can be done with a bolder explanation. The suggestion offered is that Raphael's statement is poised between two views of the structure of reality and that these views can be related to and perhaps originate in two views of the nature of language and the possibility of poetry. Both views have substantial roots in Milton's thought. Raphael does not attempt to reconcile them because their reconciliation can only be achieved by the poetic act and may indeed be said to constitute a primary endeavor of that act. The poetic act in turn can be thought of as the mimesis of a larger creative enterprise, a human and historical undertaking for which poetry provides an imaginative model.

Raphael speaks to Adam but he also speaks to an audience which has read Revelation and which is conscious, as Adam cannot be, of links between the Resurrection and the third day of battle.[3] In venturing upon a poem within a poem his difficulties can be representative as well as peculiar to his own task. When he remembers Virgil, that may be a refreshing reminder that angelic problems with language are not very different from human difficulties and that earth even in this sense can be the shadow of heaven. It is also a shadow in the more tragic sense that history on earth repeats history in heaven. It does not seem imprudent to suggest that Raphael is counseling us as well as instructing Adam and that what he says in beginning his poem may have an instructive relationship to what Milton says in beginning and proceeding with the larger poem within which Raphael stands.

Raphael's closing words relate themselves, as we have indicated, to the chain of being which he has already expounded and to that analogical universe in which the chain is a crucial structural component. In a world arranged as metaphor reflected in metaphor, poetry as a metaphor-seeking act becomes an education in the nature of reality. Language invites our confidence in its power of finding. The web of correspondence and the reenactment of structures are assurances of continuity, of our capacity to arrive at "the knowledge of God and things invisible" by an "orderly conning over the visible and inferior creature."[4] These are Milton's words but Adam's are not very different when he speaks of ascending step by step to God "In contemplation of created things" (V, 507–12). Even in the invocation that begins Book III, the natural world is described as one of the entrances not simply of knowledge, but of wisdom, an entrance "quite shut out" (50) by the deprivation of blindness. In *Comus*, Raphael's promise of body working up to spirit is anticipated by the Elder Brother when he speaks of the unpolluted temple of the mind turning by degrees to the soul's essence (461–62). The spiritual marriage of Cupid and Psyche further strengthens our awareness of continuity by liberating rather than repudiating the physical marriage of Venus and Adonis. It is from the higher union that Youth and Joy are born in a fully creative response to natural plenitude. If bearing these and other examples in mind, we return to the nuances of Raphael's wording, the line "Each to other like, more than on earth is thought" takes on additional significance. We are almost being advised that the human imagination perceives a discontinuity greater than the structure of reality warrants.

Continuity, discerned in the ladder of creation, is placed before us in a kind of ontological space. But Milton's universe is not static, as more than one Milton scholar has rightly insisted. The figure of the dance, repeatedly used, celebrates the balance of discipline and energy, order consummated in motion rather than memorialized in stillness. But even the dance remains a figure of pattern. Body working up to spirit, on the other hand, is a figure of process advising us that creative change is part of the perfection of paradise. Michael's sombre exposition of history may seem an unlikely place to look for a renewal of Raphael's promise. Yet Michael in explaining how the law yields to the Gospel does point to a prospective evolution:

> From shadowie Types to Truth, from Flesh to Spirit
> From imposition of Strict Laws, to free
> Acceptance of large Grace.   (XII, 303–05)

The double remembrance of Raphael's phrases in the first line clearly and firmly relates the prelapsarian to the postlapsarian promise. The shadow is a means of finding the light, not a betrayal of the light's nature. We move forward step by step in the continuities of self-renewal as we might have done in a better world where perfecting rather than renewing could be seen as the objective. "Light after light well used they shall attain / And to the end persisting, safe arrive" (III, 196–97) is another version of this measured progress. If earth is the shadow of heaven, the fallen world can be the shadow of paradise and language can be as music is for Thomas Browne, "a hieroglyphical and shadowed lesson of the whole world."[5] Even Michael's statement about progress from the imposition of laws to the free acceptance of grace looks back to Raphael's statement about upward evolution "in bounds / Proportioned to each kind" (V, 478–79). As the kind advances itself, the bounds change their nature. This transposition into historical time of a movement delineated in ontological space is of some importance in Milton's view of the making of order and of the relationship between pattern and process. It also answers to the needs of a poem which can often strive to be both pattern and process, sequential as well as an escape from sequence, discovery at the level of experience and implementation from the cosmic perspective.

A poem can be thought of as an eloquent affirmation of what is known or as a controlled experiment of the imagination in which turbulence is allowed to rage against the endeavors of order so that order can be made more significant by what it subdues. We can also think of a poem as an act of making and finding in which the structure of order is brought into being by the evolving consciousness rather than displayed to us, or tested and maintained under assault. When finding-making involves the recovery of a previous order catastrophically lost, knowledge both in the poem and in the larger undertakings of which it is a model will appear as both discovery and remembrance. A striking affirmation of this principle is the likening in *Areopagitica* of the state of truth to the torn body of Osiris. I have discussed this central and decisive image on a previous occasion,[6] but it is necessary to point out again how the body of truth is recovered fragment by fragment in an individual and collective effort of identification; how the process of recovery will not be completed until the Second Coming; how in an effort of seeking which is coextensive with time and by which creative action in time is therefore characterized, we move forward in a self-advancing endeavor, closing up truth to truth; and how finally, the finished form will be homogeneal and proportional like that Unity of Being which Yeats repeatedly compares to a perfectly proportioned human body.[7] The image can be considered against the background of disputes on religious toleration in the 1640s, which is perhaps to do it less than justice. It can be read more fundamentally as an account of history as a possibly creative enterprise, a magnification of that making-seeking act which is inherent in individual and in collective self-renewal. But the affinities between Osiris and Orpheus suggest that we can also be reading an account of how a poem grows, of how it discovers pattern in its processes, of how it shapes its own history and achieves its fulfillment. The image is not irrelevant as a preface to *Paradise Lost*, and that it should be pertinent is not surprising. If poetry provides us with pleasurable instruction it is not simply in a narrowly didactic sense.

We will return again to the image of Osiris and indeed it is difficult not to be made aware repeatedly of its place in the network of Milton's thought. For the moment, it is sufficient to note that the weight of implication of the image is that the unknown is not the unknowable. What we find is a trustworthy testimony to the nature of what we have yet to find. The movement of restoration mirrors the movement up the scale of nature, with each step on the ladder the shadow of the next step. The search for truth is therefore not simply consonant with Raphael's closing suggestion but is the translation of that suggestion into the creative effort of history.

We have concentrated so far on the final remarks in Raphael's preamble. We have now to remember that the preamble as a whole is poised between two possibilities. To invoke Plato, as Raphael does, is to remind us that there is more than one strand in the Platonic inheritance. If earth is the shadow of heaven, the body is also the dungeon of the soul. These images have their Christian counterparts. The firmament can display the glory of its maker, and the book of nature can be one of the texts of wisdom. But the world can also be an inn where we lodge, or better still, a hospital in which we die.[8] The world can be a perilous flood in resistance to which the true church affirms its identity, a place of darkness from which one can only be delivered by the divine rescue or the two-handed engine. Babylon and Jerusalem stand in an opposition that demands of us that we declare our true citizenship. Reality is other than actuality.

There is a strain in our imagination which takes the transcendent to lie inviolably beyond the reach of human sense, known by its unlikeness rather than its likeness to the ordinary world of our perceiving. The shadow is not an intimation but a deformity. This strain is strengthened by the Reformation insistence on the inward and transforming nature of the experience of relationship with the divine. Justification by faith calls for a crushing sense of the distance between man and God, a distance which can only be bridged by an irresistible force of remaking that lies essentially beyond human capability. Donne's *Holy Sonnets* are taut with the sense of this distance. The visible cannot guide us across this chasm to the nature of the invisible. We know the invisible only as it chooses to manifest itself—when the thunder speaks, or the siege of the city is silenced.

It is possible to locate these two ways of seeing on two sides of a crisis so that the acute sense of discontinuity is the necessary preface to renewal and the strengthening sense of continuity is the evidence that renewal has begun. But even on this assumption the mixed nature of the human battleground means that each way of seeing will continue to haunt the other. Yeats tells us that natural and supernatural are wed with the selfsame ring. He also tells us that a starlit or a moonlit dome disdains all that man is and all mere complexities.[9] He does not choose between these propositions. Rather he celebrates the world that is brought into being between them, the push and the pull of contrary understandings in the systole and diastole of the imagination. Milton is less a poet of celebration than of impassioned and reverberating comment. But for him, too, discontinuity has its fascinations, less persistent and characteristic than those of continuity, but sufficient to ensure that the main way of seeing is not unqualified.

The temptation of Athens in *Paradise Regained* can be read as an important statement of discontinuity. One of its effects is to establish a cleavage between knowledge and wisdom so considerable that the former is incapable of leading to the latter and possession of the latter makes the former superfluous. What we know is significant only in so far as it is sanctified by a source of transformation beyond the knower and the known. In *Samson* too the prisonhouse of alienation and blindness does not suggest the kind of tranquilly ordered universe in which the divine presence can be approached through contemplation of created things. Yet these distancing recognitions are embedded in poems of self-making which whether in their calm clarity or their tormented advances take us back to the legend of Osiris. If what we know cannot always lead us to what we know not, what we know not can and does guide us in the forward movement from what we know.

Milton's fascination with discontinuity is perhaps at its richest in the invocations to *Paradise Lost*. Raphael's preface, we can recall, is poised between language as discovery and language as betrayal, between a world in which metaphors give access to reality and a world in which reality can only be compromised by whatever metaphors are chosen to manifest it. Both propositions can be offered to the poet as caution and as encouragement, and in the struggle to achieve definition both propositions will find roots in the language-experience. Since for the poet the language-experience engages the reality-experience and may be a main means of entry into that experience, the formative force of these propositions can be all the more telling.

Poets are not reluctant to draw attention to the difficulty of their task, and Raphael in doing so is following a well-worn tradition. As the poet in the invocation to Book I of *Paradise Lost* prepares to attempt the unattempted and to wing his way above the classical accomplishment, the strenuous undertakings help in defining the magnitude of the assistance that is needed. Parnassus gives way to Mount Sinai and Sion hill, and the springs of Helicon to the brook of Siloa. The Heavenly Muse becomes the Muse which inspired the Shepherd by whom the chosen seed was taught. Aspiration, verging upon arrogance, dominates the poem up to this point. The muse is called on to "sing," and her "aid" is invoked in what is felt as a partnership rather than a yielding. The "And" which begins the sixteenth line coming after the taut pride of "things unattempted yet" inherits this momentum and seems designed syntactically to initiate no more than an afterthought. It leads us, of course, into the heart of the invocation. The wings descend now instead of ascending, and the wings are those of the muse and not the poet. The boundary of invocation is pushed back further by the effort of self-humbling. A special force is necessary to bridge the distance between the unprecedented task and the frail agent. The spirit which brooded over the creation must now be importuned to brood over what might otherwise be the chaos of the poem. "Thou from the first / Wast present" makes specific the thrusting to the above and before, to a power beyond the creation that is nevertheless the source of all creativeness. That power cannot be reached. It can only be implored to descend so that the upright heart of the singer can be its temple. The creative dependence thus sought is the narrow yet encompassing ground of man's being, affirmed unshakeably by Christ as he stands upon the pinnacle. But the dependence is also an admission of discontinuity, urging the necessity of the descent from above rather than the possibility of the ascent from below. To say this is not to minimize the movement of self-making which qualifies one for the descent so that the assisting response from above becomes the consummation rather than the annulment of an effort already undertaken.

Light, in the invocation to the third book, is first the offspring of heaven and then the first-born of the offspring. It is a coeternal beam of the eternal, an unapproachable radiance which God has inhabited from eternity, an effluence of essence, an ethereal steam springing from an unknowable fountain. The tentative delineations, superseded before they are fully evolved, keep the mind in movement round a still center. It is as if the mind can only know this center by the way in which the center moves the mind. Raphael's difficulties in likening spiritual to corporal things are lived out by the reachings of the verse. But the inadequacies of metaphor are not felt as defeat. The successive discardings are fitted into the flowing movement, suggesting the harmony rather than the strife of elusive possibilities. One can think of the arresting angularities in which Donne might have embodied a similar effort of definition. The sense of discontinuity is also qualified by the gradations in the invocation as a whole between celestial and physical light and by the ascent from the nonbeing of darkness to the ultimate being of uncorrupted light which is demanded of the poem at this stage in its journey.

Two invocations by the poet himself have preceded Raphael's statement in Book V about the difficulties of angels in composing heroic poetry. Hybris in these invocations has been followed by humbling. The winged assault of language on the ultimate has been succeeded by the recognition that the ultimate is knowable only as it chooses to disclose itself. Though the light is the source of all singing, there is a presumption in singing of the light. "The secrets of another world perhaps / Not lawful to reveal," on the circumference of which Raphael treads with proper caution, have already been put before us by a poet who has told us far more than Raphael will tell Adam. One of the consequences of language as discovery is the discovery of language as betrayal. And betrayal is not simply the staining of vision by metaphor. The poet, like Adam, solicits his thoughts with "matters hid" nominally because of the nature of his subject but conceivably because of the nature of poetry itself. Retribution can follow the penetration into inviolate places. As we proceed from the illumining of the mind's darkness (I, 22–23), through the irradiation of a mind surrounded by "ever during dark" (III, 45–55), to the poet in darkness and encompassed by dangers (VII, 27), the muse evolves as both instructor and protector, shielding the poet both from a hostile world and from the purity of the unmediated vision. Metaphor may be a betrayal; it is also the thin screen of a necessary safeguarding.

We are aware in the invocations of a parallel creative dependence—the dependence of man upon that divine principle which is the ground and origin of his being, and of the poem upon that ultimate muse which it invokes and by which it is instructed and governed. If the analogy is to hold firm and the poet be mimetic in this fundamental sense, the ultimate muse must be joined as closely as possible to the divine nature. In the invocation to Book VII, Milton calls upon Urania as the muse of Christian poetry; but since Urania is one of the classical muses he calls upon the meaning, not the name. She is 'heavn'lie borne," as light is in the first line of Book III. The ultimate muse was in being before the hills appeared and even before the fountain of divine creativeness was set in motion. Beyond and before generation as we conceive of it, she conversed with Eternal Wisdom and played with her in the presence of the Father. The eighth chapter of *Proverbs*, which is the basis of the imagery, does not provide Wisdom with a sister, and it is the sister, not Wisdom, who is Milton's muse. A Rabbinical commentary to which Fletcher has drawn our attention endows Wisdom with a sister, Understanding,[10] but while Urania may be Understanding in so far as she converses with Wisdom, she is more than that by virtue of her play. We do not need to succumb to Saurat's Kabbalistic interpretation[11] to accept the implied view of poetry as an act of comprehension *and* as a performance, a relationship strengthened by the subsequent reference to "celestial song." "Instruct me, for Thou know'st" is among Milton's earlier requests (I, 19). Utterance is not possible without knowledge and perhaps one should add that knowledge is not possible without obedience. "Instruct" carries more than one meaning, and one of the meanings invites us to contrast the safe-guarding obedience of the singer with the disobedience of which he seeks to sing. The act of poetry is the indivisible coming into being of knowledge and eloquence on the basis of the creative humbling of the self. In invoking the ultimate muse, this indivisibility is being recognized, but the source of song and the justification for its nature are also being pushed back as far as is metaphysically possible.[12]

Urania is called on for her version of the divine rescue, saving the committed poet from the perils and recklessness of the language-adventure. The fate of Orpheus is sufficient warning, as is the example of Bellerophon (VII, 17–39). (Shelley proceeds further when even Urania fails to save John Keats).[13] Distance between the singer and the source is necessarily part of the design of supplication. The muse must be placed away from time and from motion, must stand as light in opposition to darkness, if the inspired and instructed act of poetry is to reengage the human with the divine. To put it more brusquely, the perception of discontinuity may be needed in order to validate the finding of continuity. Milton's poetry is distinguished by its full response to both of these necessities, by the firm proportioning and interrelating of both the transcendental and historical loyalties. If his muse is Urania, the poem he writes is dedicated to Osiris. We can possibly go further and suggest that the poem itself with its searching of experience, its internal consolidations, and its step-by-step gatherings, imitates the bringing together of the torn body of truth.

Milton is not the only or even the first writer to pay his respects and pay them simultaneously to the Osiris principle of the search and the Urania principle of vision. The work of other writers falls between these coordinates, and it can even be argued that the strong and simultaneous presence of both principles, the impossibility of accepting one to the exclusion of the other, constitutes not a fundamental frustration, as might be expected, but a basic and shaping source of poetic energy. Writers must find their own ways of responding to these coordinates, of taking tenancy of the space of relationship. But Milton's articulations have an inclusive and a formative force. I make this point because one of the purposes of the kind of distinction that I have sought to adumbrate is to suggest a line of continuity in English poetry and to indicate how the work of the writer discussed registers an advance along that line and makes forward movement from its own achievement possible. Books with titles like *Milton and the English Mind* and

more resoundingly *John Milton, Englishman,* do not achieve this
placing. Johnson warned us long ago that readers opening *Paradise Lost* would find themselves surprised by a new language.[14]
Many still feel that however accurately this language may answer
to the necessities and way of life of the poem, it still remains
distant from what is unhelpfully called the run of English speech.
Ben Jonson can write a song to Celia and critics felicitate him on
having brought Catullus into the English countryside. Milton can
ask the nymphs where they were when the waters closed over the
head of Lycidas:

> Where were ye Nymphs when the remorseless deep
> Clos'd o'er the head of your lov'd *Lycidas?*
> For neither were ye playing on the Steep,
> Where your old *Bards* the Famous *Druids*, ly,
> Nor on the shaggy top of *Mona* high,
> Nor yet where Deva speads her wisard stream.   (50–55)

No one, to the best of my knowledge, has ever commended
Milton for bringing Theocritus into the Welsh countryside. It may
be argued in defense of this reluctance that Milton's effort is in a
direction different from Jonson's, that he is moving his landscape
back into the distance of universality while Jonson is bringing his
inherited subject and gestures forward into the particularities of
English life. If such a view were offered and admitted it would
make the ensuing discussion more sophisticated, but it would not
make the direction of Milton's effort un-English. Still less would it
justify the contention that Milton's language, far from standing
within the continuities of English poetry, was responsible for a
great digression of some two hundred and fifty years which was
circumvented only in our century. This view is much less influential than it was; but preoccupation with it whether in maintaining
it or defeating it obscures the recognition that the true history of
poetry lies in its continuities of concern, in the dominant fascinations to which poetry in search of a meaning addresses itself, and
in the explorations through which it moves in search of an answer,
or a form of containment.

When paradise is destroyed in the eleventh book of *Paradise
Lost*—or more correctly, converted into an "island salt and bare"
(834)—we are brought to a crucial point not only in the history of
the poem, but also in the history of the genre. In the poem the
destruction means that the way back can hereafter only be the way
forward and that given the working of body up to spirit which the

poem suggests to us through its own development, the true paradise must hereafter lie within. In the genre, the destruction points to the end of the long poem of exterior action and the beginning of the heroic poem of consciousness. The point is made because the very nature of a poem of consciousness makes it likely that it will be written in the presence of Osiris and Urania.

The historical and the visionary, the continuous and the discontinuous, language as discovery and language as betrayal, are coordinates to which Milton's poetry responds and which remain with us in literary history. Milton's sometimes overwhelming skill in the uses of the past makes it natural to look back at cultural history through the concentrations and refractions of his poems. It is less easy to look forward along the ways which a poem ought to open. Perfection is petrifying, adding to the burden of the past the crushing marmoreal weight of final accomplishment. One test of achievement is that it extinguishes the genre. If, disregarding these persuasions, we decide to look forward rather than back from Milton's accomplishment, we can ask ourselves to what extent the relationship between Urania and Osiris is reformulated in the marriage of Jerusalem and Albion. Is it accidental that one of the opening lines of the *Prelude* echoes one of the closing lines of *Paradise Lost*, or that Wordsworth's declaration of belief in man comes at the same structural point in his poem as the creation of man does in Milton's epic? Is it merely coincidental that the ascent of Snowdon takes place at the same point as the ascent of the highest hill of paradise from which Adam discerns the sombre lessions of history? Are we being no more than fanciful in linking the Urania-Osiris relationship, the discontinuous and the continuous, to the Simplon experience and the Snowdon experience or to what Professor Ferry defines as the mystic and the sacramental views of nature?[15] To the question of who killed John Keats, Middleton Murry's unambiguous and resounding answer is "Milton."[16] Nevertheless, as we read *The Fall of Hyperion*, we can ask ourselves to what extent the dialogue of the evolving consciousness that takes place between the poet and Moneta has its antecedents in the processes of self-knowing and self-making that are enacted in *Lycidas* and in *Paradise Regained*. To what extent do *The Dialogue of Self and Soul* and the other battlegrounds which Yeats arranges for himself renew the confrontations of the Osiris-Urania relationship, the commitment to time and the hunger for the timeless? Let us look at the poet whose disavowal of Milton has been so influential in forming the critical climate of the earlier part of our century. Do not the heap of broken images with which the speaker in *The Waste Land* begins, and the fragments which he finally shores against his ruins, put us in memory of a familiar Milton image? Can we not see the step-by-step advance of Eliot's oeuvre as the putting together of the structure of truth, with each poem finding and forming the basis which makes the forward movement of the next poem possible? Can we say that in the still point and in the point of intersection we find Eliot's version of the presence of Urania and that in the return to the "life of significant soil" we find his version of the commitment to Osiris? Is the movement in *Four Quarters* from language as betrayal to language as fulfillment not evocative of earlier distinctions which this paper has sought to draw? I pose these questions not to suggest that Milton's successors pay tribute to him by their imitation of him—such language defines and therefore ought to dismiss the idea of a present that is no more than the servile rerendering of the past—but rather to suggest that even in the finding of a signature, in the self-realization of the individual talent, there remains present a continuing metaphysical language. That language may be more important than the stylistic gestures the emulation of which is usually taken as the main evidence of the extent of Milton's presence. As we explore the language more fully we will come to understand better the place which Milton occupies in the continuities of English poetry. We will also understand how the place is creative.

University of Western Ontario

NOTES

1. All quotations of Milton's poetry are from *The Works of John Milton*, ed. Frank Allen Patterson et al. (New York, 1931–38).

2. *The Poems of John Milton*, ed. John Carey and Alastair Fowler (London, 1968), 710 n., 711 n.; John Milton, *Complete Poems and Major Prose*, ed. Merritt Y. Hughes (New York, 1957), 315 n.; Jon S. Lawry, *The Shadow of Heaven* (Ithaca, 1969), pp. 199–200.

3. See William B. Hunter, "The Center of *Paradise Lost*," *ELN*, VII (1969), 32–34, and "Milton on the Exaltation of the Son: The War in Heaven in *Paradise Lost*," *ELH*, XXXVI (1969), 227, for an account of these links. See also Louis L. Martz, *The Paradise Within* (New Haven, 1964), p. 124. The earliest recognition of this relationship seems to be by Greenwood as recorded in Newton's 1749 edition

of *Paradise Lost*. See *Milton 1732–1801: The Critical Heritage*, ed. John T. Shawcross (London, 1972), p. 159.

4. "Of Education," in *Complete Prose Works of John Milton*, ed. Don M. Wolfe et al. (New Haven, 1953–), vol. II, pp. 368–69. All citations of the prose refer to this edition.

5. *Religio Medici*, II, 9. George Steiner's application of the thought to "the speech of a community" (*After Babel* [New York, 1965], p. 465) is an attractive extension.

6. 'The Cunning Resemblance," *Milton Studies*, VII, ed. James D. Simmonds (Pittsburgh, 1975), 36–37.

7. I have discussed some of Yeat's more striking statements of this idea in "W. B. Yeats and the Unity of Being," *The Nineteenth Century and After*, CXLVI (1949), 150–61.

8. Browne, *Religio Medici*, II, 11.

9. "Byzantium" and "Ribh Denounces Patrick," *Collected Poems* (New York, 1956), pp. 243, 283.

10. Harris F. Fletcher, *Milton's Rabbinical Readings* (Urbana, 1931), p. 111.

11. Denis Saurat, *Milton: Man and Thinker* (London, 1946), p. 240.

12. The progressive "pushing back" is made apparent when we consider I, 19–22, which associates the muse with the creation, as superseded by III, 7–11, which invokes a light that existed before the creation. The fountain and stream imagery in which light is invoked is then superseded in its turn by VII, 8: "Before the Hills appeerd, or Fountain flow'd."

13. Shelley's Urania "chained to time" (*Adonais*, 234) differs from Milton's Urania who is insistently presented as prior to generation. In terms of *PL* VII, 5, and its context, one might say that Shelley is calling upon the name and not the meaning. A transcendental muse presents difficulties to any poet who finds himself committed to the ultimacy within. Perhaps the continuity of naming is intended to suggest that no muse, however fundamentally conceived, can protect the poet from his own creativeness.

14. Samuel Johnson, "Milton," in *Milton Criticism*, ed. James Thorpe (London, 1951), p. 85.

15. Geoffrey Hartman, *Wordsworth's Poetry, 1787–1814* (New Haven, 1964); David Ferry, *The Limits of Mortality: An Essay on Wordsworth's Major Poems* (Middletown, 1959).

16. *Keats and Shakespeare* (London, 1925).

MILTON'S HELL:
PERSPECTIVES ON THE FALLEN

Dustin Griffin

THE AMBIVALENT responses called forth in the reader by the
Satan of the first two books on *Paradise Lost* are familiar to
all students of the poem and need not be reviewed. I wish to
discuss rather the reader's multiple response to the lesser angels
of his company, not as individuals but as a group. In Books I and
II (their appearance in Books V and VI and in Book X is a simpler
story) they are sometimes the anonymous foot soldiers of the enemy, sometimes as individualized as Satan's lieutenants (in the
catalogue of false gods) and thus stamped with infamy. But elsewhere they are simply the fallen, the sorrowful damned. At
moments their stature is mythical, "godlike shapes and forms /
Excelling human" (I, 358–59), but at others Milton allows us to
recognize a fallen *human* form.[1] By altering our perspective on
the fallen angels, by varying our distance from them, he allows us
to see them now as spiteful fiends, now as harmless comic bus-
tlers, now (what has not been given due attention) as forlorn and
wandering lost souls, a proleptic and painful image of the condition of man after the Fall.

Milton's art of perspective, however, is not an exercise in the
relativism of perception, nor is his appeal for compassion simply
an exercise of his and our sympathetic imagination. Likewise, it
would be incorrect to say simply that in the opening books of the
poem sympathy yields finally to firm judgment of evil, or that
judgment gives way to an exploring sympathy with the lot of the
damned. Rather it would appear that Milton's strategy is designed to disrupt easy judgment and to force a reader to abandon
the automatic response, the simple answer, to his epic question—
"What cause mov'd our Grand Parents . . . to fall off?" (I, 28–30).
Indeed Milton's starting point is the traditional answer: it was
that inhuman "infernal serpent," moved by archangelic "envy
and revenge," (I, 34–35) who now lies safely in a "Dungeon
Horrible" (I, 61). But the rest of the poem complicates such sim-
plicities; endows the event with comprehensible and with hu-

237

man motives; envisions hell not as a physical "Furnace" but as a
spiritual place, a "dismal Situation" (I, 60–62) located in the
mind that can make its own place, even its own hell (I, 254); and
forces us to see that the real agents in the drama are human
beings (Adam and Eve and ultimately the reader himself) who
enact and reenact the fall.[2] The fallen angels play a part in this
action. For by pointing at them a judging finger and often *at the
same time* drawing out our sympathy, Milton draws the reader in
to see that the scene and the problem are ultimately his own. In
part by means of the fallen angels, Milton teaches a reader both
to see and to judge himself.

Book I, though dominated by Satan, presents his mass of followers three times—in a series of similes (301–58), in the catalogue of false gods (381–522), and as the builders and inhabitants
of Pandemonium (675–792). No single image of the fallen angels
emerges. Indeed, Milton takes pains to present a variety of images
and to call forth a variety of responses.

Take first the celebrated epic similes. The fallen angels are
like autumnal leaves (301–04), scattered sedge on the Red Sea
(304–06), the carcasses and broken chariots of the Memphian
chivalry (306–11). Ostensibly each of these similes describes how
thickly the angels are bestrewn on the burning lake, but as is
often noted, Milton brings in much more: the stillness and serene beauty of an autumnal river, suggesting the devils' utter
helplessness but also their faded splendor and God's overarching
control; the violence of biblical history, suggesting God's protection of the Israelites and his fury against his human enemies. As
leaves, the devils arouse no animus in us; they are beautiful
objects composing a scene or pattern; but as sedge they are violently "scattered," and as carcasses they are defeated enemies
thrown into chaotic disarray. In each case, however, they remain
alien from a human reader, inanimate, a lower form of life, or
biblical villains dead three thousand years. And yet, to a Bible-
reading Puritan, such villains might not be so remote. Milton
could here count on (and reinforce) the seventeenth-century
habit of mind that saw biblical patterns recapitulated in human
history. His design is to distance the devils aesthetically and
then to reenliven these images of evil, thereby to bring them
home to his readers' business and bosoms.

But contrast the effect Milton achieves with the next simile,
some few lines later:

> They heard, and were abashed, and up they sprung
> Upon the wing, as when men wont to watch
> On duty, sleeping found by whom they dread,
> Rouse and bestir themselves ere well awake.   (331–34)

The stirring devils are of course no longer inanimate. But the differences between this simile and the previous ones extend further and are not due simply to the fact that the devils are now in motion. They are now compared to men, their condition explained by reference to the common experience of fallen man. To Milton's readers the life of a sentry would have been familiar, either from Civil War experience or as sacred metaphor. As Christians, all were called on to "watch," to be spiritually awake, lest, coming suddenly, Christ might find them sleeping (Mark xiii, 35–37). Momentarily, we may even forget that the devils arouse themselves to *evil.* Surprised by Satan, they form an image of an unwary Christian surprised on his duty. The simile also looks forward to another human lapse. Like a sleeping sentry Eve too is surprised.[3] Not only does the simile have serious human relevance. Perhaps more important it also humanizes the devils. The soldiers are not caricatures; nor are they even particularly warlike. Instead, they are "abashed," stumbling groggily, trying to shake off sleep. The image is mildly comic, but gently humanized.

Milton does not long leave us with this impression. Once more the devils are alienated, compared to a cloud of locusts in biblical Egypt (338–43) and a horde of barbarians invading the Roman Empire (351–55). They are distanced from the reader temporally, spatially, morally, and biologically (the "barbarous sons" of the "populous north" are only subhuman). A reader's perspective on the devils, over the course of these fifty lines, alters markedly.

The series of similes gives way to the second major presentation of the devils, the epic catalogue of biblical false gods. Although brought firmly within a human historical context, the devils remain remote. They are gods and idols, unambiguously abhorrent. By singling them out and naming each one ("First Moloch . . . next Chemos"), Milton gives them fixed identities and stamps them with the evil that attaches to Gehenna and Sodom. Only when they are viewed as a mass, as soldiers again rather than false gods, does the tone change:

> All these and more came flocking; but with looks
> Down cast and damp, yet such wherein appeared

Obscure some glimpse of joy, to have found their chief
Not in despair, to have found themselves not lost
In loss itself.

.   .   .   .

in stead of rage
Deliberate valor breathed, firm and unmoved
With dread of death to flight or foul retreat,
Nor wanting power to mitigate and swage,
With solemn touches, troubled thoughts, and chase
Anguish and doubt and fear and sorrow and pain
From mortal or immortal minds.   (522–26, 553–59)

These are recognizable human images. The tone, likewise, is not simply condemnatory. We see human despair, joy, valor. With a touch like "mortal or immortal minds" Milton keeps before us the idea that the fallen angels are to be understood not only as followers of our great adversary, but as creatures who share with us a common condition. When Satan looks out upon

The fellows of his crime, the followers rather
(Far other once beheld in bliss) condemned
For ever now to have their lot in pain,
Millions of spirits for his fault amerced
Of heaven, and from eternal splendours flung
For his revolt   (606–11)

we can see not only the fallen angels, but (looking ahead) fallen man, the followers of Adam, by whose revolt they too are condemned "for ever now to have their lot in pain."

Once more, however, the humanized picture gives way to the supernatural or alien. Mammon's industrious crews work infernal magic, causing Pandemonium to rise "like an exhalation." Their mining and metallurgy suggest not human labors but the busy antics of a strange and lurid animated cartoon. What is alien need not of course seem wholly threatening. The famous similes of bees and faery elves, which conclude the first book, make the followers of Satan both dangerous and delightful, a cause for both fear and joy. When viewed as busy, somewhat self-important bees or as mirthful dancing elves, the devils are alien creatures, but hardly a serious threat to order, human or divine.[4] Book I, then, provides us with a variety of perspectives on the fallen angels. A reader cannot rest content with either easy judgment that externalizes and condemns the devils (what have they to do with me?) or the ready sympathy that goes out to human suffering.

For the first half of Book II the stage is occupied by Satan and his chief lieutenants. In the infernal council, one of the most dramatic scenes in the poem, our attention is focused on five speakers, each of whom enacts a role in what we discover to be Satan's carefully manipulated debate. Despite the human images, a military and political council with recognizable parliamentary (and human) tactics, despite our intense psychological interest in recognizably human responses to extreme adversity, the devils in council somehow remain titanic figures, distanced from the reader by their awesome stature and the immensity of their imaginations. Do battle against the almighty! Build an empire in hell!

As the council concludes, however, our attention is artfully transferred from the chief devils to Satan's lesser followers. The masses arise to extol their leader:

> Thus they their doubtful consultations dark
> Ended rejoicing in their matchless chief:
> As when from mountain tops the dusky clouds
> Ascending, while the north wind sleeps, o'erspread
> Heaven's cheerful face, the louring element
> Scowls o'er the darkened landscape snow, or shower;
> If chance the radiant sun with farewell sweet
> Extend his evening beam, the fields revive,
> The birds their notes renew, and bleating herds
> Attest their joy, that hill and valley rings.   (486–95)

The alteration of our perspective on the devils is striking. Lurid, stupendous Pandemonium is transformed into a storm-threatened pastoral valley basking in an unexpected sunset.[5] The devils are transmuted into fields, birds, and bleating herds (recalling the leaves and bees of Book I). Our attention is directed toward their vulnerability, their revived spirits, their relief and gratitude that the sun has extended it warmth, that Satan will undertake for them and their "general safety" (II, 481) a perilous journey which will endanger his own safety. Just as Milton can recognize the spiritual needs of the devils, so he can recognize devilish virtue. "Spirits damned," the narrator interjects, do not "lose all their virtue" (II, 482–83). Satan's motives for the journey, however mixed we later discover them to be, include a true leader's genuine concern for his followers. The lesser devils display "firm concord" (II, 497), unanimous in praise and support of their chief. Once again the narrator interjects: "O shame to men!" (II, 496) who by contrast live in enmity and strife. But we should not exaggerate the temporary sympathy and admiration for the devils which Milton evokes. He makes clear immediately that infernal solidarity has infernal ends: the devils are "hellish foes . . . That day and night for [man's] destruction wait" (II, 504–05). The corrective reminder, however, does not reestablish a single-minded view of the devils. We do not look upon them as simply damned, alien, monstrous. Groundwork is being laid, so it would seem, for the scenes that follow.

Our next (and fullest) view of the followers comes after Satan departs on his quest. Before following him to meet Sin and Death we linger in hell for some one hundred twenty-five lines (506–628). Now, undistracted by the rhetoric of revolt, defiance, or infernal empire, we see the quotidian life of hell in all its sad variety of woe. Here, perhaps more than anywhere else in the poem, we find images of the painfulness of the fallen condition. The devils' predicament is recognizably our general human predicament. By contrast, the immediate consequences of the Fall in Books IX and X are narrowly focused on betrayal and bickering, and the panorama of human history in Books XI and XII is a spectacle beheld from a distance.

This scene in hell differs from earlier scenes. It takes place not on the burning lake and shore or in Pandemonium, but in what is sometimes called his "classical hell," a broad landscape which forms the scene of games and exploration. Critics note that the underworld scenes grotesquely parody heaven on the one hand and Eden on the other.[6] Editors note too that Milton's hell is loosely modeled on descriptions of the underworld in Virgil. From the *Aeneid* Milton drew especially on the accounts of the games and pleasures of Elysium, the four rivers of hell, and the crossing of Lethe. What has not been emphasized enough is the way Milton remodeled Virgil for his own ends. Aeneas, once past the Styx, passes first through the Fields of Mourning (Lugentes Campi), where he meets Dido, "whom bitter love consumed with brutal waste" (VI, 442) and Deiphobus, a mangled and dishonored warrior.[7] Next he passes by (without entering) Tartarus, where the damned are tortured, and enters Elysium, the lands of gladness, where he meets Anchises and observes the pleasures of happy souls:

> Some exercise
> their limbs along the green gymnasiums
> or grapple on the golden sand, compete
> in sport, and some keep time with moving feet
> to dance and chant. There, too, the Thracian priest,
> the long-robed Orpheus, plays.
> . . . .

The ancient race of Teucer, too, is here.

. . . .

their spears are planted,
fixed in the ground; their horses graze and range
freely across the plain.

. . . .

And here to right and left he can see others:
some feasting on the lawns; and some chanting
glad choral paeans in a fragrant laurel
grove.   (VI, 642–58)

Milton's classical hell is a combination of all three parts of the Virgilian underworld. The games (much changed) are drawn from the joyous field of gladness; the torments of bitter cold and parching air, and the harpy-footed Furies, parallel the tortures of Tartarus; but the atmosphere of frustration and restlessness, the distinctive characteristic of Milton's hell, suggests the first region of Virgil's underworld. The devils in spirit resemble neither the blessed souls nor the traitors and murderers of Tartarus so much as the anguished inhabitants of the Fields of Mourning, which Deiphobus calls "sad and sunless dwellings, restless lands" ("tristis sine sole domos, loca turbida" [VI, 534]). Their sports and songs serve not to give them pleasure; they merely while away the time, yielding "truce to . . . restless thoughts, and entertain / The irksome hours, till this great chief return" (*PL* II, 526–27) much like the sports of the Myrmidons in Achilles' absence: "The men forlorn of their warlike leader / wandered here and there in the camp, and did no fighting."[8] Without claiming that Milton derived from Virgil's treatment of Deiphobus and Dido his tender sorrow mixed with firm censure, I would suggest that the attitude we are asked to adopt here toward the devils—a sympathetic understanding for the sufferings of the fallen—is Virgilian.

Why should Milton wish to generate such sympathy? A plausible answer offers itself when we note that despite hell's similarities to Eden, heaven, and the Virgilian underworld, it is the fallen human world that Milton's classical hell most resembles.[9] Topographically, it has rivers and hills, "Rocks, caves, lakes, fens, bogs, dens" (II, 621). The devils' activities are modeled upon traditionally heroic human activities—epic games, poetry and philosophy, exploration—just as in Virgil's Elysium, "The very same / delight that once was theirs in life—in arms / and chariots and care to pasture their / sleek steeds—has followed to this underearth" (*Aeneid* VI, 653–55). To whatever extent we can label the ferocity of these activities misguided, proud, foolish, we must also recognize that they are images of our own human efforts to survive in a world of woe. The devils may be hellish fiends, but should we repress our sympathies for their painful condition or fail to consider that they form a reflection of our own fallen state?

> the ranged powers
> Disband, and *wandering*, each his *several way*
> Pursues, as inclination or sad *choice*
> Leads him perplexed, where he may likeliest find
> Truce to his *restless* thoughts, and entertain
> The irksome hours, till this great chief return.
>
> . . . .
>
> Thus roving on
> In confused march forlorn, the adventurous bands
> With shuddering horror pale, and eyes aghast
> Viewed first their lamentable lot, and found
> No *rest*.   (*PL* II, 522–27, 614–18, emphasis added)

Belial's "thoughts that wander through eternity" (II, 148), at first an attractive image of our "intellectual being," the mind free from bounds of time and place, now more than ever becomes an image of pain, of wandering, restless thought, "condemned / To waste eternal days in woe and pain" (II, 694–95). The world was all before *them*, too, a fallen world of lonely wandering, no hope and no rest. By the time we arrive at the end of Book XII we can look back and see hell as our first glimpse of fallen human experience.

> The world was all before them, where to choose
> Their place of rest, and providence their guide:
> They hand in hand with wandering steps and slow,
> Through Eden took their solitary way.

To be sure, this passage illuminates what the fallen angels lack. For fallen man, guided by Providence, the world still contains *possibilities* for choice and rest. For the fallen angels choice only leads to perplexity; they find no truce to restless thoughts, no rest. But we should not let differences between the lamentable lots of fallen angel and fallen man obscure the similarities. Like the devils, Adam and Eve set out with "wandering steps and slow." Their lingering march too is "confused" and "forlorn." Though they provide comfort for each other, and although they are guided by Providence, their way is still "solitary." As fallen creatures they have forfeited the "rest" of heaven and Eden where "roseate dews" dispose "All but the unsleeping eyes of God to rest" (V, 647), and where "labor and rest" (IV, 613) form a grateful vicissitude. In hell "peace and rest can never dwell" (I, 65); before the war in heaven the devils, conspiring at midnight, are "void of rest" (VI, 415). In Eden after the fall, Adam and Eve cover their shame, but are not "at rest or ease of mind" (IX, 1120). Adam longs for the "rest and sleep secure" of death (X, 778). But man's final rest and native home (X, 1085) will not be dust. He will either suffer the profound restlessness of hell, or will recover eternal rest, through the help of Christ, who "shall quell / The adversary serpent, and bring back / Through the world's wilderness long wandered man / Safe to eternal paradise of rest" (XII, 311–14). So too the fallen angels must entertain the irksome hours "till this great chief [i.e., Satan] return" to lead them, so they hope, to a new paradise.[10]

Entertainment for the devils means finding ways to charm the pain of hell, in Olympic games, epic song, philosophical discourse, and exploration. Some critics have labeled these activities "pseudo-heroism" and "civilized anodynes," the materials of secular epic which Milton contemptuously places in hell.[11] But Milton has more interest in them than that. Games in themselves are not contemptible (the good angels exercise "heroic games" [IV, 552]), and Milton does not seem concerned with simply scoring points against Homer and Virgil, or against the devils. The resemblance between the fallen angels and human epic heroes surely works both ways. Secular epic acquires fallen coloration, but the devils become all the more human. Their contests are fought not to win glory but, in the furious expense of energy, to obliterate memory of pain. The races and war games, described one after another without pause, have a compulsive quality, as if the devils hasten from one moment of frantic exertion to another:

> Part on the plain, or in the air sublime
> Upon the wing, or in swift race contend,
> As at the Olympian games or Pythian fields;
> Part curb their fiery steeds, or shun the goal
> With rapid wheels, or fronted brigades form.
> . . . .
>   with feats of arms
> From either end of heaven the welkin burns.
>
>   (II, 528–32, 537–38)

"Feats of arms" may hint via "feet of arms" at the monstrous, unnatural quality of their efforts; "burns" and "fiery" suggest fierce intensity and link forward to the enraged Hercules, whose pain-prodded feats serve as an apt image of the sports in hell:

> Others with vast Typhoean rage more fell
> Rend up both rocks and hills, and ride the air
> In whirlwind; hell scarce holds the wild uproar.
> As when Alcides from Oechalia crowned
> With conquest, felt the envenomed robe, and tore
> Through pain up by the roots Thessalian pines,
> And Lichas from the top of Oeta threw
> Into the Euboic sea.   (II, 539–46)

Milton first gives a relatively distanced view of enraged giants ravaging the landscape. Their "wild uproar" resembles the "uproar" in heaven (VI, 663) when "seated hills" with "Rocks, water, woods" are uplifted and flung in battle (VI, 644–67). When the fallen angels ride the whirlwind we think of the God who spoke to Job (xxxviii, 1) or the terrible power of a punitive Jehovah envisioned by Isaiah and Jeremiah and associated by Milton with the victorious Christ, whose war chariot rushes forth "with whirl-wind sound" (VI, 749). But when Milton focuses more closely on Alcides (Hercules), implicit judgment makes room for deeply imagined pain. Human scale is reestablished as Hercules burns in the robe of Nessus. Expressive syntax suggests the stress and wrenching: "Tore through pain *up* by the roots." By withholding the object of Hercules' tearing, Milton momentarily transfers the pain of uprooting from the pines to Hercules himself, who tears through, or tries to tear up by the roots, his own pain. As the Hercules simile makes clear, the devils suffer torture in the midst of their games. Although for Tertullian and Augustine the tortured suffering of the damned may be cause for joy among the righteous,[12] Milton here suspends rigorous judgment and asks his readers to apprehend a kind of pain all too familiar in the fallen world.

While the followers of Moloch engage in feats of strength, the followers of Belial prefer the milder pleasures of song and eloquence:

> Others more mild,
> Retreated in a silent valley, sing
> With notes angelical to many a harp
> Their own heroic deeds and hapless fall
> By doom of battle; and complain that fate
> Free virtue should enthral to force or chance.
> Their song was partial, but the harmony
> (What could it less when spirits immortal sing?)
> Suspended hell, and took with ravishment
> The thronging audience.   (II, 546–55)

Although the passage in part manifests undeniably Milton's disapproval of the devils' activities, its emphasis is rather on the pain and the fallen beauty. Dennis Burden notes the Satanic theme of force, "fate," and "chance," a convenient explanation for defeat that avoids any mention of God's moral superiority.[13] Their song is partial, says Fowler, not only because it is polyphonic, but because it is prejudiced, "since they sang their own version of the Fall, in which virtue is on their side, force or chance on God's, and the ultimate power is fate."[14] "Ravishment," furthermore, suggests an improper state of mind in the listeners: not a clear-eyed understanding, but a rapt ecstasy, an excess of emotional surrender. Though fallen from grace, the devils are not stripped of all human graces and harmonies. Their music succeeds in soothing pain, in *suspending* hell. The harmony wholly absorbs their attention (*OED*, "suspend," 5a), and thereby seems to interrupt hell, to set its pains in abeyance (*OED*, "suspend," 2)—compare Satan, in Book IX, abstracted from his own evil, "stupidly good." The narrator's parenthetical interruption at this point (553) seems designed to head off surprised objections by readers, who might not expect harmony in hell, just as his earlier interruption, in the midst of the pastoral simile, is designed to insist (against expectations to the contrary) that spirits damned do not lose all their virtue. Moments later the narrator interrupts again to note that devils do not lose the power to charm the soul with eloquence (a discourse sweeter than sense-charming song):

> In discourse more sweet
> (For eloquence the soul, song charms the sense,)
> Others apart sat on a hill retired,
> In thoughts more elevate, and reasoned high
> Of providence, foreknowledge, will and fate,
> Fixed fate, free will, foreknowledge absolute,
> And found no end, in wandering mazes lost.
> Of good and evil much they argued then,
> Of happiness and final misery,
> Passion and apathy, and glory and shame,
> Vain wisdom all, and false philosophy:
> Yet with a pleasing sorcery could charm
> Pain for a while or anguish, and excite
> Fallacious hope, or arm the obdured breast
> With stubborn patience as with triple steel.   (II, 555–69)

Again, critics have too hastily assumed that Milton in these lines simply condemns and mocks infernal philosophers. True, the devils wander (the real state of all the fallen) in mazes like fallen Adam ("All my evasions vain, / And reasonings lead me still / But to my own conviction," [X, 829–31]), unlike the angels, whose understanding is intuitive, not discursive, and whose "mystical dance" resembles the "mazes intricate" of the starry dance (V, 620–22), and unlike God, who sees clearly the relation between free will and foreknowledge. But that is just the point. The devils have fallen into a *human* condition. They no longer enjoy angelic understanding (although they seem to have preserved an angelic power of harmonious song). Their reasoning is no more ignominious than all the reasoning of centuries of medieval scholasticism and Reformation theology. The efforts and powers of the devils form a picture of human powers and efforts to understand God.

The devils go on from theology to moral philosophy. It is only their discussion of "good and evil . . . passion and apathy" (secular Stoic ethics), "glory and shame" (a Renaissance ideal of earthly glory and honor), which Milton labels "vain wisdom all and false philosophy." Any secular ethics is in Milton's scheme by definition false. The weight of the passage is not on the falseness and vanity, but on the pathos of human attempts to assuage pain by means of speculation. It is "pleasing," but of course only "sorcery," a "charm" (recalling "charms" from line 556) and a specious hope. The patience it brings is not true Christian patience, but the stubborn pride of the Stoic.

A third band, the followers of Mammon, set out like explorers "to discover wide / That dismal world, if any clime perhaps / Might yield them easier habitation" (571–73).[15] As we have already seen, they foreshadow the expedition of fallen man at the end of Book XII down into the "subjected plain" and world of woe. Their wanderings bring before our eyes the physical horrors of Tartarus, a frozen continent, perpetual storms, Serbonian bog, and, as in Virgil's account of the underworld, the four rivers of hell.

> Abhorred Styx the flood of deadly hate,
> Sad Acheron of sorrow, black and deep;
> Cocytus, named of lamentation loud
> Heard on the rueful stream; fierce Phlegethon
> Whose waves of torrent fire inflame with rage.
>
> (*PL* II, 577–81)

The names of the rivers, accompanied by etymologically derived epithets,[16] bring out both the bitter passion and the sorrow of the

damned. They are filled with "deadly hate" and "rage," but also
with "sad sorrow" and "lamentation loud." The river that gets
most emphasis, however, is Lethe:

> Far off from these a slow and silent stream,
> Lethe the water of oblivion rolls
> Her watery labyrinth, whereof who drinks
> Forgets both joy and grief, pleasure and pain.
>
> . . . .
>
> They ferry over this Lethean sound
> Both to and fro, their sorrow to augment,
> And wish and struggle, as they pass, to reach
> The tempting stream, with one small drop to lose
> In sweet forgetfulness all pain and woe,
> All in one moment, and so near the brink;
> But fate withstands.   (II, 582–85, 604–10)

Here, if nowhere else in the account of hell, the sufferings of the
damned call forth our compassion. Lethe of course appears in all
the traditional descriptions of the underworld, but for his description Milton does not rest on literary forebears. He truly imagines
and re-creates the longing for oblivion. In his account, Lethe becomes merged with the pool of Tantalus (610–14); the promised
relief is ever to be sought, always out of reach. Virgil's shades, after
a thousand years of suffering, are at last permitted to drink the
water of Lethe (*Aeneid* VI, 745–51), but Milton's devils ferry to and
fro across Lethe, *augmenting* their sorrow with each crossing.

The "wish and struggle" is emphasized by this remarkable
sentence, "They ferry over . . . but fate withstands." The lyrical
looseness of the syntax is unusual. Sense, drawn out from one line
into another, suspensefully drawing the reader on, is nonetheless
complete at the end of each clause or phrase. "They ferry over this
Lethean sound . . . both to and fro . . . their sorrow to augment . . .
and wish and struggle . . . as they pass . . . to reach the tempting
stream." Completion, extension, and completion suggest the passing and repassing, the longing always put off and never satisfied,
the wish never consummated in the deed. "With one small drop to
lose / In sweet forgetfulness all pain and woe" extends the sense
one stage further. Three clauses are here collapsed into one: to
lose all pain and woe . . . in sweet forgetfulness . . . with one small
drop. Milton's order, a return to his more common practice of
inversion and delayed completion of sense, was prompted in part
no doubt by the desire for variation. But by introducing "one
small drop" as the first unit of sense and delaying the completion

of the all-important effect (to lose . . . all pain and woe), Milton perhaps emphasizes the sovereign virtues of the "one small drop," allows it, so to speak, to govern the whole clause, and allows the reader to linger in a moment of imagined relief, tempts us to hope that the drop can be tasted: "all pain and woe / All in one moment, and so near the brink." Again the sense laps forward, phrase by phrase, only to be brutally cut short: "But fate withstands."[17]

Such comfort is not available to the fallen angels, just as, for fallen man, the longed-for oblivion of death is not an acceptable solution to the problem of a life of pain in a fallen world. The longing for Lethe is indeed a foreshadowing of man's repeated desire after the fall:

> How gladly would I meet
> Mortality my sentence, and be earth
> *Insensible,* how glad would lay me down
> As in my mother's lap? There I should *rest*
> *And sleep secure;* his dreadful voice no more
> Would thunder in my ears, *no fear* of worse
> To me and to my offspring would *torment me*
> With cruel expectation.   (X, 775–82, emphasis added)[18]

Eve too proposes barrenness as a way of cheating death of future generations and suicide as a way of escaping the pains of abstention, "With desire to languish without hope, / Before the present object languishing / With like desire, which would be misery / And torment less than none of what we dread" (X, 995–98). And Adam, upon sight of the miseries in the lazar house, laments, "Who if we knew / What we receive, would either not accept / Life offered, or soon beg to lay it down, / Glad to be so dismissed in peace" (XI, 504–07). For them, too, the penalty for the fall (the taste of forbidden fruit) is continued suffering (the single "taste" which brings oblivion is now forbidden). The suffering on Lethe is even more appropriate for fallen man than fallen angel. With one small taste of the tempting tree, all in a moment of forgetfulness (as God says, "They ought to have *remembered* / The high injunction not to taste that fruit," [X, 12–13]), man brought into the world a world of pain and woe. So on Lethe, the fallen angels reach for "the *tempting* stream, with *one small drop* to lose / In sweet *forgetfulness* all *pain and woe,* / All in a moment." Now, however, the water is an active tempter, while the tree in Eden, Milton takes pains to make clear, was in itself no temptation. In the garden man had only to reach for the apple, but now the desired taste is forever out of reach.

The fallen angels on Lethe are lost souls, but their suffering is so great and so recognizable as a form of human suffering that we should not limit our response to righteous satisfaction. The devils win not only the compassion due to a helpless enemy, but the sympathy that goes out to a fellow human being, *mon semblable, myself*. Here (and in the chilling conclusion to *Samson Agonistes*, where thousands of Philistines both humane and inhumane go down beneath Samson's fury), Milton's response is multiple. Without pardoning the evil, he can imagine and lament the pain of punishment.

Moments after the Lethe passage, however, the tone shifts markedly. The discoverers of woe rove on "in confused march forlorn . . . with shuddering horror pale, and eyes aghast" (615–16), but our attention passes from forlorn souls to an increasingly fantastic landscape, a place not so much of suffering as of evil and perversion. Sympathy yields to disgust; intimate comprehension of pain yields to the detached observation of a scene or spectacle:

> through many a dark and dreary vale
> They passed, and many a region dolorous,
> O'er many a frozen, many a fiery alp,
> Rocks, caves, lakes, fens, bogs, dens, and shades of death,
> A universe of death, which God by curse
> Created evil, for evil only good,
> Where all life dies, death lives.   (618–24)

The mode of presentation has radically changed. We no longer stand in close relation to the suffering devils, imagining their plight as if it were our own. The explorers, now figures of romance, knights on a quest through some perilous land, dark and dreary vales, regions dolorous, frozen and fiery alps, finally disappear into an increasingly conceptualized landscape, in which description dwindles to mere enumeration—"Rocks, caves, lakes, fens."[19] As the scenes in hell come to a close, and as Milton prepares to shift his focus to Satan's journey through Chaos, we can almost feel ourselves being pulled bodily away. Hell as a reality recedes. It no longer seems a human place. All we now can perceive is "a universe of death," a cursed, evil place, quite literally beyond human comprehension: "Perverse, all monstrous, all prodigious things, / Abominable, inutterable, and worse / Than fables yet have feigned, or fear conceived." Where once we saw and felt the sorrow of lost souls, we now see shadowy horrors, "Gorgons and Hydras, and Chimeras dire," the traditional denizens of an alien underworld.

And yet by the end of this passage we may need to reorient ourselves. Are the Gorgons and Hydras what Milton locates in hell, or what he dismisses as the product of foolish fear and fable? The "universe of death" is distanced (by the conceptualizing mode) and yet close at hand, no fable but suddenly brought home when we realize that it literally applies to our own world, the realm of nature, and when we recognize that nature breeds far worse horrors, "Perverse, all monstrous, all prodigious things," in the human mind.

Such shifts of perspective and reorientations are sudden but (as I hope will now be clear) not mere blunders on Milton's part or failures in imagination. The shift in mode, to romance and then to allegory (with Sin and Death), would appear to exchange the vividly realized for the more literary and externalized. But we encounter these later episodes readier, perhaps, to read the inner in the outer, to receive the full human meaning of this ancient story. Shifts in perspective indeed seem part of Milton's overall design in Books I and II, if not in the whole of *Paradise Lost*. One of the prominent characteristics of the poem and one of the sources of its great strength is the multiple vision of human history which we, as readers, are invited by the narrative voice to share. It is a poem which tries to enable us to view Eden and the Fall of Man from the points of view of God, of unfallen man, of fallen angels, and of fallen man; a poem which asks us to see the loss of Eden, the triumph of evil over good, and at the same time to see the potential recovery of a paradise within, and the ultimate triumph of good over evil; a poem which subjects us to time (the uncertainties of human history, the temporal process of reading a long narrative poem) and presents us with a pattern (the ordered cosmos and God's redemptive plan, the intricate design of a highly symmetrical structure).[20]

We as readers are not asked to respond to the poem from every perspective at once. Clearly we will be more struck at one point by narrative movement (an evolving, unfolding event, fluid syntax, the sense drawn out), at another with spatial design (structural symmetries, suspensions of the action). But over a given stretch of the poem Milton typically asks us to alter our perspective, to see a different aspect of an event, to see from a different angle, to see with different eyes, not only the eyes of God or the upright heart and pure. The poem recognizes that we are fallen readers, and though it may hope to educate us, to make us "fit," does not expect us to shed our humanity, our conceptions of what is humanly good, brave, and beautiful, or our sympathies for the sufferings of the fallen. Indeed, commiseration may render more effective the process of education. We are asked not to repress or root out fallen human responses, but to recognize them, thereby insuring an animated and informed watchfulness lest sin surprise us.

New York University

NOTES

1. All quotations from *Paradise Lost* are taken from the *Poems of Milton*, ed. A. Fowler and J. Carey (London, 1968).

2. I am clearly indebted here to Stanley Fish's argument in *Surprised by Sin* (New York, 1967). As will become clear, I differ from Fish in stressing Milton's appeal to both our judgment *and* our sympathy as we read of the fallen angels.

3. VII, 545–47: "beware, / And govern well thy appetite, lest Sin / Surprise thee"; and IX, 353–55: "bid [reason] well beware, and still erect, / Lest by some fair appearing good surprised, / She dictate false."

4. Needless to say, the similes also remind us of the enormous *differences* between bees or elves and devils.

5. The simile of course also suggests the immense difference between hell and the pastoral scene, but the surface of the verse presses the reader to adopt, for the moment, a pastoral view of hell.

6. Satan comes forth from council in infernal imitation of God (I, 510–11). His fiery seraphim bear "horrent arms" rather than harps and give a "deafening shout" rather than "loud" but "sweet" hosanna (III, 344–71). Angels sing together but devils break apart (III, 370; II, 548). Eden has four rivers, a temperate climate, and a protective wall. Hell has four rivers, a climate of extremes, and a seemingly limitless extent.

7. All quotations are from *Aeneid*, trans. A. Mandelbaum (Berkeley, 1971). Line numbers correspond to Virgil's original, not to the translation.

8. *Iliad*, trans. R. Lattimore (Chicago, 1951), II, 778–79.

9. Cf. Wilson Knight's remark that "it is, indeed, our own fallen world that Milton depicts" in his description of hell. *Chariot of Wrath* (London, 1942), p. 137. But Knight sees only condemnation: "man and his total culture are condemned. . . . All this is Satan; and all are condemned."

10. On "rest," see also Isabel MacCaffrey, *"Paradise Lost" as "Myth"* (Cambridge, 1959), pp. 184–88.

11. Joseph Summers, *The Muse's Method* (New York, 1962), p. 45; Dennis Burden, *The Logical Epic: A Study of the Argument of "Paradise Lost"* (Cambridge, 1967), p. 85.

12. William Empson, *Milton's God* (London, 1965), pp. 247–50.

13. *Logical Epic*, p. 58.

14. *Poems of Milton*, ed. A. Fowler and J. Carey, p. 533 n.

15. Vasco da Gama, hero of *The Lusiads* of Camões, is one prominent example of the Renaissance explorer as epic hero.

16. *Poems of Milton*, p. 534 n.

17. Compare the hope and expectation of glory, cut short by the abhorred shears, that "slits the thin spun life" (*Lycidas*, 76).

18. Compare "Why comes not death, / Said he, with one thrice acceptable stroke / To end me?" (X, 854–56).

19. Compare MacCaffrey, *"Paradise Lost" as "Myth,"* pp. 195–97, on Satan's voyage as an archetypal quest journey. Her discussion implies that we are humanly engaged in Satan's quest. I suggest that he, like the explorers in II, 618–28, becomes a consciously *literary* figure.

20. "No poem has more propulsive power than *Paradise Lost* or conveys more of the feeling of events evolving from their own momentum. At the same time, no poem can lay claim to a more intricate or more inclusive design, a deeper establishment of energy in form." B. Rajan, *The Lofty Rhyme* (London, 1970), p. 111.

THE METAPHYSICS OF MILTON'S EPIC BURLESQUE HUMOR

John Wooten

THERE ARE two worlds in *Paradise Lost*—a tragic, fallen world and a comic universe of ultimate Christian promise. The comic obviously supersedes the tragic in the theological sense, but in the poem's narrative drama the two are held in an uneasy and tension-filled balance. This balance is the source of what I call the poem's burlesque vision of absurdity. It is this balance that Milton asks his readers to face as members of an audience and yet to transcend as believers in a divine comedy. From the theological point of view the burlesque is there only to be swept cleanly away at the end of time. But from a dramatic point of view the burlesque produces tragicomic discords which complicate a reader's experience of the epic action. These burlesque discords—which come from such juxtapositions as that of the absurd infernal trinity to its opposite, the heavenly Trinity—make possible the special mixture of farce, horror, humor, and awe which Milton achieves in his depiction of the conflict between good and evil. In the first part of this essay I will define burlesque, using the Limbo of Fools episode. Then I will consider burlesque's affinities to modern black humor.[1] The psychological and metaphysical aspects of Milton's burlesque are illuminated by a comparison to twentieth-century black humor, and important analogies between the two can be made. After establishing initial definitions, I will examine key passages which show the involvement of Satan, Sin and Death, Chaos, and even Milton's God in unmistakeable burlesque activity.

Although Ariosto's moon fantasy provides the model for the Paradise of Fools episode in Book III of *Paradise Lost*, Milton's description of Limbo's future inhabitants places his fools in a realm which lacks Ariosto's bravura comic lunacy. Milton's Limbo is dark and turbulent, and Satan, the first fool to arrive, walks

> a boundless Continent
> Dark, waste, and wild, under the frown of Night
> Starless expos'd, and ever-threat'ning storms

255

> Of *Chaos* blust'ring round, inclement sky;
> Save on that side which from the wall of Heav'n,
> Though distant far, some small reflection gains
> Of glimmering air less vext with tempest loud:
> Here walk'd the Fiend at large in spacious field.
>
> (III, 423–30)[2]

This is a macrocosmic perspective with a matching epic grandeur. The emphasis on darkness and distance from light reinforces the sense of the tragic aura which surrounds Satan as he comes on his lonely and evil quest to Eden. He brings with him chaos, storm, and cosmically inclement sky. The proleptic nature of the Limbo episode, representing as it does a glimpse into the fallen future of man, is emphasized symbolically by the image of the "pendant world" of man "starless expos'd" and encompassed by all that is "dark, waste, and wild." This panoramic gloom seems an appropriate attitude toward the event being described. But then comes a surprising shift from tragic solemnity to burlesque disorder and absurdity. Satan's arrival on the "boundless Continent" of the world's "backside" (495) is turned into a darkly comic foreshadowing of the chaos that will come—not again, but for the first time. The comic possibilities of Milton's Limbo are only slightly hinted at in the above passage by the word "blust'ring," but the mob of fools who appear in the envisioned turmoil that follows Satan's arrival does function to lighten the dark perspective. Satan's somber entrance is abruptly interrupted by an unruly menagerie of giants, suicides, and wind-tossed monks:

> Here Pilgrims roam, that stray'd so far to seek
> In *Golgotha* him dead, who lives in Heav'n;
> And they who to be sure of Paradise
> Dying put on the weeds of *Dominic,*
> Or in *Franciscan* think to pass disguis'd;
> They pass the Planets seven, and pass the fixt,
> And that Crystalline Sphere whose balance weighs
> The Trepidation talkt, and that first mov'd;
> And now Saint *Peter* at Heav'n's Wicket seems
> To wait them with his Keys, and now at foot
> Of Heav'n's ascent they lift thir Feet, when lo
> A violent cross wind from either Coast
> Blows them transverse ten thousand Leagues awry
> Into the devious Air; then might ye see
> Cowls, Hoods and Habits with thir wearers tost
> And flutter'd into Rags, then Reliques, Beads,
> Indulgences, Dispenses, Pardons, Bulls,
> The sport of Winds.   (III, 476–93)

The Fiend and the fools are linked in a satiric burlesque which acts itself out on a stage that calls to mind Lear's stormy and barren heath. Such darkness is the backdrop for all the burlesque activity in Milton's poem.[3]

The debunking which is always found in burlesque in general and in the epic variety used in *Paradise Lost* in particular is evident in the Limbo episode. Burlesque depends on a systematic letdown which travesties a systematic buildup of expectations. The Limbo letdown includes an attack on spiritual failures—pagan and Catholic spiritual failures specifically. But debunking is as much a state of mind and view of reality as it is an intellectual weapon aimed at specific targets. Burlesque debunking often has it source in questioning and disillusionment. It becomes possible only when orthodox standards and commonly held beliefs are breaking down. As Kenneth Burke has noted: "The history of debunking is interwoven with the history of liberalism. As soon as men began methodically to question the Church's vocabulary of human motivation, they gravitated towards the debunking category."[4] Burlesque ridicule can be seen as a strategy designed to deal with doubts and to sketch the foundations of new norms on the ruins of old ones. Milton's religious and political positions during and after the English Civil War put him squarely on the side of a liberalism which attempted to destroy the outworn, no longer accepted tenets of church-state orthodoxy. His liberalism is a product of the disorder which comes from rejecting and opposing old orders. Seventeenth-century burlesque is one way poets coped with the political and religious anxieties of the period. As David Farley-Hills says, "it is a confused response to a confused situation."[5] Milton's intense desire for order and harmony, so apparent in all of his poetry, is tempered by the personal traumas of regicide, civil war, and restoration. The problematic nature of Milton's epic burlesque laughter reflects the depth and honesty of his response to his own and his nation's experience. It is a laughter achieved with difficulty, accompanied by anxiety.

Burlesque as Milton uses it is not shallow or facile in its ability to find apposite fables for subjects like Catholicism, warfare, hell, or sin and death. Milton's laughter is not an easy response to incongruous phenomena. The inherently paradoxical nature of burlesque, which lends itself to oxymoronic fantasticalities, is suited to a combination not only of high style and low subject, or of vulgar actions and dignified gestures, but also to a combination of the tragic and the comic. What could be more "disproportionate," to use one of Samuel Johnson's key words

when he analyzes burlesque, than the yoking of two such opposite kinds of experience?[6] What could be more incongruous than
the requirement that a reader laugh and yet feel tragic emotions
while laughing? This strategy, however, and this mixed response
characterize Milton's burlesque in *Paradise Lost* and so give the
burlesque episodes in the poem their special tension. It is a
typically burlesque tension to join the serious and the comic and
to insist on the integrity of each while insisting, at the same time,
on their unity, indeed, their identity. The result of such a strategy is a lack of resolution and a lack of harmony. But, of course,
those are the very results burlesque strives to produce. Such
burlesque places the reader on the picket fence of paradoxical
responses and asks him to be comfortable in his straddled position. But one cannot be comfortable. There are too many disturbing thematic undercurrents in the presentation, too much darkness (to revert to that image) beneath the surface of the comedy.[7]
If Milton's burlesque humor is finally an unhappy and discon-
certing gift, it is because it sounds the depths of the most disturbing aspects of existence. To appropriate Dryden's phrase, it
"affects the metaphysics."

The burlesque described above bears a striking resemblance
to the modern absurdist tradition. One finds similar kinds of incongruity, similar irreconcilable juxtapositions, the same troubling
dilemma of reader response in each. And Milton, like Beckett,
encourages a laughter which is most usually grim. Milton speaks
specifically of "grim laughter" in his political pamphlet, *Animadversions* (1641):

Although in the serious uncasing of a grand imposture (for to deale
plainly with you, Readers, Prelatry is no better) there be mixt here and
there such a grim laughter, as may appeare at the same time in an austere
visage, it cannot be taxt of levity or insolence: for even this veine of
laughing (as I could produce out of grave Authors) hath oft times a strong
and sinewy force in teaching and confuting; nor can there be a more
proper object of indignation and scorne together than a false Prophet
taken in the greatest, dearest and most dangerous cheat, the cheat of
soules: in the disclosing whereof if it be harmfull to be angry, and withall
to case a lowring smile, when the properest object calls for both, it will be
long enough ere any be able to say why those two most rationall faculties
of humane intellect anger and laughter were first seated in the brest of
man.[8]

The grimness of the laughter Milton describes here is different
from black humor in that it is more specifically satiric, less a

reflection of a metaphysical condition. Such rational grim laughter is appropriate to satire because it functions to uncase a "grand imposture." It is an appropriate weapon for an attack on a swindler prelacy. It would also be appropriate, as indeed it is, to an exposé of Satanic evil and to a revelation of the grotesque absurdity that lies behind evil's most imposing facade. Yet the laughter in the exposé of evil in *Paradise Lost* does become a reflection of a metaphysical condition, and therein lies a deeper affinity between Milton's poetic burlesque and the black humor of our time. Both force grim laughter from a reader who is required to perceive the grotesque incongruities of existence and the tragic absurdity in the universe. Irene Samuel has argued that "Milton was not limited to the emerging neoclassical tastes of his age, but neither was he the forerunner of black comedy with its macabre relish for gallows humor." Yet she adds: "Milton asks us to perceive absurdities without forgetting horrors."[9] So it is with modern black comedy. The perception of absurdities in a universe of horrors is just what is most characteristic of modern black humor and Milton's burlesque. Both focus on unnatural phenomena, the grotesque of nature and supernature. Both exhibit a strange fascination with the warped and the perverse. The ridiculous as sublime is frequently the subject of each, and a penchant for the primitive on a cosmic stage is a shared feature. In addition, there is an unflagging concentration on sexuality and scatology. The world is reduced to its seemingly most absurd activities. Both black humor and burlesque deal with threats, psychic and real, and attempt, with doubtful success, to obliterate them with laughter. The exaggerated becomes the normal, the incongruous becomes the expected, and only confusion is comprehensible. And a central point of both is that the universe they are a response to is absurd, unreasonable.

A burlesque sounding of depths is nowhere more apparent than in Milton's allegory of Sin and Death. Sin and Death are centrally active figures, along with Satan, in a burlesque horror show that also features such absurdist comedy actors as the Limbo fools, the angelic warriors in Book VI, and the serpent angels in Book X. Sin and Death are given a burlesque treatment that has at its center a metaphysical anxiety about the values and meanings of a world order which contains such absurd realities. Satan's children are metaphysical buffoons in a philosophical comedy. But the humor in their presentation is black:

>   Before the Gates there sat
>   On either side a formidable shape;
>   The one seem'd Woman to the waist, and fair,
>   But ended foul in many a scaly fold
>   Voluminous and vast, a Serpent arm'd
>   With mortal sting: about her middle round
>   A cry of Hell Hounds never ceasing bark'd
>   With wide *Cerberean* mouths full loud, and rung
>   A hideous Peal: yet, when they list, would creep,
>   If aught disturb'd thir noise, into her womb,
>   And kennel there, yet there still bark'd and howl'd
>   Within unseen. Far less abhorr'd than these
>   Vex'd *Scylla* bathing in the Sea that parts
>   *Calabria* from the hoarse *Trinacrian* shore:
>   Nor uglier follow the Night-Hag, when call'd
>   In secret, riding through the Air she comes
>   Lur'd with the smell of infant blood, to dance
>   With *Lapland* Witches, while the laboring Moon
>   Eclipses at thir charms. The other shape,
>   If shape it might be call'd that shape had none
>   Distinguishable in member, joint, or limb,
>   Or substance might be call'd that shadow seem'd,
>   For each seem'd either; black it stood as Night,
>   Fierce as ten Furies, terrible as Hell,
>   And shook a dreadful Dart; what seem'd his head
>   The likeness of a Kingly Crown had on.   (II, 648–73)

One's response to such a description is complex. One feels, I think, variously impressed, repelled, amused, repulsed, and frightened. The stuff of bad dreams seems to have become the material for a grotesque and incongruous reality, and the reader feels disoriented as a result. This Sin and Death call up unconscious fears, yet the artificiality and self-consciousness which are characteristic of burlesque exaggeration bring about a distancing amusement. The Night-Hag simile, for example, creates a wonderful sense of the mystery and magic of evil. But, made up as it is of the stuff of popular superstition, a slight but significant undercutting of its threat is effected at the same time. A touch of the absurd lingers. The nightmarish quality of the whole is insisted on, however, and a description like "black it stood as Night, / Fierce as ten Furies, terrible as Hell" has an appropriately dreamlike vagueness and indeterminacy. But the fact remains that the unconscious fears which the double portrait of Sin and Death evokes (of the Witch Mother and Tyrant Father, for example) are mostly thwarted by the awakened intellect. Thus, nervous laughter is the usual response to the description of Sin's lower half, for the grotesque on such a lurid level and in the light of the reader's day becomes funny despite the horror contained in it and despite the threat to oneself contained in the horror. Asleep, one would find such a response impossible. Consciousness, however, brings freedom of the kind noted by Freud in his essay "Der Humor" (1927): the ego, refusing to suffer, asserts its invulnerability by means of a liberating humor and so achieves "something of grandeur and elevation."[10] The disturbing quality inherent in black humor and in Miltonic burlesque derives from the difficulty of achieving the triumphant response of laughter described by Freud. That difficulty is what makes the humor of Sin's grotesque shape or Godot's absence so troubling. The liberation from psychic and real threats and the success in gaining pleasure are so short-lived that the smile hardly appears before the fear takes over. The ego's vulnerability remains a central concern, and distress reappears. Milton's epic burlesque has the grandeur which comes from a comic triumph over sources of anxiety and danger, but it also does justice to the power of the threat represented by Sin and Death. As a result, the comic triumph is made difficult and grating. The reader is not permitted to respond in only one way to the incongruity of a woman who is a serpent from the waist down, to the outrageous image of a womb filled with howling dogs, to a being who has no substance and yet wears a crown. These are grotesque incongruities which deliberately verge on the comic, yet an open laughter which will liberate one from such images is not easily forthcoming. Milton's strategy is again clearly similar to that of black humorists. As Mathew Winston describes black humor, it "scorns the limitations of rational thought, and therefore favors the fantastic, the surreal, and the grotesque. It wishes to break down complacency and to reveal how a man's unconscious realities belie his harmonious surface, and consequently employs violent images and shock tactics."[11] These things are true of Milton's presentation of Satan's children.

Sin and Death are variously shocking, frightening, repulsive, farcical, and absurd. Their comedy is sinister, and their abnormality makes one feel insecure. For example, an insecure comic response is caused by the Satan, Sin, and Death parody of the Holy Trinity. Milton readers, of course, have long recognized that intentional parody is at work here, but the mixed nature of the reader's response to that parody has not been sufficiently emphasized. Shock and comic disbelief are paramount when one realizes that Milton has created a trinity in which the father and son threaten to destroy each other. Ironically, Sin, this trinity's second person, becomes, in this absurd moment, the spirit of peace:

> the Snaky Sorceress that sat
> Fast by Hell Gate, and kept the fatal Key,
> Ris'n, and with hideous outcry rush'd between.
>   O Father, what intends thy hand, she cri'd,
> Against thy only Son? What fury O Son,
> Possesses thee to bend that mortal Dart
> Against thy Father's head?   (II, 724–30)

The same precariously mixed response of shock and laughter follows upon Sin's description of her life in hell since she arrived:

> Pensive here I sat
> Alone, but long I sat not, till my womb
> Pregnant by thee, and now excessive grown
> Prodigious motion felt and rueful throes.
> At last this odious offspring whom thou seest
> Thine own begotten, breaking violent way
> Tore through my entrails, that with fear and pain
> Distorted, all my nether shape thus grew
> Transform'd: but he my inbred enemy
> Forth issu'd, brandishing his fatal Dart
> Made to destroy: I fled, and cri'd out *Death*;
> Hell trembl'd at the hideous Name, and sigh'd
> From all her Caves, and back resounded *Death*.
> I fled, but he pursu'd (though more, it seems,
> Inflam'd with lust than rage) and swifter far,
> Mee overtook his mother all dismay'd,
> And in embraces forcible and foul
> Ingend'ring with me, of that rape begot
> These yelling Monsters that with ceaseless cry
> Surround me, as thou saw'st, hourly conceiv'd
> And hourly born, with sorrow infinite
> To me, for when they list, into the womb
> That bred them they return, and howl and gnaw
> My Bowels, thir repast; then bursting forth
> Afresh with conscious terrors vex me round,
> That rest or intermission none I find.   (II, 777–802)

Such maternal lamentation on such a scale is burlesque at its complex best. And what is the reader to make of such violent juxtapositions as "thine own begotten" with its biblical echoes and Death with his phallic dart? This is not just satire. The purpose is not simply to attack a contemptible adversary or to establish norms by means of satiric abuse. One's knowledge of the existence of the divine Trinity, the fact on which the parody depends, is certainly reassuring when one steps back and sees Sin and Death in the larger Miltonic-Christian perspective, but the infernal trinity is designed to make one feel as forcefully as possible the special madness of a frightening world which contains such ludicrous discords. In such passages as the above, the reader is not concerned with what should be in some haven of satiric or heavenly norms, but only with the nightmarish absurdity which exists at this poetically dramatic moment. Thus Sin's recital is disturbing, repulsive, and humorous. Sin's lamenting narrative is horrific, and funny. Black laughter seems an apt description of the response that the passage encourages.

Milton's burlesque, then, does not allow one to feel at ease. The philosophic comedy of *Paradise Lost* promises triumph over the grotesque postlapsarian bondage to Sin and Death, but the immediate action of the poem confronts one with incongruity and not triumph. We are encouraged, at those moments when we share the divine perspective, to be contemptuous of the Satanic trio, yet we never are allowed to forget that Sin and Death will have us in the end. We are, as prisoners of time, slaves to the horrible necessities which they represent. We are repelled and amused by Sin's grotesque exterior and her equally offensive son, and both responses distance us from them. At the same time, we are reminded that we do sin and that we will die. Thus the distance is removed, and we recognize with renewed horror that Death's dart and his ravenous maw will work their effects on us. The rapid shifting from humor to blackness, from amusement to threat, and from farce to horror is a combination of extremes that disorients and dismays. We may be, as one of the saved, sharers in an eternity of joy, but we cannot be as certain about that personal, comforting future as we can about the personal, dangerous present of our fallen lives. There are glimpses and prophecies of an eventual salvation throughout *Paradise Lost,* and an eternity in which Death's power will be ended is predicted; but the joyful and ordered world of eschatological promise is suspended before the disordered and threatening reality of the poem's fallen universe. We may be encouraged to laugh at Sin and Death, but we are reminded that they laugh back:

                              Death
          Grinn'd horrible a ghastly smile, to hear
          His famine should be fill'd, and blest his maw
          Destin'd to that good hour: no less rejoic'd
          His mother bad.   (II, 845–49)

Our laughter trails off at the sound of theirs.

The tension between the buildup and subsequent letdown which is central to so much burlesque accounts for a large part of the ambivalence one finds in Milton's allegory of Sin and Death. A nightmare that degenerates into comic bickering and hypocritical courtesies of "Dear Daughter" and "my fair Son" is a comic reversal that has a deflating effect on characters' pretensions and readers' expectations. Such a burlesque tension is also produced in Satan's voyage through chaos. Chaos is the poem's other metaphysical absurdity, and, as Satan recognizes, his own efforts and those of his progeny are allied to the destructive forces which Milton represents in his allegory of the "Anarch old." The buildup for Satan's voyage through the kingdom of anarchy, to which he says he wishes to restore "usurped" regions (II, 981–87), takes place in the scene in which the gates of hell are opened. Sin's unlocking of the gates is a grandly dramatic gesture that creates expectations of a journey which will be equally impressive (II, 871–89). The reader is conditioned by the description to expect sonorous expansion in language and a complementary expansion in perspective. The gates are impressively wide; the view from them should be equally impressive. What is initially seen by Satan, Sin, and Death fits such expectations, for:

          Before thir eyes in sudden view appear
          The secrets of the hoary deep, a dark
          Illimitable Ocean without bound,
          Without dimension, where length, breadth, and highth,
          And time and place are lost.   (II, 890–94)

The lack of definition so strongly suggested in phrases like "without dimension" and "dark Illimitable Ocean" is consonant with a "hoary" region full of dark secrets and deep mysteries. But the grand vagueness of the initial view yields surprisingly to a rigidly precise, bothersome little allegory of armed elements. The initially awed and fearful gazing of Satan, Sin, and Death—an attitude we share as we momentarily see with them—collapses in a rubble of simplistic personification. Milton latches onto battle imagery with such abandon that a curious but, I would assert, deliberate faking in the tone is produced:

> And time and place are lost; where eldest *Night*
> And *Chaos*, Ancestors of Nature, hold
> Eternal Anarchy, amidst the noise
> Of endless wars, and by confusion stand.
> For hot, cold, moist, and dry, four Champions fierce
> Strive here for Maistry, and to Battle bring
> Thir embryon Atoms; they round the flag
> Of each his Faction, in thir several Clans,
> Swarm populous.   (II, 894–903)

Dismissing this passage as bad poetry, J. B. Broadbent asserts that the initial "simple, vast vision" from hell's gates is "split with rhetoric" and "followed by bathos," and the moral is made "ineffectually obvious."[12] Broadbent is correct about the jarring disruption of the previous effects. Nevertheless, it is possible to view the rhetoric and the histrionic allegorizing as effective burlesque letdown. The momentous grandeur is demolished when "hot, cold, moist, and dry" become four mock-epic "Champions fierce" who produce confusions which "stand." We are presented with a king who *rules* such "Eternal Anarchy." Yet the idea of order implicit in ruling a kingdom is inverted by a monarchical encouragement of disorder. Chaos is that strange monarch who "by decision more imbroils the fray / By which he Reigns: next him high Arbiter / *Chance* governs all" (II, 908–10). A king who advises conflict, and a Minister Chance who, it is suggested, has the forethought necessary for government are ridiculous. And the idea that the four elements are "Champions fierce" who give battle and gather round the flag is Renaissance *pictura poesis* made trite in order to level and thereby reduce the idea of chaos to comic oxymoronics. The use of the word "clans" with its Scottish associations reveals well enough the Englishman's contempt for the contentious "Faction" which precipitates such broils as are represented by the allegory. The kingdom of Chaos, then, is a place where mutually exclusive concepts like government and anarchy are made to coalesce. The union is violent. The result is humorous because in this allegory the literal level is wittily antithetical to the other levels. A burlesque incongruity results from allegory which comically clashes with itself.

The debunking involved in the Chaos section of *Paradise Lost* is also achieved by means of internal allusion: the factions and clans of Chaos "Swarm populous, unnumber'd as the Sands / Of *Barca* or *Cyrene's* torrid soil" (II, 903–04). These lines contain verbal echoes of two epic similes that appear in Book I. Both of the earlier similes serve to reduce the pretensions and dignity of the fallen angels. The first one, echoed by the phrase "Swarm populous," concerns the entry of Satan's followers into the newly constructed palace of Pandaemonium:

> they anon
> With hunderds and with thousands trooping came
> Attended: all access was throng'd, the Gates
> And Porches wide, but chief the spacious Hall
> (Though like a cover'd field, where *Champions* bold
> Wont ride in arm'd, and at the Soldan's chair
> Defi'd the best of Paynim chivalry
> To mortal combat or career with Lance)
> Thick *swarm'd*, both on the ground and in the air,
> Brusht with the hiss of rustling wings. As Bees
> In spring time, when the Sun with Taurus rides,
> Pour forth thir *populous* youth about the Hive
> In clusters; they among fresh dews and flowers
> Fly to and fro, or on the smoothed Plank,
> The suburb of thir Straw-built Citadel,
> New rubb'd with Balm, expatiate and confer
> Thir state affairs. So thick the aery crowd
> *Swarm'd* and were strait'n'd; till the Signal giv'n,
> Behold a wonder! they but now who seem'd
> In bigness to surpass Earth's Giant Sons
> Now less than smallest Dwarfs, in narrow room
> Throng *numberless*, like that Pigmean Race
> Beyond the Indian Mount, or Faery Elves.
>   (I, 759–81, italics mine)

The "Champions" here are fallen angels who are reduced to "Faery Elves," but these "Champions" also "swarm populous" near a gate. The second reductive simile from Book I connects to lines 903–04 of Book II through the repetition of "Sands" and through the image of unnumbered, "populous" multitudes pouring onto the earth. What is comic and reductive in this instance is that it is fallen angels who are "Pour'd," and that pouring is a euphemism for urination.

> A multitude, like which the *populous* North
> Pour'd never from her frozen loins, to pass
> Rhene or the Danaw, when her barbarous Sons
> Came like a Deluge on the South, and spread
> Beneath Gibralter to the Lybian *sands*. (I, 351–55, italics mine)

The echoes in the Chaos episode clearly connect the violent factions of warring atoms to the multitudes of fallen angels. The internal allusions identify the rebellious angels and the warring elements as confederates in a war whose ultimate aim is chaos on a cosmic level.

Chaos, then, sits as "Umpire" on his throne and "rules his unruly domain." His kingdom, like Milton's Paradise of Fools, is a fantastic place, and, specifically, a

> wild Abyss
> The Womb of nature and perhaps her Grave,
> Of neither Sea, nor Shore, nor Air, nor Fire,
> But all these in thir pregnant causes mixt
> Confus'dly, and which thus must ever fight.   (II, 910–14)

The "Illimitable Ocean" which Satan attempts to cross on his way through the region is indeed a crazy concoction of incompatible ingredients. This is a burlesque "ocean" through which Satan

> O'er bog or steep, through straight, rough, dense, or rare,
> With head, hands, wings, or feet pursues his way,
> And swims or sinks, or wades, or creeps, or flies.   (II, 948–50)

Such a manner of going takes its toll on the heroic posing which Satan has previously engaged in. He left on his journey with pompous strides, but his subsequent letdown is made quite literal:

> At last his Sail-broad Vans
> He spreads for flight, and in the surging smoke
> Uplifted spurns the ground, thence many a League
> As in a cloudy Chair ascending rides
> Audacious, but that seat soon failing, meets
> A vast vacuity: all unawares
> Flutt'ring his pennons vain plumb down he drops
> Ten thousand fadom deep, and to this hour
> Down had been falling, had not by ill chance
> The strong rebuff of some tumultuous cloud
> Instinct with Fire and Nitre hurried him
> As many miles aloft,   (II, 927–38)

Satan's "Chair" is pulled out from under him, and the devil finds himself the victim of an unexpected old joke. He survives his comic pratfall, however, and so eventually comes to Chaos' "dark Pavilion," only to find

> a universal hubbub wild
> Of stunning sounds and voices all confus'd
> Borne through the hollow dark.   (II, 951–53)

Milton's choice of words is one key to his burlesque intention. Thus Chaos, a figure potentially so frightening and undesirable, is turned into a noise polluter, a hubbuber, in a "hollow" darkness. A very similar "hubbub" will be heard when, in Book XII, God's visit to the construction site of the tower of Babel is described:

> But God who oft descends to visit men
> Unseen, and through thir habitations walks
> To mark thir doings, them beholding soon,
> Comes down to see thir City, ere the Tower
> Obstruct Heav'n Tow'rs, and in derision sets
> Upon thir Tongues a various Spirit to rase
> Quite out thir Native Language, and instead
> To sow a jangling noise of words unknown:
> Forthwith a hideous gabble rises loud
> Among the Builders; each to other calls
> Not understood, till hoarse, and all in rage,
> As mockt they storm; great laughter was in Heav'n
> And looking down, to see the hubbub strange
> And hear the din; thus was the building left
> Ridiculous, and the work Confusion nam'd.   (XII, 48–62)

Such noise, whether in Chaos or Babylon, was clearly the object of mirth to Milton, and his God.

The comic triumph, in the Freudian sense, is more easily achieved with Chaos than with Sin and Death. The reason may be that Chaos, in the Miltonic perspective, is passive and undirected. He has no will of his own. Real evil depends on the directive power of a governing will dedicated to destruction and perversion. Satan, Sin, and Death are aspects of such a will. That is why they make an appropriate trinity. Chaos and Night, however, are passive reservoirs for the refuse of Satanic evil. They are at the mercy of order because they cannot oppose it, only be other than it. Chaos has not rebelled, but he does represent absolute disorder, the state to which all grotesque irrationality and disharmony are finally reduced. The destined accomplishments of Satan, Sin, and Death will contribute to the power and dominion of Chaos and his consort, "Sable-vested Night." Chaos is what he is, and one thing he is is a potential womb of creation. The "intestine broils" of Chaos' kingdom are internal disruptions and are not effective disturbances to heaven's order. But Chaos is guilty to the extent that he does not resist the evil which employs him: he has "Tamely endur'd a Bridge of wondrous length / From Hell . . . reaching th' utmost Orb / Of this frail World" (II, 1028–30). Chaos is guilty too because in Milton's metaphysics order is good and disorder evil, by definition. But only when the materials of Chaos are given a shape, whether in the creation of the universe by the Son or the bridge-building of Sin and Death, does Chaos enter as a participant in the drama of divine glory and human failure. Because Milton views Chaos as receptive to good as well as to evil, he is less threatening. His comedy lacks the blackness of Sin and Death's burlesque. As a result, the debunking is achieved with less difficulty.[13]

The metaphysical blackness at the center of Milton's epic burlesque humor derives to a great extent from the frightening antics of Satan, his progeny, and his followers. The unease which interjects itself into the poem's universe as a whole, however, is also produced by the negative capacities of Milton's God. The infernal sources of metaphysical anxiety are complemented by a divinely caused metaphysical tension. God's speech in Book X, as he views the arrival of Sin and Death in Eden, dramatically throws into relief the threat contained in divine anger:

> See with what heat these Dogs of Hell advance
> To waste and havoc yonder World, which I
> So fair and good created, and had still
> Kept in that state, had not the *folly* of Man
> Let in these wasteful Furies, who impute
> *Folly* to mee, so doth the Prince of Hell
> And his Adherents, that with so much ease
> I suffer them to enter and possess
> A place so heav'nly, and conniving seem
> To gratify my scornful Enemies,
> That *laugh*, as if transported with some fit
> Of Passion, I to them had quitted all,
> At random yielded up to thir *misrule;*
> And know not that I call'd and drew them thither
> My Hell-hounds, to lick up the draff and filth
> Which man's polluting Sin with taint hath shed
> On what was pure, till cramm'd and gorg'd, nigh burst
> With suckt and glutted offal, at one sling
> Of thy victorious Arm, well-pleasing Son,
> Both Sin, and Death, and yawning Grave at last
> Through Chaos hurl'd, obstruct the mouth of Hell
> For ever, and seal up his ravenous Jaws.
>
> (X, 616–37, italics mine)

The emphasis on "folly" and "misrule," with their Elizabethan overtones, is no accident. Satan, Sin, Death, and Chaos are comic, but there is no immediate comfort in that. At least we do not respond to God's words with equanimity or easy comic relief. God's statement, and particularly his tone, are terrifying, horrible, and repulsive because we—fallen humanity—are the ones caught between a divinity capable of such anger and fury and "nonentities" as palpably destructive as Sin and Death.[14] Our response is made more complex because we are charged with responsibility for our own tragic position. We are, inescapably, players in the grotesque comedy of Satanic evil. Yet we are held to account for a foolish performance in a play we did not fully write. Milton's belief in man's free will is not naive. His dramatization of the great forces which are in conflict in *Paradise Lost* reveals his sense of the epically antagonistic powers which vie for a much weaker and more vulnerable mankind. Christian eschatology is a solution to man's dilemma, but Milton does not draw back from presenting the ludicrous folly and misrule which meanwhile are rampant on the stage of the fallen world. Thus, his God unflinchingly speaks of the Last Judgment in terms of dogs in heat, the licking of filth and draff, and undigested offal. The antics of Sin and Death eventually end in vile manifestations of lust, disease, and sickness. Their comedy is hollow and horrible in the extreme, and God's intemperate review of it is frightening.

The dark metaphysics of Milton's burlesque of evil presupposes a God who can tolerate great discord. This divine tolerance, of course, is the crux of Milton's theodical aim in *Paradise Lost*. How can a benevolent God let it all happen? Yes, man is free; but another aspect of Milton's "solution," if one may call it that, is to present a God who has two faces: one he turns toward the actors in the Satanic plot, the other he shows to those who participate in the divine comedy. It is as if God is a Janus-faced audience for two plays being performed simultaneously—one in the front and one in the rear of the theater. The reader is encouraged to imitate the divine spectator, to adopt the divine point of view. What happens, however, is that the reader gets a sore neck as a result of the effort to see in two opposite directions at once. We finally contemplate, with a combination of awe and resentment, the divinity who can harmonize such violently opposed realities. As in our responses to Sin and Death or to the war in heaven, we find ourselves suspended between violent extremes. We are given *one* God who is a God of anger, a God who punishes, and yet, simultaneously, a God of love, a God who forgives. He is alternately violent, scornful, serene, loving, and unknowable. In the same way, the poem as a whole is suspended between extremes. *Paradise Lost* can be thought of, as some have thought of it, as a philosophical comedy. Its Christian theology guarantees such a perspective, for, as Northrop Frye has said, "Christianity sees tragedy as an episode in the divine comedy, the larger scheme of redemption and resurrection." But he adds, "The sense of tragedy as a prelude to comedy seems almost inseparable from anything explicitly Christian."[15] The comic conclusion to man's story promised in *Paradise Lost* is, indeed, inseparable from and subsequent to the tragedy of history and time, and Milton does not cancel one in favor of the other. The poem's burlesque vision of evil is produced by the crunching pressures of the tragic as it meets the comic. The meeting of the two is the occasion for the grating and uneasy laughter which results from recognizing the incongruous poles of man's existence.

Burlesque always records a split in the perception of reality. In *Paradise Lost,* the split in the world involves the most serious matters, but burlesque remains an appropriate method for giving shape to the metaphysical schizophrenia which one finds in Milton's epic. The poem looks forward to the promised dawn of eternity, yet back to the murkiest of Satanic nights. The promises of the incarnation as Michael lists them in Book XII are warmly articulated and deeply felt, but the emotional force behind Michael's description of a world that will go on "under its own weight groaning" is equally dynamic. The famous last lines of Book XII have a consoling tone, but they also have disturbing undercurrents. Adam and Eve face a difficult future. The complexity of response elicited by the poem's concluding lines is, of course, the very source of their power. Life in the Christian universe of *Paradise Lost* is not simple, relaxing, or one dimensional. It is full of anxieties, testings, and antitheses. Milton offers his "fit audience" no pipe dreams. His imagination is not escapist, and neither is his theology. The burlesque humor found in his epic is equally complex.

United States Naval Academy

NOTES

1. The phrase "black humor" refers to a kind of traditional macabre humor which is particularly prevalent in modern world literature. Of course, Milton's attitude is shaped by older medieval and contemporary Renaissance "black hu-

mor" traditions. The medieval-Renaissance dance of death; the absurdist, gargoyled monstrosities of church art and architecture; and the vice buffoons and devil villains of early English drama are all reflections of something comically-fearfully paradoxical in the human condition. Yet the words "absurdist" and "black humor" warrant usage because Milton's burlesque shares vital features with the modern. That Milton goes beyond the modern and offers a transcending world of Christian security does not cancel the affinities between the absurdist aspects of his poem's universe and the universe of the modern black humorists.

2. All quotations from *Paradise Lost* are from *John Milton: Complete Poems and Major Prose*, ed. Merritt Y. Hughes (Indianapolis, 1957).

3. "Burlesque" is the most precise and least anachronistic term for Milton's comic-satiric strategies in *Paradise Lost*. Richmond P. Bond outlines a large context for burlesque which includes parody, mock-heroic, travesty, and Hudibrastic verse, in *English Burlesque Poetry: 1700–1750*, Harvard Studies in English, No. 6 (New York, 1932). Some modern critics have attempted to restrict the use of "burlesque" to a much smaller group of poems. For examples of the narrower application of the term, see Albert H. West, *L'Influence française dans la poésie burlesque en Angleterre: Entre 1660 et 1700* (Paris, 1931), pp. 12–17; and Ian Jack, *Augustan Satire: Intention and Idiom in English Poetry 1660–1750* (London, 1952), p. 25. West and Jack, however, ignore the loose usage of the term and the protean form of the mode in the seventeenth century.

4. "The Virtues and Limitations of Debunking," in *The Philosophy of Literary Form*, 3d ed. (1941; rpt. Berkeley, 1973), p. 169.

5. *The Benevolence of Laughter: Comic Poetry of the Commonwealth and Restoration* (Totowa, N.J., 1974), p. 20.

6. Johnson says in his *Lives of the Poets*, ed. G. B. Hill (London, 1905), vol. I, p. 218: "Burlesque consists in a disproportion between the style and the sentiments, or between the adventitious sentiments and the fundamental subject. It, therefore, like all bodies compounded of heterogeneous parts, contains in it a principle of corruption. All disproportion is unnatural; and from what is unnatural we can derive only the pleasure which novelty produces. We admire it for a while as a strange thing; but, when it is no longer strange, we perceive its deformity. It is a kind of artifice, which by frequent repetition detects itself; and the reader, learning in time what to expect, lays down his book, as the spectator turns away from a second exhibition of those tricks, of which the only use is to shew that they can be played."

7. Milton's use of black comedy should be compared to Shakespeare's in *Lear*. Two analyses of *Lear* offer stimulating material for such a comparison: G. Wilson Knight, "*King Lear* and the Comedy of the Grotesque," in *The Wheel of Fire* (London, 1949), pp. 160–76; and Jan Kott, " 'King Lear' and 'Endgame'," in *Shakespeare Our Contemporary*, trans. Boleslaw Taborski (New York, 1964), pp. 127–68.

8. *The Works of John Milton*, ed. Frank Allen Patterson et al. (New York, 1931–38), vol. III, pp. 107–08.

9. "Milton on Comedy and Satire," *Huntington Library Quarterly*, XXXV (1972), 128, 129.

10. "Humour," in *The Standard Edition of the Complete Psychological Works of Sigmund Freud*, ed. and trans. James Strachey (London, 1953–66), vol. 21, p. 162.

11. "*Humour noir* and Black Humor," in *Veins of Humor*, ed. Harry Levin,

Harvard English Studies, No. 3 (Cambridge, 1972), p. 270. Winston's essay contains a good summary of major critical attitudes on black humor.

12. *Some Graver Subject* (New York, 1960), p. 133.

13. In an essay which focuses specifically on Chaos, Robert M. Adams makes similar judgments on the ambivalence of Chaos in Milton's cosmos. See "A Little Look into Chaos," in *Illustrious Evidence*, ed. Earl Miner (Berkeley, 1975), pp. 71–89.

14. In *The Muse's Method* (Cambridge, 1962), p. 39, Joseph H. Summers has said: "Johnson believed that the ludicrous and the events and devices which shock the mind should have no place in an heroic poem, but Milton gave them a fairly central place in *Paradise Lost*. While Johnson thought that 'nonentity' could not produce 'effects,' Milton's poem is largely concerned with the 'effects' which those two 'nonentities,' Sin and Death, produce."

15. *Anatomy of Criticism* (1957; rpt. New York, 1970), p. 215.

LA TINA
THE COUNTRY SONNETS
OF
ANTONIO MALATESTI
AS DEDICATED
TO MR. JOHN MILTON,
ENGLISH GENTLEMAN

Translated by
Donald Sears

I. PREFACE

AMONG THE scattered bits of information concerning John Milton's trip to Italy in 1638–39, none is more tantalizing than his possession of the manuscript sonnets of Antonio Malatesti.[1] It would seem that before his departure from Florence in late April 1639, Milton received from the author the manuscipt of fifty sonnets entitled *La Tina, Equivoci Rusticali*. That these poems, addressed to a rural mistress and couched in imagery and words of double meaning, should have been dedicated to the Puritan poet of England suggests a social side of Milton's wit that may be broader than we have usually accepted.

What little is known of the life of Malatesti indicates that he had some repute in Florence as a student of mathematics and astronomy (perhaps studying with Galileo, and certainly visiting him), as a painter, and especially as a writer of burlesque poetry, much of it extemporaneous or circulated in private manuscript.[2] He seems to have been a special friend of Carlo Roberto Dati with whom Milton was well acquainted during his Italian stay and to whom he later wrote. In one letter to Dati, Milton makes reference to Malatesti.[3] In the academy circles of Florence, Malatesti was as early as 1630 nominated for membership in the Accademia degli Apatisti.[4] Reportedly of a happy disposition and endowed with a warm fantasy, Malatesti produced a large ar ount of fairly fugitive verse. He died in 1672 and was buried in ʰhe church of Santa Croce.

One of the few works to appear during his lifetime was his *Sfinge*, published in Venice in 1640 and republished in Florence in 1643 and 1683. This work is a collection of poetical enigmas. Published posthumously in 1673, his *I Brindisi dei Ciclopi* is in the burlesque tradition.

The history of the Milton manuscript of *La Tina* is obscure. Apparently the English poet kept the manuscript during his lifetime, after which it disappeared. About 1750, a Mr. Brand found the manuscript of the poems in a London bookstall and presented it to his friend Thomas Hollis.[5] A copy in 1758 was sent to the Della Crusca Academy in Florence. Another copy was given to a representative of the University of Padua on his visit to London. In the first half of the nineteenth century, an edition was printed in Venice. There are hints of a first edition published in London in 1757;[6] and there is a certitude about a Milan edition of 1865 which states in its preface that, lacking the first edition of London,

277

its text is based on the Venice edition of 1831.[7] Likewise based on the Venice edition but citing the date as 1837 is the edition of 500 copies published by Il Ruscello (Milan, 1945).

From information given in the catalogue of the Hollis Library, the title page of the original manuscript stated that Malatesti composed the sonnets at his Villa di Taiano in September 1637. The actual location of this villa has eluded my search of old maps of Tuscany and interviews in Italy with those familiar with the countryside. There is a Caiano in the Casentino hills east of Florence as well as a Poggio Caiano just west of Campi, a Maiano near Fiesole, a Vaiano too far out of the central Tuscan locale, but no Taiano. My conclusion is that *Taiano* is a misreading of *Caiano*, arising from the easy confusion of the capital letters *T* and *C* in late Renaissance handwriting.[8] Since the manuscript itself has disappeared, it is impossible to check the original. Assuming, nonetheless, that the poet may have written *Caiano*, there remains the choice of two locales. Internal evidence in the sonnets is provided by those place names it has proved possible to locate (see the Index of Proper Names). Of these, Castello is close to Florence on the north, Sesto and Campi slightly further removed from Florence to the northwest, and Monte Morello beyond Castello to the north. Impruneta lies about the same distance as Monte Morello from Florence, but to the south. None of the locations lies to the east of Florence, and none is as far by half as the Caiano of the Casentino hills.[9] It would seem from present evidence, then, that the best recovery of the location of Malatesti's country home is Poggio Caiano just beyond Florence and south of Prato. Lacking the manuscript, the scene of the writing of *La Tina* as well as the setting of the sonnets would seem to be the close western environs of Florence.[10]

Concerning the manuscript, Masson speculates that it may have been shown to academy friends in Florence even before Milton arrived. Further he feels that Malatesti either misjudged the character of the visiting Englishman so grossly as to think he would be flattered by the dedication and gift, or risked a joke under the guise of a real compliment.[11] It is also possible that the young John Milton did enjoy the light-hearted and ribald punning of his Tuscan friend, finding in the freer air of Florence a renewal of his earlier love of Ovid. It is likely that the manuscript of *La Tina* was shipped from Venice together with books and music sent ahead by Milton in 1639. And one may read a possible reference to the racy sonnets in the lines of *Epitaphium Damonis*, written in

1640 soon after his return to England. The lines setting forth his experiences in Florence (129–38) make reference to his participation in academy exercises and conclude with mention of Carlo Dati and Antonio Francini, both of whom wrote encomiums as parting gifts to him. While Milton makes no overt mention of the gift from Malatesti, lines 134–35 speak generally of gifts he still has by him: "nam sunt et apud me munera vestra, / Fiscella, calathique, et cerea vincla cicutae" ("for I have the gifts you gave me in reward, / rush-baskets, and osier-plaits, and waxen reed-stops"). Milton's own days in Florence when he received these gifts of pastoral poetry were fresh in his memory as he wrote of his lost friend, Diodati, of Tuscan descent. But whether Milton's pastoral images were meant to include the antipastoral sonnets of Malatesti we may never know.

Years later, the sonnets do seem to be in his mind. A *Defense* (February 24, 1651) had cost him dearly; French dates the complete loss of Milton's sight one year later on February 28, 1652. Within the next few months Milton was to be not only blind but terribly alone: his wife Mary died about May 5 and his son John about June 16, 1652. In August Milton found himself personally attacked in the anonymous *Regii Sanguinis Clamor*. His two responses against the supposed author Alexander More (*Second Defense*, May 30, 1654, and *Pro Se Defensio*, August 8, 1655) contain some of his strongest satire and some of his most explicit autobiographical statements. Bereft and blind, beset by attackers, and foreseeing the collapse of the commonwealth, Milton without self-pity lashed out against More, whom he saw—albeit erroneously—as his chief tormentor. As he defended himself, he seemed to recall especially the happy days before the Revolution when he basked in the comradeship of Florence—the circle of good friends, "living so pleasantly with each other in one city . . . to me most dear," as he had expressed it in his letter to Charles Dati of April 21, 1647. All the more in the troubled period of the 1650s Milton may have recalled the Florentine circle: "I have no greater delight all this while than in recalling to my mind the most pleasant memory of all of you" (YP, II, p. 765). Among the recollections, he may have remembered, if not actually reread, the sonnets of Malatesti. Under vicious personal attack for his defense of the commonwealth against Royalist spokesmen, Milton prepared as part of his counterblast a biographical statement. That which he included in the *Second Defense* of 1654 devotes a full paragraph to his friends in Italy. The witty academy group of Florence in particular stood in his mind for that kind of verbal play that until recently has marked the Latin scholar. Etymological punning, the teasing of morphemes into double meanings, utilizing bawdy double entendres in the cause of satire were the marks of literary wit in the Florentine circle as they had been among Milton's contemporaries at Cambridge University in their Latin addresses.[12] This playful, even bawdy, tradition of Latin humanism was fully familiar to Milton.

Indeed, as Le Comte has shown, there was a "sly Milton" who selected classical quotations for their satiric and erotic contexts.[13] Subtle verbal play, even when it touched indecency, was defended by Milton as it was by his Italian friend Coltellino.[14] As John Arthos points out, Coltellini argued that "those who wished to make ill use of a thing had only themselves to blame" and proposed that "the indecent and the obscene were as proper to language as they were to thought, and if such writing was vivacious and happy it could make the most miserable of human conditions not only endurable but interesting."[15] In this spirit Milton is nowhere more racy than in his attacks on More's flagrant behavior. In the anti-More passages lie the strongest indication that Milton was recalling Malatesti: Milton's word play in the prose satires of 1654 and 1655 parallel central word plays in the *Tina* sequence. As first noted by Allan Gilbert, the play on *coda* (tail) that concludes *Sonnet 1* and *Sonnet 18* appears in *Pro Se Defensio,* 116, 7. The rising of Malatesti's *stile* (style, stylus, pencil, penis) as exploited in *Sonnet 7* and *Sonnet 25* figures in the *Second Defense,* 32, 8 as well as in *Pro Se Defensio,* 94, 15; 108; 12; 136; 4. While these parallels might have occurred without Milton's acquaintance with Malatesti, one final parallel is the most telling: *Sonnet 45* develops the process of grafting as a metaphor for intercourse. In his wittiest attack on More, Milton in *Second Defense,* 32, 8, 10, elaborates the same imagery: "then, too, he could have shown the woman the method of grafting, that is, the way of inserting a mulberry (*morus*) into a fig, from which very soon syc*amores* would spring up."[16]

It seems likely that, far from being outraged by Malatesti's parting gift, Milton accepted it in the spirit of verbal play in which it is written, for the English poet held with Coltellini "that an obscene subject may properly be dealt with in obscene terms by the most honorable and modest men." Gilbert is thus able to conclude that "the sexual double meaning jocosely employed in the attack on More is quite such as a comic author familiar with Italian literature might employ."[17]

The gift and dedication of *La Tina* to John Milton may indeed have been a broadening experience to the young Puritan poet, but far from misjudging the character of the young Englishman as Masson suggests, Malatesti may well have detected the vein of wit and satire that appeared as early as the Prolusions, emerged in the circles of Florence, and was to await the occasion of biting satire of the 1650s for full use.

What more apt to have occurred, then? Milton is hurt by the ad hominem attacks upon him by the man he identifies as More. He prepares his answer to include (1) a defense of himself, and (2) an attack on the moral character of More. He recalls his happy days in Florence, even giving them an overly large share of his biographical defense. Those days recall the wit of the academies and indeed the special wit of Malatesti. As he turns to the attack upon More, he contemplates the scandal of More's affairs, especially with the servant girl Bontia in Salmasius' household. The parallel of a learned man's affair with a girl of the servant class recalls Malatesti's comic affair with the peasant Tina. In delivering his attack, Milton will draw on the sexual punning so brilliantly developed by Malatesti.

If my conjectures are correct, Milton the linguist and humanist was less shocked than Masson's traditional interpretation supposes. And while Milton did not publish his foreign and exotic gift, he did not dispose of the manuscript.

II. CRITICAL NOTE ON THE SONNETS

As the subtitle indicates, *La Tina* consists of *Equivoci Rusticali in Cinquanta Sonnetti* ("Country Double Meanings in Fifty Sonnets"). As such, the word plays comprise a collection of euphemisms and sexual metaphors drawn from the earthy dialect of the environs of Florence. The tone and diction are appropriately colloquial. The cleverness of Malatesti lies in his weaving the items into a sonnet sequence treating the relationship of the poet as Nencio, the Florentine dialect form of *nuncio* ("messenger"), and the ample peasant girl he calls La Tina ("the little one"), just as we might nickname a very large man "Tiny." There is also a pun on *tina*, meaning a vat (see n. 103).

To anyone familiar with colloquial Tuscan, the equivocations are generally transparent. As John Arthos has pointed out, "the poems ... far from being enigmatic ... are comically clear" in their explicit details of healthy, country sexuality.[18] The twisting of meanings as each sonnet develops is only the linguistic part of the total wit. The reader is also caught up in the teasing of Tina, presented as an unschooled, often foolish farm girl, by her upper-class wooer Nencio, who offers gratuitous advice. While Tina never speaks, it is she who ultimately triumphs. The summer sport is over as *Sonnet 50* gives us a glimpse of the incorrigible Tina: "tu abbassi il capo e voltigli le schiene," complains the poet, you lower your head and turn up your back. With a rude but effective flipping of her skirts, she is off on her country rounds.

III. A Note on the Translation

While the fifty *Tina* sonnets of Malatesti are, of course, in the Italian form, I have not consistently tried to reproduce this form in my poetic translations. English, relatively poor in rhymes in comparison to Italian, does not lend itself easily to a sonnet based on only four rhyme sequences. Thus, *Sonnet 4* represents my usual practice: the Shakespearean form of three quatrains rhyming *a b a b, c d c d, e f e f* ending with a couplet is used. *Sonnet 2* and *Sonnet 20* are typical of a different treatment. The octet is handled as if it were two quatrains rhyming *a b b a, c d d c;* the sestet follows the Italian pattern of *e f e, f e f*. It has been my feeling that the technical rhyme scheme of the translated sonnets is less important than closeness to the original sense, with puns reproduced with English equivalents to the extent possible. Such at least is the nature of my compromise with the varying demands of translation.

Since the language of Malatesti is in itself colloquial Italian of the seventeenth century, English equivalences are not always possible. Where I feel it necessary, the Italian double entendres are explained in the notes, as are local references, proverbial material, and items of Tuscan folklore.

In my interpretations of Malatesti, I have indeed been fortunate in having the aid of my wife, the Honorable Oretta Ferri Sears, who is Tuscan born and bred. During her first eighteen years she lived close to the people of Florence, of Bibbiena in the Casentino Hills, and of Volterra. She thus acquired a fund of knowledge concerning Tuscan folklore and sayings. To a surprising extent the folkloristic and linguistic material used by Malatesti is still current in the rural areas of Tuscany. I wish also to express appreciation to my late father-in-law, Colonel Corrado Nardi, for his help in interpreting some of the less decent puns. Dr. Martin Albori of Hollywood, California, has been invaluable in translating many idioms.

For older forms and meanings of Italian, the *Dizionario delle Lingue Italiana ed Inglese* (London, 1798) by Dr. Johnson's friend and protégé, Giuseppe Baretti, and augmented by F. Damiani, has been invaluable. For its strength in reporting idiomatic phrases, the *Vocabolari della Lingua Italiana* by Francesco Cerruti and Luigi Andren Rostagna (Torino, 1940) was also helpful. In the notes these are referred to respectively as Baretti, and C & R.

California State University, Fullerton

La Tina

NENCIO TO TINA

Do not marvel, Tina,[19] if—born as I was among the clods and more accustomed to handle the spade than to daub pages—I have let myself be decoyed by certain idlers (who up here in the country make earthquakes) to compose verses with a sledge hammer, since the air here around Florence inspires it. Don't you see that it is to show how much I am roasted[20] by your love, and don't you know how all night I stay pen in hand rubbing the vein of my brain, squeezing out my genius in trickles into this fustian. Accept the verses courteously, Tina; and if the style at first seems gross to you, with your efficacy you'll amend its defect, since writing at random I have made a bundle of each herb, and I have gone round and round[21] to give vent to the passion that eats at me from the exceeding love and jealousy[22] which I have in your affairs. And if you believe I have made a boast, that is to say, if in the midst of my work I be already bogged down,[23] you know that he who errs goes wrong, as the proverb says, like the priest to the altar, and I can do nothing else. If I give you all that little talent which I have, it doesn't seem to me that you should be unhappy: but well I know that your cruelty is so great and my ill fortune is such that I cannot touch the fundament of the cause of my suffering nor move you to compassion for me. In fact, the more I scratch the belly of the cicada,[24] the more you remain indifferent to provocation[25] and you stand still in the briars,[26] paying no attention[27] while I speak, letting me preach to a block of wood.[28] And I know very well that these blandishments of mine give you more tedium than levity, and that this happens because you have something up your sleeve.[29] To be precise,[30] you have found some one of these nincompoops who pretend to be sapient and all-knowing, one who admires you in secret; but if the devil causes me to note it and to put fire to the mortar, I will show that I am good enough to deal with you and with him. With the faith of ten, without stopping to tell him to go to the beggars and mind his own business, I will sing him a song[31] that perhaps will seem to him more confounded than the church music of the Armenians,[32] because you know that I do not lack the means to make an offensive jest at someone when I want to, and it will do him no good to tread with caution:[33] so often the kitten goes to the larder that he leaves his paw there, and he will then know where he ought to stay and he will see what happens to whoever baffles others.[34] While I dissemble like the cat of Masino, or to say it better, like Master Fedocco,[35] Tina, I am sharp-sighted[36] because I have pissed in more than one snow,[37] and when your devil was born, mine was already going to school.[38] Excuse me if I speak too much: passion is what moves the clapper[39] in my mouth: I cannot hear all day in this neighborhood the chittering gossips who always read in my book, because it appears to me that I have become the muckraker[40] for this region.

I have no more to tell you: read these poems that I send you, not to sate you with words, but to show you the way to come to facts.

Remain healthy, and love me as I love you.

1

These sonnets, Tina, that I have composed
Were all inspired by a comic muse,
Improvised singing[41] such as bumpkins use
When their voices are to heat of wine exposed.

If I go wrong, so be it; I'm disposed
Thus into songs to let the verse effuse.
If you'll just look on me, you may refuse
My gift; the cost was little it imposed.

All for your love did I indite in haste,
Not because the world will praise my rhyme
And not to get my cap with laurel laced.

So you'll enjoy the more, another time,
You, in whom nature's bounties all prevail,
Will get from me my sonnets with a tail.[42]

2

I can read and understand the history
Of Liombruno-Josafatte,[43] though
Born in a neighborhood a trifle low
And never steeped in the master's mystery.

And His Honor the Mayor swore to me,
When he had seen the verses I composed
That they were fine: he stamped a foot, proposed
I go to Pisa for a Ph.D.

I sing, when I am fully satisfied,
With voice and instrument to go with it
So well that Lord Apollo would not chide.

So come with me, sweet Tina, for a while;
And if upon my lap you care to sit,
You'll quickly feel the rising of my style.

3

Do not grant terms to sickness in its strife:
You've the fever, Tina, and neglect it;
It seems as if you do not care for life;
You're crazy to joke and not respect it.

In treaty-making one can't wait: you must
Take medicine, so the illness will not tarry.
Yet you will neither eat nor drink, nor trust
Yourself to take the cure-all which I carry.

I have a little marrow bone of meat
Prepared in such a way like pabulum
'Twill tickle your palate and then you'll eat.

On swallowing the meat, I put no premium;
It's enough for one whose stomach's queasy
To suck the juices from the bone; that's easy.

4

Tina, I overhear the people say
That *mal del granchio*[44] gives you griping grief
And when it does, like death, you grow so gray
And wrinkled, death itself would be relief.

I mustn't mock, for surely he's a martyr
Who, in danger, spurns the aid at hand:
And since I know a pleasant cure, be smarter;
It is both painless and ready on demand.

There is a ring where lurks the big beast's claw;
Now you can fair and safely free that nook
So every molestation will withdraw.

Give me a finger, Tina, take a look:
If you don't want the *granchio* to linger,
Modestly in the ring just place your finger.

5

It is carnival, Tina, we keep tonight,
The time when we invite in friends to eat:
And you who love to sink your teeth[45] in meat
Can satisfy, with me, your appetite.

In a kettle as big as a convent's
I'm cooking meat to whet your tooth's desire;
Right now it is simmering on the fire
With raisins, pepper, salt, and condiments.

See, here is a little piece of love chop[46]
And a bit of sausage, fennel-flavored:[47]
You've never tasted any better savored.

But to avoid your evil eye and stop
Your scolding if the meat's too hard to chew,
I'll take the chop; the sausage is for you.

6

Every time you go to your butcher store
To get that long piece of meat of his, 'll
Wager the fumbler cheats you as before
And gives you a big piece of—bull's pizzle.[48]

Now I know that it's not up to me, who'll
Seem presumptuous; all the same, please let
Me speak: Do you want to become his fool
Like the birds I catch in my fowling net?

Go home and tell your mother right out flat:
"I'll be a dirty whore if you send me
Again for meat; I'll give it to the cat. . . ."

Then shout to your father, "Now attend me,
I'll not go even if it's mandatory;
Build your own meat shop on the second story."

7

That fig[49] of yours, Tina, brown as chestnut,
Is luscious, but the branches are so high
That little use is either hand or foot;
Unless to topmost spot—all bird[50]—I fly.

As if pegged, you would stay right there all day,
Trying now with a leap, now with a string,
But getting, in the end, jump as you may,
In a sweat, but no closer to the thing.

Wait, Tina, this fig is for my taking:
I know well how to get to it, one way—
I'll give it to you with a little shaking.

Lower your head, lean on the trunk, be gay.
Make a bridge that I may ascend your back:[51]
I mount so well, a ladder is no lack.

8

Touch scarcely feels that tissue which you spun[52]
For me, for, Tina, it is flabby,
Wrinkled, like dental floss, it's shabby—
Badly woven, badly made, badly done.

The loom you have not learned to handle
And so the little bobbin feels unwound:
Error occurs because the cloth is bound
Too loose, or else you're jerking on the treadle.

The comb is insufficiently constricted
As if it were perhaps a trifle wet
And in and out the dirt goes unrestricted.

Now time has made it for you larger yet
And just to fill the bobbin with the thread
You must resize it now with starch instead.

9

Tina, my dear, when you bathe out of doors
And the patron comes upon you, in surprise
You bow "Good morning" as you quickly rise:
How your face flushes to a thousand colors!

Such a favor, though, you never do me,
Yet half a dozen times I go and come:
It must be that I am some sort of bum;
You neither rise nor yield the honor due me.

Who is well-mannered, like a diplomat,
Will rise for all; for me, a dog's chastising,
As if I'm only fit to turn one's back at.

By heav'n! I'm angry at this patronizing.
What's the difference between us two that
Always Master, never me, gets a rising?[53]

10

All the women are making robes these days
In keeping with their years or social step;
Some of cloth turned inside out, some of rep,
And some, my Tina dear, of cloth of baize.[54]

Many have a hairy nap, some are bare;
An abundance are made of finest lawn;
But those whose underside is stuffed with cotton,
While lovely, are less practical than fair.

To me it seems apparent, praise pertains
To those of wool, in texture smooth and hard,
More proper for the folks with hands work-scarred,

Because of wool they're waterproof and stains
Wipe off: therefore I shout it to the town,
Yours pleasures me by lacking hairy down.

11

Tina, I've seen how when you've taken sick
Your mother cooks one solitary egg,
Soft-boiled and bland, and will not cease to beg
Until you get it swallowed down right quick.

You don't want to, and take it with bad grace;
But when you do, it helps your appetite
So much that suddenly you feel all right—
With liveliness you show your haughty face.

Your mother's miserly, for, were I she,
When fever gnaws and cripples you with trouble,
I'd try a quicker, better cure for thee.

Why not make your dose of medicine double?
So when you're ill, please come to me for care:
I'll offer, if you wish, a perfect pair.[55]

12

The master's loaf into your oven[56] went,
And, since of whitest flour it was kneaded round,
Came out done, inside and out, fine and sound;
In short, such that you made him real content.

But mine, because it was spear-shaped, you let
It burn, beyond all joy, by over-cooking;
And now it's badly formed and ugly-looking—
You'd swept your oven in the worst way yet.

Should you tell me that this happened solely
Because his fits your oven best, to you
I would reply, I like a good piece too—

From now on, me too, by all that's holy!
To fit your oven better, I'll be bound,
And like the master, get it in the round.[57]

13

Tina, I have said and said again to boot,
When in the woods I guard the cattle,
It's the greatest pleasure in the world that'll
Let you hear me playing on my little flute.[58]

I promise if you come to me as planned,
I'll teach more playing than you can desire;
I first will play real well, then I'll require
That you take my perfect little flute in hand.

The sound is lovely but I don't believe
The music, clear as bells which toll,
Without hard work you ever can achieve.

One has to keep a finger in the hole
And, if the total secret you would sip,
You'll have to learn to keep it on your lip.

14

I have taken this hollow gourd and digger,
Since tender crabs, Tina, I go to seek.
In certain ditches round a certain creek,
He who knows how to probe, his catch is bigger.

Very few elude me; I defeat them,
Taking fair and ugly, not heeding bite.
It's true—I need not boast that I am right
Since the master knows: he gets to eat them.

Yet, by waning moon—strange to understand!
Inside they're soft, and empty shells remain
When grabbing them, you hold 'em in your hand.

Let me feel, Tina—lest I crab in vain—
If you are astrologically knowing,
And if my moon is waning, or is growing.

15

Every lock of your little grinding mill
Through age is broken and covered with rust.
Test for yourself by touching if you must;
Then if I lie, call me what name you will.

To fix a lock you must have consultation
With the locksmith—that jackass without a bit—
Unless you come to me to make it fit
So very thieves will perish of starvation.

My hands as pliers and hammer will begin
To serve me without too large a measure
Of work; thus I'll pick the staple and pin.

You then will say I am your dearest treasure
As from behind, the sliding bolt I catch
And in your lock, I oil the rusty latch.

16

Tina, on your straw sack you sleep alone,
Not fearing how the frigid breezes blow;
But when wild raving shakes you to and fro
Often sheet and quilt to the ground get thrown.

Then my compassion for you truly grows
Because when someone lies uncovered still,
He easily catches a sudden chill
And in four days to his coffin, off he goes.

If in my bed of down you come to lie,
What matter if my comforter should fall,[59]
In keeping you covered I'll prove most spry.

I'll cover you, the nicest way of all:
If futile are pillow and feather bed,
I can cover you with myself instead.

17

Tina, the bull has given me the slip;
At breakneck pace he's heading toward the stubble.
See how he runs! He'll get himself in trouble
Should he fall from there, going at that clip.

Help with the one I have in hand, at least
Until I catch up with that other one—
May he explode with rage before he's done!
It's pouring mishaps; are more to be released?

Handled or not, to me is all the same
Since I have time and can do without
What truly seems to me to be a shame.

But now, until the venom's gotten out,
If you won't lend a hand, don't let him roam:[60]
I still can handle myself at home.

18

You have docked the tails of all your chickens,
Thinking that way they'll make more eggs for you;
But, Tina, you'll find out what will ensue,
For zero returns will prove slim pickin's.[61]

The poor things you have so badly abused
They've gotten no good from the herbs they've pecked.
A trick like yours I cannot recollect,
Yet, end to end, I have a book perused.

Oh, truly now, they're sterile, every one!
How will you taste one yolk for all your pain?
Yours be the damage for the wrong you've done.

Instead of getting either praise or gain,
All year, you're bound to suffer without fail:
You get no egg from one who has no tail!

19

I have a problem, Tina, when I seek
A vessel for the scanty wine of fall,
Because my dipper is too small
Now that your bucket seems to have a leak.[62]

Besides I feel that yours has been so racked
That neither more nor less can it contain;
I'd like to know the fool who's so insane
And has so little grace as leave it cracked.

You surely knew back then, when I still had it,
It would get sprung by too much lending;
Not only me but everybody said it.

What will you do now that it's past mending?
Fool that you are! Couldn't you be satisfied
To protect the slit before it got so wide?

20

Tomorrow, Tina, all the folk are going
To Monte Morello[63] to celebrate
The Festival of Crickets.[64] At home none wait:
Campi, Sesto, Castello[65] are outflowing.

I too am going, since the weather's fine
And not a fair more excellent, I'd say.
You come too in the good old-fashioned way—
Riding on a she-ass, as I on mine.

You'll have a little cage[66] with you; I a stout
Pointer or long pin which I shall engage
To probe the hole and poke a cricket out.

Let him kick at me and spit in his rage:
He'll teach you thus the midnight stir-about
As I thrust him, live, into your little cage.

21

When I watch you sautéing fava[67] beans,
All through me, Tina, runs a thrill, till I
From too much pleasure feel that I will die,
My heart so jumps and beats beyond its means.

Now by myself I'd eat a peck of them
And always hope to feel myself replete;
For other foods, though good enough to eat,
Slip 'twixt my shirts[68] and fall out at the hem.

I might have escaped from Hunger Tower[69]
I so prick up with appetite—why not?—
When you, uncovered, show your cooking pot.

But you deliver me to anger's power
When, at that point, should someone summon you,
Through haste, you make the oil to come on you.

22

I heard you and the old crone scream and yell
Yesterday while I sowed the field with vetch.
It seemed each other's hair away you'd fetch
Because you'd dropped the bucket[70] in the well.

Forgive; she's stubborn with increasing years
And now awaits from death his final darts;
Not yet have you filled out your outward parts
And should not to her shouting lend your ears.

So the bucket has fallen in the deeps
And has no knob or handle fit to hold;
Not for that will the world collapse in heaps.

I have a hook—you need no longer scold:
Rummaging to the bottom of your well
I'll thread it right into the eye, mam'zel.

23

Tina, in my chestnut grove the other day
I knocked countless chestnuts from their jackets,
With them filling up my trouser pockets
To make you chestnut suckers on the sly.[71]

But your brother Ciapin, the indiscreet,
On seeing me wander far away, has
Seized the time—oh, what discretion is!—
To shake the peach tree by my backyard gate.

All fresh the glutton would have knocked them down;
And except for my love of you, I think,
Hard luck for him if I got him alone.

You know I will not stand for such a prank;
I'm a man who passionately reaches,
One who'll take, but will not yield his peaches.[72]

24

First Sunday of each month, I have to pay,
Tina, the fee at Impruneta[73] fair;
You know how little money I've to spare
And cannot stand expenses day by day.

With wealth I would be generous, no doubt,
But, for me, no one harvests grapes or wheat;
With just two fields, I fast instead of eat
When hail destroys the country round about.

And you desire some new attire, always
Costing the world—red ribbons by the score—
And then it lasts at most some fifteen days.

But now I tell you, I can do no more:
Before, you got my little coin[74] to spend;
Henceforth, you'll get my big one[75] in the end.

25

Two days ago I saw you, Tina, play
In my bean patch;[76] and there you took such care
That soon you had a bellyful for fair,
At least enough to stay you many a day.

The broken, ruined cods[77] you then let fall,
And scampered off with a peal of laughter;
But when you return for more hereafter,
I'd like to give you—skinned[78]—an apronfull.

Don't believe it's beans I care to guard;
Come back for more—I'll not be fussed, not I.
You may select the best: both large and hard.

But please don't send your screeches to the sky
If I should mount your ready-ripened tree:
Apples and a fig are the fruits for me.[79]

26

Tina, if beyond the vineyard we should pass
Where Albano[80] vines dot the new-ploughed land,
Bring your basket and take a pick in hand
Because I hope to get some salad grass.[81]

You don't want to have your step-mother scold
Because you used up all your day for nought;
If you return basketfull of what you got,
Her countenance won't be so sour and cold.

When it's been hoed to clear it from the soil
You then will give it to me so that I
Can wash it well in the canal nearby

And then pull it out well-rinsed after toil.
Thus you can give it to the lord, a jackass
Who likes to eat much more than plough, alas!

27

Tina, the lord today expressed the wish
That without fail he wants by eventide
The fishpond to be wholly drained and dried;
He'll make who-knows-what banquet with the fish.

Alone, I cannot get it done. Will you
Come there with me and demonstrate the way?
I know you're excellent at fish pond play,
So I'll expect tonight that you'll come too.

Then, stripped bare-foot and -armed, I'll probe the shoals
And as the level of the water sinks,
You'll see the fish I pull from out the holes.

You will stand by with basket[82] opened wide
In front of me. While I unplug the chinks,
You'll take the fish into the space inside.

28

Tina, see your brindled bullock yonder
Stray as always from where the cattle feed;
Since he is blind[83] from birth, you ought at need
To take him in hand,[84] not let him wander.

Nor should it seem so strange to you, I'd say,
To do this service for him since he's ill:
You know ingratitude's a sin of will,
One that the padré bids us keep away.

For any woman 'twould be kindly work
To lead him to the drinking trough, and then
To let him lie with others in the pen.

And if you did not all your duties shirk,
You'd see 'tis charity due even a dumb beast
To take him, blind, in hand and quench his thirst at least.

29

When I go to Vivuola[85] where I keep
The flock in pasture on the fallow land,
The wolf has always stolen one or more and
Without fear has taken off a sheep.

But yesterday by luck I caught and found
Him with a lamb almost down his throat;
In a sudden rush with the dog I smote
Him, made him drop it on the grassy ground.

Here it is, O Tina, skinned and clean.
Take it home and cook it instantly;
We'll have a supper suited to a queen.[86]

To give you the fore-part I agree,
Profits[87] and sauce be ours mutually,
With a piece of sizzling rump for me.

30

Tina, that barrel that you keep your brew in—
Filled last year with watery wine—is quite
Worn out and all the drink goes off to ruin[88]
Because it leaks a lot both day and night.

Call me, Tina, and I'll come at any hour;
Without a knife, I'll stucco up your bung,
Provided that the bottom is not sour,
The postern torn, the hoops and staves not sprung.

I'll stop your hole and fill up every slit;
Out of charity, of course, since I never
Serve this way to seek the profit in it.

While plugging from behind, I shall endeavor
To insert in front, at the self-same minute,
A rod which like my arm is big and clever.

31

Tina, my plum tree, that in the new-dug plot
Last year was shoved by me beneath the ground,
I had selected as most straight and sound
Of shoots among a hundred-sapling lot.

But where before it grew up firm and tall
With head held high, afflicted now it bends
In such a way that grief my heart distends
Until I almost pull up roots and all.

To make it right, I find no ways or means:
No matter how I straighten it by tying,
It always seems to me as if it leans;

You alone can rescue it from dying:
Your hand has such stupendous power to mend
It makes erect again all things which bend.

32

Tina, you come to work my back garden
With a pickax, but you stroke so rarely
That I'm about to tell you, unfairly
Perhaps and with scant restraint; please pardon:

But for the respect I know to belong,
By Bacchus! to your whole family fold,
I'd grab it from your hand when I behold
How much I can tell you're doing me wrong.

Don't you see you are getting me no place,
Throwing the seeds away with the tilling
Though you're reputed a woman of grace?

Leave be: I'm better equipped and willing
To work—you will see—with a digging tine
For you in your garden then you in mine.

33

Yesterday into my chicken coop stole
A fox, the window having forced and torn
(I'd woven it of willow, broom, and thorn).
He ate, flesh and bone, a capon as his toll.

Now may the master's blame fall just on me
If some day I'm the cause he lack soup stocks;
Sly and clever, or not, I'll catch that fox—
The priest for this sin too will pardon me.

But once that I have caught it, we'll rake in
Bounty by calling on the farms nearby
For eggs as gifts as we display the skin.

Then back to my room at night we will hie,
Where the fairest half you'll get as your share,
Though a pair[89] for you 's enough and to spare.

34

Tina, look where the hawk is dropping through the air;
Hear the mother hen: Chuck, Chuck, she's cried
Because beneath her wings she cannot hide
Her chicks now that they've scattered everywhere.

Go shouting over there, Shoo, Shoo, Away!
You do not move, you do not cry, O horror!
There, he's just caught one! One more, O horror!
He's sure to diminish the flock this day.

Tell me how this year you'll raise a store
Of capons for the master, and from where
You will obtain a gross of eggs or more.

I don't want to think of it, but beware:
I say that when he comes to get his due,
All his weight will fall on top of you.

35

On fresh March beans[90] I've seen you make a feast
In such a rush, your mouth stays open wide;
And though I pop them one by one inside,
Each goes straight down, not touching in the least.

What a disgrace and it doesn't look right;
It's a foolish thing for a girl like you,
Unless her mama spoons in what to chew,
Not knowing how to eat with lips closed tight.

In former days when folks weren't so precise;
They took no care of matters of this kind;
But nowadays it seems all must be nice.

So, if it's not too hard to be refined,
When you are stuffing yourself—and are seen—
Open just wide enough to take one bean.

36

My lovely Tina, I have sometimes seen
You and your doggie having a to-do;
You fill his mouth with bread and cheese to chew
And even let him lick your soup bowl clean.

See him! He sits there like a lumpish lout,
Makes no festivities as humans do,
He only bites your skirt or nibbles on a shoe,
Barks ugly-mouthed, and never jumps about.

O were I once transformed into that pup,
When the warm scent of soup stock summoned me
I'd come at once to lick your broth all up.

I'd leave my bone for something else, you'd see,
And then, when I was sated, without fail
I'd stand before you with a wagging tail.

37

All the people are noising it about
That I'm an ingrate and a country clown
And all because those nuts which I knocked down
I didn't give them all to you right out.

Yet you know I said: Take enough with you
So you won't later nail me to the cross;
For if to fill your box[91] I'm at a loss,
May I be singed with evils more than few.

But, truly, Tina, you have such a big one
That it disheartens a beggar like me
From my ever getting its filling done.

Therefore, conduct yourself more patiently:
Unless you want with acorn nuts to line
It, your box is much too big for mine.

38

I'm off to Florence, Tina, where I hope
To find the boss in mind to lend some dough;[92]
But since I've nothing to bring him when I go,
I'll enter the field and take a cantaloupe.

It must be all perfection, round and ripe,
Large and hefty, and with rarest slices;
He's hard to please, and not much suffices
Since he's unreasonable and quick to gripe.

Besides, his words are always few and terse:
If he doesn't find it full of flavor,
He'll break it on my head by way of curse.

So, watch that yours are of good scent and savor,
That where the sun strikes, they have burst and grown
Big in the stem and with the buds full-blown.

39

Yesterday, Tina, with your usual grace,
In watering my garden, from the wall
By chance you knocked over the prize of all
My gilly flowers and you broke the vase.

But charge me if you're not sorry one day;
You needn't wrinkle your nose with ire
If I want to break what's still entire
And whole—your laundry sprinkler[93] I'll make pay.

Or else next time on Christmas eve,[94] when you
Come by to beg me for the season's fee,
Though crammed with money I'll say No, you'll see,

Even if able to fill a peck or two.
When, before the manger,[95] you beg a franc,
Count on me to break your little piggy bank.

40

Tina, you make me laugh when in your pride
You visit farmers to sing in the May;
On a tambourine without jingles[96] you play,
A thing unheard of, all the county wide.

You see, you'll get so few gift eggs they won't
Sustain even two tiny kittens' cost;
Instead the neighbors are with laughter tossed.
You think you know the way to play, but don't.

Such an instrument is not made for you,
And little help from those thump-thumps you'll get
Since you lack what would make it good and true.

All in vain, Tina, you work and you sweat;
It's not your fault a lack of outcome mangles:
For unlike me, you've got no dingle-dangles.

41

Over there in the empty soaking tub[97]
I put my hand under a cloven stone
And a female crab[98] bit me to the bone,
One who'd just given birth there in the mud.

That crabs have two mouths[99] is a well-known fact;
Yet foolishly I stuck my hand into the crack
And the blood, alas, from dripping does not slack.
No help to suck and shake it, it's so hacked.

With Meo di Cecco,[100] I call to mind
That a man with a billy-goat beard
At Tetto[101] once told me what he feared:

"I see a sign in how your palm is lined,
That you're about to have crabs pinch your hand;[102]
So do not fish so much in bottom land."

42

Tina, at least ten times I've given warning
That you should cure your leaky pail with wine;
Thus you'll leave on the road no tell-tale sign
When you go fetching water in the morning.

But just like a child you are, unhearing
Of all that for your good I teach you;
Had you wit, you'd let my kind words reach you
And not set everybody jeering.

It shouldn't seem odd that thus I scold you:
Your dripping is not just a single time
But each and every time you homeward climb

And every word must be retold you—
(Oh, how stupid!) Everybody's speaking:
"O, Tina, your bucket's cracked and leaking."

43

Tina, your hedge has grown in front so much
That certainly the garden plot's enclosed;
And yet, a thing that's hard to be supposed,
The salad stuff we find half-grazed and such.

This is a sign that inside has gotten
Some animal who truly felt no fear,
One who has spoiled your shrubbery, my dear,
So that what remains appears now rotten.

O my Tina, we must plug it up anew
If from folks' laughter you're to be protected
And if I'm good enough to succor you:

Gently so that nought will be detected—
So long as you will grant me time to do—
I will entirely stop the gap for you.

44

The grapes hang black, the vats are being soaked,
So any time the clusters we may gather;
From what we have to spare we'll share together:
For so a neighbor's commune is invoked.

For what I'll give to you, I want no pay;
For what you give to me, you'll ask no stake.
Let thus be equal both the give and take,
For that's our farmers' customary way.

After we drain the vats of must, it's right
And proper that we each take back our own,
Receiving without surcharge for the loan.

But so that you'll not pick with me a fight,
I'll leave, as lent, my pestle for your task
If you'll give me your funnel and your cask.[103]

45

You know that tasteless cherry tree I've got
That grows down in the irrigated field,
I want to graft it for a bigger yield
Since now it gives a fruit I value not.

It does not pay the cost to pick it
Because it has no virtue save it's red;
To it, I want a yet small cutting wed
From a *bisciolo*.[104] That's just the ticket.

So Tina dear, don't think it strange that you
Should come and help: to keep close by my side
With wedge in hand is all you need to do.

With it, enlarge the split, and open wide
While I insert the stick and slowly fit
The skin around; then squeeze up tight the slit.

46

Going down to the brook, what do you hope
Will be the good, to squat there on that rock,
O Tina, and the laundry rub and knock,
If you forget to use a bit of soap?

Please do a better job because your lord
Has great desire that it be washed complete;
For when it's brought back to him folded neat,
He looks it over ere he has it stored.

I offer myself as wash enthusiast
To do good work; my hope is of the best
To help you wash both well and fast:

First we'll rub extremities, friend by friend,
Until we likewise later with the rest,
Between us whip up soapsuds in the end.

47

Back from Montisoni,[105] I took a stroll
Yesterday, down that cliff nearby the grove
Of chestnuts (Cecchin del Nente's[106]); I dove
Past the pits where once they hacked out coal.

Right there I found a nest of magpie's young
Atop a holm oak, and because I guessed
That people had been peeking at the nest,[107]
I took them; not one feather had yet sprung.

O Tina, if you want them as my gift,
Come take them in your hand, please come today,
Though there's no danger that they'll fly away.

When La Mea[108] saw them, her desire rose swift;
But I saved them for you altogether,
Knowing you like a bird without a feather.[109]

48

I want to come aworking for your sake,
Now that your olives have grown big and black.
We'll stay all day: no pleasure will we lack,
You beneath to take, I above to shake.

I vow, if no one spy upon our toil,
That though your basket's big, I'll fill it all;
And when throughout the farm we've made our haul,
We'll get to work expressing out the oil.

Warm them well, Tina; then between us two,
Where the machine presses them in its box,
I'll fill the hopper, you'll handle the ox.

But ere we make the oil together, you
Will see whether the screwing rod is sound,
I'll check that the vat's not trickling on the ground.[110]

49

Tina, look at that head and those small feet!
Put a pail of water on the fire, fast,
And into it, as it boils, gently cast
Them; watch that peeling, you don't scrape the meat.

If you don't want to get me mad, be quick.
Fry them well, and bring them over where I sit,
And while we eat them bit by little bit,
I'll thunder if your fingers you don't lick.

When the fat drips in cooking, lamb instead
Of young goat can scarcely be distinguished;
And thus we dine like kings on that small head.[111]

Both our hungers I want well extinguished:
All of it down your throat I want to stuff;
Since eye and tongue for me are quite enough.

50

Like turning turnips into marmalade
Is courting every day a gay young one:
What the lover does, who knows? Nothing done,
He wastes his time, the work is soon unmade.

If she'll just meet with him, he's filled with hope
That she will hold him like a linen press.
Now that I do not love, my heart beats less:
I feel, it seems, as well off as a Pope.

So, Tina, don't believe that with your talking
You'll get me to return to loving you;
I shan't with a bear to Modona go walking.[112]

I know whence arises your failure too:
If, dying for you, one asks help, alack!
You lower your head and turn up your back.

BIBLIOGRAPHIC NOTE

The following editions of Malatesti's *La Tina* sonnet sequence have been identified. Locations of copies are indicated by the following abbreviations: BM, British Museum; BN, Bibliothèque Nationale; LC, Library of Congress; UCLA, University of California, Los Angeles. No attempt has been made to accomplish a complete search for locations.

La Tina Equivoci Rusticali in Cinquanta Sonetti di Antonio Malatesti Fiorentino composti nella sua Villa de Tajano il Settembre dell' anno 1637 e da lui regalati al grande poeta inghilese Giovanni Milton Londra. A spese dell' editore. 1757. 64 pp. BM, BN.

La Tina. Venice, 1837. Unlocated. Sebastiano Blancato, in his introduction to the 1945 Milan edition, claims this edition as the basis of his text.

La Tina, Equivoci Rusticali in Cinquanta Sonetti . . . Notizia intorno all' autore . . . del Dott. G. Lami. Londra [1860?]. BM.

La Tina. Milan, 1865. Unlocated. In the 1945 edition (introduction, p. 18), Sebastiano Blancato refers to inclusion of *La Tina* in an 1865 Milan edition of others of Malatesti's works.

La Tina. Milano: Il Ruscello [1945]. 81 pp. Edition of 500 copies. No. 333, UCLA.

La Tina Equivoci rusticali in cinquanta sonetti. di Antonio Malatesti. Composti nella sua Villa di Tajano il settembre dell' anno 1637 e da lui regalati al grande poeta inghilese Giovanni Milton. (Nuova biblioteca di opere letterarie inedite o rare.) [Foligno: L. del Romano, 1946]. 63 pp. Edition of 320 copies. LC.

TOPICAL INDEX

Besides providing a key to seventeenth-century sexual euphemisms and slang idioms, the text of *La Tina* gives a rather wide-ranging picture of Tuscan farm life in its seasonal response to vegetable, fruit, nut, olive, and grape cultivation; to domestic chores of laundry and sewing, of water carrying, of baking and cooking; to outdoor recreations of crabbing, fishing, and festival keeping; to farmyard care of cattle and hens; and to the joy of romping with a dog or domesticating birds. The following index of topics is provided to aid in finding those sonnets dealing with a particular aspect of country life. Numerals refer to the number of a sonnet.

INDEX OF PROPER NAMES

Reference numbers are to sonnets, which see for identifying notes.

NOTES

Sonnet 8 first appeared in *Paintbrush*, III (Autumn 1976). *Sonnets 1, 19, 31,* and *40* first appeared in *Pulp*, II (Winter 1976/77). All are reprinted with permission.

1. See J. Milton French, *The Life Records of John Milton*, 5 vols. (New Brunswick, 1949–58) for these years. A good account of Milton's travels in Italy as well as biographical material about those he met there is found in David Masson, *The Life of Milton*, rev. ed (1881; rpt. New York, 1946), vol. I, pp. 762–831.

2. See Masson, *Life*, vol. I, pp. 780–81; and Sebastiano Blancato, introduction to *La Tina* (Milan, 1945).

3. Letter to Carlo Dati (1619–1676), April 21, 1647, in *Complete Prose Works of John Milton*, ed. Don M. Wolfe et al. (New Haven, 1953–), vol. II, pp. 762–65 (hereafter cited as YP). At the close of the letter, Milton sends his "best greetings to Coltellini, Francini, Frescobaldi, Malatesta [*sic*], Chimentelli the younger, and any other of our group whom you know to be especially fond of me— in short, to the whole Gaddian Academy" (referring to Jacopo Gaddi who had founded the *Svogliata* ["disgusted"] academy). Dati and Francini are mentioned by Milton in *Epitaphium Damonis* (1640), line 137, for their encomiums of him. See Masson, *Life*, vol. I, pp. 783–85, for English versions of these.

4. For a good and available account of the Florentine academies, see Masson, *Life*, vol. I, pp. 763–65.

5. Bibliophile and champion of republicanism. One connection with Italy was through his friendship with Guiseppe Baretti. See Alan T. McKenzie, "Two Letters from Giuseppe Baretti to Samuel Johnson," *PMLA*, LXXXVI (March 1971), 218. The Mr. Brand is probably Thomas Brand to whom Hollis left his fortune (see *DNB*).

6. The catalogues of both the British Museum and the Bibliothèque Nationale list copies of this edition. I have not personally seen either copy.

7. The difficulties of dating this early edition of *La Tina* are set forth by French, *Life Records*, entry for September 1638. A bibliography entry of 1837 establishes a *terminus ad quem*. The date 1831 is mentioned in the first Milan edition of 1865.

8. See, for example, Samuel A. Tannenbaum, *The Handwriting of the Renaissance* (New York, 1930), pp. 98, 114.

9. If, however, Milton did visit Valambroso, he would have been at the entrance of the Casentino region and not far, but over rugged terrain, from Caiano.

10. This conclusion is supported by the reference in the opening sentence of *Nencio alla Tina* to "the air here around Florence."

11. Masson, *Life*, vol. I, p. 786.

12. See Allan H. Gilbert, "Milton's Defense of Bawdry," *SAMLA Studies in Milton*, ed. J. Max Patrick (Gainesville, 1953), pp. 54–71.

13. Edward Le Comte, "Sly Milton: The Meaning Lurking in the Contexts of His Quotations," *English Studies Collections*, Ser. 1, No. 5 (September 1976).

14. Gilbert, "Milton's Defense," pp. 61–64.

15. John Arthos, *Milton and the Italian Cities* (New York, 1968), pp. 25–26.

16. I follow the translation of Gilbert, "Milton's Defense," p. 59, with its rearrangement of one clause. References in the text are to *The Works of John Milton*, ed. Frank Allen Patterson et al. (New York, 1931–38) (hereafter cited as CM).

17. Gilbert, "Milton's Defense," p. 63, in commenting on *Pro Se Defensio* (CM, IX, p. 174); ibid., p. 70.

18. *Milton and the Italian Cities*, p. 27.

19. "Nencio" seems to be Malatesti's pseudonym for himself in the role of small farmer, as "Tina" is for his country mistress.

20. *quanto io son cotto.* C&R: how great a crust I have.

21. *menare il can per l'aia:* lit., to walk the dog around the area. Hence, to beat around the bush, to go round and round.

22. *il martello:* lit., hammer. Baretti: exceeding love and jealousy.

23. *arenato:* lit., arena-ed. Stuck in the sand.

24. I.e., the harder I try to sing. One so scratches to make the cicada sing.

25. *più tu fai formicon di sorbo.* C&R: lit., the more you play at being an ant in a crab tree.

26. *sta soda al macchione.* Baretti: stand still (in a briar patch).

27. *ponendo una vigna.* C&R: lit., making a vineyard.

28. *predicare a' potri:* lit., to preach to the warts. Baretti: to talk to a piece of wood. C&R: to waste one's breath.

29. *ha paglie in becco:* to have a straw in the beak. Baretti: to have a plan.

30. *scasimodeo.* Baretti: for instance (low).

31. *canterò una zolfa:* lit., sing a set of notes of music. Baretti: reprimand.

32. *il vespro degli ermini:* lit., church music of the Armenians. Baretti: it is Greek to me (idiom).

33. *calzar' del piombo:* lit., to put on shoes of lead. To be cautious.

34. *romper l'uova in bocca alla brigate:* lit., to break the egg in the mouth of the brigade. Baretti: to baffle or disappoint.

35. *faccia la gatta di Masino.* Proverbial idiom for dissembling. The cat of Masino pretends not to observe while she in reality sees all that is going on, closing her eyes so as not to see the mice. The expression is still used in Tuscany. But *il ser Fedocco* I have not been able to trace as an idiom. Possibly a local reference to Tina's padrone.

36. *conosco il pel nell' uova:* lit., to know the hair in an egg. Baretti: to be clearsighted or of an acute wit.

37. Cf. I wasn't born yesterday.

38. *andava alla panca:* lit., going to the benches.

39. *il limbello:* lit., scrap of leather.

40. *spezzaforno,* for *spazzaforno.* Baretti: coal rake for an oven.

41. Reference to the Tuscan singing of *stornelli,* improvised peasant songs in which each singer around the circle adds a verse, often insulting and racy. Malatesti is connecting his country sonnets to the folk tradition of *stornelli.* A number of these songs are collected by Valeriano Cecconi in *Canti popolari Toscani* (Pistoia, 1972), pp. 99–117.

42. *Sonnetti con la coda* are caudated sonnets, made famous in English by George Meredith's use in his *Modern Love* sequence. The obvious pun on "tail" is an appropriate introduction to the Tina poems.

43. Characters in *Il Liombruno,* a popular *cantare* of folk legends and history which influenced Boiardo and writers of novellas.

44. *mal del granchio:* lit., sickness of the crab, a euphemism for the cramps a woman suffers when left unreleased by her mate's premature ejaculation.

45. *macini . . . a due palmenti:* to grind on both sides (idiom). Hence to eat with full enjoyment. I have used the English idiom that keeps some of the nuance of the Italian.

46. *una feta d'arista amorosa:* lit., a slice of pork chine of love. A cut of meat from the back, suggesting the delectable back curves of Tina. "Love chop" is a vain attempt to find English equivalence.

47. *finocchio:* fennel. In Tuscan slang the term—probably because of the shape of the stock and root—is applied to male homosexuals. Cf. Finocchio's, a bar in San Francisco that offers entertainment by male transvestites.

48. *tarantello* formerly meant an overabundance of edibles, but in slang it may refer to a large male organ.

49. *fico:* fig, as a fruit. Here it alludes to Tuscan slang *fica,* the woman's sex organ. Hence the appropriateness of the epithet *castagnuolo:* chestnut-colored.

50. *uccello:* bird. In Tuscan slang, it is the common term for the male sex organ. Cf. to go bird-nesting, as in the Nurse's speech: "a ladder, by the which your love / Must climb a bird's nest soon when it is dark" (*Romeo and Juliet* II.v.75–76); and *Sonnet 47* below.

51. *addosso:* on your back, from the back. A quibble.

52. In the permeating analogy of this sonnet, the household art of cloth-making is extended to indecent twitting of Tina about her large size.

53. For this final play on *rizza,* cf. modern American, "She got a rise out of him." See also *Sonnet 2,* line 14.

54. *d'un altro panno:* of another cloth. For the sake of rhyme I have translated it as "baize."

55. See *Sonnet 33* for a similar quibble on a pair of eggs, or testicles.

56. *Ieri . . . infornasti:* yesterday . . . you put in the oven. The double entendres of this sonnet rest on a sexual parallel to baking bread in an old stone oven. The bread was thrust into the oven on a peel (pie board) and dropped on the hot stone floor, which had to be carefully swept of ash prior to baking.

57. *il tondo:* the round. A quibble from the round loaf of the first quatrain to Tina's vulva.

58. The analogy between flute playing and erotic playing is at least as old as the practices of the Greek dancing girls. Cf. such modern reconstructions as those by Pierre Louys in his *Love Songs of Bilitis.*

59. *un panno ch'io v'ho grosso:* a cloth which I have for you, big. A lewd

reference is probably intended to his "big thing" which may *caschi:* fall. The quibble is suggested in the English translation, "comforter."

60. *tienlo legato:* keep him tied. The meaning hovers between the tether which would tie the bull and the latchet strings that closed the speaker's seventeenth century codpiece. A full modern equivalence is impossible. For *menarlo:* to lead by hand, see n. 84.

61. *in zeri torneranti le decine:* lit., your tens will turn up zeros.

62. "Dipper" and "bucket" are poor English substitutes for the Italian play on *peverin, pevera:* lit., a wooden vessel (masculine and feminine).

63. A street rhyme still heard in Florence provides the central images of the sonnet:

> Le ragazze di Monte Morello
> Hanno la gabbia e non hanno l'uccello;
> I giovanotti poi crepan di rabbia
> Perche hanno l'uccello e non hanno la gabbia.

> [The girls of Mount Morello, so I've heard,
> Each have a little cage but have no bird;
> The boys of Mount Morello shake with rage
> Because they have a bird without a cage.]

For slang meaning of "bird" and "cage" see nn. 50, 66.

64. *La Festa de' Grilli:* ancient Florentine festival in late May. Children collect crickets and carry them home in small wicker cages. Still celebrated.

65. Towns on the outskirts of Florence.

66. *gabbia:* cage. Typically coupled with *uccello:* to put his bird in her cage. It is here extended to the cricket festival by way of the allusion to the street rhyme regarding Monte Morello (see n. 63). This use of "cage" is common in the Scots ballads collected by Robert Burns, as in "Muirland Meg": "At thirteen her maidenhead flew to the gate, / And the door o' her cage stands open yet."

67. *faverella:* bean porridge, made of a large Italian bean (*fava*) like the lima bean. Because of its shape, *fava* has taken the slang meaning of *glans penis,* as in the following graffito recorded by me in Carrara, July 1967: "La puttana con gran bava / Ciuccia cazzo, palle e fava" ("The whore with much dribbling / Sucks cock, balls and glans"). See also *Sonnet 35,* line 14, for additional play on *fava.*

68. *mi van tra la camicia e la gonella:* lit., to fall between my undershirt and my outer shirt. Hence, to do me no good.

69. *Torre del la Fame.* A reference to Dante's *Divine Comedy, Inferno,* Canto XXXIII, especially 22–75, where Ugolino recounts his imprisonment and starvation at Pisa in the *orrible torre* (47) which he called *della fame* (23). Masson (*Life,* vol. I, p. 769) errs in conjecturing that Milton probably visited the ruins since the present Palazzo della Gherardesca was built on the site in 1607.

70. See *Sonnet 19* and *Sonnet 42* for further quibbles on Tina's bucket.

71. Consonance and off-rhyme are used in translating this off-color sonnet of homosexual overtones, although I retain true rhyme for the closing couplet.

72. *il pesco* (misprinted *pasco*) of line 8 and *le pesche* of line 14; peach tree and peaches respectively. The double entendre bottoms on the metaphoric slang meaning of *pesche:* buttocks.

73. *Impruneta:* a market town near Florence.

74. *giulio:* Roman coin equivalent to a sixpence.

75. *grosso:* coin worth about threepence. Twice the size of a *giulio*, but worth only half as much.

76. *baccegli:* (1) beans in the shell, bean pods; (2) new beans. A pun is inherent in Italian, for *baccegli* is slang for the scrotum and testes.

77. *pedali:* stems, here also the testes. The archaic English term "cods," as in "bean-cods," retains something of the Italian wordplay.

78. *sgranati:* husked, shelled. The hidden double entendre is an allusion to the exposure of the *fava* (bean, glans) if the *baccegli* are "husked." See also *Sonnet 21* and *Sonnet 35* for *fava*.

79. Lit., if I collect the already ripened fruit / That is up in your fig tree and up in your apple tree. The last two lines are translated somewhat freely in order to retain in English as much as possible of the Italian double entendres. The play between *fico* (fig tree, fig) and *fica* (pudendum) is paralleled in *melo* (apple tree) and *mele* (apples, cheeks of the buttocks). For *fica*, see also *Sonnet 7*.

80. *Albano:* an area of Italy.

81. *gramigna:* crab grass, formerly used as an ingredient of salads. Cf. "My salad days" (*Antony and Cleopatra* I.v.73). See *Sonnet 43* for similar play on Tina's hedge. Also see *Sonnet 48* for "basket," and *Sonnet 3* for "pick." According to Dr. Piero Pini of the Agricultural Faculty, University of Florence, *gramigni* was formerly given to farm animals to increase their fertility and/or potency. The final lines of the poem suggest the master's lack of potency.

82. *resta:* the rest or socket for a lance, as in the phrase *metter la lancia in resta:* to couch a lance. The sexual image of lance and socket is obvious but archaic. I have attempted to preserve the spirit, if not the original image, by substituting "basket."

83. The blindness of the steer or bullock of the poem recalls the common Tuscan saying *le cazzo e cieco* ("the cock is blind"), a more earthy version of the English "love is blind." Cf. also the English slang "blind eye" for the head of the penis. The blind steer comes in the last two lines of the sonnet to evoke the image of the "blind" male organ. In this instance I have availed myself of Alexandrines for the closing couplet.

84. *menarlo,* also *menarlo* (10) and *menare* (14): to manage, to lead by hand. The triple iteration of this word underscores the less decent quibble of Tina's fondling of a lover. I have thus translated *menare* of line 14 as "to take in hand." See also *Sonnet 17* for a parallel use of *menare*.

85. *Vivuolo:* a place-name in Tuscany (unlocated).

86. *come un banchetto:* like a banquet. I have translated freely.

87. *le rigaglie*. While the meaning is currently "giblets," Baretti defines the word *rigaglia* only as "profit." A pun was no doubt intended by Malatesti.

88. *manda in bordello:* lit., go a-whoring, thus to be ruined or spoiled. I have used the English word "ruin" to suggest the sexual ruin of maidens, so referred to by nineteenth-century authors, e.g., Thomas Hardy, "The Ruined Maid" (1866).

89. See *Sonnet 11* for the same pun on pair of eggs.

90. See n. 67 for a discussion of the play on *fava*.

91. *la sporta:* basket; now, shopping bag. The pun is kin to that of the English word "box."

92. *del gran:* lit., some grain, but here probably in the slang meaning, money. Cf. English "bread," "dough."

93. *a dove il ranno coli:* whence you drip lye, that is, the container of lye sprinkled on clothes in the process of washing. A quibble on Tina's pudendum.

94. *Pasqua di Ceppo:* Feast of Origin, Christmas.

95. *greppo:* variant form of *greppia* (manger), used in order to play upon *greppo,* which may mean a broken pot.

96. *senza dinderlini:* without the small cymbals or jingles that are usual around the edge of a tambourine. Cf. the Tuscan idiom *senza dinderli non si balla:* without the jingles (money) one doesn't dance; hence, without cash you can't have it.

97. *mollaia:* place for soaking laundry under ashes to bleach it before washing. Here with a possible quibble on *mollame:* a soft, fleshy part.

98. *una granchiessa:* a female crab. See also *Sonnet 4* and *Sonnet 14* for plays on *granchio:* crab.

99. Common Italian saying, referring to the two pincers of a crab, compared to jaws. I have kept the metaphor of *bocca* (mouth) because of its obvious application to Tina.

100. *Meo di Cecco:* name of an acquaintance.

101. *Tetto dei Pisani:* Tuscan place-name, probably of a mountain.

102. *pigliar dei granchi a secco:* to pinch one's finger (idiom).

103. See *Sonnet 19* and *Sonnet 30* for similar double entendres with wine vat, as well as the play on *La Tina:* vat, cask.

104. *bisciolo:* a superior kind of cherry.

105. *Montisoni:* Tuscan place-name (unlocated).

106. *Cecchin del Nente:* name of a neighbor.

107. Reference to the folk belief that birds will desert fledglings if people look at them in the nest.

108. *La Mea:* name of a rival girl.

109. The "bird without a feather" refers to *uccello:* bird, penis. See n. 50.

110. A number of by now familiar quibbles fill this poem, e.g., *cesta* (6): basket; *menarlo* (11): lead by hand; *Stanga* (13): bar, bolt, rod. Most central, of course, is the pun on *la tinella* (14): little Tina, little vat. The ox (11) is operating the olive press but a quibble is probably intended.

111. *la testicciuola:* lamb's head. Cf. *testicolo:* testicle, a hint of the off-color interpretation of lines 13–14.

112. *A Modona . . . menar l'orso:* to lead a bear to Modona. Idiom meaning to go in circles, to get nowhere. The spelling seems to be a variant of, or error for, Modena.